Retelling U.S. Religious History

Retelling U.S. Religious History

Edited by Thomas A. Tweed

UNIVERSITY OF CALIFORNIA PRESS

Berkeley • *Los Angeles* • *London*

The publisher gratefully acknowledges
the contribution provided by
The Pew Charitable Trusts.

University of California Press
Berkeley and Los Angeles, California

University of California Press, Ltd.
London, England

© 1997 by
The Regents of the University of California

Library of Congress Cataloging-in-Publication Data

Retelling U.S. religious history / edited by Thomas A. Tweed.
    p.   cm.
    Includes bibliographical references and index.
    ISBN 0-520-20569-3 (alk. paper). — ISBN 0-520-20570-7 (pbk. :
alk. paper)
    1. United States—Religion.   2. United States—Religion—History.
I. Tweed, Thomas A.
BL2525.R473   1997
200'.973—dc20   96-8106
                                        CIP

Printed in the United States of America
9 8 7 6 5 4 3 2 1

To our teachers and students

Contents

II. CONTACT AND EXCHANGE AT GEOGRAPHICAL SITES

Acknowledgments

This book is the product of a multiyear collaboration among scholars who teach and write about the history of religion in the United States. We held our first planning meeting in 1991 and sent the completed volume off to the press in 1995, and along the way we had two briefer meetings and two weekend conferences. Both the project's length and its collaborative nature multiplied our debts. It is a delight to get the chance to thank some of the people who were most helpful during the four years of our work. Some of the authors of this volume acknowledge scholars who commented on individual chapters. See the notes for those words of thanks. Here it seems most appropriate to express our gratitude to those who shaped the character of the volume as a whole—and there were many.

Our collaboration would not have been possible without the generous financial support of the Louisville Institute for the Study of Protestantism and American Culture, the American Academy of Religion (AAR), and the Pew Charitable Trusts. James W. Lewis of the Louisville Institute, Warren Frisina from the AAR, and Joel A. Carpenter of Pew all offered encouragement as well.

Several scholars were kind enough to comment on the project proposal or volume introduction, including William R. Hutchison, Martin Marty, Conrad Cherry, Grant Wacker, David Hackett, Stanley Hauerwas, Elizabeth Clark, Bart Ehrman, Jack Sasson, José deVinck, Tomoko Masuzawa, and George M. Marsden.

Our ideas were formed and re-formed in conversation, and many scholars who participated in one or more of our meetings, or had some relation to the project, had some impact on our thinking. Among those are David Wills, Albert J. Raboteau, Colleen McDannell, Robert A. Orsi, Leonard Primiano, Michael Chiarappa, Tod Swanson, Davíd Carrasco, and Daniel H. Levine. They helped us to remember all the geographical and social sites that we were not considering as fully—from the African coast to Latin America, from domestic interiors to public monuments. They made vivid for us the limits of what we might be able to accomplish in any single volume.

The three outside reviewers for the University of California Press and our editor there, Douglas Abrams Arava, helped improve the book in its final stages. All five of the invited respondents for our two main meetings played a decisive role in our conversations: Mark A. Noll, David D. Hall, Leigh Schmidt, R. Laurence Moore, and Edwin S. Gaustad read our work carefully and offered their nuanced judgments. As with the scholars whom we consulted more informally along the way, it is not their fault if we have not taken all of their sage advice. At the same time, it seems clear to us that these critics improved the book. For that we are very grateful.

Our collaboration would not have gone as smoothly without the assistance of several graduate students at the University of North Carolina who worked on the project. David Zercher ably planned our second meeting and helped with many other details as well. Jennifer Wojcikowski and, later, Thomas Pearson took over the role of administrative assistant in the project's final year. They helped with everything from keeping financial records to checking chapter notes. Sean McCloud, Lynn Neal, and Robert Waller served as research assistants.

Finally, to this long list of acknowledgments we add an expression of gratitude to our teachers and students. We dedicate this volume to them. That seems appropriate since our teachers taught us to tell stories about the religious past and inspired us to search constantly for better ones. And it is our concern for our students that makes our efforts to construct other historical narratives so rewarding. We hope that our students see regions of the past that are now concealed from us and that they illumine what our narratives have obscured.

Contributors

CATHERINE L. ALBANESE is Professor of Religious Studies at the University of California at Santa Barbara. She has served as president of the American Academy of Religion and has authored or edited six books and many articles. Among her recent works are *Nature Religion in America* (1990) and *America: Religions and Religion* (2nd ed., 1992).

ANN BRAUDE's first book, *Radical Spirits: Spiritualism and Women's Rights in Nineteenth Century America,* appeared in 1989. She also has written on a variety of topics concerning gender and ethnicity in American religion, including American Jewish women. She is Associate Professor of Religious Studies at Macalester College.

ROGER FINKE teaches Sociology at Purdue University. He has written extensively on the sociology of religion and coauthored the award-winning study of church adherence in America, *The Churching of America, 1776–1990* (1992).

TAMAR (SANDRA S.) FRANKIEL, who teaches at the School of Theology at Claremont, has authored four books and many articles on the history of Christianity, American religion, and contemporary Jewish spirituality. Her books on U.S. religion include *Gospel Hymns and Social Reform* (1978) and *California's Spiritual Frontiers: Alternatives in Anglo-Protestantism, 1850–1915* (1988).

LAURIE F. MAFFLY-KIPP, who was trained in the History Department at Yale University, now teaches Religious Studies at the University of

North Carolina at Chapel Hill. She has written about religion in the American West and African American religious history. Her book, *Religion and Society in Frontier California,* appeared in 1994.

JOEL W. MARTIN, Associate Professor of Religious Studies at Franklin and Marshall College, has specialized in the study of American Indians, especially those of the southeastern United States. *Sacred Revolt: The Muskogees' Struggle for a New World* was published in 1991. Building on other research interests, he also has edited a book on religion and film.

ANN TAVES, Professor of American Religious History at the School of Theology at Claremont and Claremont Graduate School, has written on a variety of topics, including ritual, religious experience, gender, and sexuality. *Household of Faith: Roman Catholic Devotions in Mid-Nineteenth Century America* appeared in 1986, and *Religion and Domestic Violence in Early New England* followed three years later.

THOMAS A. TWEED teaches in the Religious Studies Department at the University of North Carolina at Chapel Hill. He has written about the history of Asian religions in America, the history of the study of religion, and Roman Catholicism in the United States. *The American Encounter with Buddhism, 1844–1912* appeared in 1992. *Our Lady of the Exile: Diasporic Religion at a Cuban Shrine in Miami* is forthcoming from Oxford University Press.

WILLIAM WESTFALL is an Associate Professor of Humanities and History at York University in Toronto. He has written widely on Canadian culture and religion, authoring many articles and editing three books. His most recent study, *Two Worlds: The Protestant Culture of Nineteenth Century Ontario,* was published in 1989.

Introduction

Narrating U.S. Religious History

THOMAS A. TWEED

"God created America and took three persons with Him from Heaven," begins a Seminole story called "Indian History." "Out of the soil He created four more people, and from these seven people all Indians descend." The narrator, a Seminole who relayed the story in the 1950s, explained further: "Some white people think that the Indians came from another country and traveled over a narrow piece of water in boats, but that is all wrong, for God created the Indians just as He had created Adam and Eve." The account continues as God founds and sacralizes the features of Seminole daily life. God gave five things and showed Indians how to use them—the flintrock; the tomahawk pipe; the medicine herb, Wild King; corn; and tobacco. God also established the religious and political order, appointing one of the Indians as chief, another as floor speaker, and a third as medicine man. Extending the chronology until and after the first contacts with Europeans, the story continues. "From then on and until Columbus came, America was a wonderful place to live," the narrator suggests. "The weather was always just right. . . . They never had any hurricanes or cyclones and things like that until after the white people discovered America."[1]

Unless you are a Seminole, you probably did not hear this account of America's origins in school or at home, yet it conveys several personal truths and makes several moral claims for those who narrate and hear the tale in their ancestral homeland in what is now the southeastern United States. The story reclaims the dignity of American Indian peoples by narrating their sacred origins and their common bonds with whites. It challenges the usual account of the peopling of the continent, which suggests that Indians journeyed across the Bering Strait tens of thousands of years ago, and in so doing it establishes Indian rights to confiscated land. The contrast between the utopia before the arrival of Europeans and the dystopia afterward captures another truth of American Indian history. Perhaps the weather was not perfect before European conquest and Indian displacement, but certainly the social, political, and economic "climate" worsened afterward.

As with this Indian narrative, the stories that fill history textbooks are important because they negotiate power and construct identity. They situate us in society and tell us who we are. Historical narratives often reflect, and shape, the social and economic order: individuals and groups excluded from narratives are excluded from more than stories. Those who do not find themselves or their experience represented in the most widely told stories engage in struggles—private and public, quiet and noisy—to make sense of themselves and locate their place among others in the wider society. Historical narratives, then, never are "just" history. There always is a great deal at stake for narrators and readers, always much to gain and lose in power and meaning.

In part this helps to explain the origins of this book—as well as the impassioned and widespread debates in the humanities about the "canon." Current teachers of U.S. religious history, including the contributors to this volume, have been shaped by several cultural and professional shifts in the past three decades. The religious landscape of the United States, first of all, has changed since the mid-1960s. The nation's diversity always has been greater than is usually acknowledged, yet there is some truth to the claims that around 1965 or so it intensified. The so-called religious mainstream—mainline Protestants, Roman Catholics, and liberal and moderate Jews—has decreased in number and visibility just as conservative and alternative religions—from Pentecostals to New Agers—have attracted followers and notice. This "decline of the middle" has joined with other recent developments, such as denominational switching and liberal and conservative splits, to create a "religious realignment." Another shift also intensified America's diversity. Changes in the immigration laws in 1965 cleared a path for new immigrants to travel to the United States, many of them from Asia and Latin America. The result has been that Latino Catholics and Protestants and Asian Muslims, Christians, Hindus, and Buddhists are more visible in the cultural terrain. Finally, the civil rights movement and the liberation movements among women, Chicanos, and Native Americans also were crucial for focusing attention on groups that had been neglected. For many observers, by the 1990s America's diversity seemed greater than ever.[2]

The changes in the humanities and social sciences since the 1960s have mirrored those in the culture at large. Social historians and feminist scholars, for instance, began to devise research strategies to give voice to the voiceless. More and more interpreters have emphasized diverse peoples and ordinary folks. African slaves, Irish maids, displaced Cherokees, and Victorian housewives are now as important as male presidents, generals, reformers, and novelists of British descent. Many historians have come to believe that the usual historical narratives have overlooked large numbers of peoples and that historians ought to tell other stories. Lawrence Levine, a past president of the Organization of American Historians, has made this point. "To teach a history that excludes large areas of American culture and ignores the experiences of significant segments of the American people," he argued, "is to teach a history that fails to touch us, that fails to explain America to us or to anyone else." For Levine and most other U.S. historians, the old "grand narrative" of consensus and progress in American history, which was peopled by white males and set in public spaces, no longer makes sense of the national past.[3]

I believe that the same is true of the grand narratives of U.S. religion, and—although there are differences among us on some issues—so do all of the contributors to this volume. Textbook narratives that attempt to tell "the whole story" of U.S. religious history have focused disproportionately on male, northeastern, Anglo-Saxon, mainline Protestants and their beliefs, institutions, and power. In recent years those of us who teach and write U.S. religious history have participated in lively, and occasionally acrimonious, debates about the scope and history of white, male, mainline Protestant influence. Our students and many others have joined the debate. To oversimplify a complex conversation, on one side are those who think that comprehensive narratives of American religion ought to highlight these elites, since their political and cultural influence has been so great, although other characters should be included as they intersect with them and, so, enter the plot. On the other side are those who, while acknowledging mainline Protestants' public power, suggest that the standard stories obscure a good deal of U.S. religious history. New stories, they suggest, are needed.[4]

This book, which is a collection of stories about America's religious past, began as a response to that challenge. And it *is* a challenge. As teachers and authors try to incorporate the innovative monographic literature of the past several decades that has dealt with diverse peoples and ordinary adherents, some have wondered aloud whether coherent stories are possible. Diversity threatens to overcome all narrators who are sensitive to it. If coherent stories *are* possible, can we compose narratives that make sense of the religious past yet draw on new motifs and plots and include a wider range of settings and characters?[5]

I decided that was possible, or at least worth attempting. Such an imposing project, however, seemed to call for collaboration. So several of us who shared a commitment to recasting the usual stories of U.S. religion gathered together. But more than that commitment was needed if we were to succeed—or at least fail imaginatively and usefully. We needed to think through the issues together. The contributors here have had much more contact with each other than usually is the case in most edited collections of this sort. We had a planning session in 1991 and more sustained discussion in two longer weekend meetings in 1993 and 1994. At the first weekend meeting we discussed abstracts of each of the chapters; at the second we directed our encouragement and criticism at first drafts of the essays. Before and after those encounters, we communicated by letter, telephone, and electronic mail, offering each other citations and suggestions. To help us anticipate possible objections to the project and further clarify our own thinking, we also invited several "friendly critics," as one of them labeled their role. Five prominent scholars in the field—Mark A. Noll, David D. Hall, Leigh Schmidt, R. Laurence Moore, and Edwin S. Gaustad—participated in our conversations. I urged those respondents to tell us what we were doing wrong, and they obliged. We did not follow their advice on all matters, but they refined our thinking in many ways.

During our second meeting one of the respondents, turning playful, teased us by suggesting that we seemed a bit like a band of marauding revisionists. I think that there is some revision in the book, and readers will decide whether we have been marauding. But we are hardly a "band." We disagreed with each other about several issues along the way. If we agreed that we wanted to nudge our colleagues (and ourselves) toward different stories, we wondered—at least initially—whether we should write case studies or the more synthetic essays that appear here. If we all granted that there are some parallels between historical and fictional narratives, we disagreed somewhat about how much they resemble one another. If we agreed that we would not try to replace the old grand narrative with another, we remained somewhat divided about whether such metanarratives are possible, or desirable, anymore. But if we were not a homogeneous group speaking with one voice, neither were we so divided that we could not find common ground. What struck me about our meetings was that a group of scholars with different research interests and distinct personal histories could manage to allow differences to stand and, at the same time, find some commonality of viewpoint.[6]

By temperament and training, historians usually are focused on the particulars of the past, but our chosen task demanded that we consider larger issues as well—the history of scholarly writing about U.S. religion and, broader still, the nature and assessment of historical narratives. Before our first major meeting we read articles on both topics, and as a starting point for our conversations I circulated an initial draft of this introduction, which is more focused on historiographical patterns and theoretical issues than most prologues to studies of U.S. religious history. I take it that my interest in the history of narrative surveys of U.S. religion needs little justification: if we are trying to work our way toward other narratives, it makes sense to look at earlier attempts to tell the story. Some readers might wonder, however, why I discuss the character and assessment of historical narratives, as I do later. They might protest that I thereby raise irrelevant theoretical questions or distract from the main business of introductions—introducing the chapters. But I believe it is useful to consider these theoretical issues because all historians hold presuppositions and beliefs about what they do and what narratives are, whether or not they identify those for readers (or themselves). Self-consciousness and clarity about method and theory are important in all historical work, but they seemed indispensable in a volume like this—if we were to avoid unwittingly replicating the old narrative patterns, which situated some Americans on the margins of the story and the society. Further, it would be odd, even irresponsible, for us to call for other stories about the past and not offer a working definition of "historical narratives" and a preliminary set of criteria for evaluating them. As director of the project and editor of the volume, I took it as my task to propose a conceptual framework that might form a basis for our discussions. Revising that framework in conversation with my collaborators and the invited critics, I arrived at three convictions about some of the most fundamental conceptual issues of the project. These shaped not only the content of this introduction but also the character of the chapters and the organization of the book.

First, although significant differences distinguish fictional from historical narratives, emphasizing the common features between the two and analyzing historical narratives in literary terms—considering motif, plot, characters, and setting—are useful in both the assessment of others' stories and the construction of our own. Second, narratives trace changes over time, so it makes sense that scholars have emphasized the temporal in their analyses. I suggest, however, that it is helpful to attend to the spatial more fully. Historical narratives orient individuals and groups in space as well as time. They not only place readers in a stream of events but also locate them in natural terrain and social space. As I have suggested with my analysis of the Seminole story, narratives themselves also become social sites at which readers negotiate meaning and power. Third, narrators, and the tales they tell, never stand nowhere in particular or everywhere at once: they always are situated. Narratives, then, are "sightings" from particular sites. From this perspective, the essays in this volume are attempts to self-consciously narrate U.S. religious history from a variety of geographical and social positions. Our aim is not to reconstruct a single grand narrative, but to offer several situated stories and ask readers whether these illumine regions of the past that had remained obscured in the older surveys.[7]

I divide this introduction into three main sections, and the titles of the subsections play with homophonous terms that inform my thinking about narratives—sight, cite, and site. We began our collaborations in the first meeting by considering the nature and assessment of historical narratives, or *sightings,* to use my term. That is where I begin here also. In the following section I refer to—or *cite*—the textbook surveys of U.S. religious history and identify patterns in the narrators' choice of ordering elements. I conclude by describing the contributors' attempts in this volume to consider other motifs and settings, and so illumine other characters and sketch other plots, as they *site* the narratives of the religious history of the United States at varied positions in the social and geographical landscape.

Sightings: On Historical Narratives

Historians often have chosen narrative form to write about the past. Of course, there are other effective ways of writing history, including the thematic analysis often favored by social historians. All historical knowing and writing is not narratological. Rather, following the philosopher

William Dray, I believe that the "construction of narratives is an admissible and prominent, although not universal, aspect of historiography."[8]

If we can assume that narrative history is at least one effective mode of representing the past, what are historical narratives? Narratives may include the other three forms of composition—argumentation, exposition, and description—but most fundamentally they are stories that move beyond mere chronicle. Chronicles, sometimes called "plain narratives," are only chronologically arranged lists of events. The only ordering relation in chronicle is, as Louis Mink noted, "and then . . . and then . . . and then." Historical narratives, in contrast, are *ordered* chronicles, usually with a beginning, middle, and end, that construct meaning out of the human past. They highlight some features and obscure others, according to the interests of the narrator, as each of the chapters in this book does.[9]

Historical narratives, like fictional ones, establish interrelationships among actions recounted by using *ordering elements*. Like novelists, historians employ these elements to show "how a situation at the beginning of a temporal series leads to a different situation at its end." These ordering elements include the author's description of the setting and characters and the choice of motif and plot. In the movement between historical evidence and narrative framework, historians consciously and unconsciously draw on their individual imaginations and cultural resources to choose a motif and construct a plot that makes sense out of the selected evidence. In the narrative that emerges from this imaginative process, historians offer readers one ordered account of what the selected evidence means. The reader, as an active participant in the narrative situation, completes the process of meaning-construction and storytelling by tugging certain interpretive threads in the narrative fabric or, to change the image, by filling in the silent spaces of the story.[10]

If there are parallels between fictional and historical narratives, the two must be distinguished, as our common language usage indicates. The historian's work is imaginative construction. Facts, and the plot structures about them, do not await discovery. Storytellers and readers constitute facts and construct plots. At the same time, I pull back from the strongest versions of the constructivist view. Historical narratives are constructions, but they are more than constructions too. Almost all historians will report that "evidence" also is experienced as an "other" that stands apart from us. Evidence seems so independent of our constructions at times that we are drawn to language which attributes agency to it as we describe our work to each other. The evidence "led me" this way or that, we tell our students and colleagues. Of course, we do not mean this in any crude way; letters, documents, and artifacts usually do not *do* much of anything. In context, however, this language makes sense. It points to the ways in which "evidence" often appears to us as more than our constructions.[11]

Put another way, there are constraints on interpretation and criteria for assessment. Anything does *not* go. Historians have a role-specific obligation to be accountable to the past—however we might understand that duty—in ways that novelists do not. In my terms, then, historical narratives are sightings from particular geographical and social sites that employ various ordering elements to construct meaning out of the human past. In addition, although criteria are culturally constructed and no universal standpoint for assessment is possible, readers can give reasons for preferring one narrative over another.

Readers can use at least three kinds of criteria to assess historical narratives—aesthetic, moral, and epistemological—and all three are relevant as we try to analyze traditional stories and construct different ones. First, readers can use aesthetic norms to assess historical stories. Narratives can be more or less skillfully constructed. To use literary terms again, the setting, or background against which the action takes place, can be more or less vividly recounted. Characters can be drawn more or less fully and their motives can be more or less clear. A motif, a simple recurring element that serves to unify the extended narrative, can be interwoven into the text more or less effectively. Finally, some plots, or patternings of the chronicle of events, are more imaginative than others.

Aesthetic standards are important for some readers, but they rarely spark critics' passions as the application of moral standards do. This, I think, is the source of much of the emotional intensity witnessed in recent debates about the standard narratives in literature, history, and religion. Muscles tighten and faces flush because critics find some narratives inadequate on moral grounds. The often unspoken criticism of some earlier synthetic narratives of U.S. religion, as in other fields, is that they mirror and perpetuate unjust social or economic conditions by condemning some historical groups to play only minor supporting roles in the story.

These sorts of moral challenges usually are grounded in other, epistemological, critiques. The most fundamental criticism of a historical account is that the interpreter "got it wrong," however that might be understood. The proposal, explicit or implicit, that we should use moral

or pragmatic criteria to assess narratives often rests on a more fundamental conviction—that the standard narratives distort the past. Narrators can commit two sorts of transgressions in this regard—sins of
commission and sins of omission.

On the first point, readers can challenge the truth value of a narrative's empirical claims. Every historical narrative includes any number
of assertions about the past. For instance, consider an account about the
Civil War that places the key battles in the northwestern states. Historical sources, verbal and material, suggest that the Battle of Gettysburg
was not fought in, say, Oregon. No matter how aesthetically pleasing or
morally uplifting the story might be, that narrative is inadequate. It is,
we want to say, simply wrong. We could offer other examples, more or
less ridiculous, to make the point: George Whitefield was not a Jesuit
missionary in New Spain and Dorothy Day was not the founder of the
Mormons. We would challenge any accounts that made such claims. It
seems commonsensical to say, then, that the constituent assertions of
narratives each must offer persuasive interpretations of the historical
evidence. Historians tolerate an error or two on minor matters, such as
a wrongly recorded date of birth for a minor character, or an inaccurate
quotation from a primary text, but each such error diminishes the persuasiveness of the story.[12]

Narrators also can commit sins of omission. Readers can challenge a
historian's treatment of the setting, characters, and plot on epistemological grounds by suggesting that the story is not as inclusive as it
claims to be. Historians portray more or less completely the characters
or quasi characters—such as nations, cities, and ethnic groups—that
are relevant to their announced subjects. For example, as social historians have argued in recent decades, to claim to tell the story of "the
American people" without attempting to make sense of the experience
of so-called ordinary historical actors is to constrict the past and mis-
represent the subject.

To criticize narrators for "constricting" and "misrepresenting" the
past is to assume that historical knowledge is possible. Naturally, I
believe it is, as do the other contributors to this volume. Such knowledge always is limited, in part because historians inevitably stand in a
particular place as they view the past; but this knowledge is no less reliable for being situated. As the feminist philosopher of science Donna
Haraway has argued, all reliable knowledge is situated. Extending
Haraway's analysis, I suggest that self-conscious geographic and social
positioning, not pretenses to universality or detachment, is the condi-

tion for making knowledge claims. Both epistemological absolutism and relativism, in different ways, claim to locate the knower everywhere or nowhere. On the contrary, it is precisely because we stand in a particular location that we are able to see, to know, and to narrate. We cannot see everything, and we cannot even simultaneously notice everything that a single vantage point allows. As one geographer has suggested, "it is not possible to look at a scene in general; our eyes keep searching for points of rest." Narrators can claim neither omnipresence nor omniscience. At the same time, however, this view of historical knowledge allows us to avoid epistemological absolutism while reclaiming one root meaning of the verb *narrate:* it is related to *gnarus,* knowing. Narrative, in this view, is one mode of representing what we know. Narrative sightings from particular sites tell the reader not only about the narrator and the site, although they do that too, but also what can be seen from there.[13]

Citing: The Narrative Surveys

The placement of the narrator and the narrative determines what can be seen, what stands in shadow, and what disappears from view. By almost any standard, the sightings recorded in the narrative surveys of American religion since Robert Baird's *Religion in America* (1844)—those that have attempted to tell "the whole story"—have allowed readers to see a great deal. Yet much stands in shadow and much disappears from view. To develop this critique it will be helpful to consider the surveys, which are listed in the bibliography, in a bit more detail. I cannot review nearly 150 years of survey writing here. Rather, I offer an analysis of some of the patterns I see in terms of the authors' choices of motif, plot, setting, and characters. This approach can help us gain more clarity about the stories that have been told and, by highlighting the importance of the narrators' choices of ordering elements, can provide a starting point for the construction of different stories. Appealing to epistemological criteria, I suggest that the main problem with most surveys of U.S. religion is a lack of inclusiveness. To put this point differently, narrators and narratives have been positioned in ways that obscure important dimensions of America's religious past.[14]

The position of the narrative—that is, the setting of the story—obscures as much as it illumines. Several recent survey writers have given some attention to the significance of geographical setting. *America's Religions* (1990) by Peter Williams includes a nine-page chapter on religion in the South, and he briefly considers other regions elsewhere in the book. Edwin Gaustad, who has been especially sensitive to geography, also covers people, texts, and events from multiple regions in his textbook. Catherine Albanese's survey, *America: Religions and Religion* (1992), the most satisfying of the recent works in many ways, calls attention to the significance of regional variation in a case study of religion in southern Appalachia. But Winthrop Hudson and John Corrigan's popular *Religion in America* (1965; 1992) is more typical. The fifth edition does note in passing the significance of region, quoting Albanese's textbook, but most of the action takes place in the northeastern states by natives of New England and the Mid-Atlantic region. "The West" appears in the index, but it refers the reader to a two-page treatment of the "frontier" of 1800. The same index refers the reader interested in New England to nineteen different locations in the text. When the western states do appear in the narrative they, like American Indians, do so mostly as the objects of eastern missionizing or civilizing.[15]

With few exceptions, survey writers have not explored fully the significance of local particularities or regional discontinuities. This omission, recent research suggests, distorts the past. Californians, for instance, never have been as Protestant, or even as conventionally religious, as residents in the northeastern states. The contours of religion in the Southwest, the Rocky Mountain region, and Florida also have diverged from those of the East and Midwest in important ways. Indeed, a historian might compose a narrative of U.S. religious history that moved regionally rather than chronologically or thematically; or, at least, a narrator might situate events and characters—and, so, assertions about them—geographically.[16]

With a few notable exceptions, especially the works by Robert T. Handy and Mark A. Noll which include Canada, survey writers also fail to place the story within wider geographical contexts. Jon Butler has argued that American religious historians ought to locate U.S. developments in a transatlantic context. David Wills and Albert Raboteau, broadening the narrator's vision further, have suggested that U.S. religious history makes sense only in the context of the Atlantic world, understood as stretching back to the western coast of Africa. As early as 1932, historians such as Herbert E. Bolton had advocated that historians of "America" situate their stories in the hemisphere. This sort of comparative context can be illuminating. I cannot argue this point fully here, but interhemispheric comparisons of religious history not only reveal the expected particularities of time and place but also bring into focus themes that have transnational significance for the "New World," including colonialism and postcolonialism, slavery and race, natural landscape and civilized frontier, civil religion, and European-native contacts. A similar case can be made for the significance of the Pacific Rim and the potential usefulness of transnational themes for making sense of that geographical area. So far, however, few textbooks on U.S. religion highlight geographical variation within the nation's borders after the colonial period or emphasize the wider context of the history of the hemisphere, the Atlantic world, or the Pacific Rim.[17]

Narrators map social as well as geographical space, and this distinction allows us to see another way in which the settings of the standard surveys have been too restricted. Narrators often have situated the characters' actions in certain public spaces and elite sites. The church pulpit, the revival altar, the reform society, the denominational headquarters—and to a lesser extent the courtroom and voting booth—have been the backgrounds against which religious actors have worked out their history in the United States. To some extent, this historiographical pattern is understandable, but other social spaces—and the artifacts that have filled them and the rituals that have sacralized them—have been underemphasized or overlooked. Religions are cultural processes whereby individuals and groups map, construct, and inhabit worlds of meaning. They involve power as well. Mapping a symbolic landscape and constructing a symbolic dwelling involve negotiations for meaning and power in natural environments and at social sites. Understood in this way, the possible social settings of narratives expand. Stories about religion, then, might be situated at cemeteries and hospitals, fairgrounds and malls, parades and festivals, elementary schools and nursing homes, museums and choir lofts, and kitchens and bedrooms. These social sites are not private as opposed to public since those boundaries dissolve as all of these spaces interpenetrate. What happens in pulpits, boardrooms, and election booths shapes and is shaped by what happens in streets, parlors, and bedrooms. In the same way, the distinction between natural and social space blurs. Mountains and rivers—components of the so-called natural landscape—are culturally constructed and socially contested spaces, as attention to any of the disputes about native peoples' rights to their sacred land shows.[18]

The settings of narratives are important because they allow sightings of some of the people who inhabit the social and geographical landscape. They determine which characters will appear in view. To give only the most obvious example, stories told from the pews rather than the pulpit or in adherents' homes rather than denominational headquarters foreground different individuals and groups. Despite contrary impulses in the last few decades, the protagonists who people the comprehensive narratives of American religion continue to be mature, white, Anglo-Saxon, elite males. How would the story shift if narrators focused on Africans instead of Europeans, women instead of men, children instead of adults, or the working class instead of economic elites?

In the same way, it can be instructive to consider how the story would change if we shifted our attention from mainline Protestants. Almost all surveys composed since Sydney Ahlstrom's magisterial *Religious History of the American People* (1972) have acknowledged religious diversity. Survey writers have come a long way from Baird's classification of American religions into two groups, "Evangelicals" and "Non-Evangelicals." Ahlstrom might have been "possessed" by Puritans, as Sidney Mead claimed in his famous review, but Ahlstrom, and most authors who have followed him, have scripted scenes for the "others" to play. Perhaps the surveys by Albanese and Mary F. Bednarowski are most notable in this regard. If we overlook the introduction, Protestants do not appear in Albanese's text until the fourth chapter. So Catholics and Jews, as well as members of new religious movements and Asian religions, now find a place in the story.[19]

Nevertheless, the central characters of the surveys continue to be mainline Protestants. In many ways, the focus on Protestantism, and its control of "highbrow" culture and public power, is both understandable and appropriate. There has been a Protestant establishment in America into the 1960s and even beyond. Mainline Protestant denominations and personal networks have exerted disproportionate public influence. The influence and national numerical dominance have seemed so great that most scholars have felt compelled to focus on the story of Protestant victories in contests for public power. In his survey, George Marsden expresses a common view: "The story of American religion, if it is to hang together as a narrative, must focus on the role played by certain groups of mainstream Protestants who were for a long time the insiders with disproportional influence in shaping American culture." I disagree. That story is important because Protestants have had great power; but, as I argue later, it often has been presented as the only story. Concomitantly, other stories, with other motifs and plots, have not been told.[20]

The choice of a foundational motif for a historical narrative is as important as the selection of the story's setting, in part because narrators stitch the plot from that thread. Historians have drawn on a variety of motifs to tell the tale of U.S. religion, including two that Ann Braude and Roger Finke challenge in their chapters in this book—declension and secularization. Others have ordered their stories around the themes of irony and democracy. I suggest that four themes have been especially influential among survey writers since Robert Baird in the 1840s: the organic, frontier, contest, and identity/difference motifs. Although the span of their greatest influence does not divide neatly into precise eras and each continues to have interpretive power, these themes held sway in roughly successive periods.

In an age dominated by evolutionary models and organic metaphors, several nineteenth-century chroniclers of American religion turned to images from nature. For instance, in his *History of American Christianity* (1897), Leonard Woolsey Bacon traced how the "germs" of Christianity were "planted" in different "seed plots" along the Atlantic seaboard, and "diverse growths were made." Bacon, a Congregational minister, believed that the "growth" of churches sprang, in part, "through wonders of spiritual influence." Whether or not narrators appealed to divine providence in their interpretations, the prevailing image they drew on was biological and horticultural. Such narratives appeal to images of the growth of humans or plants, and the plots that use this motif concern the growth or transplantation of religious groups, mostly Protestant, in the American environment.[21]

As Americans—at least those who were not displaced from their native lands—pondered the closing of the "frontier" in the 1890s, U.S. historians like Frederick Jackson Turner appealed to that image to shape narratives about the past. Their guiding image was geographical, and in the narrowest sense the "environment" to which religious groups adapted was the emerging and closing of the frontier. Although this theme continues to find its way into surveys of American religion, it had its greatest influence in the accounts by Peter G. Mode in the 1920s and William Warren Sweet in the 1930s. As with historians who appealed to organic metaphors, the frontier was understood in broad terms, cultural as well as geographical. The plots that emerged recounted not just the gaining and losing of land and resources but also the attitudes and behaviors associated with that environment, including the influence of individualist and democratic impulses on the fate of American denominations.[22]

Since the end of World War I, as some Americans turned their attention to international conflict and class struggle, the contest motif has structured narratives. This approach is clear in the work of Progressive Era historians such as Henry K. Rowe, who wrote *The History of Religion in the United States* in 1924. Although his perspective was quite different in some ways, George Marsden wove the contest theme into the plot of *Religion and American Culture* (1990). Ahlstrom also appealed to this motif indirectly as he emphasized the cultural power of Protestantism, especially Puritanism. The basic image in this motif can be understood in political terms using the analogy of an election or a war, or it might be understood in economic terms using the language of class struggle and market economy. The plots that have been composed using this contest motif have varied, but most have cast religion in the United States in terms of a history of struggles for political, economic, or cultural control. Stories using this theme could highlight other actors—the economically displaced or the politically marginalized—but this choice of motif (as with the organic and frontier themes) has tended to lead to a focus on mainline Protestants.[23]

A fourth motif has been used in some form since the first surveys but, like the contest theme, has been especially prominent since the 1970s. It concerns identity and difference. This theme, or really a cluster of related ones, concerns the relations among entities in a field or, more narrowly, the unity and diversity of American religion. Convinced that earlier narratives overemphasized unity, narrators have tried to make a place for diversity while acknowledging that there has been some commonality too. The plots that draw on this motif tend to trace how America became so religiously diverse. The narratives differ in terms of how much diversity narrators find at the start of the story, but all weave their way toward, or back from, the "pluralistic" contemporary setting.

Authors have played with variations on this motif. It can be viewed abstractly in the mathematical terms of set theory as the relations among various sets. For me, the image lurking beneath the surface of some texts is that of a Venn diagram, representing the relations of overlapping sets in terms of identity and difference. Some narrators appeal directly or indirectly to other abstract spatial images, especially that of a center and a periphery. Sometimes narrators who also draw on the contest motif and focus on public power envision the field of American religion with a center constituted by the groups exerting the most public power and a periphery dotted with marginalized groups. The historian plots the peripheral groups in concentric circles, at varying distances from the center of public power. In turn, he or she classifies the characters as "insiders" or "outsiders."[24]

Narrators also employ this identity/difference motif by alluding to other metaphors—textile, musical, or aquatic. Julia Corbett, in her *Religion in America* (1990), refers to "America's religious fabric" to narrate diversity. She announces her plot in the introduction: "the rich fabric of American religious pluralism has been woven slowly." She makes clear as well that the pieces of cloth that constitute the larger fabric of diversity are sewn together with unifying threads, the separation of church and state and civil religion. In the introduction to her textbook, Albanese, who draws on the identity/difference motif, describes the relations between the "manyness" and "oneness" of American religion in musical terms. She compares American religious diversity to "the short notes of musical staccato, a series of sounds, touching each other but not necessarily blending." But those who listen to the symphony of American religious history hear another, unifying, musical theme sounded. That theme is expressed in civil religion, Public Protestantism, and "the larger cultural religion of the United States."[25]

One of the most popular formulations of the identity/difference motif appeals to the analogy of rivers. In this analogy, an American religious "mainstream" flows through the cultural landscape, its surface rippled by various swirling "currents" and by other "streams" merging and forking. This image dominates the narratives by Corbett and Marsden and appears in others. In some ways, this aquatic motif has been used since the first scholarly surveys. What has changed for most contemporary narrators is the width and character of the body of water. More recently, as Corbett emphasizes, many agree that Roman Catholicism and Judaism now flow in the mainstream.[26]

Still, in practice if not in principle, the identity/difference motif in most of its varied forms has tended to foreground white mainline Protestants and to shape plots that trace the rise and decline of Protestant cultural influence. In those surveys other quasi characters—for instance, Catholics or Mormons—must construct meaning and negotiate power in relation to Protestants. Whether narrators imagine Anglo-Protestantism as a center around which the peripheral groups situate themselves or as the mainstream from which the other bodies of water diverge, the point is the same.

These four influential motifs have led to plots that illumine some characters and events as they obscure others. My point here is not that these motifs and plots offer no insight into the religious past. They do. Our goal in this volume is not to displace these standard motifs and plots. For example, the contest motif—and the identity/difference theme when its plot is focused on struggles for public power—has structured stories that highlight the beliefs and behaviors of elite Protestant males and narrate their successful struggles for political, economic, and cultural control. To say that this narrative is not, by itself, inclusive enough is not to say that it should not be told. Rather, my point is that the story should not be told as if it were the only one worth telling. Stories about national contests for public power offer insights, but they would be less vulnerable to criticism if narrators claimed less. To be more specific, if Marsden's narrative is taken as one worthwhile story composed by a narrator with particular interests that informed his choice of motif and setting, his story about mainline Protestants and public power is rich and compelling. It would be more resistant to criticism, however, if the author did not claim that it was the only plot available to narrators who want comprehensive and coherent narratives.[27]

Siting: Toward Other Narratives

If one aim of this volume is to encourage authors who construct comprehensive narratives to claim less for them, another is to clear the way for other stories to be told. Focusing especially on the choice of setting and motif, and recognizing the limits of what authors can accomplish in one chapter, the contributors to this volume try to sketch the outlines of different stories, ones that we hope will illumine some regions of the past that earlier narratives have obscured.

MOTIFS: CONTACT, BOUNDARY, AND EXCHANGE

In the eight chapters that follow, the contributors draw explicitly and implicitly on a variety of themes to order their accounts. Readers, no doubt, will find among the essays continuities as well as discontinuities that I have not noticed. As I see it, however, three related motifs appear most prominently: contact, boundary, and exchange. One of the most important conclusions that many of us arrived at in our discussions was that "contact" might serve as a useful foundational motif for renarrating U.S. religion. We are not the first to use that theme. Several fine monographs have appealed to it, many of which trace native-colonist encounters or African-European interactions in the Americas. In this book, the theme of contact is most prominent in the provocative essays by Catherine L. Albanese, Laurie F. Maffly-Kipp, and Joel W. Martin. It also appears clearly in William Westfall's insightful analysis of Canadian-

American interactions, Ann Taves's rich reconstructions of intergroup negotiations about sexuality, and Tamar Frankiel's engaging exploration of cultural contacts at ritual sites.

As groups encounter each other they cross geographical and social boundaries, and "boundary" and "crossing" also appear in these essays as organizing themes. So many Americans have understood themselves as migrants who have crossed political boundaries to settle in the nation that it seems to be an obvious choice for an organizing theme. As I have argued elsewhere, "place" more broadly and "migration" more narrowly are two of the most useful themes for renarrating American religious history. Even though every comprehensive account since the late nineteenth century has acknowledged the importance of migrants, these related themes have had remarkably little influence in the standard surveys of American religion. The most notable exception is Martin Marty's lively *Pilgrims in Their Own Land: Five Hundred Years of Religion in America* (1984). Marty focuses on the attempts of those who journeyed to, and in, America to make this landscape their own. He suggests that, despite all efforts, "pilgrims they have remained in their new land." The experiences of ordinary folks are obscured somewhat in that story since Marty focuses on the "pathfinders," the male and female leaders of the pilgrim communities in America. Some readers might argue that the emphasis on leaders is inevitable if we are to have coherent stories. After all, it is difficult to use the themes of boundaries and crossings—or any other motifs—to sustain a narrative about so many ordinary folks over such a vast span of history. Still, I believe that these motifs are illuminating enough to warrant more effort toward that end.[28]

In this volume, Westfall highlights the border that separates the United States and Canada, as he traces crossings in both directions. No chapter in the volume focuses on migrants or elevates migration as the dominant theme, but Maffly-Kipp does emphasize the movements of peoples across political boundaries—northward from Mexico, southward from Canada, and especially eastward from Asia. Both of the chapters that focus most centrally on contact, those by Albanese and Martin, also discuss boundary crossings of various sorts. Many of those are, in Martin's phrase, "social and symbolic boundaries." Groups in contact have met across lines of language and custom, Martin and Albanese remind us. In a similar way, Frankiel talks not only about how revivals crossed political borders in colonial America but also, more metaphorically, about how participants can meet across cultural lines in ritual practice. The chapters by Ann Braude, Roger Finke, and Ann Taves explore the territory within and across traditional social boundaries—private and public, male and female, and church and state.

When individuals and groups meet across social and political boundaries they exchange things. They give and receive beliefs and artifacts, practices and people, and (more abstractly) meaning and power. The theme of exchange has been important in the writings of ethnographers like Bronislaw Malinowski, ethnologists like Marcel Mauss, and, more recently, ethnohistorians like James Axtell. It has been less influential among American religious historians. Although this third motif is sometimes more and sometimes less explicit in the chapters that follow, it informs many of the contributions. Although Finke does not emphasize the term *exchange,* his call for a "religious market approach" to American religious history draws heavily on economic metaphors; and, for him, American religious history is a series of exchanges between religion's "producers" and "consumers." Using cultural rather than economic images, Westfall reminds readers that the United States and Canada have exchanged people and ideas. In different ways, by using the term *colonialism* both Martin and Maffly-Kipp emphasize the power differentials in cultural exchanges within the contemporary political borders of the United States. Albanese also notices that "the gift givers and receivers" have arrived at and left from zones of contact with different amounts of social power. Still, she shows in her wide-ranging story that religious "combinations" have resulted from such exchanges. American religious history, Albanese proposes, is richer for that.[29]

exchanges

SETTINGS: SOCIAL AND GEOGRAPHICAL SITES

As we tried to sketch the outlines of other stories we considered not only the motifs but also the settings of the narratives. If the scene of the action and the position of the narrator determine what can be seen and told, then self-conscious selection of the setting of historical stories is crucial. The contributors to this book situate themselves in several social and geographical sites and report their sightings from there.[30]

In the first section of this volume, authors consider social spaces, including mission fields and revival tents, museums and memorials, bedrooms and courtrooms. Bodies, laws, and churches are especially prominent social sites in these first four chapters. Finke locates himself in a traditional social space, the church, but reports different sightings from there. Moving between the church and the state, especially legal codes, he reinterprets the shifts in the number of religious adherents over time by attending to "supply-side" factors that scholars often have neglected in interpreting religious innovation and sectarian growth, especially the role played by state regulation of churches through subsidy, suppression, and "deregulation" (the separation of church and state). "Market openings" caused by state regulation have driven the religious competition in the United States at least as much as consumer demand has, Finke argues.

Although Braude suggests that narrators of the history of women need to follow their central characters wherever they move in the social landscape, she too focuses on religious buildings. By concentrating on the disproportionate and enduring female presence in religious institutions, Braude recasts the traditional plots of religious decline. Emphasizing female presence rather than male absence, she tells a tale of the increasing vigor of women's participation and the widening scope of their roles. Americans have not left the churches at certain points in the nation's history, men have. In America, as Braude proposes in a memorable phrase, women go to church.

Like Braude, Taves moves between private and public spaces; and, like Finke, for her the public sphere mostly means legal codes. The law is "the quintessential marker" of the state. The scene of action in the story of religion and sexuality that Taves unfolds shifts between two main social sites—the body and the law. As she reminds us, the story of sexuality is first an account of the sexual body. But the body is a social space, public as well as private. Americans have encoded bodies and negotiated sexuality in courtrooms and legislative halls as well as bedrooms. Just as, for Finke, state regulation influences religious innovation and sectarian growth, for Taves changes in the laws about sexuality, marriage, and contraceptives mark key shifts in the plot. For instance, she argues, in the twentieth century the deregulation of contraceptives helped contribute to the diversification and privatization of religion that so many observers have noticed.

Frankiel also foregrounds the body. She renarrates American religious history by focusing on rituals instead of beliefs or institutions; and whatever else rituals are, they are bodily practices. Those "patterned strategic practices," to use her phrase, orient and empower communities. Rituals are social sites where participants construct identity and negotiate power. As Frankiel shows, the setting of a story situated at ritual sites—a story she divides into four periods, each dominated by different patterns of ritualization—must shift from one social space to another. Much ritualization takes place in the more traditionally religious spaces such as church buildings and camp meetings, but other sites—such as domestic spaces, museum galleries, and even lynching trees—can be as important for understanding how religions work and what they mean.

The chapters in the second section of this volume also locate the story's action in varied social settings, but they stand apart from the other essays because of their special emphasis on the importance of geographical setting. Laurie Maffly-Kipp positions herself on the Pacific Rim and reverses the east-to-west spatial movement of most accounts of American religious history. From the Pacific Coast Maffly-Kipp offers a different periodization of religious history and a different cast of characters. Russian Orthodox Christians and Japanese Pure Land Buddhists, for instance, are more important in this story of contact, even though they hardly appear in the narrative surveys that view events from the northeastern states.

In her four-part periodization of American religious history from the Pacific Coast, Maffly-Kipp emphasizes not only contact but also colonization, European and American. So does Joel Martin in his essay for the volume. Focusing especially on native peoples and, to a lesser extent, mainline Protestants, Martin sites his narrative of contact and colonialism in the ancestral homeland of the Muskogee Creek Indians, the territory that now is within the states of Alabama and Georgia. There in the Deep South, Spanish, French, English, Native, and African peoples encountered each other. By assuming that vantage point, Martin encourages readers to consider the long history of contacts and exchanges in that area, and elsewhere in the territory that is now the United States. As Maffly-Kipp does as she traces the early migrations across the Pacific Ocean, Martin begins his account in the distant past, suggesting that a full narrative would trace, as best as the sources will allow, ten thousand years of contact. Needless to say, most narrative surveys have shortened the time-span considerably, starting the account with the arrivals of the British or, slightly better, the Spanish. In the last section of his essay, Martin widens his view beyond the Deep South and proposes two ways that narrators might structure a comprehensive story of religion and contact.

Moving the setting northward, William Westfall positions himself on the Canadian border, offering a view from "the attic." From that geographical site the many crossings of the political boundary that separates the United States and Canada come clearly into view. This vantage point not only reveals the intimate relations between peoples from those two nations but also highlights crossings that have been overlooked in the standard surveys of U.S. religion. As Westfall argues, "While American religious history has celebrated all those who have come to America seeking freedom, the religious journeys of Americans *leaving* the United States rarely appear (if at all) in the standard accounts of American religion." From the Canadian border, however, not only the loyalists, slaves, and pacifists who fled to Canada but also other Americans who left their native land seem more central characters in the narrative. More broadly, Westfall suggests that narrative sightings from the "edges" rather than the "center" of national history are most illuminating, as he and other Canadian historians have found as they have tried to narrate the events of the diverse regions and peoples of Canada.[31]

In the volume's final essay, Catherine L. Albanese reports what she sees from a variety of sites of contact. Using Marcel Mauss's theory of gift exchange as a conceptual guide and, like Roger Finke, appealing to economic metaphors, Albanese analyzes "the economy of religious exchange." In an expansive narrative, she considers a wide range of characters and settings as she sketches the outlines of a story of contact. Where there is contact, Albanese reminds us, there is change and combination. Her essay, and most others in the volume, presents a different view of U.S. religion: the story is not a tale of isolated and immutable traditions sharing geographical space and national identity. Rather, there is contact from the start, and all traditions, and the nation too, are made over and over again in encounters with others. From this ongoing interaction and exchange, old religious movements change and new ones form. Albanese, and the other contributors who highlight contact, have taken us far from the classification scheme, and concomitant plot, of Robert Baird, the first survey writer. Not only are the divisions in her map of the religious landscape more numerous than Baird's, but if we use the motifs of contact, boundary, and exchange to order our stories and site the narratives in varied social and geographical spaces, even the lines that distinguish one religion or sect from another begin to blur.

This story from contact zones is illuminating, and so are the other narratives in this volume. But other compelling accounts of U.S. religion might be told from social and geographical sites that the contributors do not map here. Although Taves's story about the history of sexuality alludes to what happens in bedrooms, most of the characters in these chapters spend little time in domestic spaces. An illuminating story of American religion might be told from homes. A story sited at workplaces might focus on class (and racial) issues more than we have; a tale situated in hospitals might emphasize healing; and a narrative from public spaces such as war memorials, movie theaters, and sports arenas might highlight quasi religions in popular culture. Just as rituals are social sites, so too are artifacts and music, both of which are underemphasized in the monographic as well as the survey literature; rich accounts might be narrated from those social sites. Other geographical settings would provide vantages for useful accounts, too—for instance, stories from the Louisiana coast, the Miami skyline, the Mexican border, or the Brazilian countryside. In a similar way, we might have drawn on other motifs. There are many stories to tell, many sites from which to narrate them, and many motifs to order the plots. Our goal in this volume, then, is to be suggestive, not exhaustive. This book is another contribution to an ongoing conversation, not the first word or the last. Still, I believe that even if some stories await telling—and the old narratives retain some interpretive power—the accounts in this book provide interesting angles of vision on the history of religion in the United States. The contributors suggest other motifs and identify other settings. Characters who had remained in shadow now come into view—from Russian Orthodox missionaries in Alaska to Pueblo berdache in the Southwest, from escaped slaves in Canada to Creek ancestors in the Southeast. This can only help as we look for ways to tell more inclusive stories of America's complex religious past.

PART ONE

Meaning and Power at Social Sites

ONE

Sexuality in American Religious History

ANN TAVES

During the early decades of the seventeenth century, Anglican Thomas Morton and his friends, British and Native American, erected a huge maypole at Ma-re Mount, in the Massachusetts Bay colony, around which they danced, drank, and otherwise "Revelled." A few decades later, masked Pueblo Indians performed the traditional kachina dances with the permission of a Spanish governor, Bernardo López de Mendizábal, who reportedly said that he too would have danced "if it were not for the necessity of upholding his dignity as governor." In both instances, opponents associated the dances with "paganism" and with sex. In the words of William Bradford, governor of Plymouth colony, Morton and his friends danced around the maypole "many days together, inviting the Indian women for their consorts, dancing and frisking together like so many fairies, or furies, rather; and worse practices."[1] During the kachina dance, the Franciscan inquisition records report that the Indians appeared naked, wearing only "a kind of hood, or mask, having a small hole through which they can see a little." Afterward, again according to the Franciscans, the Indians "sometimes . . . enter whatever house they wish and have carnal intercourse with the woman whom they desire."[2] Attempts were made to suppress both dances, the former successful, the latter not.

While the two stories unfold rather differently, we have similar characters—Indians, Christians, and government officials—in each. In the first, Morton, an Anglican layperson, is depicted as the "Lord of Misrule" by the Puritan governor, William Bradford, while in the second, Mendizábal, the Jesuit-educated governor of the colony of New Mexico, is the villain in the eyes of his Franciscan inquisitors. Both Morton and Mendizábal were removed from their respective situations as a result of their flagrant violation of Puritan and Franciscan sensibilities. Nonetheless, the outcome for the respective native peoples was vastly different. In New England, the native peoples were largely exterminated by a combination of displacement, disease, and war at the hands of the Europeans. In New Mexico, however, the Pueblo successfully revolted against Spanish colonial and missionary rule in 1780 and remained independent for many years thereafter. They retained much of their traditional land (the right to which was protected by the Crown and defended by the friars) and religion (although attacked by the friars), and effected a vigorous synthesis between the Pueblo and Catholic traditions which has lasted down to the present.[3]

Juxtaposing these two stories about the body reveals themes we might not see otherwise. In the story about New England, Indians for the most part die or retreat with the frontier, renegades are "tamed" or expelled with the coming of "civilization," and New Englanders of British Protestant descent maintain a sense of their genetic and religious "purity." In the story about New Mexico, the Indians and their culture survive in place, and the mixing of peoples and religions occurs and is acknowledged, if not applauded, from the start. In time, Euro-American Protestants conquer New Mexico, but the voices of the colonized— Indian and Mexican—do not disappear. When we begin with the body as the site for our story, and specifically with sexuality (biological and symbolic), several themes are highlighted—contact and boundary, "purity" and "mixing."

In the Protestant-dominated histories of American religion, British Protestant attitudes toward sexuality are largely taken for granted and their use of sexual imagery is for the most part ignored. Martin Marty and Robert Handy focus explicit attention on Protestant attempts to forge a Christian America, but do not highlight the role that the regulation of sexuality played in that process. The most recent textbooks of American religion tend to discuss sexuality explicitly only when it "deviates" from the norm. For example, Sydney E. Ahlstrom, Mark Noll, Winthrop Hudson, and John Corrigan all discuss the unusual sexual practices of the Shakers, the Oneida Community, and the Mormons. Ahlstrom alone alludes to the sexual imagery common in nativist writings about Roman Catholics, Mormons, and Masons. In contrast, Catherine L. Albanese's shift to an emphasis on spirituality allows matters of sexuality to surface at regular intervals throughout her narrative.[4] In most recent accounts, however, sexuality remains as a persistent but mostly hidden subtext. References to Protestant morality and moral reform encode tacit assumptions about normative sexual practices, while non-normative sexuality surfaces, most often through allusion and association, on the margins of the narrative, as a characteristic attribute of nondominant groups.

To take sexuality as a starting point for rethinking American religious history is to place discourse about the body, and more specifically the sexual body (here defined in terms of the biological capacity for arousal), at the center of the narrative.[5] As religious history, the narrative is thus centered at a point where religious traditions engage with human biological capacities. As American history, the narrative is centered on the engagement among traditions within the legally defined boundaries of what now constitutes the United States. Within these parameters, I have structured the narrative around questions of legitimacy. First, what is legitimate (or illegitimate) sex? Second, since legitimate sex is so frequently limited to marriage, what counts as legitimate marriage? And third, to focus on the more symbolic dimensions, who exemplifies or is associated with legitimacy or illegitimacy and on what basis?

I have taken as my task to sketch the outlines of a story that illumines the interconnections between religion and sexuality within a framework of state formation. Although such a framework runs the risk of reproducing a traditional narrative structure, I do not see how we can escape at least an implicit linkage between questions of state formation and the task of *American* religious history in its synoptic mode, since without state formation we have no Americans. What makes the traditional Puritanism-to-pluralism narrative traditional is not its emphasis on state formation, but the way it depicts that process. By beginning the narrative with native peoples and Europeans in New Mexico as well as New England, I try to avoid reading later British-American dominance back into my account of the colonial era. Additionally, focusing on state formation illumines relationships of power in the resolution of questions of legitimacy. Such a framework highlights the law as a quintessential marker not only of the "state," but of that which is constructed as normatively "American." Given this task, I argue that although various cultures with diverse laws and customs regarding sexuality came together in what is now the United States, that which has been normatively American until the 1960s has been rooted, though not exclusively, in a heritage of medieval canon law and later attempts on the part of Euro-American Protestantism to maintain its purity and power in the face of pluralism.

The narrative is divided into three sections. The first explores issues of sexuality in the seventeenth-century encounter between Europeans and Native Americans, with a specific focus on New England and New Mexico. The second section traces the impact of racial and gender ideologies on dominant conceptions of legitimate marriage and sex-within-marriage during the eighteenth and nineteenth centuries, and analyzes how mid-to-late nineteenth-century black Protestants, Catholics, Mormons, and Jews, faced with the projections of the dominant culture, as well as their own internal dynamics, variously accommodated, resisted, and divided internally over issues of sexuality. In the third section, I analyze the twentieth-century movement to legalize contraceptives, which, in conjunction with the later civil rights movement, led to a series of legal decisions that began to unravel the intimate relationship between religion, sex, and the law in the United States.

Religion, Sex, and Social Order in the Seventeenth Century

EUROPEANS

Much in Euro-American understandings of sexuality, both Christian and Jewish, can be traced back to the Greco-Roman world. David Biale notes that rabbinic Judaism often has been singled out for its "moderate, this-worldly affirmation of sexuality," as opposed to the asceticism of Stoics, Cynics, Jewish sectarians, and early Christian church fathers. In contrast to Christian ambivalence on these subjects, marriage was central to rabbinic teachings and sex was commanded within marriage for both procreation and pleasure. Indeed, rabbinic Jewish men were commanded to have sex with their wives even if they were pregnant or past menopause. Nonetheless, Biale argues that the contrast between rabbinic Judaism and other religions of the Greco-Roman world has been overdrawn. He points out that while permitting a variety of sexual practices designed purely for pleasure, the rabbis at the same time forbade intercourse while the woman was menstruating and condemned coitus interruptus and, most vehemently, male masturbation. Moreover, marriage and, for men, the study of Torah were understood as means of channeling or sublimating excessive and potentially disruptive sexual energies. Biale concludes that "although early Christianity took a much more radical course than did rabbinic Judaism, sexuality was deeply troubling for both and had to be subordinated to loftier goals."[6]

While there were similarities as well as differences between Jewish and Christian understandings of sexuality, it was primarily the complex of Christian teachings regarding sex and marriage codified during the later Middle Ages and transmitted through civil and ecclesiastical law that shaped the legal traditions of the Americas. Some aspects of these legal traditions did have much earlier roots. In the first centuries of the common era, programs of moral reform initiated by emperors, such as Julius and Augustus Caesar, led most inhabitants of the empire, whether pagan, Jewish, or Christian, to expect monogamy and sexual fidelity in marriage from both partners. At the same time secular leaders legislated penalties for violations of this ideal and began to discourage divorce.[7] Polygamy, although practiced by the Germanic peoples of Europe, generally was abandoned within a few generations of conversion to Christianity and by the late sixth century had become uncommon.[8] The idea that the purpose of marriage was procreation also can be traced to the Roman era. Christianity inherited the idea from a variety of sources, including Hellenistic Judaism, Stoic thought, Alexandrian Neo-Platonism, and Roman popular prejudice. By insisting on the idea "more consistently and vehemently than any other ethical tradition," in time the link between marriage and procreation came to be viewed as a distinctively Christian principle.[9]

Nonetheless, in a tradition in which celibacy was the ideal and marriage was viewed with considerable ambivalence, it was not until the thirteenth century that the Roman Catholic Church declared marriage a sacrament and developed elaborate canonical rules for performing it.[10] By the mid-thirteenth century, a century of intensive efforts to codify canon law resulted in a fairly clear consensus on matters of sexuality. This consensus was grounded in distinctions between what is natural and unnatural. It distinguished between sins against nature (bestiality, sodomy, nonprocreative heterosexual intercourse, and masturbation), which included all acts in which ejaculation occurred apart from the possibility of insemination, and sexual activity outside of monogamous marriage (fornication, adultery, rape, and incest), which, while not "unnatural" in the narrow sense of nonprocreative, was framed as both sinful and criminal in canon law by the mid-thirteenth century.[11] As James Brundage has shown, the legacy of this consensus has lasted well into this century in the form of laws proscribing fornication, adultery, sodomy, and bigamy and in the legal rationales underlying marriage and divorce law.[12]

Although sex and marriage were significant issues for the Protestant reformers, the focus of their attack was the Catholic understanding of celibacy, and particularly priestly celibacy. In attacking celibacy, they did little to undermine Catholic teaching that legitimate sex was sex for procreation within marriage; they simply elevated the value of heterosexual marriage. While the Protestant emphasis on marriage as a source of intimate companionship may have led to an appreciation of marriage for purposes other than procreation and, thus, created a climate ultimately favorable to contraceptives, the first generation of Protestant reformers, like their Catholic counterparts, were inflexible in their condemnation of contraceptive use.[13] Advocates of celibacy would surface intermittently in the later history of Protestantism, among them early Methodists, such as John Wesley and Francis Asbury, and Ann Lee, the founder of the Shakers. But marriage remained the norm for Protestants.[14]

INDIANS

Among the peoples native to the North American continent, sex and marriage were interwoven with cosmology and social relations in ways that made them integral to the maintenance of traditional social orders. Thomas Morton's description of the Massachusetts Indians and Roger Williams's description of the neighboring Narragansett both attempt to counter prevailing English views of Indians by stressing the "modesty" of the native peoples of southern New England. While the bodies of the Narragansett were far more exposed than those of the English colonists, Williams notes that "they seeme to have as much [modesty] . . . as civilized people." By modesty he evidently means a reluctance to expose their genitalia; he indicates that all postpubescent men "hide their secreats of nature," and although prepubescent boys went totally naked, the girls "in a modest blush cover with a little Apron . . . from their very birth." He acknowledges that while indoors both men and women leave off their outer "beasts skin . . . and so (excepting their little Apron) are wholly naked . . . Custome hath used their minds and bodies to it" such that they are "free from any wantonnesse." In fact, he concludes, "I have never seen that wantonnesse amongst them, as, (with griefe) I have heard of in *Europe*."[15]

Williams's account further indicates that while sex prior to marriage was "count[ed] no sin," couples were expected to remain faithful to one another after marriage. According to Williams, adultery was much less common among the Narragansett than among the English and, when it did occur, "the wronged party" had the choice of either keeping or "putting away" the offending partner. Although most Narragansett were monogamous, high status men could take more than one wife.[16] Williams's observations on modesty notwithstanding, sexuality was undoubtedly less hidden and circumscribed in the native cultures than among the Europeans. Dwellings of the southern New England Indians usually housed two or more nuclear families and were without internal walls.[17] Children slept in the same quarters with their parents and could observe their parents' sexual activity and, as Williams noted, parents accepted sexual relations among unmarried adolescents.

While Pueblo, like the Indians of southern New England, were for the most part monogamous, high status Pueblo men also might take more than one wife. Pueblo attitudes toward marriage and divorce appear to have been more casual than those of the Narragansett. According to one early seventeenth-century observer, the Pueblo "make agreements among themselves and live together as long as they want to, and when the woman takes a notion, she looks for another husband and the man for another wife."[18] Nor was all sexuality among the Pueblo heterosexual. Early accounts of "berdache," biological males who performed female roles, suggest that they often engaged in homosexual relations. As a third gender, a man-woman who combined male and female, the berdache were often accorded special religious status, particularly among the Indians of the Plains and Southwest.[19] Among the Pueblo references to berdache date back as far as the sixteenth century.[20]

SEXUALITY AND CHRISTIAN CONVERSION

The sexual mores of Native Americans and Africans were viewed by European Christians as scandalous and uncivilized, yet not unlike the desires of the unconverted European heart. Because in both cases "deviant" sexuality and heresy were closely linked, the transformation of sexuality lay at the heart of the conversion process for Catholics and Protestants.

Thomas Shepard, a first-generation British-American Puritan, illustrates the widespread Christian use of marital metaphors to depict the intimate relationship between the faithful Christian and God as well as the related use of images of sexual "deviance" to describe the corruption of the human heart. For example, Shepard characterizes the heart as "a foul sink of all atheism, sodomy, blasphemy, murder, whoredom, adultery, witchcraft, buggery." At another point he avers that "though thy life be smooth . . . thou art full of rottenness, of sin, within. . . . guilty thou art therefore of heart whoredom, heart sodomy, heart blasphemy, heart drunkenness, heart buggery, heart oppression, heart idolatry." In Shepard's mind all these sins of the heart could have been subsumed under the heading of infidelity. At a time when he felt estranged from God, he refers to this as a "widow-like separation and disunion from my Husband and my God."[21] Marital imagery (the "bride of Christ") was used to describe both male and female converts. Fidelity, with its rich layers of religious, marital, and sexual meaning, was expected of all converts in their relation with God. Heart sodomy, heart whoredom, and heart idolatry were all forms of infidelity or unfaithfulness.[22]

While Shepard was not alone in his use of such imagery, in relation to either other Puritans or Christians more generally, his use of these terms was not merely a rhetorical device intended to illustrate the fundamentals of reformed theology. This rhetoric also gives shape to his own conversion narrative. The account begins with an episode of drinking and feasting in a fellow "scholar's chamber" from which he awakes "sick with [his] beastly carriage" and departs in "shame and confusion." In a marginal note, he adds, "I was once or twice dead drunk and lived in unnatural uncleanness not to be named and in speculative wantonness and filthiness with all sorts of persons which pleased my eye (yet still restrained from the gross act of whoredom which some of my own familiars were to their horror and shame overtaken with)."[23] The references to "unnatural uncleanness" and "filthiness" short of the "gross act of whoredom" suggest that Shepard was sexually involved, while drunk, with his fellow students without actually committing the act of sodomy. In classic fashion, he indicates that God used these, his worst acts, as a means of bringing him to make his peace with God.

Making his peace with God meant confronting the depths of his own "vileness," including his suicidal impulses in the face of unrelenting atheistic and blasphemous thoughts. He emerged from his despair having learned to loathe himself and depend wholly on Christ for his redemption. As he did so, he began to "forsake [his] loose [companions]" and found his heart willing to "receive [Christ] as Lord and Savior and Husband." While in the past, he says, "Christ was not so sweet as my lust. But now the Lord made himself sweet to me and to embrace him and to give myself up unto him." In the end, he says, "I saw the Lord gave me a heart to receive Christ with a naked hand, even naked Christ, and so the Lord gave me peace."[24]

Presuppositions about marriage and sexuality, following long-standing Christian tradition, were embedded at the heart of the conversion process. Sexual fidelity in monogamous marriage was a primary metaphor for the relationship between the converted Christian and a monotheistic god. Sexual infidelity in marriage (adultery), nonprocreative sex (sodomy, buggery), and sex outside marriage (whoredom, fornication) were metaphorically linked to religious infidelity or heresy (blasphemy, atheism, witchcraft).

As Shepard's image of "giving himself up to Christ" suggests, orthodox Puritans did not conceive of the relationship between the convert and God in egalitarian terms. Like the relationship between wife and husband on which it was modeled—and like most relationships in colonial New England—the relationship between convert and God was hierarchical.[25] In a hierarchical system, subordination of lower to higher was assumed. In keeping with law and theology, the clergy taught people to submit to God in much the same way they submitted to others above them in the social hierarchy. Within the self, the clergy expected rightly ordered passions (including both sexual desires and emotions) to relate to the soul (reason) in much the same way that they expected wives to relate to husbands and converts to God. Sexual desire was not sinful in and of itself, but became sinful only when "insubordinate."

Placing the marital metaphor at the heart of the conversion process, then, linked the unconverted not only with heresy, but also with illicit sexuality and insubordinate women. If we add to this the presupposition that for most Europeans Christianity, and conversion thereto, lay at the heart of what it meant to be civilized, we have a constellation of ideas in which particular beliefs about sexuality, gender, marriage, and Christian civilization are intimately linked. This constellation of ideas, albeit overlaid with some later notions, comes down to us in the "traditional family values" rhetoric of contemporary conservative

Christianity. We also can see why European Christians would have a propensity to view the unconverted (heathen) and uncivilized (savages) as inevitably characterized by all the "perverse" sexual desires that plagued the heart of the unconverted and/or unfaithful Christian. Just as conversion subordinated the lustful and atheistic heart of the Puritan to Christ as Lord and Savior and Husband, so too the conversion of native peoples subordinated their heathenism and savagery to the salvific patriarchal dominance of Christian civilization.

In both northern New Spain and the British colonies, the initial social distinctions between "us" and "them" were primarily, but not exclusively, religious and drew on categories that emerged in efforts to conquer Old World enemies—the Moors in the case of Spain and the Irish in the case of Britain. According to Ramón Gutiérrez, "the conquerors were honorable because they were Christians, Spaniards, 'civilized,' and white," while Indians were dishonorably characterized as "heathens, Amerindians, 'uncivilized,' and dark." Sexuality, too, played an important role in defining Indians as "other" than their conquerors, especially in the case of women. "Because," in the words of Gutiérrez, "slave women bore illegitimate children, failed to establish stable unions, were frequently sexually assaulted, and reputedly licentious, to be a Spanish woman, regardless of one's class, was to be concerned for one's sexual purity and reputation, to guard one's virginity, to marry, and to be continent in matrimony."[26]

The English names for the native peoples listed by Roger Williams— "*Natives, Savages, Indians, Wild-men . . . Abergeny* [aborigine] *men, Pagans, Barbarians, Heathen*"—indicate that for the English, like the Spanish, the primary distinctions between the native peoples and the colonizers were religious (pagan, heathen), cultural (savage, wild-men, barbarian), and geographical (native, Indian, aborigine). Williams's stress on the modesty of the Narragansett, the relative absence of adultery, and the relative infrequence of polygamy may have been intended to counter the popular English comparison of the American Indians with their other colonial conquest, the "Wilde" Irish. According to Audrey Smedley, in the eyes of the English, "both the Irish and the Indians seemed to lack shame in that they went about naked with little care as to the visibility of even their 'most private parts.' " In addition, both were polygamous and, in the English conception of the cosmos, this combination of nudity and plural marriages was inextricably linked with sexual immorality.[27]

With a few exceptions—the Jesuits in New France being the most

notable[28]—the evangelization and "civilization" of the native populations were closely linked in the American colonies.[29] British, French,
and Spanish governments and most missionaries expected Native Americans to convert to Christianity, adopt European customs, and submit to
European laws. Conversion and relocation to New England "praying
towns," for example, were accompanied by the imposition of civil law
with respect to sexuality. Although the civil laws made polygamous
marriages, adultery by married persons, and fornication by single persons illegal, it was the last, according to James Axtell, that represented
the greatest challenge to local native cultures. New Englanders were disturbed not only by sex outside marriage, but also by unconcealed sex.
Thus, they encouraged natives to build larger dwellings such that, in the
words of Thomas Shepard, "they may have their partitions in them for
husbands and wives togeather [sic], and their children and servants in
their places also, who formerly were never private in what nature is
ashamed of, either for the sun or any man to see." Finally, at catecheti-
cal examinations of sachems or chiefs who had pledged their loyalty to
the Massachusetts Bay colony, the native leaders were introduced to the
familiar litany of European sexual sins, including "fornication, adultery, incest, rape, sodomy, buggary, or bestiality," and enjoined "to
commit no unclean lust."[30] Williams's description of native culture
would suggest that many of these concepts were new to the indigenous
Americans.

The disruption of traditional understandings of sexuality figured
centrally in the Pueblo resistance to Spanish colonization and conversion. Native testimony collected by the Spanish in the wake of the
Pueblo Revolt in 1780 attests to long-standing Pueblo resentment of the
Spanish. Repeatedly the Pueblo testified that in the wake of the revolt
Christian baptism, devotional practices, and marriage were rejected.
Josephe, a Spanish-speaking Indian, declared that the "apostates," after
burning "the God of the Spaniards, who was their father . . . Santa Maria, who was their mother, and the saints, who were pieces of rotten
wood . . . they all went to bathe in the rivers, saying that they thereby
washed away the water of baptism." The Pueblo captains and chiefs,
Josephe went on to say, "ordered that the names of Jesus and Mary
should nowhere be uttered . . . that they should discard their baptismal
names, and abandon the wives whom God had given them in matrimony, and take the ones they pleased." Then the "estufas" (kivas) were
erected and they "danced throughout the kingdom the dance of the caz-
ina [kachina], making many masks for it in the image of the devil."[31]

*Sex, Race, Gender, and Religion in
the Eighteenth and Nineteenth Centuries*

RELIGION AND SEX BETWEEN THE "RACES"

European Americans gave explicit articulation to the idea of distinct "races" in the context of the colonial encounter and granted these supposedly innate distinctions between peoples the status of scientific truth in the nineteenth century.[32] In its emphasis on innate differences, racialized discourse was at odds with, and eventually undermined, older Christian beliefs in the power of conversion to create "one people." Attitudes toward interracial sex and especially marriage—that is, the possibility of licit sex between persons of different "races"—provides a window into this transformation.

Africans only gradually came to occupy the bottom rung in the racial ranking system that came to dominate in the United States, a position initially occupied by the Irish and the Indians. In time the rhetoric of heathenism and savagery developed in relation to the latter groups was applied to Africans as well. Thus religious ("heathenism") and cultural ("savagery") differences rather than physical ones such as color provided the first rationale for the enslavement of Africans. By the end of the seventeenth century, however, "dark complexion had become an independent rationale," and during the eighteenth it "became a symbol of savagery and heathenism and all the other negative features that these terms connoted in the English worldview. . . . As the eighteenth century wore on, their [African] savagery became intrinsic and terminal."[33] As Jon Butler has shown, eighteenth-century Anglican missionaries anxious to offer salvation to slaves participated in the creation of a racially based worldview by assuring slaveowners that, contrary to popular belief, Christians could enslave other Christians and that baptism liberated the soul but not the body.[34] The repudiation of the connection between conversion and physical emancipation marks a significant shift in the conceptual basis of slavery. As long as persons were enslaved because they were heathens, they could be freed through conversion. Once their enslavement was rationalized on the basis of race—on the basis of a "divinely ordained" hierarchy of biologically distinguishable human groupings—then salvation and enslavement could coexist.[35]

The racial ideology that developed in the United States was more rigid than in the rest of the Americas. This difference has been most apparent with respect to interracial sex and marriage. In 1691 Virginia took the internationally unprecedented step of banning "all forms of inter-racial marriage by providing that any white man or woman who married 'a negro, mulatto, or Indian . . . bond or free' was liable to permanent banishment from the colony." Other colonies, including Massachusetts, North Carolina, Pennsylvania, and Georgia, followed Virginia's lead, so that by the mid-eighteenth century six of the original thirteen colonies had made interracial marriage punishable by law.[36] Although the reasons for the difference are still disputed,[37] it is clear that the degree of sexual intermixing of the various peoples of British America was far less extensive than among the various people inhabiting Latin America and that British attitudes toward interracial marriage were far less tolerant.

Antimiscegenation laws, of course, did not prevent interracial sex. What they prevented was the legitimization of such relationships and the offspring they produced. While these laws applied to free and slave alike, sexual liaisons were especially common between white male slaveowners and their female slaves. Whereas in Latin America, slaves who bore children by their masters often were freed or at least protected from sale, in the United States, laws prevented the manumission of slaves and the legal acknowledgment of the paternity of children born to slaveowners and their slaves.[38] The most famous of the female-authored slave narratives, Harriet Jacobs's *Incidents in the Life of a Slave Girl* (1861), describes a young woman caught in the binds that such a system created. Sexually pursued by her master, who was the father of at least ten children by his first and second wives and at least eleven children by his female slaves, Jacobs initiated an affair with another slaveowner to arouse her master's jealousy and hopefully initiate her sale. All of her master's children by slave women and Jacobs's children by her slaveowning lover were slaves because their mothers were slaves. Neither father recognized his children as his own.[39]

Jacobs describes the ethic of obedience that permeated the Christianity of white slaveowners, such that her master could join the Anglican Church and even encourage Jacobs to join, all the while pursuing Jacobs sexually and telling her that her virtue as a slave lay in her obedience to him. Jacobs's own understanding of Christianity, by way of contrast, reflected a female-oriented tradition that linked sexual purity, freedom, and justice. This countervailing tradition, passed on to Jacobs by her mother, her grandmother, and her first mistress, seems to reflect the resistance of both slave and free women to the sexual promiscuity of slaveowners. For Jacobs, true Christianity demanded moral purity, but that required a level of personal autonomy antithetical to the slave system. Because slaves had neither the authority to reject sexual overtures outside marriage nor the legal sanction of sex within marriage, men could violate slave women with impunity and deny them access to what they took to be true Christian virtue.[40]

While prohibitions against interracial marriage undergirded the slave system in the South, prejudice against such marriages was strong in the North as well. Although an assimilationist approach to missions led logically to intermarriage, northern Protestants made it clear that Christianizing and civilizing "heathens" did not mean marrying them. When Elias Boudinot, an exemplary Cherokee Christian earmarked for the Congregationalist ministry, proposed to Harriet Gold, a young Congregationalist woman of British descent from Cornwall, Connecticut, her relatives and her community were scandalized.

This was the second such scandal that had rocked the town of Cornwall. The town was home to an experimental school that was founded by the American Board of Commissioners for Foreign Missions and attended by missionized youth like Boudinot. The first marriage involved John Ridge, Boudinot's cousin and fellow student, and Sarah Northrup, daughter of a school official. Although John Ridge's father was a wealthy Cherokee slaveowner and the new Mrs. Ridge became a plantation mistress, Isaiah Bunce, the editor of the local paper, emphasized "the affliction, mortification and disgrace, of the relatives of the young woman . . . to have her thus marry an Indian and taken into the wilderness among savages." He describes Northrup as having "thus made herself a *squaw,* and connected her ancestors to a race of Indians."[41] Here we have the mutable image of the savage-in-the-wilderness assimilated to an immutable image of race, such that all standard markers of "civilization" (class, wealth, education, cultural assimilation) become irrelevant.

Bunce believed Northrup's desire to marry Ridge was a product of the *"missionary spirit,"* as he referred to it, and held the "agents" or trustees of the school, most of whom were ministers, liable for the "unnatural connection" between the couple. The agents, among them such notables as the Reverend Lyman Beecher, immediately condemned miscegenation and forbade any further marriages at the school across racial lines.[42] John Ridge and Sarah Northrup, both apparently unconverted, were at best indirectly affected by the missionary spirit that so disturbed Isaiah Bunce. Harriet Gold and Elias Boudinot, however, fully realized the editor's suspicions. In their disregard for the school's newly stated policy forbidding "miscegenation," Gold and Boudinot exemplified both the logic of an assimilationist model of missions and their commitment to bring "civilization" to the "savages."[43]

The closing of the mission school in response to these and other less provocative challenges to a thoroughgoing assimilationist approach signaled a shift to a missionary strategy that emphasized conversion independent of "civilization."[44] While mid-nineteenth century attempts to distinguish between the Christian gospel and Western culture partially undercut the cultural imperialism of the assimilationist approach, they also allowed Christians to step back from the question of intermarriage in an increasingly race-conscious and racist era.

RELIGION, SEX, AND (WHITE) PROTESTANT DOMESTICITY

As the general absence of prohibitions against intermarriage between "persons of color" suggests, the purpose of miscegenation laws was to maintain the purity of "whiteness." Due to patriarchal concerns with property and inheritance, purity also had long-standing associations with the female "virtues" and traditional notions of "femininity." During the course of the nineteenth century, the association of purity with whiteness and femininity was embedded in a wider set of dichotomies—state and church, work and home—brought on by industrialization, urbanization, and disestablishment. European Americans constellated these dichotomies along gendered lines such that the state, work, and men were associated with the public or civil "sphere," and church, home, and women with the private or domestic "sphere." Purity, racial and feminine, linked pure sex to legitimate marriage and thus located it in the domestic realm. These ideological polarizations—public/private, white/black, masculine/feminine, pure/impure—led to private lives that did not necessarily fit their public images. This also encouraged attempts to undercut or diffuse the tensions and produced anxieties about "purity" which were projected on to various "others."

The twentieth-century assumption that the Victorian language of purity correlated with sexual repression or "passionlessness" in practice has been widely questioned by historians. A number of recent studies stress the gap between the public rhetoric and the private practice among middle-class Victorians. Indeed, some interpreters have suggested that the history of sexuality in the United States from the Victorian era to the present is less a history of progressive sexual liberation than a progressive narrowing of the gap between public discourse and private behavior.[45]

The gap between public and private is most apparent in relation to the use of artificial contraceptives. Publicly, the first wave of the women's movement rejected both abortion and contraceptives because these practices separated sexuality and reproduction, a separation associated with prostitution. The fundamental problem was economic. In an era when "respectable" women depended on marriage for financial security for themselves and their children, many women believed that a publicly sanctioned link between sex and reproduction provided an incentive for men to marry and stay married.[46] Nonetheless, there is considerable evidence from diaries, letters, and declining birth rates that native-born Euro-American married couples privately used contraceptives and abortifacients and understood sex as a means of marital intimacy, not just reproduction. Historians have speculated that the passage of the Comstock law in 1873, which labeled drugs for abortions and materials used for contraception as obscene and limited their importation and distribution, was passed in response to concerns about the widespread use of both by American women.[47]

The love letters of Pasadena clergyman Robert Burdette and his wife, Clara, a prominent clubwoman, encoded the split between the public and private. Publicly, Robert was described in the newspapers as one whose "language was as clean as his thoughts are pure." Privately, the letters written during the couple's courtship reveal an unabashed sexuality and a frank enjoyment of bodily pleasure, up to and including sexual intercourse before Clara accepted Robert's proposal of marriage. Although Robert suggested burning their letters and Clara later censored them extensively, enough uncensored material survived to provide a startling contrast to Clara's account of their courtship in her published autobiography. Karen Lystra argues that this disjunction was less a matter of hypocrisy than evidence of the Victorian emphasis on limiting the full disclosure of passionate feeling to the private sphere.[48]

Such letters show how the ideal of romantic love flourished in the private sphere during the nineteenth century and, due to its emphasis on sex as an expression of love and intimacy, tended to undercut the association of sex and reproduction. Moreover, if we do not equate sexuality with intercourse, we find that the emphasis on romantic love encouraged a broad range of passionate, erotically tinged relationships, not only between courting men and women, but also between persons of the same sex. Whether these relationships are best described as "passionate friendships" or erotic relationships depends both on the relationships themselves and on the definitions we bring to them.

However such relationships are characterized, it is clear that they provided an emotional infrastructure that animated both the radical and the evangelical wings of the nineteenth-century woman's movement. Frances Willard, active Methodist lay woman and the second president of the Woman's Christian Temperance Union (WCTU), comments in her autobiography that "the loves of women for each other grow more numerous each day" and memorializes a series of "attachments . . . so much less restful than friendships, that [she] cannot fairly call them by that consoling name." Recent research on her diaries reveal that the first great love of her life was her friend Mary Bannister. While Mary went on to marry Frances's brother Oliver, the intensity of feeling Frances had for her own fiancé paled in comparison to her feelings for Mary and led her to break off her engagement. According to Carolyn DeSwarte Gifford, Willard rejected marriage partly because she believed herself to love women, rather than men, with the depth necessary for marriage and partly because she was unwilling to sacrifice her ambitions to a husband's aspirations in the way that she felt that married women should.[49] While many married women maintained intimate friendships with other women, such friendships provided primary relationships for many single women such as Willard and freed them to devote their lives to careers in church work, social reform, and teaching.[50]

The idealization of romantic love also infused the theology of Henry Ward Beecher, the mid-nineteenth century's most popular Protestant preacher. According to William McLoughlin, it was Beecher's great achievement to "amalgamate Romanticism, religion, and science . . . [with] a firm faith in the national destiny of Anglo-Saxon America." Beecher's romantic Christianity replaced the stern and distant Calvinist God of his childhood with a God known through nature and manifest as love. Although he avoided systematic theology, he laid out his theological views in his best-selling novel *Norwood*, which McLoughlin describes as "the first fully developed statement of Liberal Protestantism to appear in popular form."[51]

In Beecher's theology, romantic and divine love merged. As in the love letters studied by Lystra, falling in love took on the language of conversion and being in love the language of worship.[52] Although the language of romantic love has an egalitarian ring to it, it was rooted in the reality of gendered social spheres. For men, romantic love was a part-time activity, embraced when they entered the privacy of the home, whether literally or metaphorically. Women, literally and metaphorically associated with domesticity and motherhood, "loved" as a full-time occupation. Love, even romantic love, had its roots for Beecher and many other nineteenth-century Americans in maternal love.

The conflation of romantic and maternal love underscores the difficulties involved in interpreting the seemingly erotically charged language of intimacy. Indeed, some nineteenth-century women and men expressed confusion as well. According to McLoughlin, Beecher offended some of the reviewers of *Norwood* with what sounded to them like "coquettish and almost incestuous love play" between a male character and his widowed mother. Sounding rather naively pre-Freudian, Beecher responded that "not every angel even is given to know the full meaning and sacredness of a mother's and son's inner most communion, *in a love utterly without passion,* without color of selfishness, deep as life and stronger than death."[53]

In true or higher love, according to Beecher, sexual passion is absent, as in the case of parents and children, or strictly controlled, as in the case of adults. Not all people, in his view, had the same capacity for love in its highest forms. Just as he thought love in its highest forms developed slowly even with persons of a higher nature, so too the capacity for "higher" love was understood to evolve as "less-civilized" classes, cultures, nations, and races were progressively civilized and Christianized.[54] The selfless love associated with a mother's love for her children was most fully realized, of course, in the self-sacrificial love of Jesus. Belief in the purity of the Protestant home, in the crucifixion of Jesus as an act of self-sacrificial love, and in the hierarchies of race, class, nation, and culture provided the ideological underpinnings for late nineteenth-century Protestant efforts to Christianize America and civilize the world.[55]

While in private, and especially within the confines of marriage, romantic love aspired to link love and sex and infuse both with an air of purity and sacrality. Yet fears of unchecked lust and unprotected womanhood loomed large in the public rhetoric of nineteenth-century Protestant missions and social reform.[56] At midcentury, images of "barbarism" and "lust" were gendered. Popular fiction and social reform literature depicted men as the threat—in accounts of priests violating young women in the confessional and convent, lustful slaveowners raping their female slaves, brutal Indians capturing innocent white women, and polygamous or alcoholic husbands degrading their wives.[57] The twin themes of this literature—tyranny and sexual excess—defined the antetypes of Christian and heathen, Protestant and Catholic, free and slave, wife and husband. They also tacitly linked Protestantism with freedom and femininity. European American Protestants associated most of these images with missionary or social reform movements—the common school movement, abolition, Indian removal, anti-Mormonism, and temperance. Some of these images were specific to northern Protestants and some had Republican overtones. The image of the lustful slaveowner, for example, while popular in abolitionist literature and Republican rhetoric, obviously did not play well among southern white Protestants.

The crusade against polygamy illustrates the rhetorical overlaps and disjunctions that could occur. The Anti-Polygamy Society, organized by Protestant women in Utah in 1878, was consciously modeled on the antislavery societies of an earlier era and, following the Republican party, linked slavery and polygamy as "twin relics of barbarism."[58] Harriet Beecher Stowe gave her support to the movement, describing Mormonism as "a slavery which debased and degrades womanhood, motherhood, and family," while Frances Willard compared the Utah territory to Islamic Turkey, "doubtless the most debased country on earth," and lamented that the United States, "the 'bright consumate flower' of Christian civilization," should allow this "montrous lust" to continue in its midst. A New England paper invoked the specter of "Romanism" when it editorialized that, as in the case with slavery and the South, it soon will be "discovered . . . that the essential principle of Mormonism is not polygamy at all but the ambition of an ecclesiastical hierarchy to wield sovereignty; to rule the souls and lives of its subjects with absolute authority, unrestrained by any civil power."[59] From these superimposed rhetorics of slavery and freedom, heathenism and Christianity, tyranny and restraint, we learn little about Mormonism and a great deal about Protestant perceptions of themselves as free, Christian, and republican.

Mormon women, not surprisingly, mobilized soon after the formation of the Anti-Polygamy Society, declaring that they had been "misjudged and misrepresented . . . by those in our midst of our own sex, in regard to our most sacred rights . . . of wife-hood and mother-hood." One male observer commented that "the speeches gave evidence that . . . the so-called degraded ladies of Mormondon are quite equal to the Women's rights women of the East."[60] While mainstream Protestant activists such as Willard and Stowe had little positive to say about Mormon women, leaders of the more radically oriented National Women's

Suffrage Association (NWSA) forged a link with Mormon women after they were enfranchised at the state level in 1870. Elizabeth Cady Stanton and Susan B. Anthony both traveled to Utah shortly after the vote was granted, and some years later Mormon delegates began attending NWSA conventions. While Anthony and the NWSA did lobby against proposed federal antipolygamy legislation that would have disenfranchised Utah women, the most vehement, but ultimately ineffectual, support for the Mormon cause came from southern Democrats, who turned Republican rhetoric on its head and defended polygamy on the grounds of states' rights.[61]

By century's end, Protestant sexual rhetoric was less gendered, less regionally polarized, and more overtly racist. Theories of social evolution and "scientific" racism allowed Protestants to project their fears of unchecked lust on to animal-like "primitives." This racialized stereotype, although most persistently associated with black men, also was applied to Indians, southern and eastern Europeans, Mexicans, and Asians.[62] Rebecca Latimer Felton, a member of the WCTU and the Women's Home Missionary Society of the Methodist Episcopal Church, South, illustrates the depths to which Protestants could descend in their defense of "white womanhood." In a letter to the editor of an Atlanta paper, Felton referred to black men as "half-civilized gorillas" and advocated lynching if that was what it took to "protect woman's dearest possession from the ravening human beast."[63]

At the same time, women of color, non-Protestant women, and working-class women, often cast as victims in the earlier literature, increasingly appeared as sexually degraded by virtue of their race or class rather than innocent by virtue of their gender. The presence of a substantial mixed-race population, for example, no longer was linked to the depravity of slaveowners and the sexual vulnerability of slave women, as it had been in some abolitionist literature, but to the innate promiscuity of black women. According to Evelyn Higginbotham, "racist representations of black women as unclean, disease-carrying, and promiscuous conjoined with representations of black households as dirty, pathological, and disorderly" to make black women *the* turn-of-the-century icon of sexual and domestic deviance to which others were assimilated.[64]

While white Protestants most commonly associated their fears of unchecked lust and unprotected womanhood with nonwhite or non-Protestant "others," newspapers still reported allegations of sexual misconduct on the part of Euro-American Protestant clergy throughout the nineteenth and twentieth centuries. These allegations occasionally resulted in spectacular trials, such as that of Methodist minister Ephraim Avery in the 1830s, charged with seducing and murdering Sarah Cornell, and that of Henry Ward Beecher in the 1870s, charged with "criminal conversation" or sexual intimacy with Elizabeth Tilton, wife of his longtime friend Theodore. M. E. Billings, a nineteenth-century freethinker who assiduously compiled newspaper reports of clergy crimes, the majority of which turned out to be sexual, viewed ministers' access to their parishioners' homes as providing much the same opportunity for criminal conduct as the confessional allegedly provided Catholic priests. According to Billings, "the danger of such 'pastoral visits' [was] strikingly exemplified in the Beecher-Tilton scandal."[65]

Despite widespread public belief in the guilt of both Avery and Beecher, jurors acquitted both in civil and ecclesiastical trials. In the latter case, modern historians have remained as divided in their verdict as the nineteenth-century jury. Suspicions regarding guilt or innocence tend to loom large in interpretations of the incident. Altina Waller, for example, presents Beecher as unequivocally guilty; in her reading, rumors of previous affairs are taken as fact and Beecher is implicitly cast in the modern mold of the charismatic minister who repeatedly seduces female parishioners. More recently, Richard Fox downplayed the issue of guilt, emphasizing that all agreed that whatever the relationship may have become, it undoubtedly began as, and may have remained, the sort of "passionate spiritual romance . . . enlivened with physical affection . . . that was common in their circle among friends of both sexes." While Waller's reading makes it hard to avoid accusations of hypocrisy, Fox's reading raises the possibility that Elizabeth Tilton's own vacillation regarding her guilt or innocence may reflect less on the weakness of her character than on the fuzziness of the boundary between romantic friendship, spiritual romance, and marital infidelity.[66]

ACCOMMODATION, RESISTANCE,
AND CONFLICT AMONG THE "OTHERS"

For a variety of reasons, some internal and some external to their traditions, sexual issues came to the fore among black Protestants, Mormons, Catholics, and Jews during the latter part of the nineteenth century. In each case, issues of "Americanization," or adaptation to the dominant Protestant culture, loomed large. Faced with the projections of the dominant culture, as well as their own internal dynamics, these traditions accommodated, resisted, and split.

Within the bourgeois black church tradition, Baptists and Methodists—and especially Baptist and Methodist women—identified Christianity with "temperance, cleanliness of person and property, thrift, polite manners, and sexual purity."[67] The emphasis on respectability was a rhetoric simultaneously of resistance and of accommodation to white stereotypes and norms. In claiming the high ground of "respectability," black women, according to Higginbotham, "boldly asserted the will and agency to define themselves outside the parameters of prevailing racist discourses," while also revealing their "assimilationist leanings." The emphasis on "respectability" created a bridge between "respectable" black church women and progressive white women, while tacitly distancing them from the masses of urban blacks still steeped in rural traditions that they sought to reform.[68]

The writings of journalist and African Methodist Episcopal churchwoman Ida B. Wells attest, as did the writings of Harriet Jacobs, that the association between Christianity and sexual purity was not simply a product of the postwar period. Wells recounts that she encountered a black clergyman, while traveling through the South after the Civil War, who opined that "there were no virtuous [black] southern girls," presumably due to the legacy of slavery. Challenged by an outraged Wells, he apologized from the pulpit and quoted Wells to the effect "that many a slave woman had fought and died rather than yield to the pressure and temptations to which she was subjected." She commented that growing up, "I had heard many tales of such and I wanted him to know at least one southern girl, born and bred, who had tried to keep herself spotless and morally clean as my slave mother had taught me."[69]

Wells, however, is best known for launching the crusade against lynching. Her research, based on published newspaper accounts, led her to conclude that not all persons lynched were males and that the majority of persons lynched were not actually accused of rape. Moreover, in the minority of cases where there had been involvement of a black man with a white woman, she came to the highly inflammatory conclusion, given the prevailing racist mythology, that the involvement was frequently voluntary on the part of the woman. Wells's largely single-handed crusade was taken up by the National Association for the Advancement of Colored People in the teens and by reform-minded

white southern church women in the thirties. The involvement of the
white women, whom lynching was ostensibly supposed to protect,
marked a turning point in the movement. Because doing so challenged
their self-perceptions, it took white women some time, even after they
became involved in the movement, to acknowledge white women's voluntary sexual involvement with black men.[70]

If the struggles of black Protestants were rooted primarily in differences of color, and to some extent culture, Catholic struggles were
rooted primarily in theology. The flashpoints for Protestant fantasy and
projection about Catholicism—the celibate priesthood, secret confessional, and enclosed convent—were grounded in fundamental theological disagreements. These undergirded Protestant and Catholic differences with respect to the value and indeed the possibility of celibacy and
the number and definition of the sacraments. In contrast to classical
Protestantism, which created a radical conceptual gulf between matter
and spirit, Catholic theology, in the words of Peter Gardella, "pictured
God bringing people to redemption through the physical world, teaching about invisible things by means of the visible, and imparting grace
through material objects in the sacraments." What Protestants viewed
as a shocking (and simultaneously titillating) interest on the part of
Catholics in sexuality was, in the eyes of Catholic theologians, a logical
outgrowth of a natural theology that assumed a purpose for all aspects
of the created order, including genitalia. Traditional Protestants assumed that matter, including the material body and its sexual organs,
while not evil, was nonetheless without positive religious significance;
Catholic theologians meanwhile developed highly specific doctrines to
illumine its positive meaning and purpose.[71]

The moral theology elaborated in Latin textbooks read by priests and
seminarians was disseminated widely, as Protestants suspected, through
the confessional. Bishop, later Archbishop, Francis Kenrick's *Theologia
Moralis* (1843), the first major American handbook of moral theology,
stated that a husband who did not remain sexually active until his wife
reached orgasm committed a venial sin of omission, that a wife who
distracted herself during intercourse in order to avoid having an orgasm
sinned mortally, and that a wife who did not reach orgasm during
intercourse had the right to bring herself to orgasm manually after-
wards.[72] Such passion, in keeping with an orthodox line of reasoning
running from Thomas Aquinas through Alphonsus Liguori, was free
from sin only in the context of marital intercourse "informed by rational purpose," that is, intercourse for conceiving children, fulfilling

duty, and avoiding sin. Sex simply for the sake of pleasure still was considered sinful.[73] Although Kenrick's frankness about sexuality was in keeping with tradition, he recognized that the publication of such a book in the American context left him vulnerable to criticism. Resisting Protestant norms, he defended his discussion of marital sex against those who, "pretending to moral purity, abhor scrutiny of the facts of marriage."[74]

Ironically, American Catholic moral teachings on sexuality became more conservative, just as liberal Protestants began to find positive meaning in married sexual passion. This new conservatism was apparent in the second major treatment of moral theology by an American Catholic, St. Mary's Seminary professor, Adolf Tanquerey, whose recommendations were published during the first decade of the twentieth century and remained influential for many years thereafter. The prudish tone of Tanquerey's moral theology reflected a more conservative reading of Liguori than either Kenrick or the European moral theologians of his day and, at the same time, an accommodation to the anti-Catholic and antisensual character of late-nineteenth century American public discourse about sex.[75]

With or without plural marriage, the Mormon understanding of marriage was theologically distinct from that of both Protestants and Catholics. Unlike Protestants, who viewed marriage as a civil contract, Mormons sacralized it; unlike Catholics, who sacralized marriage but valued celibacy more highly, Mormons privileged marriage over singleness. For Mormons heterosexual unions, "sealed for time and eternity" by the church, assumed a central place in Mormon theology in the wake of Joseph Smith's revelation on plural and celestial marriage in 1843. While civil marriages ended with death, marriages sealed by the Mormon priesthood bridged the material and spiritual worlds and structured human relationships in heaven as they did on earth. Such marriages provided the means by which humans could progress to the highest heavenly status and ultimately to godhood. Within this theological framework, plural marriage modeled on that of the Hebrew patriarchs was a particularly exalted form of eternal marriage. The intimate connection between sealed marriage and full salvation meant that in some cases women were sealed as plural wives in marriages that never were consummated sexually.[76]

Recent studies of the diaries of the nineteenth-century Mormons who entered into plural marriages suggest that their primary motives for doing so were religious and that they had to abandon the romantic notions popularly associated with monogamous marriage in order to maintain these unions. Plural marriage required women to relinquish exclusive claims to their husbands and required husbands to avoid favoritism. Plural marriage, along with the extended absence of husbands involved in missionary work, subordinated sexuality within marriage to overarching religious ends.[77] The maintenance and defense of plural marriage can be viewed as the primary manifestation of a general subordination of personal aims to the building up of a distinctive corporate religious life in the Great Basin Kingdom. While this weighed most heavily on the highly placed minority who actually entered into such relationships, the legitimacy of plural marriage and the distinctiveness of the kingdom was maintained collectively, not individually. It was the collective assent to the moral legitimacy and theological centrality of plural marriage that, according to Jan Shipps, "explains why all the citizens of the kingdom—those who were involved in plural marriage and those who were not—were willing to defend to the last possible moment the practice of polygamy that kept them set apart."[78]

Within Judaism divisions over sexuality were as wide-ranging as within Christianity. Reform Jews, products of the German Enlightenment and well assimilated to American culture, dismissed newer, generally more religiously conservative eastern European immigrants as backward and superstitious. The newer immigrants, in turn, viewed their more established compatriots as having abandoned the tradition. Disagreements about sexuality surfaced with respect to marital practices, specifically the traditional practice of early marriages arranged by a matchmaker, or *shadkhan*. These disagreements concerned gender roles, and more fundamentally, the nature of Judaism.

Within the Orthodox Judaisms of eastern Europe, the yeshiva movement and Hasidism shared an emphasis on the sublimation of sexual energies in service of God. For the yeshiva movement, Judaism revolved around the study of Torah. Young men, typically in their first years of marriage, would leave home often for several years at a time to study at the yeshiva. One description of an eastern European yeshiva described the young men as "reject[ing] all the pleasures of life before they have had a chance to enjoy them. Their young, beloved wives stay at their parents' homes and take pride in their husbands."[79] Young married men within the Hasidic movement entered into a similarly intense relationship with a Hasidic holy man or *tzaddic*, often again at some distance from their wives and families. The unusually strong drive within Hasidism toward sexual asceticism within marriage was balanced by a mys-

tical theology that emphasized the erotic union between the Hasid and
God. Drawing on the Song of Songs, the Baal Shem Tov taught that
prayer, the central act of the Hasidic Jew, is "a form of intercourse with
the Shekhinah and just as in the beginning of intercourse one moves
one's body, so it is necessary to move one's body at first in prayer.
. . . The power of his movement causes a great arousal, for it causes him
to think: 'Why am I moving myself?' [And he answers himself:] 'Because perhaps the Shekhinah is actually standing in front of me.' And
from this great power, he comes to a great passion."[80]

As Ann Braude has pointed out, gender roles within Orthodox Judaism were inverted relative to Victorian Protestant norms, such that men
fulfilled most of the religious obligations for the family, while women
supported the family materially, as well as supporting men in the
fulfillment of their religious obligations.[81] Reform Judaism, a product
of the Jewish Enlightenment, rejected the traditional practice of early
arranged marriages and rejected traditional Jewish gender roles. According to David Biale, "while the maskilim [Enlightened Jews] directed their polemics against a specifically Jewish system of marriage
and family, their goal was the same as that of other nineteenth-century
advocates of domesticity—upholding such values as privacy and chas-
tity."[82] Within the American context, the Orthodox, although not static
in their approach, retained more traditional understandings of sexuality
and marriage, while Reform Jews conformed most closely to the norms
of the dominant culture. Moreover, the Jewish Enlightenment combined with the traditional value placed on sex for pleasure within marriage prepared Reform Jews to take the lead, along with the most liberal
Protestants, in publicly advocating the legalization of contraceptives for
use within marriage.

Religion, Sex, and Society in the Twentieth Century

DIVISIONS OVER CONTRACEPTIVES

The twentieth-century movement to legalize contraceptives for use
within marriage marked a turning point in the history of religion and
sexuality in the United States. Its significance lay not in making contraceptives available, since, as indicated earlier, they were widely used
throughout the nineteenth century. Nor did it lie simply in increasing
access to contraceptives. Rather, the drama lay in the explicit and public

attempt to sever the legally protected and religiously sanctioned connection between sex within marriage and reproduction. While the romantic emphasis on sex within marriage as an expression of love had been undercutting private resistance to the use of contraceptives for decades, especially within the more liberal wings of the various traditions, the movement to legalize contraceptives forced religious traditions marked by profound ambivalence with respect to the role of sex within marriage to take public stands on the issue. The way they responded set the tone for the rest of the century.

Margaret Sanger, a Catholic by upbringing, a nurse by training, and a pragmatic sexual radical by disposition, was well positioned to lead the movement for the legalization of contraception. Having witnessed the lethal effects of illegal abortions on poor women during her nursing career, Sanger sought to give poor women equal access to contraceptive information and supplies by establishing birth control clinics. Sanger's fellow Catholics were the first to mobilize in response, and according to Ellen Chesler, birth control became "a vehicle for the church's institutional organization and political empowerment in this country." Father John A. Ryan, Catholic spokesperson on issues of public policy, began writing against the movement in the teens. In 1919 in their first joint pastoral letter, the American Catholic bishops prohibited Catholics from using artificial means of family limitation, and in 1930 Pope Pius XI followed with the encyclical *Casti Conubii* codifying official Catholic opposition.[83]

The mainstream consensus around sexuality began to show signs of disintegration in the thirties when Reform Jews, Unitarians, and Universalists in the United States followed the Anglican Lambeth Conference of Bishops in endorsing the use of contraceptives by married couples. Shortly thereafter a widely publicized committee report of the Federal Council of Churches also broke ranks with Catholics to support the legalization of contraceptives, although the member bodies of the council were sufficiently divided to prevent its formal endorsement.[84] While denominations influenced by the currents of theological modernism, such as the Congregationalists and Presbyterians, lent their support to the movement, more conservative denominations resisted. By mid-century, however, few Protestant denominations vehemently opposed the use of contraceptives by married couples.[85] Within Catholic circles, the changes wrought by the Second Vatican Council and the introduction of the birth control pill, both during the sixties, empowered a high

percentage of the American laity to ignore papal teachings on contraceptives.[86]

THE SECULARIZATION OF THE LAW

The fight over legal access to contraceptives eventually led to the Supreme Court and to a series of legal decisions that began the process of
unraveling the intimate relationship between religion, sex, and the law
in the United States. In a 1965 decision in *Griswold v. Connecticut,* the
Supreme Court overturned a Connecticut law banning the sale of contraceptives. In doing so they articulated "a right to marital privacy,"
later extended to two consenting adults, that was to serve as the basis
for the Court's decision in *Roe v. Wade* in 1973.[87] Two years after *Griswold,* the Supreme Court overturned a lower court ruling that defended
the state of Virginia's right to prohibit miscegenation, ruling that persons could not be prevented from marrying solely on the basis of race.[88]
This case, aptly titled *Loving v. Virginia,* subsequently formed the basis
for Judge Stephen Levinson's ruling in what has come to be known as
the "gay marriage case" brought to the Hawaii State Supreme Court in
May 1993. The judge, noting that Virginia had unsuccessfully tried to
defend its long-standing ban on interracial marriage by declaring that
the "Deity" found such marriages "unnatural," argued that the state of
Hawaii could not prevent persons from marrying solely on the basis of
gender.[89]

While laws limiting access to contraceptives and banning abortion
and miscegenation have been ruled unconstitutional, sodomy laws have
proved the most resistant to change at the national level.[90] In 1985, the
Eleventh Circuit Court of Appeals declared the sodomy law of Georgia
to be unconstitutional in the case of *Bowers v. Hardwick,* on the
grounds that "homosexual activity is a private and intimate association
that is beyond the reach of state regulation" based on the precedents
established in *Griswold v. Connecticut* and *Roe v. Wade.* The following
year, however, the Supreme Court overturned the lower court ruling in
Bowers v. Hardwick and refused to extend the right of privacy to sexual
activity between consenting adults of the same sex.

The state of Georgia in its case and Chief Justice Warren Burger in
his support of the majority view appealed to Christian tradition to support their position. Burger wrote that "decisions of individuals relating
to homosexual conduct have been subject to state intervention throughout the history of Western civilization. Condemnation of those prac-

tices is firmly rooted in Judeao-Christian moral and ethical standards."
In a powerful dissent Justice Harry Blackmun argued that "the assertion that 'traditional Judeo-Christian values proscribe' the conduct involved cannot provide an adequate justification for [the Georgia law]."
He concluded that "far from buttressing his case, petitioner's invocation
of Leviticus, Romans, St. Thomas Aquinas, and sodomy's heretical
status during the Middle Ages undermines his suggestion that [the
Georgia law] represents a legitimate use of secular coercive power."
Noting the "almost uncanny" parallels with *Loving v. Virginia,* he declared that "a State can no more punish private behavior because of religious intolerance than it can punish such behavior because of racial
animus."[91]

RELIGION AND COMPETING SOCIAL VISIONS

(The primary opposition to the Supreme Court rulings that repealed
laws restricting marriage and sexuality has been religious. Repeal has
been viewed rightly as a process of secularization. This does not mean,
however, that secularization of the law has not received religious support. In fact, the polarization within religious traditions around issues
of marriage and sexuality highlights a thoroughgoing shift in attitudes
toward sexuality within the more liberal wings of these traditions.

Since the sixties, the focus of controversy within Christian and Jewish religious bodies has been first on the legitimacy of sex outside marriage, then abortion, and most recently homosexuality. For most religious groups these are not peripheral issues. As James Davidson Hunter
has noted, "conflict within traditions has extended beyond the realm of
theology and ecclesiastical politics to embrace many of the most fundamental issues and institutions of *public* culture: law, government, education, science, family, and sexuality."[92] Conflicts over sexuality have
generated the most emotion and underlie many other issues of concern.
Convictions about the nature of legitimate sex (homosexuality and pre-
marital sex) and the control of fertility (contraception and abortion)
presuppose definitions of the family and assumptions about gender
roles that often play a part in controversies over education, science, law,
and government.

As in the nineteenth-century crisis over slavery, congregations have
mobilized on either side of the issue. Religious bodies have been threatened with schisms, and new denominations, such as the United Fellowship of Metropolitan Community Churches, have been founded in pro-

test. "Parachurch" organizations dedicated to advocacy on these issues have multiplied among Protestants, Catholics, and Jews since World War II. Moreover, as Hunter and others have argued, unprecedented alliances have formed across traditions to resist or promote change. Orthodox Catholics and Evangelical and Fundamentalist Protestants have aligned with one another as well as with Mormon and traditionally oriented Jewish organizations. Similar alliances, while not as unusual, have formed to link progressives across the lines of traditions.[93]

Two fundamentally different worldviews regarding the nature and purpose of sexuality and its relation to the sacred surface in these opposing alliances. The "orthodox" alliance would highlight the continuity between its own views and those of the Old World and the impact of "paganism" on liberal, feminist, and liberation theologians. The "progressives" would emphasize the ever-changing nature of theological traditions and the negative connections between orthodox beliefs and the creation and maintenance of patriarchal systems of race, gender, and class oppression. Both positions are oversimplified. The "orthodox" often fail to recognize either the pagan roots of many Christian and Jewish traditions or the range of opinion historically present within their traditions, while the "progressives" often underplay the radicalness of their break with the past or the extent to which traditional beliefs have been mobilized against the forms of oppression they oppose. Granting such oversimplification, nonetheless there is from a historical perspective considerable truth in both points of view.

If what has been normatively "American" with respect to religion and sexuality has been rooted in medieval canon law and later attempts by Euro-American Protestants to maintain their "purity" and power in the face of American heterogeneity, the secularization (and effective liberalization) of the law with respect to sexuality reflects and codifies changes within and among America's religious traditions. Within traditions, publicly expressed positions on sexuality are now far more diverse and contentious. In the relations among traditions, Euro-American Protestant sexual norms no longer hold their once privileged position. For many Americans, perhaps most, matters of religion and sexuality still are tightly linked, but the nature of those links is of less concern to the state.

TWO

Ritual Sites in the Narrative of American Religion

TAMAR FRANKIEL

In August 1994, my family and I took an excursion to Watts Cultural Center in south-central Los Angeles, where the current attraction was a series of workshops for children, titled "Healing Violence through Art." It featured sand painting by Tibetan monks. When we arrived, a pleasant "Anglo" woman greeted us, explained the exhibits briefly, and offered to show us the sand painting. In a room all to itself stood a large, about six-by-six-foot square, waist-high table where the painting was emerging. On three sides stood the three monks, each holding a pair of metal funnels that were about ten inches long and smooth except for one serrated strip of metal along their length. Each monk put colored sand in one funnel and then stroked it repeatedly with the other, so that the vibrations created by the metal rubbing on the serration caused grains of sand to drop out in a tiny stream. This flow of sand "painted" an intricate design.

The monks were in the middle of a two-week span of work, spending about six hours a day, five days a week on a four-sided mandala design. We watched for several minutes as they spun tiny lines from their tubes. One monk then stopped painting to offer a commentary for the visitors. The design was, he explained, the Palace of the Four Enlightened Beings of Compassion. The monks were painting from memory, in two dimensions, but the design truly represented a palace, in three dimensions. He described the names of the enlightened beings and showed us rooms, walls, and pillars on the painting.

Our guide took us to another very large room. Along three walls were altars, fashioned by the Watts community on West African models. In the center children sat at a long table, busily coloring mandala outlines on paper. The African American program director welcomed our younger children, explained the drawing project to them, read a poem, and began talking about stories of Africa and slavery. His people were in "exile," he explained, and the Tibetans in the next room were too.

While our younger children busied themselves coloring, my husband, our older children, and I moved into a third room where another mandala sand painting stood on a table. This one was being created by Watts teenagers. It featured in its four lobes a variety of symbols suggestive of Africa and nature, together with a dozen or more names of African Americans (for example, Malcolm X, Rosa Parks, Martin Luther King, Jr.) who, our guide explained, had been identified by the children as heroes whose lives were significant for them. Then she offered us the opportunity to learn and practice the sand painting techniques ourselves at a small table nearby.

After some hours of talking, drawing, painting, and watching, we departed. The intricate sand paintings would be completed in another week. Then, in a traditional ceremony, both the Tibetan monks and the Watts children would sweep up the sand, gather it together, and return it to the sea with a blessing.

Thus, in one of the more violent sectors of the African American community of Los Angeles, an extraordinary event of cultural contact was occurring, focused around learning and adapting a ritual. Both communities explicitly intended to cross geographical and cultural boundaries. The Watts community offered the space; the Tibetans offered the practice, negotiating a ritual setting in which the two groups could, temporarily and partially, share their traditions and enlarge their horizons. The director, who identified himself as a Jewish Buddhist, had chosen the concept of "exile," which both communities had experienced, to help bridge the gap. In practice, however, the monks and teenagers were not discussing common themes (indeed, only one Tibetan could speak much English at all) but were meeting one another through ritual. The community was constituting itself less by ecumenical dialogue than by common practice.

Creating a new community was, moreover, only part of the story. Watts participants also immersed themselves in a new experience by creating their own sand painting. This meant not merely acquiring the basic skills and discipline of hand necessary for a new art form, but entering into the psychological space of a Buddhist ritual marked by concentration and quietude. They painted in a silence broken only by the pleasant clinking of metal on metal as the tubes were rubbed together. Except for exchanges with visitors, there was no talking. The African American youngsters worked in silence with the same solemn visage as the monks, focusing intently on the work at hand. They were learning a practice that had as its intention "healing violence through art."

This example illustrates two of the fundamental functions of religion—defining a community and effecting inner change. These occur in the ritual act itself. Until recently, however, scholars of American religion would not likely have bothered to study ritual events like this one—and not only because it occurred in an urban ghetto, featured a group (Tibetans) who are quantitatively a small presence in America, and was focused on children. Rather, a scholar who happened on this scene a few decades ago might have admired the skill of the "artists," but then looked for the cognitive content of the adult dialogue—perhaps about exile—that would "explain" the meaning of this cultural exchange. Until very recently, our cultural and scholarly bias toward words, beliefs, leaders, and institutions would have made it difficult to recognize any other significance in the ritual event.

Fortunately, this situation has changed. One of the most exciting developments in American religious and cultural studies in the past decade or so is the proliferation of excellent studies of ritual. Some initial moves in this direction came from scholars of American "civil religion," beginning with Robert Bellah's work in the late 1960s. The field expanded rapidly to include many theoretically sophisticated and historically sensitive monographs on particular rituals, as well as historical studies that include ritual as part of the analysis.[1] The theoretically oriented work of anthropologists and historians of religion helped break new ground in deciphering ritual on its own terms.[2] The result is that we now can imagine narrating American religious history with a focus on ritual, illuminating previously obscure aspects of that history.

The task of this chapter is to illustrate how this end might be accomplished. It is not possible to present in such a brief space a full description of the processes of ritualization, or apply it to every period and movement. I stipulate certain features of ritualization without defend-

ing or explaining them at length. Then, to hint at the potential usefulness of writing American religious history from ritual sites, I offer the
outlines of a broad-brush historical narrative.

Ritualization and Empowerment

Like other components of culture, ritual actions continually reconstruct
the human situation in particular terms. Ritualizations are different
from discursive verbalizations, however, in that they rely primarily on
the physical embodiment of both actors and things used in the ritual
environment. As many scholars have noted, the effect of coordinated
ritualizations often resembles that of drama, which relies heavily on
body, positioning, and props on a stage.[3] Yet the effects of ritualizations
seldom achieve closure (in contrast to drama acted on a stage) and frequently are not even systematic. Ritualizations are sets of interlocking
practices by which the participants orient themselves to one another, to
aspects of their own selves, to outsiders or nonpractitioners, and to the
"other" which they often identify in religious terms (for example, divinity or spirit).[4] Ritual practices are frequently repetitive or habitual;
they are always strategic. They are bodily actions that dynamically and
continually define individual and community space through implicit or
explicit contrasts: we stand (instead of sit); we sit in circles (rather than
in rows).

Religious ritualization, further, orients the person in "spiritual
space," beyond the immediate social context: even the king kneels before God; one washes one's feet before entering the mosque; the priest
dons a special robe. Rituals can be very straightforward and "everyday," as when a Jew selects kosher over nonkosher food. Or they can
develop into elaborate sets of contrasts and analogies, forming complex
and even paradoxical networks of interlocking practices that do not
readily yield to analysis. Most important, however, the ritual act itself
communicates the "message" of ritual, telling participants what cues to
attend to. In church, one is not told "kneel because you are supposed
to express humility"; rather, one kneels because this is the way it is
done. As we learn the "right way" to perform the ritual, our bodies
become ritualized, thus embodying and internalizing the meaning of,
for example, humility. In our opening vignette, the Watts students were
not taught to "be quiet so you can attain peace of mind," but rather
they imitated the monks, painting in silence, and thereby, if the ritual

learning was successful, internalized a sense of meditative concentration.[5]

One of the principal accomplishments of ritualization is empowerment. Each strategic move enables individuals or groups to reorient themselves in relation to the powers that be. Imagine, for example, varieties of empowerment in the following actions: taking a seat on the dais next to the visiting lecturer; wearing flowers in your hair; taking time for personal prayer in the church service; washing your hands on leaving the cemetery; saying the password. These acts respectively enable one to align with the powerful, assert one's distinctiveness, carve out an individual space in the midst of a crowd, purify oneself of contact with the defiling, become an insider and reject the outsider. One can embody different selves by becoming socially "liminal," paradoxically gaining power by identifying with the powerless,[6] or, just as paradoxically, by entering into trance states that empower by separating the self from ordinary bodily experience. In our original example, the Tibetan monk—here the ritual expert teaching students the art of the mandala—empowers ritual apprentices in the art of inward peace and self-integration, offering an alternative to the rough-and-tumble life of the streets. At the same time, as the two groups work together on their own mandalas, designing symbols that help them imagine their historic traditions, they empower themselves as members of a larger community that extends over space and time.[7]

The range of ritualization is immense, limited perhaps only by the number of movements a human body can make or imagine. Nevertheless, it is possible to describe them as patterned strategic practices, responding to other actors' practices, within the immediate cultural context. On the macro level, each act of ritual empowerment opens up a direction that, when successful, can define a subculture or even an era. In the following pages I sketch out this process of orientation for American religious history.

Toward a New Historical Narrative

We can divide American religious history roughly into four periods, each dominated by different patterns of ritualization: independent ritual communities in interaction, 1600–1730; enthusiasm and the ritualization of passion, 1730–1850; national conformity and diversity, 1850–1950; and experiments in embodiment, 1950 to the present. As with all periodizations, these eras overlap. As broad generalizations, they serve heuristically as a framework for narrating the story of dominant trends.

INDEPENDENT RITUAL COMMUNITIES IN INTERACTION, 1600–1730

When Europeans began their attempts to colonize North America, they met Native Americans as complete strangers, each unprepared for one another's very existence. Yet each culture had standard ritualizations of encounter with the stranger—whether polite bows, presenting gifts, or preparing for war. Despite some early conflicts in the English colonies, including a few incidents in which Indians destroyed entire settlements, war was the last resort before 1689. Both sides explored many other alternatives.

Native Americans recognized potential as well as threat in the new settlements, and therefore attempted to incorporate Europeans in ways familiar from intertribal affairs, where each tribe's separate identity and way of life were respected. Tribal alliances had ensured territorial stability and allowed social, economic, and cultural exchanges (for example, learning the dances and rites of other tribes). Ritually, Indians sealed their alliances at gatherings of representatives from each tribe, meetings where mutual respect was ritually refined to such a degree that a person would never disagree publicly with another. Native Americans also attempted to create these kinds of relations with Europeans, a kind of egalitarian incorporation into new or existing alliances. In the long run, however, Europeans did not treat the indigenous system of relations with respect.

Another alternative was to incorporate Europeans as individuals. When Native Americans brought home captives, they usually adopted them into one of the families of the tribe to replace a lost family member. After an initiatory scenario to ritually eliminate the captive's "whiteness," the person became part of the tribe. So long as the European captive did not betray the group's trust, she or he would have complete freedom and appropriate privileges. Particularly with children, Native Americans invested a great deal of energy in teaching them their ways, treating them with patience and respect. Indeed, the Indians' reputation for kindness and patience spread back to the colonies, making some religious leaders fear the influence of Indians on New England.[8]

Most European settlers saw little value in Native American ways of life and, as Indian settlements became decimated by disease while European immigration increased, the newcomers expanded where they could. This often meant war. Protestant leaders sometimes had genuine concern for the Native Americans, but the best future they could imagine for Indians was for them to become Christian and civilized. But Protestants, as sectarians and separatists, had no group incorporation rites, and the only way for people to join was individually by conversion. Especially in New England and the Middle Colonies where conversion efforts were most intense, Protestants demanded numerous qualifications before admitting Native Americans into their churches. Essentially, the Native American had to be "civilized" before he or she could convert, and this involved a series of social-ritual adjustments ranging from giving up the "wandering" way of life and living in a "praying town" to wearing short hair and attending school. Such acts indicated a willingness to submit to discipline, understood as the "yoke" of Christian life. Notably, the English did not take Indians into their homes as Native Americans did their captives.

After separating American Indians from their traditional way of life, their Christian guides prescribed a more specific and demanding ritual education. In the schools, Indians were "sexually segregated, morally guarded, classically oriented, rigorously disciplined, patriarchally dominated."[9] Protestant ritual reliance on the Word—focusing on preaching and the understanding of preaching, reading and being able to reflect on and converse about the Bible—meant that the process of ritual incorporation could take years. In addition, the New England way required an ability to reflect and speak about one's own spiritual struggles. Puritans oriented themselves to being one of God's elect by means of a ritual language far more familiar to medieval mystics than to Native Americans—the drama of introspection. The construction of the "visible saint," in Edmund Morgan's classic phrase, required imagining God's judgment on oneself as sinner, ritual confession of one's distance from God, intense personal prayer and, eventually, a testimony of hope to the minister or congregation.

The Puritan also had to identify closely with the organic community to which he or she was bound in covenant, as part of the New Israel. The minister in the late seventeenth century frequently led communal introspection, in the form of the "jeremiad," full of warnings and urgings to repentance. Therefore, even to be baptized, a convert had to become fairly fluent in the Word, mastering many verbal ritual formulas

of self-examination as well as embodying appropriate emotional responses. This requirement was quite different from most indigenous
cultures, where normally only ritual experts such as shamans developed
special competence in orienting themselves inwardly. Moreover, for the
Native American to feel truly a part of most Protestant communities
would ultimately require identifying with the cultural history of the
Reformation and the exodus from England—a most difficult transformation.[10]

Until recently, historians interested in Protestant attempts to convert
Native Americans usually attributed failures either to the external situation (war, disease, and treaty breaking) or to the difficulty in accepting
Christian beliefs. Indeed, Indians sometimes did challenge Christian
theology, or listened politely while disagreeing privately. Highlighting
ritual shows, however, that the difficulty was not so much understanding new religious concepts as embodying a different practice.

Roman Catholic missions to Native Americans operated with different expectations. While the intellectual framework of Catholic doctrine
was as complex as that of Protestant teaching, ritual entry into the community was far simpler. The approach of Catholic regulars in North
America (mostly Franciscans or Jesuits), based on centuries of Catholic
encounters with pagan cultures, involved contacting prospective converts, learning their languages, and either moving into the community
and becoming adopted (as with the Jesuits) or bringing Native Americans into a mission to form a separate community (as with the Franciscans in California and the Southwest). There the friars would instruct
them. As Axtell has pointed out vividly in regard to Jesuit missions, this
instruction involved all the senses:

> In native hands he put attractive silver and brass medals, rings, crucifixes,
> and rosaries as mnemonic devices to recall his oral messages. . . . To their
> noses he introduced the mysterious fragrances of incense. To their lips he
> lifted holy wafers. To their eye he offered huge wooden crosses, candle-lit
> altars rich with silk and silver, long brocaded chasubles, and pictorial images
> of the major acts in the drama of Christianity. And into their ears he poured
> sonorous hymns and chants, tinkling bells, and an endless stream of Indian
> words, haltingly, even laughably pronounced at first, but soon fluent and ca-
> denced in native measures.[11]

The Franciscans in California, with their structured towns or "missions," offer perhaps the closest Catholic parallel to the Puritan "praying towns."[12] An Indian who was willing to separate himself by living

in the mission compound had taken one step toward salvation. If he could, at minimum, acknowledge one God and a consciousness of "sin" by recognizing wrongdoing in his earlier life, he could be baptized. Fuller instruction in theology could come later. Meanwhile, the friars could offer additional involvement, such as altar service for the church or, since the missions were total communities, becoming trained in European technologies. For example, some Native Americans became expert in the making of musical instruments. Therefore, it was not difficult, ritually speaking, to have access to some benefits of belonging to the community. In many ways the empowerment might seem considerable. It meant supplies of new kinds of food and clothing, as well as opportunities for learning in music and art, even if one never learned to read.

For these reasons California missions attracted more Native Americans, proportionately, than did the Puritan "praying towns." Yet the missions were not entirely successful because, as the Indians soon learned, the problem with a California Indian becoming a Roman Catholic was not getting into the community, but getting out. The friars seldom converted large groups, so the convert was isolated from familiar social relations. Because the friars feared pollution of the shallow-rooted new faith by contact with the "idolatrous" practices of the native community, they discouraged contact with the tribe. They sometimes used coercive rituals such as whipping, both to make converts work at the missions and to prevent new converts from leaving.[13] A particular source of stress developed when a neophyte or convert wished to attend the funerary ceremonies for a deceased family member. This was a powerful draw to return, at least briefly, to the traditional community for the rites. To many Native Americans, there was no necessary conflict between their ancestral practices and the rituals to the new Christian god, but the friars could not abide the two together. Thus ritual entry was easy, but converts learned, sometimes after the fact, that the exclusivity of Christianity often blocked the paths back to their old ways and relationships. In addition, they had to live under threat of punishment from the Franciscans.

These examples illustrate that patterns of ritualization were as important as modes of belief in the failure of Europeans and Native Americans to relate successfully. Christian missionaries either made ritual competence hard to attain—so that few Indians could experience the empowerment of truly belonging—or failed to accommodate sufficiently the Native Americans' desire to convert gradually, adding new practices and dropping the old little by little. The result was that, from the period of colonial empires in North America down to the mid-eighteenth century (and later in California), largely independent communities struggled to perpetuate themselves and to incorporate or dominate one another.

The struggle of Indian communities to reach working agreements with Europeans, and the Europeans' efforts to convert Native Americans are only two examples. In addition, each transplanted European settlement had, at first, its own dominant religious body that attempted to exclude or dominate others. Getting in and getting out—or being driven out—were regular issues within colonial Protestantism. At the extremes, Congregationalists persecuted and killed Quakers; separatists refused to commune with the impure. With each religious group striving to maintain its own separate patterns of ritualization, its own embodiment of the pure community, religious exchanges functioned mainly to defend the group's boundaries.

ENTHUSIASM AND THE RITUALIZATION OF PASSION, 1730–1850

The patterns of ritualization in Anglo-Protestant tradition itself were gradually changing so that, by 1730, we can speak of a new era in Protestant ritual. Our periodization here coincides roughly with the years from the beginning of the First Great Awakening to the enthusiasm that flooded the Northeast in the 1830s and 1840s. Notable throughout this period is the tendency for towns, cities, and regions to nourish revivalism and revolutionary enthusiasm, each with novel ritualizations.

The First Great Awakening was in part the result of a long process of erosion of the Puritan and early Protestant ritualizations that had empowered people through the practices of an organic, hierarchical community. The church, led by its clergy, stood at the center of a deferential society. These ritualizations had included requirements for proper social behavior such as codes of dress and demeanor, but also, and most specifically in Puritanism, for that complex mode of introspection and imagination known as the conversion experience. Already in 1662, the Halfway Covenant implicitly acknowledged that the ritual process did not always produce the desired experience, as did Solomon Stoddard's admission of the unconverted to the communion table. The jeremiad as a sermon form came to the fore as a kind of communal substitute, presenting current events in terms of God's judgment and proclaiming communal prayer and fast in times of declension.

In this way the community came to ritually mediate divine empowerment for those many who did not have their own personal experiences. This also meant that young people born after, say, 1700 had fewer mentors in the rituals of conversion, which made it even less likely that they would find a way to reaffirm their spiritual status as part of the New Israel. At the same time, power in society at large was shifting away from the "saints" to the newly aggressive merchant community, many of them not defined by their holy demeanor. Gradually the "reform of manners," a ritualization of civility, replaced what the devout believed to be the true foundation of morality, the personal relation to God that developed only through deep introspection. This trend toward an emphasis on civility and manners as attributes of the good person worried the more devout; by 1740, the "Log College" minister Gilbert Tennent could attract approval in many quarters by proclaiming that even many ministers were "unconverted."[14]

The "surprising conversions" of the Great Awakening, sparked by dramatic preachers like the Tennents, Jonathan Edwards, and George Whitefield, were ritual acts that empowered converts and challenged not only the immoral behavior of the larger society, which Whitefield especially attacked, but also the constraints of the local church. Their "enthusiasm" drew much criticism, but in the end religious communities grew stronger. Attention to ritual can illumine how practices challenged traditional community and how revivals strengthened the churches.

The kinds of manifestations found in the Great Awakening were not new: they had appeared long before in the British Isles, also in the context of challenges to the prevailing religious situation. As Leigh Schmidt has shown in his award-winning *Holy Fairs,* revival rituals evolved among Presbyterians in seventeenth-century Scotland during the annual summer and fall communion seasons. In great outdoor gatherings, people fasted, heard preparatory sermons on Saturday, took communion on Sunday, and held thanksgiving services on Monday before departing home. Fasting, confrontational sermons, vivid depictions of the "wondrous" drama of salvation appeared in revivals not only in Scotland but also in America, and continued in Presbyterian contexts until the nineteenth century, as in the work of Scottish preacher James McGready and the famous Cane Ridge revival in Kentucky.[15] Such gatherings in America became, in effect, pilgrimages to the great preachers and implicitly challenged sacred community and, more specifically, the established minister who had been "called" by the local congregation.

Pilgrimage to the revival preacher served to create a sacred community beyond the local church, through the act of leaving one's home and engaging in a complex series of rituals designed to empower the individual through direct contact with God.[16]

At the same time, the often extreme bodily manifestations of the revivals transformed the bodily experience itself. They could have been rejected as demonic (as similar manifestations had been in the era of the Salem witch trials); but, when accepted by at least part of the community, they encouraged a radical rejection of prevailing orientations of the self. These strategies of ecstasy defined the participants in direct relationship to God, as different from both the "civil," rational-ethical religious community and those who indulged in the material temptations that were flooding the colonies. In the aftermath, the "enthusiastic" conversions gave individuals their authentic entry into a church, strengthening the churches numerically. The newly converted also insisted on stronger rituals of moral discipline and, thereby, constructed for the enlarged community a bulwark against the temptations of the outside world.[17]

Another unintended consequence was that the creation of a larger revival community softened boundaries between denominations, suggesting that the bonds among Christians who felt the divine power were more significant than their differences. Schisms were, to be sure, as common as ecumenical feelings; but the debates were less over canonical rituals than the ritualization of enthusiasm itself. These debates continued over the next hundred years and more. As Terry Bilhartz has pointed out, still in the early 1800s Episcopalians in Baltimore were castigating those who "instead of controlling their passions . . . are continually expecting visionary attestations of divine favour," while Methodists continued to criticize the lukewarm "formalist" and attested to the reality of "the power."[18]

The diminishing of the significance of boundaries applied also to borders between colonies. The waves of enthusiastic revivals empowered individuals to act beyond their local communities, and their first joint moves were political and military. During the French and Indian War that followed on the heels of the First Awakening (1745–63), the colonists identified themselves as the pure community against France, the "scarlet whore," and Canada, the "North American Babylon." As Sacvan Bercovitch has observed, the ritual of the jeremiad, adapted to this millennial scenario, extended to the Revolution. John Adams could write in traditional ritual formulas (on 3 July 1776) that "Americans

shall suffer Calamities still more wasting and Distress yet more dread-
ful," but later predict that "deliverance be wrought out . . . as it was for
the children of Israel." Likewise, one of the first proposals for the Seal
of the United States, from Franklin and Jefferson, showed Moses leading the chosen people; in fact, the adopted symbol, the eagle, represented the eagles of the books of Exodus and Revelation.[19] Political "enthusiasm" fell into disfavor after the violence of the French Revolution,
but millennial ideas erupted dramatically again after the turn of the century.[20] Moreover, as many observers have noted, when party politics began in earnest in the 1830s, that new "enthusiasm" had similarities with
revivals of the period. Here were the beginnings of "civil religion," a
grand new ritual drama to be acted out in many variations over the next
century and more.

In short, the evangelical revival empowered participants by adapting
familiar ritualizations—from the Puritan conversion and the Scottish
fair—to new situations. The unintended results were dramatic. Instead
of the Puritan approach in which divine power was mediated through
small communities of the elect, and ultimately through the "little commonwealth" of the family where election ideally passed from parent to
child, now God empowered individuals directly. At the end of the eighteenth century, the emotional and physical realms became the locus of
individual empowerment, even more than in the First Awakening, while
weeping, fainting, and more extreme manifestations characterized even
urban revivals.[21] A major issue in the scholarship on the Second Great
Awakening has revolved around whether the awakening was an "organizing process" or a destabilizing force. A ritual perspective suggests that
the emphasis on empowerment through individual ecstasy, in the open
context of the early 1800s, was likely to be revolutionary.[22] This supports the contention of some scholars that, while church membership
increased, the Second Awakening undermined traditional authority and
gave far more scope to individuals, sectarian groups, and churches that
encouraged lay participation.[23]

Lay participation began to include African Americans. Even the
southern slaves were able to merge their African heritage with evangelical belief in the ritual setting of the revival, but with a different style of
empowerment from that of whites. As Walter F. Pitts has explained in
his analysis of Afro-Baptist ritual, the structure of African ritual allowed for a rather smooth amalgamation with evangelical practice. The
African initiatory structure of chanting produced a passive-receptive
frame of mind, followed by rhythmic drumming and dancing to induce

spirit-possession (in American revivalism called the "shout"). This was structurally analogous to the preparation period with prayer and quiet hymn singing, followed by dramatic, rhythmic preaching which was intended to bring the "sinner" to a religious experience. The difference was that African Americans looked to this experience of being overcome by the Spirit as a regularly desirable religious experience (although its duration was much shorter in the New World), while evangelical whites regarded it as a humbling one-time experience, rather to be feared than welcomed. This confirms Donald Mathews's interpretation some years ago that "while whites might rightfully be said to have 'broken down' under preaching, blacks were lifted up, enabled to celebrate themselves as persons because of their direct and awful contact with divinity." The black/white divisions did not remain so clear, however. Some black churches later dropped the ecstatic aspects of ritual, while some whites later in the century, notably Pentecostals, adopted them for regular ritual use.[24]

In particular, African Americans contributed to the musical style of the revivals. A disapproving observer testified to this phenomenon: "We have too, a growing evil, in the practice of singing in our places of public and society worship, *merry* airs, adapted from old *songs,* to hymns of our own composing: often miserable as poetry, and senseless as matter, and most frequently composed and first sung by the illiterate *blacks* of the society."[25] Methodists had used hymns, particularly those of John Wesley, while Puritans began to introduce Isaac Watts's hymns in the late eighteenth century. Often a testimonial in simple lyric form, the hymn became a new lay cultural form, with tunes frequently adapted directly from popular music. In addition, lay people learned to organize orderly meetings that previously had been in the hands of the clergy alone. They led public prayer and used testimonial, a ritual form evolved from Puritan self-examination, to replace or supplement the sermon (or lay exhortation).[26] All of these elements constituted a new ritual form which transformed evangelical religion.

An increase in negative attitudes toward the clergy undermined the range of their authority. Ritually speaking, authority figures are those who are themselves proficient in ritualization and/or who can teach others. They also may be individuals who can negotiate differences in order to hold the community together. The decline of the covenanted, established church and the cultural demotion of the minister made room for the "prophet." Prophets use information and insights which they access while (presumably) in altered states of consciousness—

dreams, visions, and the like—to prescribe and model solutions to a community's problems. The late eighteenth and early nineteenth centuries brought forth, for example, Ann Lee of the Shakers, Alexander Campbell of the Disciples of Christ, Joseph Smith of the Mormons, Ellen G. White of the Seventh-day Adventists, and John Humprey Noyes of the Perfectionists.[27]

These more radical, "prophetic" movements illustrate by their extremes a significant feature of ritualization. The trance manifestations of the revivals had encouraged a spontaneous, "uncontrolled" physical body. The visions of the prophets taught new ways to ritualize the body. They regulated excitement and "enthusiasm" through new social rules, frequently focused on sexuality and the family. Shakers, Adventists, Mormons, and Oneida Perfectionists all regulated relations between men and women. Concurrently but less dramatically, new medical and health alternatives emerged (such as vegetarianism, which the Adventists later adopted) to purify or perfect the physical body.[28]

In the 1840s, as the more radical groups were re-ritualizing the body, especially its sexual aspects, mainstream evangelicals faced the same issues. The greatest threats to evangelical purity were physical acts that "excited" or "overstimulated" the passions. The leading contenders were alcohol, slavery (believed to encourage violence), and materialism. In addition, as Ann Taves points out in Chapter 1 of this volume, mainstream Protestant culture defined as deviant many forms of sexuality, ranging from too much sexual activity in marriage to Roman Catholic celibacy. Any such behaviors were a threat to the pure community, many believed, and indulgence in them could drive a person crazy.[29] While the radicals created new versions of family and society, mainstream Protestants put their faith in what they considered the "traditional" home, the still center in the maelstrom of a passionate society. In fact, however, they created a new version of the home where the woman was domestic priestess, who learned (from numerous housekeeping and family manuals) the rituals that would, together with her faith, empower her to create the perfect home and haven for her husband and children.

Yet openings for the laity who were empowered by their direct contact with God meant far greater opportunities for women in the outside world. While women always had been a majority in the churches, as Ann Braude argues in Chapter 3, they now began to employ organizational talents and devote their energy to creating a more holy community.[30] Beyond the home, in reform associations comprised largely of women and clergy, northerners created a white Protestant network that aimed to purify the national community of its vices, particularly the passion-exciting practices of drinking, prostitution, and slavery. The reformers' ubiquitous tracts and impassioned lectures promoted an intense concern for social morality within the millennial community. As a corollary to the increasing emphasis on the home and transdenominational reform movements, many churchgoers belittled denominational ritual differences in areas like the church service, baptism, and the Lord's Supper.[31]

In the South, separatists under local leaders tended not to form large denominational movements or reform societies. They differentiated within small communities, as for example the Baptists did. There too, lay people redefined their churches by developing or elaborating, within a biblical-evangelical framework, ritual practices such as the love feast, laying on of hands, anointing the sick, devoting children to Christ, the right hand of fellowship, the kiss of charity, and the washing of feet. The prominence of the body is clear, particularly in crossing established boundaries of intimacy. "Separates," comments Donald Mathews, "touched each other with hands, arms, and lips, actions which were completely at odds with conventions that maintained invidious distinctions among people in part by maintaining social distance." Changes in ritualization undermined the power invested in the South's social class system and replaced it with tight communal bonds.[32]

Thus the long struggle over how to orient self and community in a New World, a struggle marked by the repeated abandonment of established identities in favor of contact with God, seemed to have come to a new consolidation by 1850. What Marilyn Westercamp has called the "triumph of the laity" in the First Great Awakening became even more pronounced. Enthusiasm faded, and the generation born after 1840 would not stir up the same kinds of revivals as their grandparents had. God now worked through the nation as a millennial instrument, in the meantime counting on woman, home, and family to socialize every individual into the rituals of pure living. Whether living in a Shaker utopian community or toiling in a reform group, American Protestants were promoters of a new order.

NATIONAL CONFORMITY AND DIVERSITY, 1850–1950

The revivals of Dwight L. Moody and Ira D. Sankey in the 1870s were a consummate expression of the predominant evangelical ritual form.

They emphasized lay prayer meetings, Sankey's "gospel hymns," and mothers' weeping for their wayward sons. Moody saw domesticated, revival Christianity as the bulwark of hope in the stormy sea of urbanizing America. Yet his sense of a national community centered around evangelical religion, family, and home was necessarily incomplete, and soon it became the ritual practice and ideology of only one faction, albeit a powerful one.

The nation's new challenge was diversity. By the middle of the nineteenth century, large numbers of Roman Catholics from Ireland had moved into urban centers, while Mexicans challenged American efforts to control California and Texas. The Mexican War may have seemed a minor affair, but only because it was soon overshadowed by the intense national suffering of the Civil War. A "Yankee" victory heralded new expansion, but also brought new wars—the Indian Wars, ending in the consolidation of the reservation system, and the Spanish-American War that made the United States an imperial power. Internal stresses arose from immigration, particularly Jews fleeing from Russian pogroms and other eastern Europeans from economic and political distress. World War I brought the United States into collusion with a larger European community, yet it also brought more immigrants until, in the 1920s, Congress established strict immigration quotas. Intense antiforeign, racist, and anti-Semitic sentiments followed, ironically, on the heels of the war to "make the world safe for democracy." During the same period, class divisions became more intense, while secular pastimes became more acceptable (for example, in entertainment, sports, and the arts), diversifying Americans' behavior even more.

Mainline Protestants, who still dominated numerically and wielded cultural influence, were sharply aware of the rapid expansion of the power of the United States westward and internationally. They developed new kinds of ritualizations to orient the expanded community, in what could be called the commemorative phase of American civil religion. Northerners, by 1900, transformed the horrors of the Civil War into sacrifices that fulfilled a providential destiny. They saw the succeeding wars of territory and ideology as fulfilling the promise of the millennial community. These developments took ritual form in devout observance of Thanksgiving in the home, enabling identification with the Pilgrims and their mission as the New Israel, while simultaneously connecting the domestic priesthood to civil religion. Self-sacrifice on behalf of that mission was taught in Memorial Day parades in virtually every town, where young children marched, carried American flags, and placed flowers on soldiers' graves at the town cemetery.[33] In the arena of church-religion, missionary work became a highlight of Protestant public relations, with reports of missionaries heavily featured in evangelical magazines. The founding of the new journal entitled, significantly, the *Christian Century,* heralded the glories to come. Unfortunately, there was also a dark side to this aspect of American ritualization: antiblack and anti-Semitic sentiments flourished. Attempts were made to quash Native American dance. Lynchings became communal rituals in the South and, by the 1930s, protofascist groups appeared who equated "America" with "Anglo-Saxon."

The aspiring upper and middle classes initiated new efforts, often outside the religious institutions, to reorient themselves to a larger world. Philanthropy in the late nineteenth and early twentieth centuries made possible the establishment of several major museums, from the American Museum of Natural History to the University of Pennsylvania Archeology Museum to the Southwest Museum in Los Angeles. One of the most popular features of a ritual museum visit, for the cultured American, was the tour through archeological exhibits. These reminded the visitor of the glories of Egypt and Peru and introduced our own "ancient" peoples, the Native Americans, through ancient and contemporary artifacts. Americans could walk through history and see the vanished and supposedly vanishing races and, at the same time, recognize themselves as at the pinnacle of civilization. This period also saw new definitions of society's relationship to nature (often through imitation of Native American culture) in such varied movements as the Sierra Club, Boy Scouts, Campfire Girls, and conservation groups.[34]

Meanwhile, the lower and middle classes became a market for new kinds of entertainment. The circus and vaudeville achieved great popularity with their celebrations (or parodies) of diversity. The "dime novel" offered models of American heroes, the best-known among them being Horatio Alger's self-made man. Baseball and football emerged as popular sports that, in addition to providing diversion, celebrated a manliness and competitiveness that the prevailing evangelicalism had not much encouraged. (Significantly, one of the great revivalists of this era, Billy Sunday, was a former baseball player.) Fraternal societies such as the Masons and Lions Club flourished. What would eventually become a major imaginal ritual by which Americans oriented themselves—the entertainment of the "movies"—emerged in the early twentieth century. That industry was the product of entrepreneurs who were willing, unlike the established wealthy investors, to play to the working

classes. Many of the creators of the film studios and movie house empires were immigrants, an unusual proportion of them Jews.[35] Like African Americans in the religious world of the early nineteenth-century
revival, such "outsiders," along with their black contemporaries, continued to shape American religion and culture.

"Outsiders" were becoming more important numerically in this period, even as they debated among themselves how to Americanize. The
growing Roman Catholic population chose, for the most part, to maintain their ritual distinctiveness through parish and private devotional
life. The Catholic Church rapidly developed ecclesiastical organizations
to incorporate unchurched individuals through a system of private
schools that attracted some liberal Protestants as well. The Jesuits in
particular transformed education and founded colleges. Priests, sometimes imitating revivalist techniques, gathered the unchurched in the
cities or on the frontiers. The system of ritualizations into which they
were incorporated was essentially the traditional one of masses and confession, feasts and fasts, and devotions to the saints, largely uninflu-
enced by the Protestant majority. However, as Catherine L. Albanese
points out in Chapter 8, Catholics argued over acculturation issues such
as the school system, the dominant language, the use of alcohol, and the
appropriateness of fraternal societies. New immigrations also raised
tensions within Catholicism. For example, the dominant Catholic community, the Irish, found it disturbing when Italians immigrated in large
numbers, since the Italian customs brought more dramatic emotional
and bodily rituals into public view.[36] But most Catholics accepted the
possibility of remaining a practicing Catholic and, at the same time,
affirming an American identity through the rituals of the civil religion
such as Thanksgiving and the Fourth of July.

Jews were in a somewhat different situation. Those who immigrated
in the nineteenth century were mostly from Germany, where the Enlightenment's influence on educated Jews had led many communities to
adopt a Reform practice. The Reformers understood themselves not as
imitating non-Jews but simply as "modernizing" in the light of reason
and in pace with civilization. Their watchword in reforming ritual was
"decorum" or, as one congregation described it, "that high standing of
respectability which the world has a right to expect." In practice, this
meant adopting synagogue ritual styles similar to those in "cultured"
Christian churches. In the American case, it meant white northern Protestant styles that were dominant in the major cities. Jewish Reformers
used unison readings instead of individual chanting, adopted more

refined hymns, and added choirs. They changed the traditional *d'var Torah* (word of Torah) into an inspirational sermon rather than a discourse on Jewish law, moved the reader's desk to the front instead of the center of the synagogue, and gave their rabbis titles such as "Lecturer and Preacher." Amid much controversy, they adopted mixed seating (an innovation of late eighteenth century Protestants).[37] They gradually dropped ritualizations that they judged to be primarily social-cultural (kosher food and distinctive dress) and substituted confirmation for bar mitzvah. In making these choices, they oriented their communities through synagogue services that paralleled those designed by mainline, upper-class Protestants for their churches. They also maintained distinctiveness by recognizing implicitly that their channel of empowerment was not the personal-salvation model of Christianity, but their special communal relationship to God mediated through the holidays they chose to emphasize, particularly Rosh Hashanah, Yom Kippur, and Passover.

Orthodox Jews arrived from eastern Europe in small numbers in midcentury, and by the tens of thousands a few generations later (mostly 1880–1920). It is significant that most of these Jews were from Russian-controlled areas where, even before the pogroms, they had learned about the temptations and the effects of assimilation.[38] In addition, traditional synagogues of eastern Europeans tended to be small gatherings primarily for men. As such, the shuls not only helped to maintain the habits and lifestyle of the home country, but also functioned as communal supports. In their small groups, they strengthened the internally empowering aspects of Jewish life, insisting on the religious value of every element of Jewish distinctiveness. Their sense of election went hand in hand with purity and seclusion, much like Puritans in the early days of the colonies. They made few changes except that, being sensitive to accusations of a lack of "decorum," they often hired cantors.

Still, they rapidly lost ground with the younger generation. Despite attempts by new turn-of-the-century organizations like the Orthodox Union and Young Israel to offer English sermons and classes, Orthodoxy rapidly became the smallest Jewish "denomination." Conservative Judaism, beginning in the 1890s with attempts to strike a balance between Reform and Orthodoxy, was more successful with the younger generations. Conservatives used more English in services, emphasized Hebrew schools, and tried, like many large Protestant churches around 1900, to make the synagogue a versatile community center for many activities ranging from school to recreation. In this respect the Conservatives were more like the immigrant Catholics, insisting on distinctive rituals but Americanizing all the while. Like all Jews of this period, they emphasized family and community rather than the individual in their ritualizations, in this way distinguishing themselves from Protestants.

Within traditional Protestantism, another division was emerging with the movement known as Fundamentalism. Accusing the Protestant denominations of becoming "modernist" to the point of denying the Bible, the Fundamentalists provoked a crisis that pitted the Bible against science and materialism in all forms, demanding that Americans join one of two opposing camps. The public significance of the movement was clear since the crux of the debate centered on the primary issue of education: were children to be taught to imagine themselves as descendants from monkeys or as creations of God? The 1925 Scopes trial of a public school teacher became a national drama that ended in the (temporary) public defeat of Fundamentalism.

Ritually, there was far more diversity than is suggested by the dichotomy assumed by Fundamentalists. In the late nineteenth century, several diverse metaphysical religious movements had emerged, first in the Northeast and later spreading rapidly to urban areas in the Midwest and California. Spiritualism, which began with the famous "rappings" in upstate New York, was one of the first of these. After being scandalized in the post–Civil War era by revelations of fraudulent séances, Spiritualism continued to grow in a low-profile way. Another series of movements emerged from the forging of mesmerist and healing traditions—Christian Science and a variety of New Thought organizations (Church of Divine Science, Church of Religious Science, Unity, and others). Each claimed to harness the power of mind to produce positive effects on the body and the material world.

Notable in the metaphysical movements was a loose relationship to community. In a communal ritual where contact and interaction are significant, the individual makes a bodily connection to other participants and to material reality. Whether the ritual acts are a common meal with prayers or a choreography of kneeling, bowing, and processing, the practices create a shared physical reality. In groups with a more tenuous communal structure, the "spiritual"—with its physical manifestations in various states of consciousness from dream to ecstasy—appears to separate from the material. The Spiritualist séance oriented participants to other realms through its meditative atmosphere. As participants sat in a circle around a table, their community enlarged. It became a heavenly one because it included nonphysical beings who manifested themselves in these rituals. These figures did their part for the community as they advised and consoled those who remained in the material world. Christian Science and New Thought, using the recital of formulas known as "affirmations," oriented people to a world where everything was "Mind" or "Energy." It was not family Bible study, but the private affirmation (a last remnant of the testimonial) and the "reading room" visit that empowered individuals. Despite the apparent isolation from the ordinary world, however, the aim of such practices was mastery of the material world, so that many affirmations spoke of physical strength and bodily health as well as material wealth.[39] Logically enough, both Spiritualists and New Thought proponents proclaimed universalist, nonsectarian messages. As body did not "matter," group membership was not significant either. Thus, these groups attracted occasional Catholics or Jews who broke away from their traditional communities. In addition, American versions of Buddhist and Hindu thought began to appear, particularly among the more educated.[40]

On another track in the same era, the Holiness movement emerged from revival origins and developed into new denominations. Holiness churches emphasized a stricter moral code than the mainstream churches, which they believed had accommodated too much to the customs and fashions of the secular world. They focused on rituals of appropriate dress, emphasized behavioral codes such as avoiding dance halls and sensual entertainment, and separated themselves from the worldliness around them (without forming economically separate communities). In addition, they often had strong "spiritist" inclinations, as appeared in the early Church of the Nazarene. Those who were suspicious of "matter" opened themselves to the presence of "spirit."[41] The search for a deeper connection with the Holy Spirit also came to fruition in another movement, Pentecostalism. This movement flourished both in rural areas, as in its Kansas origins, and in urban enclaves, as in the Azusa Street revival in Los Angeles in 1906. Pentecostalism ritualized altered states of consciousness which resulted in "gifts of the Spirit," most notably glossolalia or speaking in tongues. In ways similar to metaphysical movements, but with a different style and communal context, Pentecostals ritualized individual behavior to promote inner transformation.[42]

The century from 1850 to 1950, then, saw an increasing materialism and elaboration of rituals of the secular sphere, together with an increasing "spiritualism" in religion. The idea of a single nation with a mission in the world promoted outward conformity, often on a military model with successful generals as the heroes. This Protestant and civil-religious orientation remained dominant throughout the period, largely defining the meaning of "American." Yet those who oriented themselves by means of an inward spirituality offered vigorous alternatives for empowerment through intense or unusual experiences. These ranged from infusions of divine energy to possession by the Holy Spirit. These explorations of other realms underwent considerable modification and, in some ways, went underground during the two World Wars and the Great Depression.

EXPERIMENTS IN EMBODIMENT, AFTER 1950

As suggested earlier, dance, music, and film began to transform Americans' bodily orientation as early as the 1920s (the Jazz Age). These popular trends eventually affected religion and spirituality as well. In dance, the flappers of the 1920s gave way to dancer Fred Astaire in the 1930s and 1940s, while the Big Band sound captivated the public. African American culture was the direct source of these cultural phenomena, and it is no accident that African Americans themselves first gained recognition in the field of music, in blues and jazz. The film industry, particularly in promoting the romantic stars of the 1930s, produced imaginal ritualizations of more permissive sexual relationships. Simultaneously, the temperance movement's century-long attempt to control Americans' passions died with the repeal of the Eighteenth Amendment (Prohibition) in 1933.[43] During the Great Depression and World War II, however, people tended to reaffirm traditional values. In the popular imagination, African Americans and their jazz music came to be associated with degeneracy and drugs, just as Jews became linked with (anti-American) socialism.

The traditional ritualizations that constituted evangelical culture continued to be powerful counterweights to new explorations throughout the 1950s, the era of the "man in the gray flannel suit." Conformity was the watchword in politics and social relations as well as religion. But the emergence of rock music, epitomized in Elvis Presley and expanded by the Beatles, introduced new, less controlling attitudes toward the body, which reflected the influence of both African American and working-class styles. Some intellectuals alienated by the conformity of mainstream America produced the Beat Generation culture which modeled new lifestyles. One of the most critical religious developments, which also deeply affected American society at large, was the practice of nonviolent resistance, adapted by Dr. Martin Luther King, Jr., from Mahatma Gandhi. The combination of African American preaching style and communal energy with influences from India produced revolutionary ritualizations—the sit-in and the protest march. None of these became core elements in new or old church rituals. Even rock music did not enter the churches for two decades or more. But the cumulative effect of these secular and religious practices was twofold: they shifted the focus toward the *integration* of body and soul, rather than toward the spirit/matter distinction that had characterized the previous period, and they connected spiritual pursuits with moral ideals and political action.

One of the most widespread forms of mind-body ritual integration appeared in what was first called the human-potential movement. Springing from psychological practice in the late 1940s and 1950s (especially Gestalt psychology), this movement reached its apotheosis in the famous retreats at Esalen on the Big Sur coast of California. A wide variety of ritualizations attempted to integrate the "whole self" through individual and group psychotherapy, massage, and meditation. This holistic movement, led primarily by psychologists and self-proclaimed spiritual teachers, was one example in a multifaceted exploration of the connections between psychological and physical health. It later inspired a large collection of self-improvement groups, workshops, and literature. At the same time, pastoral counseling became a new ritual practice in some mainstream (particularly Methodist) churches as early as the 1960s, bringing psychological know-how to bear on individual spiritual growth.

Some of the self-improvement movements either claimed religious credentials or advocated spiritual healing. Probably the most widespread in its influence was the network of what came to be called "twelve-step programs." Beginning with Alcoholics Anonymous, which had originated in the 1930s to address the medical problem of alcoholism from a spiritual perspective, this network expanded enormously after the 1960s. It became a multipronged attack on many personal problems labeled as addictions, from drug use and compulsive eating to anger and obsessive gambling. Similar to the New Thought movements in their emphasis on positive thinking and self-directed development, they went beyond their predecessors in offering a structured plan based on abstinence, that is, control of the body in the area of the problem being solved. A full program of social support via telephone and meetings made these twelve-step programs systems of multiple, mutually reinforcing, verbal affirmations.

These movements were just the beginnings of an approach to spirituality that was highly eclectic, using a variety of techniques from different sources to orient the individual in a pluralistic universe where community and family ties were highly unpredictable. The result was a kind of cultural revolution in the 1960s that led to diverse practices in the 1970s and 1980s. Without major changes in traditional religious affiliation, people came to tolerate a wide range of physical expression in body and dress. After the initial shocks of the fifties and early sixties, rock groups and protest marches had become part of American culture. Some Americans accepted a variety of Asian religions, with Buddhist and Hindu forms of meditation becoming a significant feature even for many people who retained loose affiliations with other traditions. In this new atmosphere, the jockeying of various religions for people's allegiance did not necessarily create conflict. A religious person in the 1980s could sit in Buddhist meditation, eat a Japanese macrobiotic diet, practice ta'i chi, attend Alcoholics Anonymous meetings, and elicit no reaction at all from neighbors in the pews of her suburban Methodist church. In a parallel way, a Catholic could practice a much wider variety of ritual—endorsed by the Second Vatican Council in the 1960s—and not be condemned as a heretic.

Earlier movements also reawakened during this period. Some religious groups who had not embraced the ritualizations of emotion and encounter in earlier periods began to do so. The charismatic movements in Catholic and Episcopal churches introduced ecstatic encounters with the Holy Spirit as accompaniments or supplements to the more usual means of grace, the sacraments. The traditional rituals did not disappear, but participants in "charismatic" services now could orient themselves by direct religious experience. Thus traditions that already had emphasized "embodiment" now added another ritual form that allowed a more intense and personal spirituality. Even more telling, many contemporary Pentecostals, whether Catholic or Protestant, made physical-psychological healing prominent among the "spiritual gifts" they celebrated in communal ritual. Indeed, a range of religious leaders, from Pentecostal preachers to psychic healers, emphasized therapeutic practices for mind and body.

Eclecticism for its own sake was not the goal. The aim of most of these movements was to deepen individual spirituality and connect participants to the physical world. In some ways, this effort resembled that of nineteenth-century Evangelicals to harness the energy of the Second Great Awakening to drive efforts for social reform. But the groups acting on new ideals after 1960 had no one framework (such as the domestic model that had united many nineteenth-century reformers). Many "reforms" espoused by the spiritual movements of the late twentieth century were private and personal, such as physical fitness and psychotherapy.

Many movements, nevertheless, looked beyond the individual, the church, and even the nation to a larger sphere of moral responsibility. This was true of those who joined Martin Luther King in the civil rights movement and protested against the Vietnam War. Ecologically oriented movements frequently tried to connect spirituality and political action as they worked to preserve the environment. Some of these adopted a model of human connection to nature inspired by John Muir; others created neopagan groups or borrowed Native American rituals. Implicitly, such ritualizations created an imagined global moral community. But in this view, that moral community should be imagined not as a melting pot, but as one that preserved and celebrated differences. Jews, Native Americans, African Americans, Latino Americans, and others could hope to define a social space in which they could recover their roots, reinterpret their traditions, and negotiate their place in American culture. This orientation was enshrined in two major museums of the era—the Holocaust memorial in Washington, D.C., and its West Coast counterpart, the Museum of Tolerance in Los Angeles. On one level, these sites focused on Jews and other minorities, commemorating people who died at the hands of Nazis; but, as the name of the Los Angeles museum indicates, the more important message was that prejudice of all kinds must disappear.

Changes in Judaism and Catholicism during this period provide an example of how these various trends worked together. On the one hand, for Jews the trauma of the Holocaust resulted in significant disaffection from religious identity and increased inclination toward religious intermarriage. On the other hand, among those who remained formally connected to Judaism, emotional-spiritual emphases showed marked change after World War II. Hasidic teachings that emphasized prayer, music, and joyous service, which were brought to the United States with the twentieth-century waves of Jewish immigration, began to attract attention in mainstream Judaism during the 1950s.[44] One sect in particular, Chabad-Lubavitch, trained rabbis to move out of the traditional

study halls into communities and colleges where Jews were highly assimilated and reintroduce Jews to ritual observance in an energetic,
positive, and emotionally satisfying way. Significantly for our understanding of this period, these same Hasidic traditions emphasized the
sanctification of everyday, material, and bodily life through spiritual intentions. As a result of this and other similar movements that modeled
themselves on this kind of outreach, the number of Orthodox adherents
began to grow rather than decline for the first time in two hundred
years. A Jewish renewal movement, modeled on Hasidic fellowship but
not necessarily Orthodox, began in the late 1960s, attracting many who
had participated in the civil rights and antiwar movements. In the
1980s, teachers emerged to introduce one or another form of Jewish
meditation, sometimes incorporating Hasidic along with modified Buddhist or Hindu practices. If we recall that a Jewish program director
spearheaded the teaching of Tibetan Buddhist sand painting to Watts
teenagers, we can see an unusual way in which, for some Jews, the connection between spirituality and political concerns manifested itself.

As Jews faced disaffiliation, Catholics too lost the loyalty of many
members of the younger generations. Far fewer entered the priesthood,
and many of those who remained officially affiliated abandoned traditional practices such as devotion to the saints and refused to follow papal injunctions on such issues as contraception. The Second Vatican
Council, however, helped shift the tide by allowing for greater lay participation, and this encouraged spiritual growth and liturgical experimentation beginning with the "underground church" of the late 1960s.
Soon after, ferment in many other Roman Catholic populations, notably
in Latin America, brought U.S. Catholics to an intensified moral consciousness. Protests and boycotts on behalf of Spanish-speaking farm
workers brought the message home to the United States. Liberation theology encouraged followers to identify with the poor, making that the
criterion for authentic Christianity. Thus spirituality, morality, and
changing attitudes toward embodiment marked some forms of Catholicism as well.

In contrast, this also was a period, like the early nineteenth century, of religious experimentation in prophet-led groups. Some groups,
such as Sung Myun Moon's Unification Church and L. Ron Hubbard's
Church of Scientology, attracted widespread condemnation from mainstream religions for their evangelistic techniques or their adherence
to prophets. Other groups gradually have achieved acceptance with
less fanfare. Of greatest concern, however, were those that seemed to

threaten violence or terrorism. The 1978 collapse of the communitarian experiment at Jonestown, Guyana, in a mass suicide was a shock felt throughout the United States. The experiment had roots in a promising religious development—the People's Temple, which initially had a high moral purpose and a strong interracial base. The apparent degeneration into a "cult" focused around the charismatic Jim Jones, who demanded complete allegiance, was all the more disturbing. Other groups also developed millennial expectations with doomsday scenarios that sometimes became self-fulfilling prophecies. In 1993 the Branch Davidians, an offshoot of Seventh-day Adventism, died in a blaze provoked by confrontation with federal agents. Parallel events in other countries, together with fundamentalist-inspired international terrorism, made Americans more wary of unusual religious groups even while they were becoming more culturally tolerant.

National identity seemed less important to many Americans in this period than a higher moral purpose and a transcendent religious ideal. Many of these tendencies toward diversity challenged the civil religion and provoked a corresponding response. In the 1960s, protests against the Vietnam War showed that the sacredness of the American government could be challenged: people burned the flag instead of saluting it. While the power of civil religion, and even its "holy days," declined, the great Protestant communal empowerments such as revivals also were losing much of their force. By the 1990s, Billy Graham was, for some, the last nationally respected mass evangelist.

Counterforces emerged to reinstate "American" and "Christian" standards. A family values movement led by conservative Protestants developed in the 1980s and early 1990s. Adherents promoted both true womanhood, along the lines of nineteenth-century domesticity, and true manhood, with male authority and committed fatherhood being the main themes. Whereas in the nineteenth century the advocates of domesticity condemned both excessive arousal and celibacy, in the late twentieth century advocates of family values focused on homosexuality and abortion as their principal foes. People who deviated from prescribed gender roles were the principal sinners. Yet these efforts to reinstate behavioral codes of an earlier, more homogeneous country were themselves far more diverse than before. They rarely involved the ethnic slurs associated with such causes in the nineteenth century (against African Americans and Roman Catholics, for example). They also were religiously pluralistic. Conservative Protestants made common cause with conservative Catholics and Jews, and whenever possible included

African Americans prominently in their campaigns. Such campaigns were explicit efforts to resanctify America as a pure community that might also be inclusive—so long as "liberals" were excluded. A strong Fundamentalist current accompanied this movement, advocating school prayer, respect for the Bible, and teaching creationism in the public schools.

In short, religious "liberals" developed practices that minimized group boundaries and maximized individual body-spirit integration, creating what they saw as universal communities supportive of individual spiritual goals. "Conservatives" focused on moral behavior, emphasizing the preservation of traditional American social and family structures as the unifying factor.

All the movements described in this section are still in the process of development as this essay is written, and none is, by itself, representative of American religion. Nevertheless, the distinctive movements of the late twentieth century help us identify certain themes in ritualization. Sometimes they have offered temporary palliatives, an escape into spiritual bliss. Rarely have they attempted to build stable churches or communities, and those that did often have been messianic groups that appeared threatening to the dominant culture. Despite their self-absorption and loose communities, however, most recent religious groupings have been predominantly this-worldly, using practices that orient people to the sacred "other" in direct relationship to this world. Most American Buddhists studied child-rearing methods and engaged in political action rather than joining monasteries. Environmentalists sought a spiritual base in Native American rituals of the earth. Suburban churches adopted psychotherapeutic practices, while support groups prayed to a Higher Power. In many ways, healing became a dominant theme of American religion in this period, which emphasized the body and celebrated supraphysical powers that are efficacious in the world.

I began this essay with an account of Tibetan monks teaching a ritual to Watts teenagers in a program created by a Jewish Buddhist. In retrospect, that story is remarkably apt for understanding the contemporary scene. Its characters were diverse. Its theme, "healing violence through art," championed the ideal of a global moral community and appealed to the therapeutic tone that has predominated in the most recent period of American history. Creating the art was a rite of communal healing through an act of collective remembering. The ritual itself offered participants an intense personal experience in a quiet meditative atmosphere. Its movements were eminently physical, the body constantly en-

gaged in the act of painting. At the same time, the sponsors and participants created a spiritual process whose ultimate aim was to deal with
that most physical of activities, violence. As with many other practices
of the era, by integrating the physical and the spiritual, emphasizing
emotional and physical healing, and exhorting the community to moral
and political action, this ritual oriented individuals in a world that
seemed larger and more complex than ever before.

In my analysis of this ritual, and the many others I have considered,
I also have tried to show that the orientational processes that constitute
ritual can be central to understanding individuals and groups. A focus
on bodily actions as orientational processes illumines new areas of historical interest and allows new angles of vision. This concern with ritual
reflects, of course, our own cultural setting, and particularly the heightened interest during the last forty years in embodiment. Yet it is not
merely an expression of cultural trends or an attempt to correct the previous generation's preoccupation with ideas. Ritualization is a central,
though still understudied, theme in American religious history.

THREE

Women's History *Is* American Religious History

ANN BRAUDE

In America, women go to church. This essay explores how we would tell the story of American religion if we took as our point of departure the fact that women constitute the majority of participants in religious activities and institutions. It reexamines from this vantage point three influential motifs that have been used to structure the narrative of American religious history—declension, feminization, and secularization. Each of these, in turn, rests on the respective historical claims that religion declined in the colonial period, was feminized in Victorian America, and gave way to a secular order in the twentieth century. I believe that attention to gender helps to explain why these motifs, and the historical claims that ground them, have held such explanatory power for historians even though, from an empirical perspective, they never happened. Interpreters have turned to these themes to narrate American religious history not because they point to demonstrable demographic or institutional shifts. Rather, their popularity as organizing ideas seems to reveal more about historians' and churchmen's anxieties about the role of religion in American society, anxieties closely tied to women's numerical dominance in churches, synagogues, and temples. From this perspective, the historical developments that these three themes attempt to explain concern increase, not decrease. To put it differently, the motif of the story I narrate is female presence rather than male absence. The plot, which I can only suggest here, traces the increasing vigor of women's religious lives and roles, discerning some of the same chronological shifts as older narratives, but interpreting them differently. The story shifts, I argue, as women move toward spiritual equality with men in the colonial period, as they assume public roles because of their positions as guardians of private morality and piety during the nineteenth century, and, in the twentieth, as women exercise public moral authority first as voters and as shapers of the welfare state during the Progressive Era, then as members of the ordained clergy following the rise of feminism in the 1970s. This essay suggests that narratives focusing on the absence of men reflect theological concerns of Reformed Protestantism, and that a more useful theme for the story of American religion may be found in the presence of women.[1]

The Female Majority

One cannot tell a story unless one knows who the characters are. Women constitute the majority of participants in religion in the United States, and have wherever Christianity has become the dominant faith in North America. Indeed, the numerical dominance of women in all but a few religious groups constitutes one of the most consistent features of American religion, and one of the least explained. Beginning in the early seventeenth century, more women than men could give convincing accounts of the rigorous dealings between God and the soul prerequisite to membership in Puritan churches. Women have outnumbered men in Protestant churches among whites and blacks, in the North and the South, and across denominations.[2] Among Catholics, women's vocations to the religious life have far outnumbered men's, while lay women have participated disproportionately in diverse devotional practices.[3] Women's religiosity still exceeds men's when studies control for educational level and workforce participation. While there is no comprehensive study analyzing sex ratios in religious affiliation, all of the available case studies indicate female majorities: there is no counter-example in which men are found to sustain a substantial religious group over a significant period of time. Studies documenting increases in male participation usually show only a temporary decrease in the size of a consistent female majority.[4] The only exceptions are groups in which religious affiliation is contiguous with membership in an organic community (Hasidic Jews, Native American tribal groups), or small groups that draw unusually sharp boundaries between themselves and the larger culture (Unification Church, International Society for Krishna Consciousness, Nation of Islam).

These exceptions go a long way toward proving the rule: they define group identity by rejection of the dominant values and structures of American society, explicitly dissenting from American gender roles. Likewise, for some immigrant groups increased participation by women in religious institutions has been an important feature of Americanization (for example, Reform and Conservative Jews).[5] We do not yet have adequate information about the response of Muslim, Hindu, and Buddhist immigrant groups to American gender norms for religious participation. However, already there are indications that women's participation in mosque services (discouraged or prohibited in many Islamic countries) plays an increasingly important role in the religious identity of American Muslim women in immigrant communities. It also is clear that among non-Asian Americans who have adopted Buddhism, Asian gender norms have been rejected in favor of American expectations for women's institutional participation.[6]

To say that women go to church in the United States is not to say that other national cultures may not present similar or even more extreme patterns, but the goal of this essay is to examine the significance of women's numerical dominance for telling the story of American religious history.[7] Women have made religious institutions possible by providing audiences for preaching, participants for rituals, the material and financial support for religious buildings, and, perhaps most important, by inculcating faith in their children to provide the next generation of participants. There could be no lone man in the pulpit without the mass of women who fill the pews. There would be no clergy, no seminaries to train them, no theology to teach them, and no hierarchies to ordain them, unless women supported all of these institutions from which they historically have been excluded—and still are by Catholics, conservative Protestants, and Orthodox Jews. To understand the history of religion in America, one must ask what made each group's teachings and practices meaningful to its female members.

While women have been the mainstays of the largest and most powerful American religious groups, they also have been leaders of dissent. Throughout most of American history, women have been barred from leadership as clergy, elders, or theologians, or, until the twentieth century, as lay leaders. Because women have been excluded from religious leadership at the same time that they have been elevated for their natural piety, it is not surprising that they have played a prominent role in religious dissent. Well-known leaders such as Mary Baker Eddy, Ellen Gould White, Ann Lee, Helena Blavatsky, and Aimee Semple McPherson played key roles as religious innovators.[8] It is precisely the consistency of the religious establishment in restricting women's leadership and confining their self-expression that ensures that the rejection of conventional gender roles and of conventional religious beliefs often will go hand in hand. From Anne Hutchinson to Ann Lee to Starhawk, examples abound in which women's articulation of distinctive religious views have been perceived as presenting fundamental threats to the well-ordered (patriarchal) society. Thus women's religious leadership, itself a dissent from prevailing norms, will be especially visible among dissident religious groups. Elsewhere I have explored the role of such groups in encouraging women's leadership and the role of women in promoting religious dissent.[9] This essay, in contrast, focuses on women's role as the backbone of the vast majority of well-established religious groups whose values constitute the status quo of American morality. Women's significance in groups considered marginal must not be allowed to obscure their centrality in maintaining what scholars traditionally have called the "mainstream." Women's history *is* American religious history.

Having established that women will be the main characters, the task of constructing a narrative of American religious history remains extremely difficult. Women are present in every class, race, and ethnicity: they are immigrants and natives, old and young, educated and illiterate, northern and southern, Mexican and Canadian. They reside in every geographical area, they are urban and rural, single and married, theologians and devotees. They belong to every American religious group. In short, American women are as diverse as the country itself, and as difficult to categorize. They stand somewhere within every "site" from which American religion can be viewed. What women share is a differential in power between themselves and their male peers, and the common experiences of the roles to which society has assigned them. American religious history is founded on a paradox: its institutions have relied for their existence on the very group they have disenfranchised. The willingness of women to participate in the institution that enforces their subordination and provides the cosmological justification for it requires explanation, but women have done more than participate. They have embraced the churches and the belief systems they teach, finding special meaning there for their lives as women and defending them against a variety of threats from without.

If women are to be the main characters, then, power must be the subplot, whatever the main events. The numerical dominance of women among the laity always must be viewed in tandem with the exclusion of women from institutional religious authority. Robert A. Orsi's observation about devotional Catholicism—that it is practiced *by* women in the presence of male authority—has relevance to a broad spectrum of American religion. The theme of many stories of American religion is a strong association of lay piety with femininity and of clerical roles with masculinity. As Mary Maples Dunn puts it, "passive females, ruled over by ministers . . . personify Christian virtue."[10] Church structures reified gender hierarchies: just as women failed to receive recognition, authority, or remuneration for domestic labor that made the household possible, their role as the backbone of the church went unnoticed and unrewarded. The wealth of scholarship produced over the last twenty years showing the centrality of women in sustaining American Christianity cannot be interpreted as demonstrating publicly acknowledged female dominance. The conceit of male dominance has been essential to the logic of American religion.

This is not to suggest that women did not exert other types of power as a result of their religious beliefs and activities. For example, the biographies of exceptional female historical figures are filled with accounts of how personal piety led to spiritual empowerment. Piety also has provided ordinary women with a source of moral power in the family, in the community, and most important, in their own lives, where religious practice has enabled generations of women to endure apparently unendurable situations. In assessing women's involvement in religion, we should not limit our perception of power to those forms that are publicly recognized within religious institutions. New narratives then must both expand accepted notions of power *and* deal seriously with the meaning and consequences of women's exclusion from official or institutional power. Furthermore, we must not confuse the ability to endure with the opportunity to influence. Religion may provide one without the other—and to understand women's experience we must distinguish between them.

For the most part, scholars of religion have accepted the claims made by church hierarchies that it is the types of power that men wield that are important, and that men's monopoly on institutional authority means that the characters of the story of American religion should exclude the majority of participants. Over and over, studies have perpetuated through their subject matter the contention that the views of one man in the pulpit are more important than those of the many women in the pews. Ironically, this characterization applies equally to recent accounts focused on "democratic" religious movements that "empowered ordinary people."[11] No survey history of American religion has taken women's presence into account in structuring its narrative; most have ignored women's role completely.[12]

This essay takes both women's centrality in American religion and their lack of authority as its points of departure. The first step required by this reorientation is a simple one—to view the story of religion in America as the story of women's presence. The story begins when women are there. Where women are present, religion flourishes, where they are absent, it does not. While this formula seems overly simple, it is a necessary corrective to the distortions caused by the absence of the central characters from standard narratives. Such a crude statement cannot tell the whole story of any American religion, but few stories can be told without it. Similarly, once women's presence is acknowledged, few stories can be told without reference to the gendered power dynamics of religious systems. This does not mean that women have been passive victims of religious ideologies. Rather, it means that the way women negotiated their roles within the ideologies always must be kept in view. Holding these two lenses simultaneously before the data of history requires a reevaluation of nearly every story of American religion. To illustrate how such reevaluation can proceed, I begin by examining influential narrative motifs derived from the "master narrative" of American religion, the story of reformed Anglo-Protestantism. The lens of women's history brings into focus both the gender specificity and the cultural and religious particularity of the themes.

The History of the Minority

The story of Anglo-Protestantism in North America has been told as a story of linear progress and, conversely, as a tale of constant decline since an edenic Puritan moment when religious and civil authority combined in perfect harmony. Here I focus on the second interpretive tradition, the ideological agenda of which is less transparent than that of the first. I turn the lens of gender on three interrelated narrative fictions that have been used to structure accounts of American religious history: declension, feminization, and secularization. I call these "narrative fictions" because the processes they describe cannot be discerned from empirical data about church membership or structures. Churches did not decline in Puritan New England; they did not experience a new female majority in the nineteenth century; nor did they disappear in the twentieth. All three fictions result from the assumption that the public influence of the Protestant clergy is the most important measure of the role of religion in America society. All assert that there was a time (immediately before whatever period is being studied) when Protestant ministers enjoyed a degree of authority that has since been undermined, and that this constitutes a stage in the decline of religion in the modern world.

Mary Maples Dunn has suggested of Puritan New England that "what was seen as a 'declension' was only a loss of *male* piety."[13] Numerous additional studies document that concerns about declension among both seventeenth-century divines and twentieth-century historians correlate not with decreases in church membership but rather with decreases in the proportion of men among church members. What needs to be added to Dunn's statement is that female majorities are the norm in American religious groups, so the perception that they constitute a "declension" is a normative assertion about the superior value of male church membership rather than an empirical observation. It is the temporary gender equity characterizing some first-generation Puritan churches, not the development of a predominantly female laity, that departs from American norms. Gender balance in religion seems to result from gender imbalance in the population. The disproportionate number of men among the first generation of English immigrants artificially inflated the proportion of male church members, a pattern that was repeated in many immigrant and frontier populations.[14] Permanent female majorities appear within twenty years in New England churches, and their stability has been documented for the subsequent three hundred years. While the size of the female majority may vary, its presence is a constant, not a trend.[15]

Declension has been a primary theme of American religious history since Cotton and Increase Mather merged historical narrative and jeremiad to criticize the "great and visible decay in the power of Godliness among many professors in these Churches."[16] Even Perry Miller, who made declension a central theme of modern Puritan studies, warned that we should not take literally accounts of religious decline penned by clergy who used self-denunciation as an exhortation to piety.[17] Nevertheless, the term entered the historiography to connote a falling away from the intellectual rigors of a consistent Calvinism expressed in relaxed standards for church membership indicating a loosening of the doctrine of predestination. While subsequent generations of historians contested particulars of Miller's account, they accepted the fundamental dynamic that fueled it—the view that the primary threat to religion in American culture came from the marketplace, and from a Protestant ethic that placed worldly endeavors in competition with otherworldly concerns. This way of telling the story of American religion anticipates the notion of "separate spheres," so widely debated among historians of American women, and the concept of "feminization."

The term *feminization* has been used to describe a refashioning of church teachings in response to a rise in the female membership, usually identified as occurring between the Revolution and the Civil War. Barbara Welter applied the term *feminization* to American religion, explaining that after the American Revolution the critical importance of political and economic activity made them "more competitive, more aggressive," that is, more "masculine." At the same time, "Religion, along with the family . . . was not very important, and so became the property of the ladies . . . more domesticated, more emotional, more soft and accommodating—in a word, more 'feminine.' " The most influential use of the term was in Ann Douglas's *The Feminization of American Culture,* where the word referred to a loss of nerve on the part of the Protestant ministry who conspired with their female supporters to cut the spine out of American culture. Just as her teacher Perry Miller coined the term *declension* to describe a falling away from the difficult doctrines of Calvinist theology during the Puritan period, Douglas found the same process in the nineteenth century, but blamed it on women. As we have seen, however, female majorities were nothing new in the nineteenth century. Nor were they a secret. Cotton Mather knew that "there are far more godly women in the world than godly men" in the seventeenth century, and he made sure his congregation did too. So if female majorities alone could lead to a specific type of theological change, they ought to have done so before the nineteenth century. What Richard Shiels describes as "the feminization of American Congregationalism" consists of an increase in the size of the female majority from 60 percent during most of the eighteenth century to 70 percent during the early National period. This was a notable change, but was it a "feminization"? His finding that the "final decades of the Second Great Awakening checked the feminization process but did not reverse it" is characteristic of historians' use of the term to describe something like a contagious disease.[18] The term *feminization,* then, is a misnomer when applied to religious demographics. Like the term *declension,* it expresses a nostalgia for a religious landscape that never existed.

Once we have severed feminization from its demographic implications, we still must ask whether it has utility in describing ideological change. Here the concept has been used to join together the rise of domesticity and the rise of liberal theology in Protestantism. While this link does seem to hold true for the liberal denominations studied by Ann Douglas, those denominations were losing ground to other groups during the nineteenth century, and so cannot be said to represent American culture. But domestic ideology never was limited to advocates of a single theological persuasion. American Catholics adopted all the accoutrements of domesticity without notable theological change, and conservative Protestants took to it at least as well as liberals. If the historiography of the nineteenth century has not demonstrated amply that religious groups can laud domesticity and conservative theology, then the data of the twentieth makes it abundantly clear. Betty De Berg, for example, has argued that the rise of Fundamentalism in the 1920s may be seen as an attempt to provide a theological foundation for the preservation of domestic values.[19] Since the 1960s, domestic values have been associated much more closely with religious conservatives than with liberals. Perhaps this simply reflects liberals' greater receptivity to change: when domesticity was new it was championed by liberals, when it had become the status quo it found favor with conservatives. Nevertheless, the sympathy between domestic values and certain theological doctrines cannot adequately explain its rise and persistence in American culture.

Of the three themes I have proposed to view through the lens of gender, secularization is the most far-reaching in its implications. It also has been the most influential among American intellectuals and has by far the largest scholarly literature. It forms an aspect of the theory of modernization that lies at the basis of modern sociology. Secularization theory has been called a myth by some contemporary sociologists, defended by others, and reinterpreted with ever-increasing subtlety.[20] It lies far beyond the scope of this essay to offer a full (or even brief) treatment of the debate over secularization. However, I include it here because it continues the tradition of discerning declines in the influence of religion that are not reflected in declines in church membership or institutional strength. In contrast to the expectations of sociologists, statistics show that per capita church membership in the United States increased steadily throughout the nineteenth century, beginning at less than 10 percent and reaching stunningly high rates (67 to 76 percent) that have persisted throughout the twentieth century.[21]

Does the discrepancy between the perception of secularization and rising rates of church membership have anything to do with gender? The apparent paradox often is explained by describing a relocation of religion's influence from the public realm to the private. The theme of secularization is thus closely related to another narrative fiction—the highly gendered concept of "separate spheres," in which a public/private dichotomy is used to describe the distinctive roles of men and women in society. While the terms *public* and *private* have been used to mean different things by historians debating the existence of a "woman's sphere" and by sociologists trying to describe the process of modernization, both depend on a dichotomy that has strongly gendered associations. John Murray Cuddihy, for example, has described the process of assimilation for nineteenth-century Jews as learning to be "private in public" by adopting the decorum and respectability of bourgeois culture.[22] In other words, the price of admission to the public realm of civil society was leaving one's religion at home, where it would influence only private behavior. Secularization can mean the same thing as feminization, a decline in religion's efficacy in a public realm associated with men's activities, concurrent with persistent or increased influence in a private realm associated with women and the family.

I have argued that declension, feminization, and secularization never happened, if the terms are understood in their most overt sense. They can be said to have happened only if they are understood as referring not to demographic shifts but rather to anxieties caused by the belief that such shifts were occurring or the fear that they might occur. In each case, the term expresses nostalgia for a world that never existed, a world in which men went to church and were as moved as women by what they heard there, a world in which the clergy felt they had precisely as much public influence as they should. Perhaps it is not women who have sentimentalized American Protestantism, but rather the male clergy who have cherished a romantic notion of a patriarchal past.

The History of the Majority

If American religious history is viewed from a perspective in which women are assumed to hold the central position in the narrative, the possibility arises that the aforementioned anxieties result not from declines in religion but rather from advances, advances in both the quality and the quantity of women's participation in American Protestantism. Attention to power discrepancies further reveals that all three narrative fictions incorporate a judgment that the health and integrity of a religious group are seriously threatened by any increase in the visibility or influence of its female members. Because women are viewed as the less powerful half of society, their numerical dominance is interpreted as a decline in power for a religious institution. Thus declension, feminization, and secularization incorporate into the story of American religion assumptions about women's powerlessness derived from the value systems of American Protestantism. If the assumption of women's powerlessness is rejected (or at least bracketed), and women's participation is viewed as a neutral or conceivably even as a positive contribution to a religious institution, then the story of American religion might have a very different shape. The cultural transitions referred to as declension, feminization, and secularization might be seen as positive developments in American Protestantism: the colonial period saw an increase in the spiritual status and role of women; the nineteenth century saw a vast increase in the activities and influence of the female laity; and the twentieth century, in a process that is still ongoing, has witnessed the rise of female clergy and a reorientation of liturgy and theology based on women's experience.

Historians of American women have interpreted these transitions primarily in terms of a shift away from the long-standing Christian view of women as temptresses in league with the devil toward a view of women as models of Christian virtue. Throughout Christian history women have been associated both with Eve, symbol of human disobedience to God, and with Mary, model of Christian submission. Puritan scholars have argued that reformed theology's rejection of celibacy and elevation of the family marked a watershed, shifting the balance toward a positive view of women's nature. If grace was to be attained within marriage and the family, mothers must join fathers as religious exemplars. While the newly spiritualized family elevated the authority of the father, it did so at the expense of the church hierarchy, increasing the role of the laity in general, so that women's religious role also was enhanced. Likewise, women shared in the religious empowerment of a newly literate laity, who could read the Bible for themselves. Puritan ministers portrayed women as formed by God in order to serve as helpmates to their husbands, in both material and spiritual goals. To support such a view, they had to defend women against the charge that they drew men into sin, and argue instead for women's spiritual equality with men.[23]

On an institutional level, the Puritan notion of church membership demonstrated the importance of women's religious role. Church membership was in itself a new concept. Before the advent of Protestantism all residents of a geographical area surrounding a church belonged to that parish, saints and sinners alike. The Puritan notion of a church gathered out of the world, composed only of those few whom God had predestined for salvation, drew attention to the fact that more women than men could meet the membership requirements, providing a convincing account of the evidence for their own salvation.

During the eighteenth century, the rise of Evangelicalism enshrined a religious style that elevated qualities associated with femininity as normative. The model conversion experience of the Great Awakening encouraged an emotional and sensual surrender in which both male and female saints became "brides" of Christ. The relative spiritual equality of the period produced remarkably similar accounts of the conversion experience from men and women—but both partook of qualities considered feminine.[24]

By the nineteenth century, the balance between Eve and Mary in Protestant prescriptive literature had tipped so far that women were portrayed as inherently pious by nature. A society nervous about the implications of moving production and economic activity out of the home elevated domestic virtues into a religious calling for women. In Barbara Welter's classic formulation, a True Woman of the nineteenth century was pure, pious, passive, and domestic. Each of these characteristics was seen as mutually reinforcing: women were believed to protect their purity by restricting their activities to the so-called domestic sphere. There they could maintain pristine homes untainted by the men's sphere of the marketplace, where competition and self-interest would breed immorality if not tempered by the influence of pure wives and mothers. In the home, mothers provided a Christian atmosphere through loving example and self-sacrifice, not through the exercise of authority. For women, teachings about family life and social relations harmonized exactly with religious instruction. "Thy will, not mine, be done" summarized the appropriate attitude for the ideal wife and daughter as well as for the ideal Christian.[25]

While more subtle observers acknowledge that positive and negative valuations of women's nature have coexisted throughout American religious history, many agree that among Protestants the balance had shifted in favor of a positive view by the Victorian period. Rather than assigning this shift to a particular demographic moment, Nancy Cott sees it as a gradual transition occurring between the seventeenth and nineteenth centuries. Most important, she sees the religious notion that women as a group shared a positive moral "nature" as a prerequisite to the gender consciousness that allowed the rise of women's movements. While domestic ideology reflected Protestant anxieties about religious, cultural, and racial diversity, it was by no means limited to a single social or religious group. Historians most frequently associate domesticity with middle-class Anglo-Protestants in the mid-nineteenth century, but substantial evidence indicates that its impact crossed economic, racial, and ethnic boundaries and continued into the twentieth century, reasserting itself in a modern version following World War II. A growing literature documents domestic ideology among Catholics, Jews, African American Protestants, Asian American immigrants, and white working-class Protestants.[26]

Yet the story of religion in nineteenth-century America cannot be told simply by replacing "feminization" with "domesticity." Domestic ideology, as I argued earlier, ran wide and deep through American culture, and did not require a specific theological outlook. It could be—and was—used to argue for or against the ordination of women, for or against women's education, for or against woman suffrage. The rise of Evangelicalism both reinforced and challenged the notion that a woman's place was in the home. The urgency of evangelical imperatives in revivalist denominations authorized new roles for women both within and outside the home.[27] Even as women departed daily from the unrealistic ideology of the Cult of True Womanhood, they used its assumptions about women's natural piety to assert authority in the home and in the public realm. From the antebellum American Female Moral Reform Society to Another Mother for Peace in the 1960s, women embraced claims about moral superiority based on religious gender ideologies.[28] In the ideology of separate spheres for men and women, the church occupied an awkward indeterminate status: while it was clearly beyond the privacy of the home, it was a religiously sanctioned place for women.

Evangelical morality allowed women to criticize, and sometimes control, men's behavior. It extended the sphere of women's influence far beyond the home. But women also had to live by the values through which they asserted public authority, so the transition from temptress to moral model was not without cost. In the old view of woman as temptress her power to threaten male virtue resulted from her sexuality. Consequently, women's moral elevation required their sexual disempowerment. Frank acknowledgment of sexual desire in women during the colonial period gave way to a vigorous denial of its existence in the nineteenth century. Nancy Cott has argued that women gained a great deal by accepting the restrictions on their behavior required by an evangelical moral code. "Passionlessness," in her view, "was on the other side of the coin which paid, so to speak, for women's admission to moral equality."[29]

But women's sexuality (and the religious problems it posed to men) did not, of course, disappear when it was denied in prescriptive literature; nor did all women live up to Protestant ideals of femininity. The view of woman as temptress, then, did not dissolve with the rise of Evangelicalism and domestic ideology. In fact, the more responsibility the churches assigned to women for the spiritual welfare of their families, the greater the repercussions of any lapses in feminine purity. Any moral failing on the part of husband or child might ultimately be laid on a woman who failed to be "true." Thus women's moral ascendence did not mark the demise of negative views of women. As Carol Karlsen has shown in the context of colonial New England, the two views needed each other. The risk of being found guilty of witchcraft for evincing traits such as anger or avarice, which were unfeminine and un-Christian, functioned to encourage obedient Christian character in all women. Likewise, in the nineteenth and twentieth centuries, demonic images of women who fail to live up to their "nature" play a crucial role in defining normative Christian roles by contrast. While Puritan scholars have demonstrated that the idea of women as "Handmaidens of the Lord" was not a Victorian invention, scholars of twentieth-century Fundamentalism have shown that a view of women as "Handmaidens of the Devil" could be applied to a World War II pin-up girl as easily (if not as harshly) as to a seventeenth-century woman accused of witchcraft.[30] While the shift toward positive views of woman's nature is a major event in the story of American religion, it is crucial to remember that it remains by definition incomplete, that it is not a positive valuation of women qua women, but rather of an ideal that few women ever can attain.

Nevertheless, the increased emphasis on women's presumed natural piety marked a major transition in American religious history, because it meant that women could begin to use religion to assert moral authority. Rather than a decline in religious institutions, this shift inaugurated a stunning proliferation of organizations composed exclusively of women intent on promoting Protestant values. These were the groups that facilitated the existence of religious institutions by supporting the training of clergy, sponsoring missionaries and evangelists, maintaining the sanctuary, and providing a host of other unglamorous services. While some, such as the ubiquitous Maternal Associations, had private goals like praying for the conversion of members' children, even this served an institutional function, because converted children would become church members, supplying the most fundamental institutional need. But many of the new women's groups hoped to have a direct impact on public life. Antebellum Female Moral Reform Societies, for example, organized not only to rescue fallen women but also to control the behavior of men who patronized prostitutes. In contrast to the prescriptions of domestic literature urging women to rely on private influence to change men's behavior, religiously motivated reform women understood the public sphere as an appropriate arena of activity and as a site where they might promote their moral agenda. The New York Society, for example, published the names of men who patronized prostitutes or seduced unmarried women.[31]

Beyond these more subtle evidences of women's centrality to the progress of religious institutions in the nineteenth century, women's organizations were crucial to the three most important reform movements of the nineteenth century—antislavery, temperance, and missions. Each of these movements effectively promoted evangelical Protestant values as a basis for political action, the first two resulting in constitutional amendments and the third becoming intertwined with United States foreign policy. In each case, organizations of Protestant women developed influential gender-based theoretical justifications for the reform, as well as providing financial support. Leaders like Frances Willard articulated a "social gospel" to a broader spectrum of Christians than those affected by the later, male liberals more identified with the term. Women's religious activism advanced the presence of Protestantism in public political discourse and advanced new priorities that would transform the denominations.[32]

By the beginning of the twentieth century, women's organizations had become so successful as promoters of Protestant churches that they were perceived as a threat by male church leaders. With membership far outnumbering that of denominational counterparts led by men, women's missionary societies pursued a distinctive agenda based on women's values, support for women missionaries, and social services for women in the mission field. Because women's missionary societies were organized on a national level, they offered a female alternative to the exclusively male hierarchies of their denominations. Denominations occasionally acknowledged that these groups represented the disenfranchised majority of members by turning to missionary societies when they wanted to communicate with the women of the church. In the early decades of the twentieth century, male church hierarchies moved to take control by subsuming women's organizations into "general" missionary societies. Although this change was touted as a move toward equality, the result for the most powerful women's groups was a loss of control of their organizations, budgets, and programs.[33] In spite of the efforts of denominations to restrict women's public roles, the early twentieth century saw significant success for women's public promotion of Protestantism. The maternalist values that contributed to Progressive reform and the rise of the welfare state built on the foundations of nineteenth-century women's religious culture.[34]

In the second half of the twentieth century, women's religious commitments have contributed remarkable vitality to the churches during a presumably secular age. With the rise of feminism in the 1970s women flooded the ranks of ministerial candidates. While even those denominations that ordained women had few female candidates before the 1970s, women have comprised 50 percent or more of seminary students in the liberal denominations (including Reform and Conservative Judaism) since the early eighties. In addition, the women's movement spurred debates leading to the ordination of women among additional religious bodies, most notably Lutheran, Episcopal, and Jewish. The Catholic Church, which continues to limit ordination to men, has had a drastic shortage of priests, and has been forced to shift a variety of religious functions to laypeople (most often women).[35]

According to the secularization thesis, the increasing presence of women in religious leadership could be seen as an indication of a decline in the status and influence of religious institutions. If one looks at the internal impact of feminism on the denominations, however, it is difficult to portray it as a symptom of decline. The feminist movement has served as a catalyst to liturgical creativity, inspiring new inclusive-language hymnals, prayerbooks, and lectionaries. It has rekindled interest in theology, giving rise to whole new areas of theological inquiry and to a new generation of women theologians. Names like Rosemary Radford Ruether and Elisabeth Schussler-Fiorenza have become household words among American church women who may not be able to name a single male theologian.

In addition to the new leadership roles assumed by women clergy, the ordination of women may be significant in breaking down the long-standing association of the clergy with men and the laity with women—

an association that may inhibit religious participation by men in lay roles. There are some indications that the gender gap in church membership is declining, not because fewer women go to church but because more men do.[36]

It also can be argued that debates about gender roles have increased the vigor of conservative religious groups. Some studies suggest that women are attracted to conservative religious communities precisely because they offer access to traditional roles of wife and mother.[37] Opposition to changing roles for women and to specific feminist proposals such as abortion rights and the Equal Rights Amendment has galvanized religious commitment among conservative Catholics, Mormons, and, especially, Evangelicals. Antifeminist or pro-family positions have inspired new attempts by women and men to promote Christian values in public.

Religion and Masculinity

In spite of the ideological difficulties presented by the identity between piety and femininity in American culture, many men do go to church. But the presence of men does not negate cultural associations between women and religion, rather it allows them to be acted out in a public arena. The dual identification of Christian women with both Eve and Mary made patriarchal authority essential. If women could be either good or bad, male authority was necessary to assure that they chose to be good, and that they did not tempt men toward sin.

Which men go to church? Biographies of America's famous theologians frequently attribute their subject's religious concern to their mother's piety.[38] But it is not only great divines who profess the faith of their mothers rather than their fathers. Mary Ryan's study of the Second Great Awakening in Utica, New York, found converts were twice as likely to follow a female relative into church membership as a male relative. Theodore Dwight Weld's account of how he experienced conversion after his aunt "followed with several ladies and shut me in" to a pew to hear evangelist Charles Finney supports Ryan's picture of revivals at which women literally led their husbands and children into church by the hand. Her findings have been confirmed by other studies.[39]

Because the men who do go to church most often do so in the presence of female relatives, men's participation in religion can be illumined if it is seen in relation to women's. Men may attend church as heads of families, whose ability to coerce attendance from dependents reinforces their authority. Or men may agree to worship at the behest of more involved wives or mothers, in which case their participation is a secondary effect of women's piety. Gay men or men without families also may embrace lay religious roles incompatible with conventional masculinity. In general, however, the strong association of clergy with men and laity with women seems to have a chilling effect on the participation of male laity. One recent study documented the paucity of male youth in African American denominations, suggesting that the identification of piety and femininity continues to expand today.[40]

Because women's dominance in the laity has been accompanied by a devaluation of female participation, male church members have been highly valued, and well rewarded for attending church. The most visible and powerful lay roles have been reserved for them. In most denominations women could not vote as members of the laity until the twentieth century. This meant that Protestant churches had a greater power discrepancy between male and female laity than in the Catholic Church, in which no lay members had substantial authority. In many denominations women could not vote until long after they were enfranchised by the Nineteenth Amendment to the Constitution in 1920. Men who did attend church enjoyed a setting in which their participation—especially as heads of family—was highly valued, regardless of contrary evidence. In assuming that female dominance is an aberration to be explained or a problem to be solved, historians have accepted the theological and institutional traditions' privileging of men's participation.

Men who assumed lay roles as religious leaders were bolstered by a tradition of muscular Christianity that portrayed religious virtue as compatible with normative masculinity.[41] The gender ratio of church membership, however, suggests that this tradition never held the influence of the association of piety with femininity. For men, ideals of masculinity often conflicted with Christian virtues rather than reinforcing them. American men frequently have found themselves in the position of abrogating religious values to make it possible for their women and children to practice them. Whether exemplifying manhood by competing in the marketplace, the battlefield, or the playing field, the goal for men was to win, not to offer examples of self-sacrificial love. (Although winning often required self-sacrifice, this was the means, not the end, of normative masculinity.) The numerical dominance of women in the churches as well as the identification of piety with femininity reinforced the idea that the church was not part of men's world. Following disestablishment of the Protestant churches during the early National period, clergy had less and less appeal as role models for American men.[42]

Impediments to men's religious participation sometimes have been offered as explanations for the presence of female majorities. C. Eric Lincoln and Lawrence H. Mamiya, authors of the massive sociological study *The Black Church in the African-American Experience,* entitle a three-page section on the numerical dominance of the female laity "Where Have All the Black Men Gone?" The section says nothing about women, but focuses on the devastating demographic realities that remove men from the black community, as well as the cultural factors that discourage them from going to church.[43] Assuming that a female majority could be the result only of racist violence is disturbing for several reasons. First, as the reader probably has wearied of being reminded, such a view ignores the prevalence of this pattern throughout American religious groups. Second, and more important, it assumes that there is something wrong with a majority female church, and that it is a symptom of social dysfunction. If this is the case, it will require a broad reevaluation of American religious history.

Catholicism and Feminization

The limitations of narrative devices equating women's presence with a decline in religion resulting from a loss of male authority become even clearer if they are applied beyond the Protestant groups from which they derive. The term *feminization* rarely has been applied to American Catholicism, although it espoused many of the same gendered religious norms that characterized nineteenth-century Protestantism. Rosemary Ruether has used the term *secularized mariology* to refer to domestic ideology among nineteenth-century Catholics—a term indicating continuity rather than decline in religious beliefs. The Marian Century, from 1850 to 1950, coincided in many ways with the Cult of True Womanhood. From the point of view of Protestant historiography, Catholicism always was "feminized." Nineteenth-century Catholics, after all, had never stripped their churches of the rich sensual environment or intercessory figures whose absence constituted the "masculine" style of reformed theology and worship. The concept of "feminization" expresses the normative claims of the Protestant reformation. The cult of the saints and especially the veneration of the Virgin presented just the type of loving mediators that "feminized" Protestantism presented in the figure of Jesus. It is not surprising that the greatest "feminizer" of them all, Harriet Beecher Stowe, hung paintings of Italian Madonnas over her fireplaces and abandoned the extreme anti-Catholicism of her family to laud the virtues of *Agnes of Sorrento* (1862). The term *feminization*, then, retains the anti-Catholic as well as the antiwoman bias of the standard narratives of American religion.

The significance of the presence of women in American Catholic history is less studied than the Protestant case, but the data are quite suggestive. The Irish, who came to dominate American Catholicism during the nineteenth century, had a greater rate of female immigration than any other group. These women quickly became the economic backbone of the American Catholic Church.[44] The Irish immigration was especially remarkable for the large number of single women it included.[45] Single women religious made the parochial school system possible by providing a labor force whose subsistence wages constituted a massive economic subsidy. Following 1884, when the Third Plenary Council made the establishment of parochial schools the priority of every diocese in the country, female vocations skyrocketed. Teaching in parochial schools became the primary occupation of women religious, and sisters became the primary educators of Catholic children. Because contact between student and teacher far exceeds that between priest and parishioner, nun's roles as teachers made them central as religious socializers of Catholic children. Sisters instructed children in the rudiments of their faith, and prepared them to receive the sacraments and to establish Catholic homes. By the end of the nineteenth century there were 40,000 nuns in the United States, outnumbering priests by four to one. By 1950, there were 177,000 American women in 450 religious congregations. Without the women who felt a vocation to the religious life, the Third Plenary Council could not have made parochial education the hallmark of preconcilliar American Catholicism.[46]

Girls were much more likely than boys to attend Catholic school before the Third Plenary Council, because immigrant families often relied on their sons' labor to survive. Thus girls who would grow up to raise Catholic families were likely to be more thoroughly imbued with the values of the church than the men they married. For instance, the number of boys enrolled in Catholic schools in Massachusetts did not approach the number of girls until well into the twentieth century when child labor had been outlawed. Once again women's presence and lack of authority must be viewed in tandem. Catholics placed a higher priority on educating girls in a milieu that would in many ways encourage their subordination.[47]

Conclusion

In my analysis of Catholics, as in my treatment of other groups, I have argued that the historiography of American religion depends on a host of undocumented normative assumptions about religion and gender. As a corrective, in this essay I have sketched the outlines of a narrative of U.S. religion that is organized around the themes of female presence and male power. Many questions remain. For instance, it is unclear exactly why women, more than men, have found religions to be effective avenues for understanding their experiences and constructing their identities. Informed readers will notice omissions. Many groups do not appear in my abbreviated account. My aim was to be suggestive, not exhaustive; provocative, not conclusive. If I am right, however, focusing on the cluster of motifs that concern gender—especially female presence—promises to allow other characters to come into view. And we cannot expect to understand the history of religion in America until we know at least as much about the women who have formed the majority of participants as we do about the male minority who have stood in the pulpit.

FOUR

The Illusion of Shifting Demand

Supply-Side Interpretations
of American Religious History

ROGER FINKE

This essay focuses on a traditional "site" of American religious his-tory—the churches. General surveys of church life have until recently provided a masterful synthesis of past research, taking the stories of many and making them one. Over the last twenty years, however, this task has become increasingly difficult. Evidence from a growing num-ber of new historical studies has unveiled the rich complexity of Ameri-can religion and the limitations of the story told by earlier surveys. The general explanatory principles of past surveys are being questioned, with little evidence that a new master synthesis or metanarrative is emerging.

In this chapter I propose a new interpretation for one aspect of America's religious past—church growth and decline. Unlike many of the new studies that consider religious life outside of Christian denomi-nations, this chapter retains the earlier scholarship's focus on churches. In contrast to the earlier interpreters of American religion, however, I offer a religious market approach to explain religious change over time and the shifting fortunes of various religious movements. My emphasis is on supply-side explanations. Rather than explain religious innovation and church growth by pointing to a shifting cultural climate or the changing demands of the people, I stress supply-side explanations focus-ing on regulation, market openings, competition, and pluralism. Thus I argue that religious innovation and sectarian growth are often a re-sponse to opportunity, not a reaction to changing consumer demands.

With a high regard for the challenge general historians face, I offer a call
for revision.

The Voluntary Principle Revisited

When nineteenth-century European scholars and church leaders visited
America, they were quick to comment on what they called the "voluntary principle." Using explicit market terms, they described the unique
"religious economy" and the open competition that resulted from separating church and state. Andrew Reed, sent by the Congregational Union of England and Wales to assess the church of America, offered this
bold pronouncement on America's religious economy: "Deliberately,
but without hesitation, I say, *the result is in every thing and every where
most favourable to the voluntary, and against the compulsory principle.*"
Basing his conclusions on visits, interviews, and an extensive collection
of quantitative data on churches, communicants, and ministers, Reed
explained that "the ministry has been supplied with better men; the
men have been better maintained. Churches have been revived where
they languished, and they have been created in abundance where they
did not exist." And, though many nineteenth-century visitors would
warn of the evils of revivalism and denounce sectarianism as splintering
the unity of God's kingdom, they each recognized the powerful changes
resulting from the "voluntary principle."[1]

Two of the earliest surveys of American religion, not surprisingly,
place the voluntary principle at center stage. Initially written for European audiences, *America,* by Philip Schaff, and *Religion in the United
States of America,* by Robert Baird, used the voluntary principle to explain the unusually high level of religious activity and the growing number of sects in the United States. Swiss-born, German-educated Philip
Schaff quoted with favor an "impartial" Austrian editor: "The United
States are by far the most religious and Christian country in the world
. . . because religion is there most free." Baird devoted one of the eight
sections of his book to explaining the voluntary principle. At the close
of this section he concluded that the voluntary principle "has brought
gospel influences to bear in every direction."[2] For Baird and Schaff the
"facts" seemed obvious: religious freedoms increased the involvement
of the people and stimulated evangelical activity.

But Schaff and Baird were keenly aware of the charges coming out of
Europe against the new voluntary principle. Schaff acknowledged that
the "shady side" of the new sect system "changes the peaceful kingdom

of God into a battle-field, where brother fights against brother." Yet both writers came to the defense of the new system. Schaff promised that the new system "will produce something far more grand and glorious, than Catholicism," and Baird devoted an entire chapter to address the "Alleged Want of Harmony Among the Evangelical Christians of the United States." He argued that many of the charges were based on "gross misrepresentation" and gave personal testimony on how the "enlightened members of one denomination respect and esteem those of another."[3]

In the surveys of American religion that followed, the voluntary principle motif fell from favor and only the hope for unity remained. As the audience for general historians shifted from Europe to the United States, the peculiar American system and the religious activity it generated required less explanation. The "new" sect system was now the norm for author and audience. Despite the attempts of Sidney Mead, Franklin Littell, and others to display the transforming power of religious freedoms, these freedoms never regained a central role in explaining religious change for the surveys of American religion.[4] When reviewing Sydney Ahlstrom's monumental history of American religion, Mead laments that the " 'Puritan Epoch' motif seems to provide the standard for judging the historical significance of everything in the religious history of the American people . . . while somewhat less than two pages are given to the sections on 'Church-State Relations and Religious Freedom.' "[5]

For a religious market approach, church-state relations are the starting point. State regulations, or the lack of regulation, define the rules of the game.[6] To discuss how a market operates, we must first understand how church-state relations alter the supply of religions available to the people. How do regulations curb the development of new religions, restrict the behavior of member and minister, and subsidize religions approved by the state?

Before I turn my attention to supply-side principles, however, I want to stress that this approach does not dismiss the importance of religious demand. To the contrary, this approach is built on the premise that the diversity of religious demand requires a diversity in supply. No single religion can meet the demands of all segments of the population. Later I argue that even in small towns and rural villages, a single faith can not satisfy the variety of demands present. The medley of American religions, both past and present, reflects the diversity of the population it serves.

This essay stresses supply-side principles for two reasons. First, the diversity of demands is far more stable than past arguments suggest. Due to variations in the population, religious markets always will contain distinct segments seeking more and less worldly versions of faith. While some will seek a message that relies on a refined and rational theology, others will seek a message appealing to emotions and experience. Some want an exclusive religion that harbors them from the world, others want an inclusive religion that allows them freedom in the world. Throughout American history there has been demand for a variety of sectarian and mainstream religions.

Second, supply-side explanations often are ignored. When there was a surge in new Eastern religious movements in the late 1960s and early 1970s, scholars quickly discovered a new demand for Eastern religion. But the more telling story was the changing supply of Eastern religious teachers. When exclusionary rules against Asian immigrants were quietly dropped in 1965, the door was opened for Eastern religious teachers, and the long-standing demand for Eastern wisdom was met. Even the growth of the Catholic Church in the late nineteenth and early twentieth century (the most dramatic demand-side shift in American religious history) was prompted by more than a shift in demand. Explaining this growth requires scholars to give careful attention to supply-side principles. Although the growth relied on immigrants from predominantly Catholic nations, many immigrants were, at best, potential recruits when they arrived. Mobilizing them into the parish required an adequate supply of diverse ethnic parishes, priests, and religious orders to market the faith aggressively.[7] If demand alone were adequate to explain this growth, the revivalistic parish mission never could have gained the prominence it held in the latter half of the nineteenth century. Attention to demand alone fails to explain the growth and decline of religious movements, even for Catholics.

When Europeans visited America in the nineteenth century, they quickly recognized that America's "exceptionalism" was due to more than a shift in demand. Returning to the motif of Schaff and Baird, I want to explain how the lack of religious regulation (the voluntary principle) contributes to the "exceptionalism" of American religion.

Regulating Religion

In the preface to *The Nation with the Soul of a Church*, Sidney E. Mead states that the "only good reason . . . for giving a lecture is that one is concerned to present clearly and persuasively a proposition, the accep-tance or rejection of which one deems important."[8] For the sake of clarity, I begin with one of the key propositions underlying a supply-side explanation of religious change: Religious regulation restricts the in-volvement of the people by changing the incentives and opportunities for churches, preachers, and revivalists (religious producers), and the religious options for the people (religious consumers).[9] The religious regulation referred to in this proposition comes in two common forms: subsidy and suppression. Both forms of regulation restrict competition in the market by redefining rules governing the operation of the reli-gious economy. Subsidy rewards only selected religious groups, and suppression penalizes unauthorized groups.

Suppression, the most obvious form of regulation, frequently targets the new and powerless religions.[10] The consequences of these regula-tions seem slight, at first, since the groups suppressed are initially small and attract members from the "fringes." Yet these groups are a source of innovation and growth for any religious economy. Not only do they appeal to a segment of the population not reached by the more "refined" religions authorized by the state, but they also serve as a test-ing ground for religious innovation. Though most will fail, a few suc-ceed. Indeed, in the case of America, today's religious majority is formed from yesterday's minority.[11]

Suppression also changes the incentives for dominant religions. When state-supported religions can restrict competition through sup-pression, they find it far easier to suppress the activities of new religions and their itinerants than to compete with them (for example, colonial establishments). Incentives for institutional change or popular appeal soon fade when the option of suppressing alternative religions is avail-able.

Although suppression is the most obvious form of regulation, sub-sidy is equally powerful and far more deceptive. Initially, subsidy ap-pears to stimulate activity by supporting religious institutions and re-ducing the cost of involvement for the individual. On closer inspection we find that subsidy reduces the incentives of churches to gain popular support, and serves to limit competition by restricting the subsidy to a few select religions.

Church subsidies make a striking change in the incentives of the clergy. When the state pays clergy salaries, the clergy have little incen-tive to mobilize popular support.[12] In 1837 Francis Grund of Austria offered this pithy assessment of American clergy: "In America, every clergyman may be said to do business on his own account, and under his own firm. . . . He always acts as principal, and is therefore more anxious, and will make greater efforts to obtain popularity, than one who serves for wages." He contrasted these clergy with the "indolent and lazy" clergy of Europe's established churches, and explained that "a person provided for cannot, by the rules of common sense, be supposed to work as hard as one who has to exert himself for a living."[13] When the market is unregulated, religious groups must garner popular support to survive.

Finally, suppression and subsidy also change the incentives of the people. Suppression can burden dissenters with persecution, loss of privileges, fewer religious options, and the cost of concealing their membership. Subsidy inflates the cost of joining alternative religions. Just as parents choosing a private school must pay the full cost of the private education, forego the option of a "free" public education, and still make tax "contributions" to support the public schools, individuals selecting an alternative religion must forego the "free" or partially subsidized religion provided by the state. Thus the state's preference for one religion reduces the individual's incentives for joining another.

Whether the regulations involve subsidy or suppression, the result is a change in the incentives and opportunities for churches, preachers, revivalists, and the people. I next apply this proposition to the story of early American religion and the prominent shifts in religious regulation.

AWAKENINGS AS SUPPLY-SIDE CHANGES

General histories of American religion devote much attention to the "Great Awakenings" that occurred from approximately 1730 to 1760 and 1800 to 1830. The so-called First Great Awakening is best known for the enormously successful revivals of George Whitefield during 1739 and 1740, when Whitefield attracted unprecedented numbers to his revivals throughout the colonies. As for the Second Great Awakening, the revivals of Charles Grandison Finney and others are well chronicled, but the most remarkable feature was the rapid growth of upstart sects and their ability to expand the market. Between 1776 and 1850 the national rate of adherence doubled, from 17 to 34 percent.[14] What explains the success of Whitefield's revivals or the phenomenal growth of the upstart sects? I argue that deregulating religion gave itinerants and sects new opportunities for marketing their faith and gave the people greater freedom to choose.

As the term *awakening* suggests, some scholars have viewed the Great Awakenings as times of surging or changing demand—times when demand for religion arose after a period of religious decay, or when a new demand surfaced for a style of religion better suited to an emerging culture (for example, frontier, market economy, or spirit of freedom). I would argue, however, that this surge in revivals and the growth of organized religion were due to a shift in supply, not demand. As the colonial establishments lost support, itinerants and sects gained freedoms. When the state reduced regulations on new sects and itinerants, a new wave of religious suppliers emerged: preachers and sects that aggressively marketed their product to the masses. American religion flourished in response to religious deregulation.[15]

By the mid-eighteenth century, the religious toleration practiced throughout the colonies made Whitefield's revivals possible. As an Anglican clergyman with a degree from Oxford and no aspirations of starting new churches, Whitefield was tolerated by colonial governments. But religious toleration is not the same as freedom, and remnants of religious regulation remained.[16] Despite the credentials and popularity of Whitefield, the General Consociation of ministers convinced the 1742 Connecticut legislature to prohibit itinerants "from preaching in any parish without the approval of the minister of that parish." In 1774 James Madison claimed that persecution persisted in Virginia: "There are at this time in the adjacent county not less than five or six well-meaning men in close jail for publishing their religious sentiments, which in the main are very orthodox."[17] And, though little open persecution was reported in New England during the late colonial era, dissenting groups (in most colonies) still were required to qualify for religious certificates to exempt members from paying religious taxes, and the established groups still benefited from state subsidies. The eroding establishments tolerated Whitefield, but they were not ready for Lorenzo Dow and the band of uneducated Methodist itinerants that would follow over fifty years later. The religious freedoms unleashing the itinerants and allowing sects to compete on equal footing with the colonial mainline were still evolving in the latter half of the eighteenth century.

By the early nineteenth century, however, the sects were gaining free rein throughout the new nation and subsidies for establishments were nearly gone.[18] When colonial mainline churches objected to the presence of sectarian itinerants, the itinerants appealed for the support of the people, not the state. In his autobiography, the famous Methodist itinerant Peter Cartwright recalls how the colonial mainline sought to retain the old territorial system of regulating competition. Arriving in a new community, he was approached by the local Presbyterian minister, who did not object to his preaching but requested that he make no effort to form a church in this neighborhood, because it was within the "bounds of his congregation." Cartwright responded: "I told him that was not our way of doing business; that we seldom ever preached long at any place without trying to raise a society. He said I must not do it. I told him the people were a free people and lived in a free country, and must be allowed to do as they pleased. . . . He said that was true; but if we raised a society it would diminish his membership, and cut off his support." Cartwright concludes the chapter by reporting that "public opinion was in my favor . . . the minister sold out and moved to Missouri, and before the year was out I had peaceable possession of his brick church."[19] The rules of the game had changed: all must compete for the support of the people, rather than seek favor from the state.

The revivals of Whitefield and the growth of organized religion in the early nineteenth century were both the product of newfound freedoms for the marketing of faith. Whitefield's crowds did not materialize out of nowhere, they responded to the publicity, press releases, and sermons circulated in their communities up to two years in advance.[20] The so-called Second Great Awakening was nothing more (or less) than the successful marketing campaigns of "upstart" evangelical Protestants. The "thundering legions" of popular and often unpaid preachers brought religion to every nook and cranny in the new nation. In his introduction to *The Democratization of American Christianity*, Nathan O. Hatch describes "America's nonrestrictive environment" as the "engine that accelerated the process of Christianization." With the likes of Cartwright and Francis Asbury at the throttle, this engine ran full speed throughout the early nineteenth century.[21]

WITH OR WITHOUT REGULATION

As the surveys of American religion were increasingly written for an American rather than European audience and the content was isolated to religion in the United States, the comparison of America's religious economy to other options began to cease. Yet these comparisons are essential for understanding what was and what might have been. Here I offer one example of how religious regulation can shape the development and design of religious movements.

The divergent paths of American and British Methodism offer a pointed example of how regulation can alter the formation and growth of a single religious movement. At the end of the eighteenth century when state regulations were fading for American Methodists, British Methodism was facing the threat of increased regulation. The Church of England had initially tolerated the Methodists' rigorous behavioral standards, exclusive membership, and lay and female itinerancy because Methodists had organized as a society within the Church of England and because John Wesley could guarantee their allegiance to the English church and state. But by the 1790s, Wesley's death and the growth and independence of Methodist societies pushed Methodists beyond the protective shelter of Anglicanism. The Methodists could no longer call themselves the "Church of England at prayer"; they were dissenters. According to British historian David Hempton, the English "Methodists realized that their preaching privileges depended upon continued loyalty and good order."[22]

The Methodists' concern with loyalty and good order soon led Methodist leaders to discourage emotional revivalism, curtail the activities of itinerant preachers, and promote loyalty to the state. Whereas the American Methodists quickly embraced itinerancy and camp meetings in the early nineteenth century, the Methodist hierarchy in England opposed these, viewing both activities as a threat to the "fragile nature of religious toleration." When the dissident Methodist Hugh Bourne and his brother James organized a camp meeting in 1807 based on the American model, the Methodist Conference quickly responded "that even supposing such meetings to be allowable in America, they are highly improper in England, and likely to be productive of considerable mischief: and we disclaim all connections with them."[23]

The threat of state intervention did more than curtail revivalism, however; it reduced British Methodists' appeal to the growing urban working class. W. R. Ward reports that "in the days when Methodists participated largely in Anglican rites they were ferociously denounced by high-churchmen for destroying the establishment; in the [eighteen]'thirties when separation was virtually complete, they were fawned on for propping it up." Dissenters began to complain that their movement "had forfeited a birthright of political activism."[24] British Methodists also had the practical problem of offering few free seats for the urban poor. According to the 1851 British census, the Methodists relied heavily on pew rentals and often had a lower percentage of free seats than the Church of England.[25] Whether by design or perceived necessity, the Methodists were gradually appealing to the rich rather than the poor.

As British Methodism forged an alliance with the state to promote order and loyalty, American Methodism forged an alliance with the people to promote an unbridled evangelism. The result: Methodists in Great Britain struggled to keep pace with population growth, as the percentage of Methodists in America soared. From 1776 to 1850, Methodist membership in America rose from less than 3 percent of all church adherents to 34 percent, and the number of Methodist congregations skyrocketed from sixty-five to more than thirteen thousand.[26] Such meteoric growth could never have occurred under a hierarchy that restrained its itinerants and opposed camp meetings.

Principles of Religious Markets

The proposition on religious regulation helps to explain why regulation changes the level of popular support, but it does not explain how the religious market operates. Why does the level of religious activity vary for communities experiencing the same level of regulation? Why do some religious movements prosper while others fall into decline? The religious market approach has offered many propositions to address these questions, but I want to give attention to only a few.[27] Each offers important revisions to the standard story of American religion.

WHY THE UPSTARTS WIN, AGAIN

When "mainline" denominations began showing membership declines in the late 1960s and conservative churches displayed growth, general historians quickly concluded that this was a major turning point in American religious history. Ahlstrom described a "transformatory process [in the United States] . . . an eclipse of the Protestant Establishment which presided over its early colonial life, its war for independence, and its nineteenth-century expansion." Martin Marty labeled the declines a "seismic shift" and explained that "mainline churches suffer in times of cultural crisis and disintegration. . . . So they looked good in the 1950s as they looked bad in the 1970s." Winthrop Hudson wrote that the declines which "had begun in the 1960s . . . constituted a marked reversal after a century and a half of steady growth." In his third edition (1981) of *Religion in America,* Hudson devoted the final chapter to explaining "The Turn to Conservatism in the 1970s and 1980s."[28]

More recent surveys have acknowledged that the conservatives grew
in the 1940s and 1950s too, but interpretations of this growth are often
vague or resort to explanations relying on a transformation in the sixties. Mark A. Noll offers the clearest presentation of the rapidly growing "Newer Denominations" and the declining "Older 'American' Denominations," and recognizes the restructuring as a product of several
decades, but he struggles to interpret this finding. After reviewing
societal and organizational explanations, he concludes that "whatever
reasons lie behind the different growth rates of the American churches
over the last half-century . . . [a] major reorientation has taken place."
George M. Marsden also notes that the Southern Baptist Convention
and evangelical institutions were growing long before the 1960s, but
when he begins his explanation on the "remarkable spread of evangelical and conservative Protestant movements" he returns to the 1960s
and resorts to a cultural crisis interpretation. He writes that a "cultural
factor" explaining this growth was that "beginning in the 1960s Americans were becoming increasingly dissatisfied with the materialistic and
rationalistic definitions of reality . . . [and] were increasingly open to
spiritual dimensions of reality."[29]

But the notion of a sudden shift in the 1960s, used by many surveys,
is based on the fact that it was only then that the decline of mainline
denominations was noticed. When the membership totals of each denomination are treated as a market share (a percentage of all religious
adherents), this "recent" trend is part of an enduring cycle that has been
present for at least two centuries. The proposition offered by the religious market approach is: When the tension between major religious
movements and the dominant culture is reduced, rapid membership
growth will be concentrated among religious movements holding a high
level of tension with the dominant culture. Thus, growth occurs in areas with market openings. Religious movements frequently reduce their
tension with the dominant culture by relaxing their standards for membership, beliefs, and behavior.[30] Over time, tension might be reduced as
the movement tolerates drinking and dancing, accepts alternative interpretations of scriptures, and discourages religious emotionalism.[31] Another way of stating this proposition is that when large religious organizations secularize, market openings are available for less secularized
faiths.

This view is the basis for the sect-church cycle Rodney Stark and I
present in *The Churching of America, 1776–1990.* Sects begin in sharp

opposition to the secular culture, but if they are successful, they gradually decrease their tension with the host culture and reduce the demands they place on their membership. At first this shift might increase growth because it reduces some of the onerous costs of membership, but over time this process will compromise the movement to such an extent that it will fail to meet the religious needs of its members. As the former sect drifts into the mainline, new sects seize the opportunity for growth. Thus new sects arise as old sects accommodate to the dominant culture.[32]

Notice that supply, not demand, explains the rise of sectarian groups and the fall of mainline denominations. Sectarian growth relies on market openings rather than cultural crises or troubled social times. As former sects drift into the mainline, the supply for sectarian religion decreases and the supply of mainline religions increases. When this cycle occurs for several denominations, the inevitable result is an overabundance of mainline religions and market openings for new sects.

This recurring pattern becomes clear when denominational totals are converted to percentages of all religious adherents. The colonial mainline—Congregationalists, Episcopalians, and Presbyterians—claimed 55.1 percent of all church members in 1776, and it seemed certain that they would continue to dominate for the foreseeable future. By 1850, however, their market share plummeted to only 19.1 percent. Meanwhile, the Methodists' and Baptists' share soared from 19.4 to 54.7 percent, the Catholics found a market opening with new immigrants, and the Christian movement showed substantial gains too.

But changes were on the horizon. As Methodists quickly revised their organizational design and reduced the distinctive demands they placed on their members and ministers, they were beginning to resemble the old colonial mainline and their rate of growth was beginning to fall. Even in the South, where immigration was low and Catholicism weak, the Methodists were rapidly losing ground to their rival upstart, the Baptists. Whereas the Methodists held 42 percent of all adherents, compared with only 30 percent for Baptists in 1850, the advantage was reversed by 1926 when the Baptists' share jumped to 43 percent and the Methodists dropped to only 28 percent. Like the colonial mainline, the southern Methodists continued to show numerical increases, but they could no longer appeal to a growing segment of the population. They began a descent that shows few signs of reversal.

Today, as this process continues for Methodists, Baptists, and other mainstream denominations, market openings continue to show for a variety of sectarian groups, including a wide range of Pentecostals, Jehovah's Witnesses, the Mormons, and new groups such as Calvary Chapel and the Vineyard. This process could (hypothetically) reverse itself, with churches becoming more sectlike and market openings occurring for new mainline churches. The weight of historical evidence suggests the opposite, however: churches will continue to compromise with the culture over time and market openings will continue for the revivalistic, high-tension upstarts.

Failure to recognize the enduring vitality of the upstarts and the continuous sect-to-church cycle has led general historians to interpret sectarian growth as a product of troubled social times, rather than a response to market openings.[33] The underlying assumption is that a changing demand for sectarian religion explains the changing supply. A supply-side explanation suggests that religious demands are far more stable than past research implies, and the shifts in supply are due to changing state regulations or the gradual drift of popular religious movements from upstart sects to mainline churches. Thus the upstarts of the early nineteenth century appealed to a massive market opening as the state allowed them to compete without constraint and the colonial mainline continued to accommodate to the culture. Today's upstarts continue to find opportunities for growth as the sect-to-church cycle continues.

THE POWER OF PLURALISM AND COMPETITION

Schaff and Baird recognized the close link between religious freedom and religious vitality, but they were careful to distance this vitality from the pluralism and competition allowed by the freedom. Schaff explained that Protestant divisions were "only a temporary transition state" and would eventually produce the "noblest harmony." As late as the 1970s many surveys continued to offer a similar promise of cooperation. Reviewing twelve church mergers between 1906 and 1940, William Warren Sweet proclaimed "there is hope for a better day." In *Righteous Empire*, Marty highlighted the importance of the "competitive principle" for Protestant mission work in the nineteenth century, but saw a change in the twentieth. Describing the momentum of Protestant churches as "centrifugal" in the nineteenth century and "centripetal" in the twentieth, Marty writes that "they noted the limits of their competition and division, experienced frustration in mission around the world, and began to draw back together in the ecumenical, or Christian unity, movement."[34] Sweet's and Marty's assessments were accurate for the mainline, but the mainline mergers and cooperative efforts could not keep pace with the growth of competitive sects.

For the market approach, the diversity of religions is a product of population diversity and religious deregulation. Because a single faith can seldom shape its appeal precisely to suit the needs of one segment of the population without sacrificing its appeal to another, the supply and diversity of religion rise as regulations are removed. Rather than a "temporary transition state," competition and pluralism are the inevitable result of religious freedoms. For the market approach, pluralism helps to explain the vitality of religion in America. This approach leads to two propositions about religious pluralism. First, due to the underlying differentiation of the population, religious competition and pluralism will thrive unless regulated by the state. Second, to the degree that a local religious market is competitive and pluralistic, the level of religious participation will tend to be high.

The argument is as follows. A variety of religious groups, each catering to the unique demands of specific population segments, can mobilize the population to higher rates of membership and commitment. This arises because of the inherent inability of a single religious organization to be at once worldly and otherworldly, while the market will always contain distinct segments seeking more and less worldly versions of faith. The social markers of ethnicity, race, social class, and region will further divide the population into segments with unique demands for their religion. It follows that many religious bodies will, together, meet the demands of a much larger proportion of a population than can be the case where only one or very few faiths have free access.

Attempts to rid towns and villages of their "wasteful ecclesiastical economy" in the early twentieth century reveal the persistent power of competition and pluralism.[35] Rural reformers were confident that church unity was the wave of the future, and the salvation of rural churches and communities. Writing in the *American Journal of Sociology* in 1914, John Robert Hargreaves predicted that rural churches would soon follow a trend of consolidation similar to that of rural schools: "The community churches of today are very few in number, but before ten years have passed they will be all over the land, and the countryside will have come to its own." A decade later, however, the

1926 religious census reported only 301 federated churches out of a total of 167,864 churches in rural areas.[36] Country churches might be
small, but they were not merging.

The harsh reality for reformers was that involvement in churches
sharply increased as pluralism flourished. On the basis of his surveys
of 140 village communities during the early 1920s, sociologist Edmund
de Schweinitz Brunner, a strong proponent of merging village churches,
conceded that a village with an "organized church for each small sectarian group enlists more people." He found that when the relative
number of churches began to rise, the rates for church membership,
Sunday school enrollment, church attendance, and local church expen-
ditures sharply increased. Yet Brunner vehemently opposed this pluralism because it reduced support for full-time resident ministers, increased competition, and allowed emotional sects to grow. Although
Brunner and other reformers viewed the sects as only a temporary aberration, they still feared that the emotional sects might break down the
"established denominations." For the reformers, the "new" upstart
sects not only resisted any form of mergers, but also threatened the survival of the village mainline.[37]

Recent surveys have abandoned the hope for a greater unity and now
report on a "new pluralism" in America, one that covers a much
broader religious spectrum.[38] But this new pluralism should not distract
from the basic principles governing the competitive and pluralistic
American market throughout the century. Even at the peak of ecumenical activity, most mergers occurred between denominations in the same
denominational family (for example, Lutherans merged with other Lutherans), new religious movements continued to arise, and the denominations with an increasing market share showed no interest in changing
the status quo. Sociologist H. Paul Douglass devoted much of his career
to explaining how cooperation and unity between Protestants could be
achieved, yet his own data (collected in 1932) revealed that support for
ecumenism was limited to denominations with a declining share of the
religious market.[39] Even in small villages, where reformers argued that
the community could be united by a single church and the population
was homogeneous, pluralism mobilized higher levels of participation.

Population diversity, competition, and changes in regulation continue to drive the "new pluralism." Regulations permitting, each new
religion is meeting the needs of a specific segment of the population.
Recent changes in immigration policy resulted in a new ethnic pluralism that was soon reflected in a changing religious pluralism.[40] Mean-

while, rapidly growing upstarts appear on the horizon as mainline churches make peace with the dominant culture. The argument remains: if religion is unregulated, religious pluralism will continue to thrive and religious participation will remain high.

Conclusions

Although research historians seldom rely on the general surveys of American religion, the surveys provide evidence and explanation of America's religious past for scholars and students outside American religious history. The general surveys are the initial, often the only, port of entry into the history of American religion. Because the general surveys define American religious history for so many segments of the population, we should pay careful attention to the contributions and shortcomings of the general interpretative framework offered by these surveys.

Throughout this chapter I have sought to make a case for a market approach, emphasizing supply-side interpretations of American religious history. I recognize, of course, that religious change often mirrors shifts in both supply and demand, with America's religious pluralism reflecting the diversity of demands in the religious marketplace. But I emphasize the supply-side explanations because standard surveys of American religion too often ignore these explanations and treat each new development as a cultural realignment or a new religious demand.

Using the propositions of a religious market approach provides a new interpretation for many significant changes and trends in American religious history. The so-called Great Awakenings are an expected consequence of deregulating religion. When establishments lose their support and all movements are granted religious freedoms, the new opportunities and incentives of deregulation favor popular religions and lead to a rapid growth in organized religion. Moreover, with the fear of regulation or reprisal removed, new religious movements continue to emerge throughout American history and pluralism flourishes. This pluralism increases religious participation by catering to each segment of a diverse population.

This approach also shifts the center of attention away from the traditional mainline religions.[41] When general historians held out a hope for increased unity, they saw this vision through the eyes of the mainline. And when they expressed surprise, even alarm, at the growth of sectarian movements in recent decades, they failed to see this phenomenon as a trend that has proceeded unabated for over two centuries. Rather than stressing the dominance of mainline Protestantism, the market approach reveals the popular appeal of the upstarts and the ongoing trend of upstart growth and mainline decline. As I stated earlier, today's majority is formed from yesterday's minority.

This chapter offers only a glimpse at the religious market approach, an approach that helps explain many religious changes not highlighted in this essay.[42] For example, it explains the importance of religion for promoting the cause of small and powerless groups. When religion is independent from the state, churches can serve as the institutional base for a minority group's identity and call to action; African American churches and ethnic churches serve as the most obvious examples.[43] This approach also stresses the role of the laity as active religious producers. Whether the popular movements are contemporary Mormons and Jehovah's Witnesses or early nineteenth-century Baptists and Methodists, the laity have spread and shaped the faith. When churches rely on the resources of the people, not the state, the laity play a key role in generating and supporting religious practice.[44]

Supply-side explanations also go beyond the growth of religious movements and the private practice of religion. Stephen Carter's recent book *The Culture of Disbelief* illustrates how court decisions guarding the separation of church and state exclude the voice of religion from the public arena.[45] In *The Churching of America, 1776–1990,* Rodney Stark and I show how American evangelical preachers rushed to the airwaves when a new Federal Communications Commission ruling facilitated their entry. Whether the religious change involves private practice or public expression, supply-side explanations look for changes in regulations, opportunities, and incentives.[46]

The religious market approach moves beyond the mainline to stress the significance of the upstart sects, and beyond cultural crises to focus on changes in regulation, diversity, and competition. As documented by European visitors over a century ago, to understand the American religious economy you must first understand the voluntary principle and the "new sect system."

PART TWO

Contact and Exchange at Geographical Sites

FIVE

Eastward Ho!

American Religion from the Perspective of the Pacific Rim

LAURIE F. MAFFLY-KIPP

Narrators of American Protestant missionary success love the story of Henry Obookiah. To be sure, renderings of his story contain all the elements of a good tale. In 1809 Samuel J. Mills, a recent graduate of Williams College and one of the founding members of the Brethren, a cohort of mission-minded students, discovered an orphaned and homesick boy from the Sandwich Islands (present-day Hawaii) in New Haven, Connecticut, living at the home of Yale president Timothy Dwight. Obookiah had been rescued from tribal warfare in his pagan homeland and transported to New England by a sea captain. Mills, sensing an opportunity, removed Obookiah to his father's parsonage in Torrington, a small community in the northwestern part of the state, assisted in his education, and oversaw his conversion to Christianity. Writing that year to a former classmate at Williams, Mills noted happily that Obookiah's presence had turned his attention to the great challenge afforded by missionary work in the Pacific: "What does this mean? Brother Hall, do you understand it? Shall he be sent back unsupported, to attempt to reclaim his countrymen? Shall we not rather consider these southern islands a proper place for the establishment of a mission?"[1] Ironically, Obookiah's martyrlike death from typhus in 1818 helped the missionaries more than Mills could have predicted. The pagan convert's life was memorialized in a published funeral sermon by Lyman Beecher and popularized in a memoir that ran through twelve editions. It set the stage for the establishment of the first American Protestant mission to

Hawaii in 1820, arguably the most notable evangelical success of the nineteenth century.[2] America had discovered the Pacific Rim.

To scholars of American religious history since the 1960s, much of the language of this narrative—essentially an account of Protestant triumphalism encountering "pagan" passivity and happy acceptance of a superior culture—chafes. And it should. The native Hawaiian in question, whose real name was Opukahaia, was apparently older than the youthful Mills who took the "pagan boy" under his wing. Having fled his home and traveled halfway around the world to the Atlantic seaboard, Opukahaia certainly had seen more of life than had his spiritual mentor. Rather than being a lone representative of his culture on the American continent, moreover, Opukahaia was one of a number of Pacific Islanders who ventured eastward in this era, including fur traders and laborers in the Pacific Northwest, sailors in the international Pacific trade routes and the United States Navy during the War of 1812, and at least four other Hawaiians in Connecticut by 1818.[3] The Pacific Rim, it seems, already had discovered America.

This final fact becomes most important for a reconsideration of religious history from the perspective of the Pacific Rim of the United States, which for my purposes includes present-day California, Oregon, Washington, Hawaii, and Alaska.[4] Recent narrators of American religious history have by and large learned to avoid the more egregious confessional pitfalls that governed accounts for well over a century, and they now employ metaphorical vectors more in keeping with a pluralistic story. Yet the spatial vector of westward movement, of gradual and inexorable discovery of things farther west by people from the eastern states, of the American "discovery" of Henry Obookiah, has yet to be challenged seriously as a dominant motif. This is not to suggest that westward movement did not take place or that we should avoid talking about it. Indeed, we should talk about Euro- and African American religions as they spread west of the Mississippi much more than we do presently. But ignoring other movements—northward from Mexico, southward from Canada, and especially eastward from Asia—as well as the history of the prior presence of those who never wanted to move at all, furnishes us not simply with an incomplete historical narrative, but with unsatisfying accounts of religious experience.[5]

Consider, briefly, the treatment of several subjects in recent surveys of American religion that have the most relevance for the Pacific Rim world. Several textbooks make mention of Hawaii and one of its principal religions, Buddhism. Although Winthrop Hudson and John Corrigan's *Religion in America* contains no entry for Hawaii in its index, the state shows up in the chapter "New Americans" about the postbellum period, with a mention of the formation of the Young Men's Buddhist Association in Honolulu in 1898. Buddhism also is discussed in a section on Theosophy, and under the heading "Separatist Tendencies" in a chapter that deals with the effects of the 1965 immigration laws. Martin Marty's *Pilgrims in Their Own Land,* admittedly a more condensed narrative, does not contain references in the index to Hawaii, Alaska, or California. But Marty does juxtapose "Americans," those restless, unsettled souls on a constant pilgrimage, to "most of world religion" and "most eastern religions" which "seek timelessness and constancy or even escape from history." Zen Buddhism is covered in his discussion of Alan Watts, a Euro-American Buddhist convert. No mention is made of the tens of thousands of Asian Buddhists who apparently did not feel settled in spite of their timeless religious beliefs and practices, and who sought escape from history by fleeing their native lands.[6]

These accounts are all problematic chronologically because of when they introduce us to this Eastern tradition. Buddhists emerge as a feature of the narrative when they are "discovered" by "Americans," that is, by Euro-Americans. The World Parliament of Religions of 1893, the appropriation of Eastern religions in the Theosophical Society, and the interest in Buddhism shared by the Beat poets in the twentieth century may tell us plenty about Euro-American appropriations of Buddhism, but they offer little insight into the vast majority of American Buddhists who had been in this country since at least the 1850s.[7] These stories are also problematic because they indicate by their silences that Asian Americans either are not important for the larger story or are not American. This kind of problem is most evident in Marty's account, but it also emerges in less likely places. Edwin Gaustad, whose *Religious History of America* contains by far the most complete description of religious activities in the trans-Mississippi West, including mention of Chinese immigration, and whose groundbreaking *Historical Atlas of Religion in America* (1962) still stands as the definitive overview of religious affiliation in the western United States, occasionally employs language that posits an exclusively east-to-west orientation. "While most of the country did not encounter Asian religion until the World's Parliament of Religions met in Chicago in 1893, California knew Chinese emigrants before the Civil War," he writes. Yet his description of Hawaii's historical cultural and religious ties to the United States, "dating back to the 1820s when New England dispatched Congregational missionaries to this Pacific outpost," with its overtones of Euro-American westward activism and Hawaiian passivity, sounds all too reminiscent of the tale of Henry Obookiah. We are once again traveling westward with the pioneers.[8]

It is easy enough, of course, to find fault, particularly with grand narratives. It is much harder to propose a new narrative that takes all of these criticisms into account and corrects them. All that most of us know and learn about American religion keeps us firmly moored in an east-to-west framework, and the farther west we go, the less important the religious events seem to become, in part because the vast majority of us know much less about them. How many Buddhologists, after all, have written synthetic narratives of American religion? Even some historians of the American West, for example, have confessed with chagrin that Hawaii and Alaska make only fleeting and disjointed appearances in their course outlines. As Patricia Limerick cautions us, it is now accepted to find fault with traditional narratives of "English-speaking, westward-moving, literate, record-keeping, middle- and upper-class, pre-twentieth-century, white men." The real problem, she continues, is that nothing has emerged to fill the void left by the collapse of that grand narrative; the new agenda simply escorts "one to the edge of one's ignorance and then leave[s] one to contemplate the vacancy."[9]

In the long run, integrating the history of religion on the Pacific Rim into our larger narratives will entail a series of (admittedly enormous) steps. First, we must learn about the Pacific Rim and its peoples ourselves, and then synthesize the religious stories of Alaskan Aleuts, Nootkas, Tlingits, Pacific Coast Indians of all sorts, indigenous Hawaiians, fur traders and whalers (Spanish, French, Russian, British, and American), missionaries (Spanish, French, Russian, British, American Protestant, Mormon, and Japanese), and migrants (European, American, and Asian). If this were not a tall enough order, we must then weave all of these actors and events into a larger narrative of American religion that relates them to an Atlantic world and an emerging hemispheric community. We will have, in short, a world history of American religion.

Pacific Geography and Colonial Encounters

For the time being, we must by necessity proceed incrementally. In this essay I sketch an account that pays particular attention to religious activities on the Pacific Rim. In doing so, I highlight the importance of placing these new (to most of us) actors and events in their proper chronological context, and attempt to shape a narrative that imparts equal powers of choice and will, if not equal time, to a variety of participants. The relative novelty of the subject necessitates a prefatory discussion of method, in an attempt to impose order on the variety of historical experiences that are mentioned in this account. Because of my attention to a specific physical space, and to human migrations into and within that space, one of the most important tools employed here is a theoretical framework borrowed from humanistic or cultural geography, an academic discipline that pays close attention to the human perception and use of space. As Yi-Fu Tuan describes it, humanistic geography studies "how mere space becomes an intensely human place," with specific attention to "the nature of experience, the quality of the emotional bond to physical objects, and the role of concepts and symbols in the creation of place identity."[10]

This approach has several distinct advantages for illuminating a broad and varied range of religious phenomena. In examining the use and perception of space, one can be attentive both to the shaping power of beliefs, or the religious "mapping" of a world, and to the religious practices that mark and delimit a given space, be it a nation, a town, a home, or the bodily space of an individual. Thus we can see these processes of "sacralization" at work not simply in traditionally religious spaces, such as churches or temples, but also in other overlapping or concentric sites. Often, sacralization will include the binary demarcation of "sacred" and "secular" sites within a given area, in keeping with an Eliadean categorization; but it may just as often refer to the sacralization of a conceptual space, such as John Muir's romanticization of the wilderness of the American West as an object and site of reverence, or to the nonbinary perception of space on a continuum that moves through gradations of sacrality or religious significance. The Pacific region of North America as a whole served varying symbolic and practical functions within the religious systems of settlers, and those functions often greatly affected participants. For example, of what significance was it to Protestant migrants that the economic and political power of Euro-American Protestant denominational organizations was centered in the northeastern states, thousands of miles from the Pacific? Would a Japanese migrant see the world differently from a site in Honolulu, rather than from the sacred center and spiritual homeland of her mental world? When and how (if ever) might she modify or transform her comprehension of which spaces she considered sacred? Scholars of religion have been slow to take up these geographical questions, presuming all too readily that religious traditions themselves are both conceptually and spatially coherent entities. This essay is premised on the notion, which Thomas A. Tweed also articulates in the introduction to this volume, that geographical placement is an important factor in understanding religious behaviors and beliefs. A connected question about the ordering of space concerns issues of contact and power: religiously, it matters greatly who one's neighbors are, and who controls the cultural, political, and economic resources of a given region. While these factors do not entirely determine the shape of religious experience, they frequently circumscribe the intellectual, cultural, and material tools available to a community, thereby affecting the choices people are able to make about the sacralization of space.[11]

Cultural geography also suggests that it pays to be attentive to the significance of topography, climate, and other physical features of the earth that have dictated human behavior and movement. The constraints of the natural environment have played a vital yet neglected role in American religious history. The Pacific Coast of the present United States, which was for many centuries the part of the world most isolated from both European and Asian centers of population and political prominence, remains in the shadows of historical and environmental consciousness to this day.[12] Yet for many North American inhabitants along this rim, the structural realities of the world are shaped by proximity to a vast liquid desert, encompassing roughly one-third of the surface of the world, that has served as both a barrier to, and facilitator of, communication and contact for thousands of years. As oceans go, the Pacific is extremely large, measuring 9,200 statute miles from the Bering Strait at its north to the Antarctic Circle at its south. It is also wide, with some 10,400 statute miles separating Ecuador and Indonesia at the equator. Finally, the Pacific is relatively empty, especially its northern and eastern regions, those closest to the North American continent.[13] Yet looking at a map does not reveal much about the practicalities of overwater voyages in the days before steam-powered transit, or about the relative importance of any given location, because trade routes were determined by the caprices of prevailing winds, treacherous currents, and uncharted waters. For example, the most perilous sailing route to the Pacific Northwest and southern Alaska is the approach from the coast of California, despite its relatively short distance; boats ordinarily would sail far to the west to pick up prevailing winds, thus allowing them to make an easy track to Nootka. This meant, in practice, that the

Hawaiian Islands became the most important trading and reloading point for Pacific Rim commerce by the late eighteenth century. The relatively isolated chain thereby served for several centuries as a crucial point of economic and cultural contact between Hawaiians and Russian, Asian, British, Spanish, French, and American travelers.[14]

These multidirectional contacts across the water begin our story, although details of the earliest movements are elusive. The Asian ancestors of the American Indians found their way over the Bering Strait some fifteen thousand years ago, and began to spread out across the North American continent. Sometime in the last eight hundred to thousand years, Polynesians began arriving in the Hawaiian Islands. At least some came by way of Tahiti as part of what may have been an active trade route between the two island chains. Most scholars also agree that Polynesians were in contact with Native Americans at some point.[15] By the eve of first contact with Europe, the native peoples spread out along the Pacific Coast (present-day Mexico, California, Oregon, and Washington) and in the Hawaiian Islands occupied the most densely inhabited part of North America.[16] It is otherwise difficult to generalize about precolonial American peoples, particularly with respect to the wide variety of cultures and religions they encompassed. But they shared one important feature historically: all of these peoples, at one time or another beginning in the late fifteenth century, came into contact with "discoverers"—Europeans, Americans, and/or Asians, some accompanied by slaves from Africa or other parts of the New World, who moved in from a variety of directions and began to claim the land for themselves.

As was the case in the precolonial Atlantic world, the impenetrability of the Pacific from the outside and its elusive promise of new worlds gave rise to all manner of religious visions and aspirations. In China during the second and third centuries B.C., maps articulated a cosmology that located China at the center of the world, surrounded by four seas. Early Chinese geographical exploration of the Pacific was based on religious beliefs and astronomical speculation; the coastal inhabitants of Hopeh and Shantung provinces, for example, wanted to search for the "immortals" that lay beyond the ocean to the east. In 219 B.C. the Ch'in Emperor sponsored the Taoist Hsu Fu on a mission to seek a "longevity herb" that grew on the "Great Immortal Island of the Eastern Sea."[17] Christian Europeans and later Euro-Americans were drawn westward and northward by, among other things, an evangelical desire to spread their beliefs and practices to the rest of the world. Many came to see the Pacific Coast as the gateway to a new world, promising economic, political, and/or religious gratification.

A geographical overview reveals the complexity and variety of cultural contacts catalyzed by those desires beginning in the 1400s. The Spaniards first attempted exploration and settlement of the Pacific on a large scale. For over three hundred years they dominated trade and settlement in the region. In 1493, through their treaty arrangements with the Portuguese and without consulting any of the local inhabitants, they claimed the "Mar del Sur" (or Pacific Ocean) as Spanish territory. By the late fifteenth century, Iberian technology enabled ships and men to sail for long distances across open stretches of water. They too were led in part by the promise of spiritual fulfillment. Early maps and accounts of Spanish exploration on both the Atlantic and the Pacific oceans reveal a world of Christian piety and state-sponsored organizational efficiency fueled by the *reconquista* (the reclaiming of the Iberian peninsula from the North Africans), which coexisted with a popular religious realm of "enchanted islands, Amazons and fountains of youth" inspired by romantic novels of the day.[18]

Meetings between Spaniards and indigenous peoples from Manila to Acapulco touched off a series of overlapping encounters over the subsequent five hundred years, in which people moved in all directions around the oceanic basin. The Catholic Iberians came not just from the east but from the south, where prior experiences of contact and evangelization in a Latin American empire that comprised nearly two-thirds of the Americas by 1600 shaped strategies on their northernmost frontier.[19] Beginning in the mid-eighteenth century, Russians established their easternmost "remote and raw outpost of empire" in southern Alaska, baptizing the small colonies with names replete with spiritual import such as Three Saints Harbor, New Archangel, and St. Paul's Harbor.[20] British and French fur traders built settlements in present-day Oregon, Washington, and British Columbia in the early nineteenth century, staking claim to the land as the westernmost extent of European imperial dominance. Newly nationalized Americans began their westward course of empire on the Pacific, which included a well-organized Protestant missionary presence and later an equally energetic Mormon outreach to the South Pacific, in 1820. At the same time, increasingly mobile Pacific Islanders migrated eastward, moving as far inland as Idaho (and even Connecticut) in the nineteenth century. Mobilized by eco-

nomic and political transformations in the 1850s, large numbers of
Asians, first Chinese then Japanese, moved eastward to Hawaii and then
the Pacific Coast of the United States in a migration that continues today. In the late twentieth century, Latino and Asian in-migration has
accelerated dramatically, while the exportation of Protestantism in
many forms, and Mormonism, have begun in turn to alter the religious
landscapes of the South Pacific, Latin America, Asia, and Africa.

This brief inventory of Pacific contact is messy and incomplete. It is
intended to convey both the wide range of movements through space
that have allowed for cultural encounters and the extreme shortsighted-
ness (despite its tempting simplicity) of limiting our attention to a paradigm of Euro-American westward migration. Simply listing and describing
the religious traditions imported during each of these migrations would
tax the patience of any historian, without trying to analyze the effects
of intercultural contact on religious beliefs and activities. Still, the cata-
loguing of migration tells an important part of the story of American
religion on the Pacific, an area where travel and contact have served as
dominant and enduring motifs in historical experience.[21]

Specific features of these movements afford a more nuanced glimpse
of their religious contours, and also allow us to shape this sprawling
story in more detail. Although all of these peoples shared experiences
of encounter, certain types of meetings and vectors of movement predominated at particular points in time. The choice made here is to highlight aspects of American religious history that have been largely overlooked in the east-to-west account and that are particularly salient for
understanding the historical development of the Pacific states. If we take
1513 as our starting point for colonial contact (the year that Vasco
Núñez de Balboa first sighted the Pacific Ocean), our narrative can be
separated into several overlapping parts: the European colonization of
the Pacific, 1513 to 1821; the emerging American colonial presence,
1820 to 1898; and exchanges with Asian and Latin American worlds,
1850 to the present. All three periods witnessed different kinds of contacts and colonizations; for our story, the accompanying sacralization of
space and region was their defining and consistent characteristic. Colonialism plays a crucial but complex role in the narrative. It refers, on the
one hand, to the simple notion of colonization, of the inhabiting of a
particular space by a people. On the other hand, it signals the dynamics
of political, economic, and cultural power with respect to relations between groups; in turn, those relations have direct bearing on the reli-

gious life of the peoples involved. In each of these eras, the connections between economic expansion, imperial aspirations, and religious beliefs and activities comprise a central feature of the story.[22]

At the same time, we must not lose sight of other sorts of power, an omission that often occurs with even the most noble of intentions.[23] We must attend to other renderings of religious experience and narrative in the midst of the din of nationalistic movement and expansion. For example, if we focus exclusively on the migrations of European merchants and soldiers in the period prior to 1821, a focus surely important to our understanding of the political reconfiguration of the Pacific Rim during this period, we may miss entirely the religious activities in the local Hawaiian, Aleut, or Tlingit populations that were related to, but not exclusively determined by, their relations to Europeans. Conversely, our own national narrative of internal expansion may prevent us from assessing the cultural complexities of American colonialism. Thus, in our second period, placing the "American colonial world" alongside an earlier era of European colonization is intended to highlight the extent to which the nineteenth-century United States was an imperial power, rather than merely a fulfiller of its own internal destiny. Yet this story, too, has its human intricacies, and it would be inaccurate to dismiss Catholic, Protestant, or Mormon attempts to sacralize Pacific colonies as simply the extension of hegemonic political aspirations.[24]

European Colonizations of the Pacific, 1513–1821

Spain was far and away the dominant political presence in the New World prior to 1821. In the Spanish period, the *encomienda* and later the mission system governed the religious life of both native peoples and Spaniards, from Cabo San Lucas in Baja California (in present-day Mexico) to San Francisco.[25] Scholars often have contrasted the notions of the "Spanish pick" and the "English hoe," and have thereby exaggerated the distinction between the presumably transient, limited Spanish exploration and conquest of the New World and the purportedly more stable and enduring British settlement patterns in the Americas. Spaniards settled, too. Not only did they settle, but they built schools, universities, towns, and churches in the New World nearly a century before the Puritans arrived in New England.[26] A far more useful and important distinction between Spanish and British patterns is that in New Spain, the majority of the Crown's subjects were mestizo, mulatto, Indian, or African.[27] The Spanish granted this status not out of any intrinsic love for these peoples, but because of the need for tax revenues (which could be levied only on royal subjects) and an understanding of religion and its relation to the state that required conversion to proceed alongside political domination. As early as 1526, two priests were required by royal decree to be sent along with exploring parties. The Spanish Crown provided first Jesuits in Baja California (prior to their expulsion in 1767) and later Franciscan friars in Alta California with resources and military support. Money was taken from war funds for missions well into the eighteenth century because the missions were deemed a relatively inexpensive way to subdue native populations.[28]

Many arguments have been made regarding the relative humanity or inhumanity of the Spanish mission system. Although the Crown did not wage war against the natives in traditional political terms, Indians did die in large numbers. European diseases killed many. The friars, although they did not believe in forced conversion, inflicted severe physical punishments on converts who lapsed into their former ways. Culture wars thrived in New Spain. Following their own notions of Christian benevolence and evangelism, Spaniards smashed, burned, and confiscated idols and other sacred objects, and did everything possible to suppress native ceremonies.[29] Natives, for their part, went about the business of weighing the costs and benefits of negotiating with the missionaries. Different cultures chose different points of acquiescence, depending on their own needs and values.[30]

Toward the end of the period of Spanish domination of the land, beginning in the early eighteenth century, the fur trade introduced new peoples to the Pacific world. Russia, France, and Britain began to exert political and cultural force in the Pacific. The indigenous societies of what would later become the states of Alaska, Hawaii, Washington, Oregon, and California also communicated systematically with one another by way of the growing trade in skins, which connected merchants in Canton, Nootka, Astoria, Monterey, and Hawaii.

While experiences differed among the peoples of varying faiths involved in the fur trade, the fate of Russian Orthodoxy in Alaska presents a valuable and largely overlooked case study of missionary efforts on an economic frontier. Between 1743 and 1799, merchants and *promishlenniki* (fur traders) established small settlements in Alaska, near some of the most profitable sources of otter and seal skins. Seeing the need for spiritual renewal of both Russian migrants and indigenous Alaskans, the Russian Orthodox Church dispatched a delegation of eight monks and two novices to the area in 1794. They were prompted, in part, by a rumor of Kodiak natives a decade earlier who had requested baptism and conversion to Orthodoxy.[31] Despite considerable native opposition, the monks worked at converting local populations, halting the practice of polygamy, and removing children from their families in order to place them in Orthodox schools. They claimed extraordinary success: in 1795, barely a year after the establishment of the mission, Archimandrite Joasaph claimed that they had baptized 6,740 natives and performed 1,573 weddings.[32] Yet in the small Kodiak community of approximately 225 Russians and 8,000 natives, they faced their stiffest opposition from Russian traders, who openly mocked the monks and contributed little to the mission's survival. Tensions ran deep. Clerics and *promishlenniki* accused one another of depravity, and the mission limped along until the Russian American Company was officially charged with its support in 1825.[33] Missionaries also attempted the settlement of areas as far south along the Pacific Coast as Fort Ross in northern California, but it was not until the purchase of Alaska in 1867 by the United States and the transferral of the See from Sitka to San Francisco that Russian Orthodoxy gained significant strength in the lower states.

Like the Spanish settlement system before it, the Russian trade, along with other enormously profitable trade-based settlements of coastal areas along the Pacific Rim, began as almost exclusively male migrations. This fact had far-reaching cultural and religious consequences—for European men, as well as for indigenous women and men and the métis children that resulted from intercultural sexual encounters. Some laborers and traders, like the Europeans and New Englanders involved in the hide and tallow trade between California and Hawaii, married into local Latino Catholic families and adapted to regional mores. Others openly resisted the imposition of any religious controls by their own missionaries, reveling in a male culture free of familiar domestic restraints. And many simply relied on female family devotions "back home" by pious wives, mothers, and daughters to fulfill their religious obligations for them in absentia.[34] Sites of religious encounter and exchange, from missions to the rituals of birth, marriage, and death, were shaped by the relative mobility—and thus the freedom to choose, religiously and culturally—of European men. Yet whatever their choices, their increasing presence led to reconfigurations of the sacred world by all parties: by migrants, who, even if they did not appear traditionally pious, nonetheless often established ritual patterns that reflected some meaningful worldview; by local populations, who had to account for the arrival of newcomers in their understandings of sacred space and time; and by children, whose very existence represented cultural exchange at its most fundamental level.[35]

American Colonial Movements, 1820–98

European colonizations also initiated a second dynamic, a characteristic mode of local moral conflict, that affected the religious development of Pacific Rim communities. A common triangular pattern involved European (and later American and Asian) missionaries experiencing tensions with both indigenous populations and the entrepreneurial members of the very governments that the missionaries claimed to represent, who often resented the restrictions that missionaries sought to impose on their behavior. The ensuing moral battles were a defining feature of the American colonial period as it began its Pacific phase in 1820. The story of Euro-American Protestant missions is certainly the most familiar aspect of religious history on the Pacific Rim.[36] Therefore two illustrations must suffice for our understanding of America's colonial era, which ended, at least in its Pacific phase, with the formal annexation of Hawaii in 1898. In both cases, that of the American Board of Commissioners for Foreign Missions (ABCFM) outreach to Hawaii, and the cultural tumult touched off by the California gold rush of 1848, contacts between Protestant missionaries, native peoples, and settlers from across the globe reveal the multiperspectival nature of religious encounters. Although from one perspective the contacts represent the inexorable westward movement of gospel truths, for other participants religion played an altogether different role.

The years 1820 to 1821 mark a logical shift from the story of European colonial dominance to that of American dominance. The United States began its "Pacific patrol," the first systematic defense of its Pacific interests, in 1822. In 1821, New Spain lost its northernmost frontier when Mexico gained its independence. A year earlier, Asa Thurston and Hiram Bingham, two New Englanders and members of the Andover Brethren, had arrived in Hawaii with a twenty-two-member missionary expedition sponsored by the interdenominational ABCFM to establish a mission to the "heathen" of the islands. They were greeted enthusiastically by members of the royal family of Kamehameha II and subsequently forged a close relationship to the monarchy, several members of which were baptized and converted to Christianity in the mid-1820s.[37] By 1833, the mission enrolled forty thousand native students in twelve hundred schools, in which teachers emphasized instruction in the native language.[38] Protestants also sacralized the landscape, erecting churches for both natives and sailors throughout the islands. But they were not welcomed by American traders and whalers. In the mid-1820s John C. Jones, the U.S. consular agent in Honolulu (and a Boston Unitarian by birth), wrote to his friend Josiah Marshall to complain that "nothing but the sound of the church going bell is heard from the rising to the setting sun and religion is cramm'd down the throats of these poor simple mortals whilst certain famine and destruction are staring them in the face."[39]

As missionaries gained influence over the king and native leaders, and convinced them to discourage the trade in prostitution between visiting ship crews and local women, merchants and others vocally denounced the introduction of evangelical mores in the form of "blue laws." Angry at the increasing restrictions, sailors raided and destroyed missionary properties.[40] Hawaiians looked to traders for their livelihood, in order to get some piece of the huge profits from the fur and later the whaling industries that enriched the merchants' pockets. Despite the economic help of the merchants and the spiritual support of the missionaries, local populations died off rapidly with exposure to new diseases. From a high of anywhere from 300,000 to 800,000 inhabitants just prior to James Cook's first visit in 1778, the native population plummeted to 130,000 by 1832, and perhaps 70,000 by 1853. By the time Hawaii became a part of the United States through annexation in 1898, native Hawaiians represented just 36.2 percent of the population. At the same time, new settlers were coming in from Asia, dramatically transforming the cultural landscape once again. In 1866, Chinese laborers comprised about 2 percent of the population; by 1896, fully 42 percent of the inhabitants of Hawaii were Chinese or Japanese.[41]

To argue that the most important plot here is that of the Protestant missions is to miss the importance of differing views of the landscape (both the internal moral terrain and the built environment), conflicting accounts of encounter, native subjugation and near-extinction, and multidirectional movement within the region. All of these themes present opportunities for discussion of religious experience in Hawaii using a paradigm other than exclusively westward movement. We discover that even the culture brought to Hawaii by New England merchants and ministers was internally conflicted: were the islands to be an antinomian paradise or a "city on a hill"? The Hawaiian example is also significant because of the remarkable degree of cultural diversity found there: by the end of the century, no single group could claim majority status, and although a Protestant establishment (of sorts) did exist, it could not lay exclusive claims to public culture.[42]

The California gold rush (1848–56) offers many of the same themes, albeit on a much larger and even more diverse religious canvas. It is probably not too much of an overstatement to say that the gold rush was the most important cultural event in Pacific Rim religious history. The rapid migration to California of some 350,000 people from all parts of the world had enormous effects throughout the region. Hawaiians migrated to the continent. Peruvians and Chileans boarded boats headed northward. Australian, French, German, Welsh, and Irish prospectors followed close behind. Americans came by the tens of thousands to the new El Dorado, a region that (previously) had been considered too distant and far too unhealthy for permanent settlement. Native Indians discovered new opportunities and new perils among the newcomers, and the rush once again remade their own sacred landscape. For the first time in United States history, tens of thousands of East Asians, primarily Chinese, migrated to the North American continent.[43]

Religiously, California was marked early by a pride in its religious pluralism, as was also the case in Hawaii, a pride that obscured more than it revealed.[44] Imperial plans continued apace, and religion—Protestant, Catholic, Jewish, and later Buddhist—played an important part in organizing society into familiar American patterns.[45] Yet the religious landscape looked different to everyone who touched it, and these often divergent perceptions form an important part of the story. Some Catholics, for instance, viewed California as a place of moral peril because it was filled with Protestants; it had once been a sacred landscape, during the mission era, but by 1860 it was mired in heresy. Many Protestants, in contrast, saw future spiritual promise in a recently born society, and boasted that California would become the theological center of the world. Asians venturing to the "golden mountain" found themselves insulated, persecuted, and isolated, walled into small communities and met on all sides by hatred and suspicion. Their temples became tourist stops for gawking Euro-Americans. Mormons, Spiritualists, and Theosophists celebrated a surprisingly healthy climate and audiences receptive to their varying messages. African Americans found freedom, if not yet equality. Indians, pushed off their lands and venturing farther north and into the mountains, encountered high death rates and increasing poverty; for them, California had ceased to be the land of opportunity with the arrival of the many boats.[46] All of these groups, over time, imparted their own sacred meanings to the land through religious activities; California became a place, like Hawaii, of multiple and overlapping significances.

Many more decisive moments could be sketched to illustrate the increasing complexity of religious colonizations and contacts during the nineteenth century. Even as the United States set out to bring its divinely inspired form of Protestant civilization to the Pacific world beyond its shores, its nation-building activity spawned migrations from all around the globe to the emerging Pacific Rim network of communities. Although American imperialist designs continued apace into the twentieth century, 1898 marked both a physical and a symbolic moment of transition. In that year, both Hawaii and the Philippines came under the control of the United States, the latter marking the final retreat of Spain from its former position of Pacific dominance. These acquisitions seemed to signal the final victory of American cultural and economic aspirations to control access to ports from the Americas to Asia. Yet ironically, these annexations and the resulting political unrest around the region gave rise to reverse migrations from Asia and Latin America, pulling greater numbers of people eastward and northward to the United States.

Exchanges with Asia and Latin America, 1850 to the Present

If California and Hawaii were some of the westernmost and latest frontiers of Europe and the United States, the discovery and sacralization of the Pacific Rim by Asians and Latinos were just beginning. Simply recognizing that these latter cultures can be described as having "discovered" the United States moves us toward a new understanding of the religious history of the region. Moreover, highlighting this discovery does not imply that Euro-Americans stopped in their tracks. It merely emphasizes narratives that have been virtually excluded from most accounts. Perhaps the dominant motif in this most recent period of religious history has been that of exchange: while Protestant and Mormon missionaries have continued to transform the Pacific Basin in the twentieth century, increasing numbers of Asian and Latino migrants have altered not only the Pacific Coast of the United States, but also other regions of the country.

Two large waves of immigration brought the first Asian communities to America, and it is important to distinguish them from one another, religiously and culturally. The California gold rush brought Chinese laborers, whose religious world consisted of a mixture of Buddhism, Taoism, Confucianism, and popular folk beliefs. The initial immigration was overwhelmingly male (as has been the case on all of the economic frontiers we have discussed), and few priests joined in the movement. Religious life in America initially centered around private temples within the confines of the working associations that contracted for their labor.[47] After 1870, Japanese began migrating to both Hawaii and California. They brought with them their own mixtures of Buddhism, Taoism, and Shinto, among other traditions, and they, too, were laborers, headed for the New World in a pattern established first by the infamous "coolie" trade to Peru. The Japanese migrants were followed quickly by Buddhist priests of the True Pure Land sect, who erected temples, performed rites, and provided assistance and comfort to workers.[48]

The religious stories of these two cultures in America vary, but they are intertwined by virtue of their ill treatment at the hands of nearly every other group in the United States, peoples who could not tell the difference between Chinese and Japanese and who labeled both as immoral (and often unpatriotic) pagans. To a significant degree, the story of Asian Americans is to the nineteenth and twentieth centuries on the Pacific Rim what the story of African Americans is to the eighteenth and nineteenth centuries in the Atlantic world, and therefore both accounts require prominence in a balanced account of our religious past. It is no coincidence that the United States began encouraging the immigration of Asians just as African slavery was being abolished; many contemporaries looked to Asian labor to fill the need for a cheap and exploitable human resource. In both contexts, the African and the Asian, considerable religious resources were expended simply in fending off despair and utter exhaustion.[49]

A brief religious history of Japanese Buddhism in Hawaii suggests how helpful such a comparison might be, not only for our understanding of the Buddhist discovery of America, but also for our understanding of Christian traditions. In 1889 the first Japanese Buddhist priest, Soryu Kagahi, a member of the True Pure Land sect, arrived in Hawaii on a seven-month visit to oversee the spiritual welfare of Japanese migrants. Through his eyes, Honolulu was a "Puritan" village (the term used to denote all Protestant denominations by local Japanese), with its stark church spires and stifling temperance leagues.[50] The sacred landscape was indeed bare. With Kagahi's help, workers erected the first Buddhist temple in Hilo. The more pressing challenge for Ka-

gahi and the priests who followed him came in the form of aid for laborers—men who were homesick, lonely for families (without which
they could not enjoy the many family-centered rituals of their tradition),
and dismayed at not being able to save enough money to go home. The
early period of Japanese immigration was described by Buddhist leaders
(as was the case in Kodiak in the 1790s, by Russian Orthodox monks,
and again in California in the 1850s, by Protestant missionaries) as
a period of moral corruption: the spiritual climate was epitomized
by the phrase *Tabi no haji wa kaki sute,* or "throw away shame when
away from home." In many instances, Japanese priests worked with
sugar plantation owners to satisfy unhappy laborers by building local
temples.[51]

If the plight of the Asian migrants bore some resemblance to that of
other laborers on the Pacific Rim at other times, it bore perhaps closer
comparison to African American slavery. At several points in the period
of Asian movement to America, Euro-Americans have detained Asians
indiscriminately in concentration camps for varying periods of time,
taxing the cultural resources of the population. In late 1899, when bu-
bonic plague hit Honolulu's Chinatown, the local board of health ordered that all infected buildings be burned. When the conflagration got
out of control and destroyed the homes of over four thousand people,
the local government responded by placing the homeless in detention
camps for several months.[52] This brief confinement and dislocation
served as a prelude to the larger tragedy of internment during World
War II, when Buddhist activities were disrupted, schools and temples
were closed (and plundered in Hilo by American military), and priests
were imprisoned along with other Japanese Americans.

The full story of religious and cultural adaptation in the face of this
political discrimination has yet to be written, but what we have is suggestive of rich resources and comparisons. Buddhist festivals and rites
within the camps, while not part of an entirely "invisible" institution,
thrived under the constraints of physical confinement. In the wake
of war, new syncretistic religious movements arose among Japanese
Americans, including several founded by women. For example, Seichnō
no Ie, the most popular new movement during the war years, combined
Shinto, Buddhism, and Christian Science in a healing tradition. Other
Japanese converted to Christianity, even in the face of ill treatment on
the part of American officials. "Mainstream" Japanese Buddhism resembled ever more closely an American denomination in its organizational structure.[53]

In the twentieth century, Asian migration, particularly to the West Coast of the United States, has encompassed many more than Japanese and Chinese newcomers. Our narrative must take account of the significance of Los Angeles, in particular, as a port of entry for immigrants from around the Pacific Rim and beyond. This sketch cannot incorporate the many strands that must be newly woven into our history; it can only suggest avenues for further research that may someday yield studies of Southeast Asians, Hindus, Koreans (a large percentage of whom were already Christian before coming to the United States), and other Asian Americans as they have remade the American landscape into a sacred place.[54] Since the late-nineteenth century the Pacific Coast has been a relatively hospitable place for the establishment of Asian religious centers, including the Vedanta Society and International Society for Krishna Consciousness (Los Angeles), the Sikh Khalsa Diwan Society (northern California, with historic roots in Washington state as well), Zen Centers (initially founded in California), and the Buddhist Churches of North America (San Francisco). But increasingly, the significance of this story moves farther eastward, as Asian immigrants establish communities throughout the United States. Maharishi International University in Iowa, a Hindu temple along an interstate in Ohio, and a Zen Center in Rochester, New York, all attest that this religious narrative extends to the heart of American life as vitally as does the story of the Puritan migration from Europe.[55] These accounts of Asian colonization and sacralization no longer can be dismissed as a regional story.

Demographics reveal much that our narratives tend to overlook. Yet increasingly in the twentieth century, our fairly simplistic equations of national or regional identities with specific religious traditions have broken down. In our mobile world, religious exchanges increasingly take place across borders, giving lie to any easy categorizations. To some extent this has been true throughout our Pacific Rim history, but the sheer numbers of migrants in the modern world and the ensuing multiplication of religious identities complicate our task considerably. The story of exchanges with Latin America comprises a singular piece of the story that is not entirely equivalent to any other account. For Latinos on the Pacific Rim, as well as those who have migrated to the southwestern United States, border crossings are often an ongoing feature of life. The sacralization of a region, for many Mexicans in particular, includes a desire and ability to move back and forth, to live "betwixt and between."[56] Moreover, lest we think that these religious exchanges can be encapsulated by using the dichotomies of Catholic/Protestant, we must analyze the effects of several centuries of outreach from both directions across national lines: as early as 1910, for example, a small but growing number of Mexican migrants to Los Angeles had encountered Methodist, Presbyterian, Baptist, and Mormon missionaries in northern Mexico before coming to this country. The Irish-Catholic institutional hierarchy that Mexican migrants discovered on arrival was perhaps more foreign than the Protestantism they had left behind.[57] The recent growth of Pentecostalism and other forms of evangelical religion in Latin America will further affect the patterns of sacralization undertaken by newly arrived immigrants to the United States.

The rapidity with which Asians have become Christian and Latinos have become Protestant forces us to reconsider our notions of Christianity as a "Western" tradition that has encountered the mysterious East and triumphed over it. It is equally true that Christian traditions have been internationalized, thanks in large measure to impulses originating on the Pacific Rim. Pentecostalism, perhaps our best claim to an originally internationalist religious movement, began with revivals in Los Angeles. Some scholars have noted that one strain of Protestantism that emerged after the 1960s in California—best illustrated by Robert Schuller's Crystal Cathedral, Bethel Chapel of Redondo Beach, and Van Nuys First Baptist Church—blended evangelical Christianity with New Thought and other offshoots of the sixties counterculture, all of which were indebted to "Eastern" religions.[58] Mormonism represents a particularly fascinating example of this trend toward a resacralization of a religious world. The Latter-day Saints began an aggressive outreach program around the Pacific Basin as early as the 1840s, establishing an early center in the Sandwich Islands. In the last thirty years, a period in which the church has doubled in size from the increase of membership outside of the United States (primarily in the Pacific and in Latin America), church leaders were compelled to reinterpret passages of the Book of Mormon, a document that relates the history of Christianity in the Americas. Church authorities revealed that the Lamanites, the designation that had previously referred to Native Americans, also included Polynesian peoples. The sacred center of the Mormon world, in a sense, has shifted slightly westward and southward from its original mooring in the Continental United States, reflecting demographic shifts within the church itself; it remains to be seen to what extent scholars will, in the coming years, be able to describe Mormonism accurately as the "quintessential American religion."[59]

Religious exchanges are also challenging our notions of "Eastern" traditions and their "natural" constituencies, and the Pacific Rim has once again served as a site of encounter and exchange for various beliefs and practices. While Islam of various sorts is spreading quickly, particularly among African Americans, the demographics of the Buddhist movement reveal that there are currently more non-Asian participants—mostly white, middle-class, educated, urban Americans—than Asian-American.[60] This trend has led to ethnic tensions between Asian Buddhists and "white Buddhists" over questions of authenticity, and typically has resulted in the self-segregation of the two constituencies. Sacralization, as has often been the case, does not occur without conflict; increasingly, sites of encounter are moving eastward as Euro-Americans encounter "Eastern" religions and Asian Americans throughout the country.

New Starting Points

Any narrative is, by necessity, incomplete, and just as it illuminates certain historical moments, it risks obscuring others. Phrased more optimistically, however, this new illumination, rather than placing in shadow the older narratives of the westward course of Christianity and empire, will help us to see those stories in a new light by juxtaposing them to other movements, other ways in which the landscape of the United States has been mapped, imagined, and inhabited. Multidirectional and multicultural contacts have shaped the American religious experience on the Pacific from its beginnings. First conquered by a Spanish empire and later contested by European and American peoples, the region has most recently become a site for Asian and Latin American migrations. These latter events, in particular, increasingly challenge our ability to characterize complicated cultural hybridizations and reveal our fictions of continued Euro-American dominance of the eastern seaboard. Just as Protestant settlers came westward, moving eventually into and across the Pacific itself, so Japanese settlers moved east, creating sacred centers and building religious worlds that, by the late twentieth century, dotted the countryside of formerly Puritan New England as well as Los Angeles and San Francisco. Simultaneously, Latin Americans have moved northward, at times confounding our national and racial categorizations by creating a "border culture," problematizing generalizations about immigrant experiences, and transforming the American heartland, from San Diego to South Carolina, with their own sacred mappings. Out of the resulting contacts have come both violent confrontations and relatively peaceable religious exchanges and appropriations—riots and detainment camps, meditative techniques and New Age healings. Our seat on the Pacific affords a view of all of these features of the American religious landscape and stresses the ways they are bound together historically. They are all exceptional and distinctive histories that increasingly are intertwined; each must bear some of the narrative weight of our larger religious legacy. Then, with Opukahaia, with eighteenth-century Spanish Jesuits, with Russian fur traders, with indigenous Hawaiians, and others, we can discern the eastward, northward, southward, and westward paths that have contributed to our present religious situation.

SIX

Indians, Contact, and Colonialism in the Deep South

Themes for a Postcolonial History of American Religion

JOEL W. MARTIN

Two recent intellectual movements have underscored the importance of American Indian peoples across the land and throughout the history of North America. On the one hand, a new Indian history, produced in the last two decades by ethnohistorians, has altered our understanding of the American past. Far from chronicling the inevitable disappearance of Indian peoples, this history highlights the resilience and dynamism of Indian cultures and underscores their impact on the identities and cultures of non-Indians. On the other hand, Indians themselves are gaining unprecedented visibility in American public life as artists, entrepreneurs, journalists, political leaders, and intellectuals. In the academy, they have contributed an important critique of colonialism and its legacies.

Ideally, historians of American religion will learn from both of these movements and change the field of American religious history in fundamental ways. The change I envisage would be much more than a matter of simply tacking Indians on or splicing them into our narratives. Informed by the new history on Indians and stimulated by the contemporary perspectives of Indian intellectuals, we could attempt a paradigm shift. We might move from narratives that convey the notion that Indian religions were not important to those that acknowledge the importance of all traditions. We could turn from accounts that suggest Indians disappeared to those that depict Indians as constant participants in American life. We can progress from narratives that ignore uneven power relations to those that explain how these relations affected religious history and historiography. In a nutshell, this would mean a shift to postcolonial narratives.

To help encourage this shift, I begin this essay with reflections on how standard textbooks in our field currently diminish the importance of the history of American Indians and their religions. I then argue that such shortchanging can be corrected by paying more attention to two themes—contact and colonialism. Attention to these motifs can illumine not only Native American religion, but also non-native religions. Asianists and African Americanists would likely find these themes useful in their narratives. Scholars of European religions in America should consider their value as well, because Europeans initiated much of the modern history of contact and invested heavily in colonizing projects. Indeed, a full-blown postcolonial narrative would show how most religions in America have been affected by contact and colonialism. In such a narrative, Indians would be one quasi character among many others. Unfortunately, I have neither the space nor the expertise to write such a narrative.

Instead, working within my present limitations and to correct for silences in past stories, I concentrate disproportionately on native peoples and, to a lesser extent, Protestants. Specifically, to demonstrate the value of the themes of contact and colonialism as organizing foci of narratives, I offer a case study of religious history in a single region—the ancestral homeland of the Muskogee Creek Indians, whose original territory is now contained within the states of Alabama and Georgia. Originally inhabited by Indians alone, during the colonial period it became the home of Spanish, French, English, and African peoples. It continues to be a vital region in American religious life, a place where native and non-native peoples interact, argue, and sometimes create common ground. Many of the points I make in this case study have broader applicability to American religious history. To illustrate, I then move from the case study to imagine a postcolonial survey of American religion centered on contact and colonialism. In my conclusion, I sketch two possible ways to structure the story: a history organized chronologically from past to present, and a narrative that begins not with the past, but the present, and works backward. My sketches do not provide the full-fledged postcolonial narrative that I am calling for; nevertheless, they suggest its outlines.

Textbooks versus Realities

In recent textbooks on religion in America, Native American religions are typically treated in an early chapter, often the first.[1] Such placement has the salutary effect of acknowledging the chronological priority of Native American religions in America. By placing Native American religions only at the beginning of the work, however, these textbooks, as diverse as they are in methods and intents, all imply at a formal level that these religions belong only at the beginning of the story. Although the contents of that initial chapter may explicitly affirm the richness, creativity, and persistence of Native American religions, as in Catherine Albanese's survey, the very form of these books conveys to readers a different, if not contradictory, message. Native Americans appear "before the whites," but then vanish as the texts progress to treat Europeans or African newcomers. Despite their authors' best intentions, then, these books can imply that Native Americans disappear from religious history.

As anyone who reads the newspaper knows, Native Americans have not disappeared nor have they been ōverwhelmed by the challenges of modern life. In court cases throughout the country, Native American attorneys are seeking restoration of lands and resources stolen or misappropriated by non-natives. They are defending Native American religious freedom and sacred sites. In pursuing these causes, they have placed liens on homes in Connecticut, protected tribal fishing rights in the Pacific Northwest, collected millions of dollars in overdue rents on land in upstate New York, repatriated sacred artifacts from the Smithsonian Institution and other museums, contested Oregon's ban on the use of peyote, challenged a Forest Service's road project in California, and written the charters for casinos on a multitude of reservations. Many more cases are pending, many more claims outstanding.[2]

But Indian "legal eagles," chiefs such as Wilma Mankiller and Tom Porter, and gaming entrepreneurs are not the only Indians making their presence felt. A virtual literary renaissance is taking place in Indian country. Many Native American writers, such as N. Scott Momaday and Leslie Silko, have crafted stories, plays, and poems that reach large nonnative audiences, an unprecedented development in American literary history. Yet it represents only a part of the current richness of Native American artistic production. In Minnesota and elsewhere are native artists, playwrights, and poets who are not interested in attracting a national following but are influential regionally.[3]

Meanwhile, Native Americans "are pouring into colleges" as students and as teachers.[4] Native American academics such as Ward Churchill and Vine Deloria, Jr., are bringing important and unique perspectives to bear on American cultural, intellectual, and political history, Western philosophy, law, and ethics.[5] They have raised important questions concerning political sovereignty, the scope of religious practices protected by the Constitution, the definition of sacred sites, and the complicity of Christianity with ethnocentrism. Often they are raising questions no one else thinks to ask.

In Ward Churchill's perspective, for instance, the United States is an outlaw nation, a settler state living parasitically on its Native American host. Churchill argues in his essay "Perversions of Justice" that the United States "does not now possess, nor has it ever had, a legitimate right to occupancy in at least half the territory it claims as its own on this continent." He concludes his essay with a call for decolonization— "the restoration of indigenous land and indigenous national rights in the fullest sense of the term."[6] Needless to say, a history of American religion written from Churchill's perspective would differ from standard approaches. For one, it never would describe the process by which non-natives occupied North America as a settling of a wilderness by a pilgrim people. It is far more likely that a Churchillian scholar would depict this migration as an invasion of the territories of sovereign peoples by land-hungry Europeans who denigrated indigenous religions.

Churchill is but one of the many native intellectuals active in the academy, and his is but one of the challenging and diverse perspectives they are articulating. Together, these thinkers and artists have formed one of the most stimulating intellectual movements in America today.[7] Significantly, it is flowering at the precise moment when American historians have begun to take seriously the presence and activities of Indian peoples in the past.

Using various theoretical frameworks, employing diverse disciplinary approaches, and guided by different key metaphors, these historians are telling what for far too long has been the greatest story ever untold, the tale of two old worlds meeting in an encounter that irrevocably and decisively changed human history.[8] Scholars such as Jacqueline Louise Peterson, Richard White, and many others have recovered the importance of cultural contact in various U.S. regions, including the Great Lakes, the Northeast, the Southeast, the Midwest, and the West. In so doing, they have decisively altered our conception of the settle-

ment of North America. Rather than portraying it as a unilinear push
of Europeans into an unoccupied or "virgin land," the new scholarship,
because it does not ignore contact, has revealed that North America
has been the scene of highly charged interactions and complex cultural
negotiations among Native Americans, Africans, and Europeans. This
new view of the continent's history has encouraged historians such
as Gary Nash, Donald Meinig, and Ronald Takaki to write synoptic
narratives of the American past emphasizing cross-cultural exchange
and exploring the impact of colonialism on the economies, politics, and
peoples of North America.[9]

No historian of American religion has done the same. We have not
yet written narratives centered on contact or fully cognizant of colonialism and its legacies. We have not assimilated the new historiography
on Indians and the postcolonial critique advanced by Indians. And since
these two developments are still separate, even if simultaneous, we must
learn from each of them on its own terms. There are no shortcuts. We
need to consider the views of ethnohistorians and the perspectives of
Native American intellectuals. Put bluntly, we need to listen to James
Axtell and Vine Deloria, and many other diverse, sometimes conflicting,
voices.[10]

As ethnohistorian James Axtell pointed out in an essay several years
ago, historians have been slow to realize that Indians were "one of the
principal determinants of historical events" throughout colonial North
America, including Anglo-America.[11] To underscore his point, Axtell
offers an interesting counterfactual argument showing that colonial Anglo-America without the Indians would have been a radically different
place. By presenting to readers a fantasy America stripped of Indians,
Axtell conveys the powerful impact Indians actually had on the English,
the very Europeans we would normally assume were least affected by
contact. Because of the presence of Indians, the expansion of English
settlement was retarded. Consequently, British colonial society became
more stratified than it would have been if a true virgin land, the kind of
frontier mistakenly but vividly envisaged by historian Frederick Jackson
Turner, had been available. Because of the presence of Indians, the English developed a high-strung, fortress mentality centered on the contrast between savagery and civilization. Reinterpreting their religion in
light of the encounter with Indians, they intensified their own sense of
chosenness and judged Indians to be idolatrous.

Following the lead of Axtell and many other ethnohistorians, some
narrators of American religion will want to examine how contact af-

fected the religious life of Indians and non-Indians in New England and other regions. The theme of contact could become the organizing principle for synoptic histories of religion in America.[12] Yet if this motif becomes a main focus of inquiry and writing, another theme, colonialism, should not be neglected or subsumed under the theme of contact. To do so might encourage historians to neglect a motif that many of us are all too eager to avoid. Colonialism is one of the most painful, difficult, and contested aspects of American history, and we historians of American religion are not accustomed to thinking or writing about it. Yet we must. Colonialism, after all, powerfully affected American religious life. As contemporary Native American intellectuals argue, it continues to affect how we imagine our past, present, and future. Scholars of American religion need to learn from Native American thinkers how to analyze colonialism and its impact, just as we learn from the new Indian historians more about contact and its influence. Like an ellipse, our narratives should be generated around two foci—the themes of contact and colonialism. I attempt to demonstrate the value of this approach through a case study of the religious history of the homeland of one Indian people, the Creek Indians.

Ten Thousand Years
of Contact History in the Deep South

While most Creeks today live in Oklahoma (as a consequence of forced removal of their ancestors from Alabama by the United States during the 1830s), several thousand make their home in the traditional Creek homelands of Alabama, Florida, and Georgia.[13] No people has lived in this region longer. Some of the Creeks' ancestors have been there for 10,000 years or more. In contrast, Spanish Catholics first traveled through the region 460 years ago, and Protestants first visited it 330 years ago. Non-natives became the majority population only 180 years ago, or after 98 percent of the region's religious history had passed. These are important facts to remember. They call into question our standard periodization, helping us to see how our narratives have been shaped by unspoken assumptions about what and who matters. If we want to write postcolonial history, we need to extend our narratives much further back in time.

Archaeologists have learned much concerning America's pre-Columbian religious history. In the Southeast, the region of our case study, they have documented dynamic, persistent cultures that sometimes un-

derwent radical changes. Southeastern Indians experienced at least three
major religious revolutions before Europeans arrived. Indians moved
from a hunter-gatherer subsistence religion (the Archaic period, ten
thousand to three thousand years ago) to a religion that harmonized
with the settled life associated with vegetable horticulture (the Woodland period, three thousand to one thousand years ago) to the hierarchical civilization centered on intensive corn production, temple-mound
construction, and chiefly lineages (the Mississippian, 900–1550 C.E.).
Even when such epochal transitions were not occurring, significant
change was common. Individual Mississippian chiefdoms and temple-
mound complexes rose and fell. Near present-day St. Louis, the mound-
centered city of Cahokia grew to a population of many thousands and
then collapsed centuries before Columbus sailed. (In the Southwest,
around the same time, the large towns of the Pueblo civilization,
with their extensive stone apartment buildings, proved unsustainable
because of drought.) Elsewhere in the Southeast, temple complexes (for
example, Moundville, near present-day Tuscaloosa, Alabama) gained
power and then lost it. Dramatic change was part of southeastern Indian life long before Europeans arrived.[14]

Similarly, the experience of contact with other cultures was common
throughout North America before 1492. In California alone, a large
population of Indians spoke two hundred dialects. Southeastern Indians
were also diverse, spoke dozens of different languages, and inhabited
hundreds of villages. They were accustomed to meeting people who
looked, dressed, governed, believed, and buried in ways different from
their own, and they had developed rituals and protocols for dealing with
cultural "others." Not surprisingly, they employed these time-tested,
religiously charged forms to handle contact with the first Europeans and
Africans they met.[15]

During the sixteenth century, Spanish explorers and Indian town-
dwellers interpreted one another within their own religiopolitical
frameworks, trying to identify the strange "other" within familiar categories. An early significant contact between Creeks and Europeans occurred in 1540 when a Spanish military expedition led by Hernando de
Soto traveled across the Southeast searching for gold. Southeastern Indians responded to de Soto as if they were meeting a chief of a Mississippian mound complex, using the rituals and bestowing the gifts they
normally used to mollify visiting dignitaries. For his part, de Soto considered the Indian leaders he met to hold positions analogous to that of
Spanish "nobles." Invoking rights he possessed as an agent of Chris-

tianity in a land of heathens, he demanded tribute from them and took them hostage. When a town failed to produce the gold he desired, he ravaged it. Marching from town to town, and chiefdom to chiefdom, de Soto enslaved hundreds and killed perhaps thousands of Indians. In response, Indians, including ancestors of the Creeks, ambushed de Soto's army and nearly defeated it at a site located in what is now Alabama. De Soto fled west.[16]

Contact with Europeans such as de Soto spread diseases among southeastern Indians. Only within the last two decades have scholars established the extent of the devastation. In some places, Old World diseases such as smallpox, measles, and influenza killed as many as 90 percent of the people in the Southeast.[17] This demographic catastrophe led to the collapse of the chiefdom system of governance. Thus Old World diseases caused a fourth major religious revolution among southeastern Indians.

Chiefdoms had been characterized by a tension between two aspects of Mississippian religion—that practiced by an elite minority of priests and hereditary chiefs and that of the majority of Indians. Priests administered a temple-based cult of ancestors. Chiefs controlled esoteric knowledge vital to warfare and cosmological order. Working together, priests and chiefs dominated the mound center, which functioned simultaneously as an *axis mundi*, political heart, and redistribution site in Mississippian society. While subordinated to the temple-mound cult, the commoners' traditions focused also on the cycles of corn horticulture and the hunt. As the chiefdoms collapsed, many of the symbols unique to the elite religion lost their power or underwent a fundamental reinterpretation. In contrast, the broader religion retained its strength and became the basis of the postholocaust, village-based religions associated with seventeenth- and eighteenth-century Creeks, Choctaws, Chickasaws, and Cherokees. The religions of these peoples had some continuities with the Mississippian past, much as Mississippian religion itself had perpetuated many aspects of Woodland religion (for example, the symbolism of the four cardinal directions). It is tempting to say that the new religion emerging in the sixteenth century was to Mississippian religion as Protestantism was to Catholicism. The old center no longer held, and symbolic and political power was diffused much more widely, but many traditional symbols, stories, practices, and values persisted.[18]

What mattered most to postholocaust Muskogees was the life of the village, not the prestige of the chief or the cult of the ancestors. Their new ceremonial space was not the mound, but the town square: "A quadrangular space, enclosed by four open buildings, with rows of benches rising above one another." Muskogee civic and ceremonial life centered on the square ground, and almost every village was affiliated with a square ground town or *i: tálwa*. Here important visitors were received, rituals were performed, and communal decisions were formulated. One of these buildings served as the council house, where *mikos* (chiefs) and warriors assembled every day in council.[19] Dominated by men, the square ground was also the Muskogees' most important symbolic space.

With the arrival of the English in 1670 and the French in 1699, a new phase of contact history began in the Southeast. It was a phase characterized by many modes of reciprocal exchange. Meeting in the square ground and elsewhere, southeastern Indians, Africans, and Europeans learned to communicate across linguistic and cultural barriers, formed alliances, traded goods, exchanged ideas, constructed images of each other, and altered social and symbolic boundaries to accommodate that which was desirable or to restrict that which was not. Diverse peoples brought their cultures into contact, created a southeastern "middle ground," and transformed one another as a result. As defined by Richard White, a middle ground consists of "an elaborate network of economic, political, cultural, and social ties" that enable two or more societies to engage in multiple forms of reciprocal exchange.[20] Indians, European settlers, and African slaves traded deerskins, cloth, rum, corn, and horses, but they also intermarried, mixed genes, and produced bicultural peoples. They swapped ideas, songs, poems, stories, and symbols too. They exchanged and compared religious perspectives.

In the Southeast, Indians, Europeans, and Africans compared and evaluated cultures and religions not as an academic exercise, but in the heat of everyday encounters with different peoples pursuing other ways of life, ways of life that had their seductive, as well as repulsive, qualities. Southeastern peoples constructed "implicit ethnographies" of one another. As active, competent cultural agents in a context of cultural exchange, native and non-native men and women continuously sought to make sense of their lives, to remake traditions, to reinvent moral codes, to re-vision the past, to reprophesy the future. To be religious here (as elsewhere in North America) was to be involved in constant negotiation with other traditions and active reinterpretation of one's own.

Some contrasts across cultures were particularly stark and became nodes of vexed debate as the presence of Anglo-Americans increased in the Southeast during the latter part of the eighteenth century. For instance, Anglo-Americans and Indians disagreed profoundly over the proper order of gender relations.[21] These differences led to some misfired, mutually frustrating conversations and negotiations.[22] The contrast of cultures also produced moments of critical self-reflection. For instance, as Indians perceived that Anglo-American Protestants defined religion in relation to literacy and deemed the reading of the Bible to be essential to faith, some Indians felt it necessary to explain their own ascriptural spirituality. A Creek man informed a Moravian missionary, "white people have the old book from God. We Indians do not have it and are unable to read it." Even so, he averred, his people still possessed insight into the cosmic order of things. "The Indians know it without a book; they dream much of God, and therefore they know it."[23] Where Protestants turned to the Bible for archetypal figures and patterns to interpret their lives, Indians turned to dreams and natural signs. Like traditional people in many societies,[24] the Creeks formed their responses to important events by rumor-mongering, engaging in animated discussions, circulating countless anecdotes, and dreaming new visions.

Creek religion, though very different from Protestantism, was taken seriously by many non-Creeks, especially during the eighteenth century when the Creeks were still numerically dominant in the interior. We normally think of cross-cultural conversion in terms of Indians or Africans becoming Christians, but there were several cases of African American and Anglo-American men and women becoming Indians, in terms of lifestyle, values, and religion. According to an eighteenth-century trader, many English men living among the Creeks learned the "Usages and Laws" of the Creeks. Called "Indian countrymen," these "white people . . . [became] Indian proselytes of justice, by living according to the Indian religious system."[25] Some Anglo women also became Creeks and refused to return to their white families.[26] Runaway African Americans did the same and became important intermediaries between native and non-native cultures. In the historical record, they were referred to as "Indian negroes." They appear disproportionately to their numbers as translators in the deerskin trade. These and other translators were called "linksters," the Scottish word for linguists or interpreters, Scots being the leading traders. The term describes the translators' linguistic role as well as social activity: they not only interpreted speeches, but also linked peoples.[27]

Most non-natives did not make the full switch, but assimilated aspects of Creek cosmology and mythology, adding Creek teachings concerning spirits to their own European and African beliefs in haints, sprites, dragons, ghosts, witches, demons, ancestors, and nature gods. The Anglo-American trader James Adair knew whites who swore they had seen the Tie-Snake, a dragonlike underworld creature described in Creek oral tradition. And, just as Creek Indians appropriated Brer Rabbit narratives from African Americans, there is reason to think the Creeks' vast knowledge of the region's plants might have influenced the development of conjure and folk medicine among African Americans.[28]

Even self-conscious champions of Christianity, such as the Baptist missionary Lee Compere, were intrigued by Creek spirituality. In 1828, when clearing land, Compere killed a hickory tree, unwittingly violating a Creek rule of propriety. A Creek woman, who had heard and enjoyed Compere's telling of Bible stories, informed him that he had "broke in upon some of the secrets of the Indians' superstition . . . which is that the Indians consider such trees when they happen to be found in the Townfield as sacred to the Great Spirit." Pleased to learn about this belief, Compere was not sorry for his mistake. On another occasion, Compere succeeded in persuading a Creek headman, Tustunnuggee Thlucco, to relate some of the Creeks' sacred history, including how they had defeated the indigenous inhabitants of the Southeast. Indeed, Compere learned enough to write a manuscript history of the Creeks, a document unfortunately later lost. Other missionaries wrote hundreds of pages describing the belief systems of southeastern Indians.[29] In the Southeast, the flow of religious and cultural knowledge was not a one-way affair. Exchange on this "middle ground" was unavoidable, rich, and comprehensive; it changed everyone.

This point needs to be stressed. If historians of American religion adopt contact as an organizing theme for their narratives, they must be careful to show how it affected all participants, not just those who were Native American. "Contact" here is understood broadly. Sometimes it was direct and face-to-face, as when Anglo-Americans and African Americans entered Creek country. Other times it was indirect, mediated by journalism, political rhetoric, sermons, folktales, literature, artifacts, and artistic works. Sometimes it was open and emulative, expressing a positive appreciation of some aspect of the other way of life. Other times it was defensive and reactive, expressing a desire to maintain or increase cultural distance from the other way of life. Sometimes it focused on the exchange of material objects; other times it meant the transmission of values and ideologies. Most important, contact refers not only to embodied encounters between representatives of different cultures, but also to interpretations of contact manifested on the symbolic level. Indeed, the latter form of contact may be far more important, lasting, and influential, especially if we define religions, to some extent, as special kinds of symbol systems.

Defining contact in this larger sense calls attention to some of the ways the presence of Indians in the New World became important symbolically and mythically for Protestants, leading the latter to alter their interpretations of their religious traditions and even to create new traditions of meaning. For example, the presence of Indians changed how Protestants read their Bibles. Because many Anglo-American Protestants saw their emigration from Europe as a shedding of religious and social fetters, when they read their Bibles they identified strongly with the children of Israel who escaped Egyptian bondage. Yet Anglo-American Protestants also connected their experiences in the New World with the Bible stories depicting the Israelites' arrival and settlement in the promised land. Specifically, they compared Indians with the Amorites, Hittites, Perizzites, and Canaanites that the Lord blotted out so that Israel could enjoy a land flowing with milk and honey.[30] This metaphorical comparison placed Anglo-American Protestants in the position of a chosen people entering a promised land littered with the remains of unbelieving peoples subjugated by providential forces.[31] By interpreting the Bible in light of contact, Anglo-American Protestants created new interpretations of their sacred text.[32]

In the contact situation, Anglo-Protestants kept reading the Bible, but they emphasized different parts of it, interpreted its stories differently, and stretched its teachings to apply to new circumstances, including conflict with native peoples and the enslavement of Africans. In using their scriptures, they strengthened their affiliation with their Christian ancestors, producing a sense of continuity. In using their traditions in a new context, linking Canaanites to Indians and Ham's descendants to African slaves, they changed their ancestors' traditions, producing discontinuities in spite of themselves. Meanwhile, Africans continued to watch for signs of the gods in nature, but now they linked these signs to the Christian God and scriptures. As for the Creeks, they continued to tell origin stories that centered on their emergence as a people, but now these stories mentioned African Americans and Anglo-Americans as two of the Creator's unsuccessful attempts to make Indians.[33]

This was the paradox of religious reconstruction in the southeastern contact situation. Adherents of precontact European, African, and Indian religions attempted to bolster their traditions in response to the crisis of exposure to that which was novel and sometimes culturally dominant; but the very attempt to respond to contact revealed that the situation had changed irrevocably. People transformed traditions to respond to the cultural hybridity of life in the New World. Ultimately, everyone was a "linkster," helping to forge new religious orientations in the crucible of the southeastern contact zone.

Few of these links, few of these religious transformations, were merely responses to contact. They also were responses shaped by the uneven power relations created by colonialism. As Europeans gained greater power, and more and more Indian peoples became subjugated by invading colonists, the way contact was interpreted on all sides necessarily changed. Colonial power relations colored the religious imagination of natives and non-natives alike. When Anglo-American Protestants compared Canaanites to Indians, they did so as colonizers who had the upper hand politically and militarily. They told their story of triumphant invasion while enacting it at the expense of North America's indigenous peoples.

The history of contact in North America, after all, has not been the story of diverse peoples meeting as equals around a table to exchange their views on vital matters. Contact did not take the form of a free "dialogue" in a Habermasian zone of democratic exchange. For more than two centuries, Europeans and their descendants held Africans and their descendants in perpetual, total slavery, and for many generations, Europeans and their descendants have dominated Indians economically and politically. When African Americans converted to Christianity, they did so as people who had been compelled under threat of legally sanctioned violence not to practice their ancestors' religions. It was illegal for slaves to possess drums, speak African languages, or assemble without a white person present. This decisively shaped how Africans responded to Christianity and how Europeans responded to African religions, and the impact of this bitter experience continues to affect how whites and blacks interpret each other, the past, the present, and the future. Their captivity also influenced how Africans responded to Indians. After Georgia, founded by the utopian visionary George Oglethorpe in 1733, capitulated to slaveholders' pressures and opened its territory to slavery in 1750, African American slaves began running to Creek country with greater frequency. Among the Indians, according to one outraged official, "they lead an idle life and have an Idea of being free."[34] For those who remained in captivity, "Indians" became associated with freedom. As racial oppression continued, "Indians" acquired iconic value for African Americans. That this remains true today is signaled in Toni Morrison's *Beloved* when the runaway prisoner Paul D finds safe refuge with a group of Cherokees living in a mythic space.[35]

If slavery impacted how African Americans interpreted contact, so American imperialism affected how Indians responded to newcomers and their religions. During the nineteenth century, white Americans desired to terminate Indian societies altogether, to destroy them as peoples once and for all, to end any possible form of contact and exchange. These genocidal practices and desires decisively shaped how Indians responded to European religions and how Europeans responded to Indian religions. Like African Americans, southeastern Indians viewed Christianity with considerable skepticism, considering it to be the religion of the lying, drunken thief, the ideology of the oppressor. This remains true to this day for many Indians, who see Christianity as an agent of cultural destruction, a view embodied in Leslie Silko's novel *Ceremony* by the Christian character Auntie, who mistrusts her people's healers.[36] As scholars focus on religious contact, we need to emphasize that encounters occurred almost always in the context of uneven power relations and all too often in the extremes of colonialism.

Without a focus on colonialism, we cannot understand many religious movements among Native Americans, particularly those that have been termed "nativistic," but may more accurately be described as anticolonial. Such movements occurred among the Guales (1576, 1597), the Tarahumaras (1616), the Powhatans (1622, 1644), the Apalaches (1647), the Timucuans (1656), the Pueblo peoples (1680), the Yamasees (1715), the Natchez (1729), the Delawares (1760), the Shawnees (1805), and the Creeks (1811). Far from allergic reactions to contact, these were responses to militant European imperialism. Indeed, those movements occurring in the eastern woodlands took place when the forms of exchange associated with a "middle ground" were being destroyed by settlers who wanted Indian land, not Indian trade. Contact was not the problem; colonialism was. One can correlate several of these religious revolts (Powhatan, Yamasee, Delaware, Shawnee, Creek) with a sequence of maps tracing the westward expansion of Anglo-Americans in North America. The last instance of this type of movement, the Lakota Ghost Dance, occurred in 1890, the year the Anglo-American military conquest of the continent was virtually complete.[37] I return to this point in the conclusion, when I suggest the key historical markers for a postcolonial narrative centered on contact and colonialism. There remain several points to be learned from our case study.

The Creek anticolonial movement relied on extensive intertribal syncretism, significant intercultural borrowing, and bold religious innovation.[38] In this revolt, nine thousand Creeks tapped the rich cultural resources of the southeastern middle ground to create a coherent religious movement that rejected the ongoing white invasion of their lands. They blended elements present in that contact zone (the visions and ecstasies of Alabama prophets, Afro-Christian apocalypticism, a Shawnee dance, traditional Creek purification ceremonies, the European idea of the Book), and improvised new rituals, including attacks on cattle and chiefs. Restoring the symbolic boundaries between Indians and whites became a religious duty, political revolt a sacred cause. Using the old and new, fusing the native and non-native, Creek rebels attempted to show that they were still the masters of the land and all of its symbols.

After the Creek revolt was crushed by Andrew Jackson's army of Tennesseans in March of 1814 at Tohopeka (the Battle of Horseshoe Bend), the Creeks faced a new religious challenge. They had contested the rise of colonial power relations and lost. For the next several generations, religious life in this region was colored by these relations, not only for the Creeks, but for all the region's inhabitants—native, black, and white. The first sign that religious history had taken a significant turn was signaled by the arrival of Protestant missionaries in Creek country. Missionaries had traveled through Creek country before; now they settled there.

Because these missionaries arrived at the moment when the United States was ascendant and expanding, rapidly absorbing Indian lands, Creeks did not respond favorably to them. Specifically, Creeks outlawed preaching, and they made special efforts to hide their own culture of the sacred from Christian scrutiny. For instance, during the 1820s, the Tuckabatchee Creeks would not let any white person see their ancient copper plates, sacred items displayed during that town's Busk ceremony. Although Lee Compere, a Baptist missionary, lived among the Tuckabatchees from 1822 to 1828, he "would never get to see them. . . . The Indians were reluctant to talk about them." Compere did succeed in persuading Tustunnuggee Thlucco to relate some of the Creeks' sacred history, including how they had defeated the indigenous inhabitants of the Southeast. When Compere made an insensitive comparison between this ancient story of conquest and the ongoing Anglo-American invasion, however, the chief turned silent. Compere had crossed the line. "From that time I could never after induce him or any of the other chiefs to give me any more of their history."[39]

In addition to hiding their most sacred relics and keeping much of their oral tradition secret, Creeks tried to protect their ceremonies from white civilization. Confronted with hostile whites in their midst, Creeks consciously kept important artifacts, values, beliefs, and practices secret. They developed alternative stories and myths to explain the origins of the diverse races, performed rituals and dances that celebrated their identities as Indians, and carefully controlled whites' access to their interior lives. By developing and hiding an "underground" cultural life, many Creeks retained their sense of their separate identity even as their land was being invaded.[40]

Surrounded by plantation society, some affluent Creeks adopted the practice of holding African Americans as slaves. Like white masters, some Creek masters tried to control their slaves' religious life.[41] Like white masters, they could be cruel. In the spring of 1828, when chiefs learned that Baptist missionaries Lee and Susanna Compere were leading worship services that involved slaves, they took brutal action. Susanna and Jonathan Davis were leading the worship service of her family and "a few coloured persons" when "a band of savage monsters rushed in upon them, seized the poor black people, bound them with cords and belts."[42] Leaving Susanna and Jonathan untouched, they led the African Americans "one by one to a post of the yard and beat unmercifully," delivering more blows to one they deemed "the ringleader" of the slaves. Then the Creeks terrorized an African American woman, leading her out to the post, throwing her clothes over her head and beating her. They took a candle and examined her in a "licentious manner." This shocking event traumatized the African American Christians, distressed both Comperes, and ultimately led to the demise of the mission altogether. By November of 1829, the Comperes were out of the Indian country and had established the First Baptist Church in nearby Montgomery, Alabama.[43] Their single "full-blood" Creek convert, Jonathan Davis, went to the Arkansas territory to missionize among a band of Creeks who had migrated voluntarily. Within a few years, the great majority of Creeks followed. Still not Christianized, they were removed forcibly from Alabama to the Arkansas territory, where they continued to resist the efforts of missionary couples.[44]

Removal (1836) inaugurated a phase in which non-natives felt free to construct images of Indians as they saw fit, to imagine Indians without regard to the few real ones remaining in the Southeast. In a sense, this was simply the logic of colonialism carried to an extreme: the colonizer assumed the exclusive right to represent the colonized. To understand how these images possessed mythic value for non-natives, we need to review the history of their construction in the pre-Removal and post-Removal periods.

Throughout colonial North America, contact with Indians had posed serious moral and existential challenges for Anglo-Americans fascinated with and fearful of "savagery." The sense of living in a wilderness near "savages" made Anglo-Americans see the world differently from their cousins in England. Constructing their identity in relation to real and symbolic Indians, Anglo-American Protestants not only reinterpreted their scriptures, but also found it necessary to create new myths. Richard Slotkin, in *Regeneration through Violence,* argues that at the center of Anglo-American cultural life was an archetypal "myth of initiation into a new world and a new life." To be an Anglo-American one had to come to terms with the wilderness, and the wilderness was represented by Indians. He traces the literary expression of this myth back to the Puritan captivity narratives. Captivity narratives, of which there are thousands extant, usually centered on an innocent Christian held prisoner by a dark and savage Indian people. "The captive presented an exaggerated and emotionally heightened illustration of the moral and psychological situation of the community."[45] Only faith enables her to endure the ordeal. According to Slotkin, this portrait of the wilderness as a threatening, consuming power declined in the eighteenth century, although the wilderness and Indians retained tremendous symbolic power. A shift took place. It became possible to imagine mastering the wilderness and absorbing its vitality. Identification with Indians, even if the identification was achieved through violence, became the hallmark of Anglo-American nationalism.

Many of these themes were present in the ways southeastern Anglo-Americans responded to Creek Indians as symbolic figures before and after Removal. In May of 1812, a full year before the Creek war erupted, the prominent land speculator, lawyer, and slaveholder Andrew Jackson fed the spirit of war by invoking the archetype of the white female captive. Jackson wrote: "When we make the case of Mrs. Manly and her family and Mrs. Crawley our own—when we figure to ourselves our beloved wives and little prattling infants, butchered, mangled, murdered, and torn to pieces, by savage bloodhounds, and wallowing in their gore . . . we are ready to pant for vengeance . . . the whole Creek nation shall be covered with blood."[46] Once the war started, Jackson fulfilled his promise, destroying dozens of Creek villages, including some allied with the U.S. forces.

After the war, the symbolic equation of Creeks with the demonic declined, but their symbolic value did not cease. Creek Indians became associated with vital natural energies that whites could absorb through acts of violence. As Catherine L. Albanese has shown, Anglo-American literature transformed Davy Crockett from a frontier settler and soldier into a violent superhero communing with the overwhelming spirit of the wilderness by killing and eating bears and Creek Indians.[47] Graphic descriptions of his slaughtering Indian men and women were extremely popular among Protestant readers in the United States. Meanwhile, Crockett's commanding officer in the Creek war, Andrew Jackson, rode his popularity as a vanquisher of the Creeks to the White House.

In a counterintuitive development, representations of Indians proliferated *after* Removal. Having violently expelled the region's indigenous peoples, white southerners could not contain their enthusiasm for Indian themes. Indian place-names were adopted by the thousands during this period, particularly in newly absorbed areas of Georgia, Alabama, Mississippi, and Tennessee. And "Indians" infiltrated nearly every genre of writing. Indeed, the genres that are considered distinctively southern—southwestern humor and the romance novel—centered on Indians. Authors who wrote in these genres included William Gilmore Simms, Augustus Baldwin Longstreet, Johnson Jones Hooper, William T. Porter, "Davy Crockett," and many others. Other important genres in the South—historical works, reminiscences, and natural history— likewise gave a prominent place to "Indians."

After Removal, the Creeks themselves were romanticized; their heroic martial spirit was deemed worthy of emulation by non-native Alabamians. Alexander Beaufort Meek wrote (1845) and published (1855) an epic poem, *The Red Eagle: A Poem of the South,* to commemorate the Creek war and celebrate the gallantry of a "mixed-blood" Creek leader, William Weatherford. Albert James Pickett provided Alabama with its first history (1851), a book more than six hundred pages long and overwhelmingly focused on the Creeks. Toward the end of his volume, Pickett lauded the Creek rebels as positive examples of people willing to spill their life's substance to defend their lands from invasion. "Brave natives of Alabama! to defend that soil where the Great Spirit gave you birth, you sacrificed your peaceful savage pursuits! You fought the invaders until more than half your warriors were slain! The remnant of your warlike race yet live in the distant Arkansas. You have been forced to quit one of the finest regions upon earth, which is now occupied by Americans. Will THEY, in some dark hour, when Alabama is invaded, defend this soil as bravely and as enduringly as you have done? Posterity may be able to reply."[48] Is it too much to find in this passage the legitimating of warlike patriotism and rebellious nationalism, the glorification of a lost cause, and the notion that blood shed in defense of land is honorable, noble, and redemptive? Such were the moral lessons white slaveholders like Pickett drew from Creek history and communicated to readers, many of whom would take up arms soon in behalf of the Confederacy.

It would take a good deal more space to begin to develop this argument adequately, but the main points should be clear. In the Southeast, colonial power relations shaped the experiences and processes of contact and religious exchange. Among those colonized and experiencing cultural imperialism, there was a strong incentive to try to keep what was sacred hidden, safe, underground. Among the enslaved, there was a tendency to elevate "Indians" as the embodiment of freedom. And among the culturally dominant, it was possible, and perhaps even desirable, to construct identities that relied on fantastic images and mythologies of Indians. By substituting fantastic Indians for real ones, Anglo-Americans asserted control over "Indianness," domesticated "Indians" for their own use, and rendered real Indians disposable. In short, they colonized "Indianness" at a symbolic level even as they colonized Indian lands and resources.

As in so many things, the Civil War marked a watershed in the history of southern representations of Indians. After the war, white southerners' ideological needs changed dramatically. Instead of needing to legitimate Removal, whites needed to defend their prewar commitment to slavery and to justify continuing a race- and class-based hierarchical social order. "Indians" were still important, but they did not help achieve either of these goals. Accordingly, the literary genres that had focused on Indians changed. Southwestern humor picked up and moved west, leaving the South behind. Romance novels, to a much greater extent than before the war, concentrated on the plantation, portraying it with nostalgia as a happy place. A popular plot, symbolizing national reconciliation, featured a marriage between a Confederate war widow and a northern man. Contact remained important, but now the critical issue was negotiating and regulating exchanges between black and white, the North and the South.

During this period, Indians became somewhat "westernized" in the minds of southerners. As newspapers proliferated and began filling their pages with stories related to Sioux Indian "uprisings" and Apache skirmishes, and dimestore westerns became popular, southerners started thinking of Indians in the ways other Americans did, as horse-mounted, buffalo-hunting nomads roaming the Great Plains. African Americans in New Orleans adopted this view and began dressing as "chiefs" during Mardi Gras, continuing the long tradition of identifying Indians with freedom, but now equating Indians with the western peoples. In the twentieth century, Hollywood westerns completed this transformation on a national level. One result of this shift was that southerners visiting Cherokee, North Carolina, would not believe they were seeing a "real" Indian unless he was wearing a war bonnet. (Nowadays, Cherokees dressed in such bonnets make money posing with tourists. The activity is called "chiefing.")

Non-Indians continue to find significant symbolic meaning in Indians. For a few years now, I have been collecting references to Indians that appear in contemporary literature, television, popular culture, advertising, or on commercial products.[49] The volume is staggering, shows no sign of diminishing, and does not appear to be limited to regions where Indians live in great numbers. In the traditional homeland of the Creek Indians, which is now overwhelmingly non-native in population, images of Indians occur frequently. Not every image is stereotypical, but many of them are, conveying to readers or viewers the sense that Indians lived only in the past, that every one of them wore a war bonnet, that they were all nomadic, or that they had a romantic relationship with nature. In Atlanta, the largest city located in former Creek country, a major-league baseball franchise persists in calling its team the Braves, a name that cannot help but evoke stereotypes. Like a verbal magnet trolled through the cesspool of the American racial discourse, this word attracts images of Indians as ignorant fools and "blood-thirsty, tomahawk-waving savages."[50] (At Braves games, thousands of fans chop the air with plastic "tomahawks" to express their excitement.) As long as the team name remains, these kinds of images will be lifted out, amplified, commodified, and broadcast far and wide.

Black and white Braves fans who "chop" are not bad people, Indianhaters, or crypto-fascists. Rather, like almost all Americans, they are victims of colonialism, captives of cultural constructs and captivity myths created by people who were engaged in campaigns of conquest. Because these campaigns were partially successful, constructs of Indians as doomed, uncivilized, bellicose nomads have gained cultural dominance and, therefore, a kind of normative status and symbolic value for non-natives. Ward Churchill terms constructs such as these "the fantasies of the master race."[51] Except when analyzed by a cultural critic like Churchill or protested by Indian activists, these constructs rarely undergo reality checks. They represent how many Americans, if not the majority, think about Indians, and therefore, how Americans construct their own identities and meaning systems. Nevertheless, because the campaign of conquest was not completely successful, these fantasies and meaning systems do not finally go uncontested. Indian people are now resisting them. They protest, organize, lobby, vote, boycott, sue, editorialize, argue, negotiate, write novels, curate exhibits, and create art. In speaking for themselves, they attempt to demythologize "Indianness" and to decolonize America. Today in the Southeast their focus may be on the name of a sporting team; tomorrow it may concern violated treaty rights, Indian sovereignty, the repatriation of sacred objects and human remains, the use of peyote, or a host of other matters. In the Southeast—as in Wisconsin, Oregon, Connecticut, South Dakota, and many other areas of the United States—native and non-native peoples are struggling to come to terms with the sorry legacies of colonialism. In the traditional homeland of the Creeks, this struggle has recently taken an unexpected turn because the Creeks have returned from oblivion.[52]

After the United States conquered the Creeks in 1814 and subsequently removed almost all southeastern Indians to "external colonies" in Arkansas and Oklahoma, few Creeks remained in their traditional homeland. Among the few who remained were some who resided in southern Alabama on allotments of land sanctioned by the 1814 Treaty of Fort Jackson. For close to a century, they lived largely isolated and therefore somewhat independent lives. This changed with the dawn of the twentieth century and the arrival of the Jim Crow system of racial segregation and persecution. State-sanctioned racism caused the Creeks to lose some of their land, yet they persisted and began creating formal institutions to protect their identities. These included Free Will Baptist, Episcopal, and Holiness churches. After World War II, they organized politically and began reclaiming their Indian identity. They engaged in a school boycott, filed lawsuits for land claims, started an annual pow-wow that became a major tourist attraction, and, most important, in 1984 gained federal recognition as a tribe, the Poarch Band of Creek Indians. With recognition, they acquired the special sovereignty that belongs to tribes—access to community development grants, rights to open gaming establishments, and much more. Already the Poarch Creeks operate the largest bingo parlor in Alabama. Soon, they may open the first casino in the state. From an obscure, beleaguered group that numbered only 150 people at the beginning of the century, they have become a semisovereign people numbering nearly 2,000 and wielding some respectable economic and political power in Alabama.

With this increase in secular power, the Alabama Creeks have not escaped the problems and internal divisions that plague any community or polity. Yet as their secular power has risen, so has their freedom to express themselves as Indians, without fear of discrimination. In the last two decades, Alabama Creeks have attended meetings of national Indian organizations, resumed the wearing of traditional clothing during the annual powwow, learned how to make war dance costumes, performed sweat-bath rituals, and conducted Native American Church services. Alabama Creeks also have deepened their connections to Oklahoma Creeks and to classic Creek religion. They have hired a traditionalist Creek to teach native heritage and Muskogee language classes, have attended Creek religious ceremonies in Oklahoma, and have discussed "reestablishing in Alabama a traditional 'square ground' with a properly sanctified 'fire.' "[53] In sum, the Poarch Creeks have challenged the politics of removal and racism and evaded destruction and oblivion. Andrew Jackson is probably rolling in his grave.

Toward a Postcolonial Narrative

Creek religious history is unique only in its particulars. In broad ways, it parallels the history of many, if not most, Indian peoples. It also points to larger historical processes that had significance for American religious history in general. These include the emergence of the Atlantic world during the colonial period, the subsequent encounter among cultures and religions in North America, the rise and expansion of the U.S. nation-state at the expense of Indian peoples, and the ongoing struggle to overcome the legacies of colonialism. A history of American religion that paid close attention to these processes would look substantially different.

If arranged chronologically, our new history would begin by describing an initial period (circa 1200) in which little, if any, transatlantic contact occurred. In central and eastern North America, the Mississippian civilization was strong; in western Europe, Catholicism was dominant; in western Africa, traditional village-based religions flourished. Next our story would trace how, in the century before Columbus sailed, western Europe and western Africa were connected by Portuguese slavers. This connection spread Catholicism, created a hybridized coastal culture, and established a pattern of plantation slavery that the Spanish soon reproduced in the tropics of the Western hemisphere.

While much of North America remained peripheral to the Spanish tropical empire, this empire did impact North America. In our contact-centered narrative, a critical year was 1540, for it marked the simultaneous invasion of the Southeast and the Southwest by major Spanish expeditions (de Soto and Coronado, respectively). These two invasions inaugurated dramatic changes in dozens of Indian societies spread over thousands of square miles of territory. As a consequence of these expeditions and the diseases they spread, the Mississippian civilization collapsed and Pueblo peoples suffered greatly. In the Southeast, survivors such as the Creeks had to reconstruct their religion. In the Southwest, Pueblo peoples began a long process of assimilating Catholic saints to their gods, creating new, hybridized symbols and rituals.

As transatlantic encounters increased in North America during the seventeenth and eighteenth centuries, dramatic stories of religious rebirth and transformation occurred throughout Indian country. Our narrative would consider several of these. It might, for instance, describe how Sioux people accepted the sacred pipe from White Calf Buffalo Woman, mounted Spanish-imported horses, moved to the Great Plains, and began their sacramental relationship with the buffalo. It could consider how some Canadian Indians involved in the fur trade allowed Jesuits to exercise influence in their villages, treating the Black Robes as shamanlike figures. It might probe how New England Indians, overwhelmed by Protestants and defeated militarily, moved to "praying towns." It likely would consider how thousands of seventeenth-century Florida Indians converted to Catholicism in Franciscan missions, and how California Indians did the same in the next century. Our narrative would describe contact-induced change not just among Indian religions, but also among the religions of non-natives. It might, for instance, describe how New England Protestants became fascinated with the captivity narrative, making it a key form to explore the meaning of Christian faith in the New World. Our narrative would convey clearly that nearly everyone in the Atlantic world recreated their lives in the new demographic, material, and spiritual context created in the aftermath of transatlantic encounters. This approach would highlight the idea that religions are dynamic meaning systems, not static cultural formations.

The next period treated in our narrative could be called the era of the "middle grounds." These were cross-cultural networks that enabled natives and non-natives to meet and exchange goods, genes, ideas, stories, and symbols. Our history would examine their rise and fall in various colonies, as well as their more lasting impact on cultural, mythic, and religious life.

In New England and Virginia, these networks were short-lived because English settlers soon overwhelmed native populations.[54] In both colonies, the turning point came in the 1630s. In New England, the Pequot massacre of 1636 and in Virginia the Powhatan revolt of 1633 marked the death of the middle ground and the beginning of a long period characterized by brutal oppression and dispossession of Indians, climaxing with King Philip's War in New England (1674–76) and Bacon's Rebellion in Virginia (1676). It is not coincidental that the Puritan missionary John Eliot founded fifteen praying towns for Indians in the second half of the seventeenth century or that he wrote his *Indian Dialogues* in 1671.[55] These activities, resettling Indians for the purpose of conversion and assuming the right to speak for them, presupposed cultural and political dominance; they were antithetical to a true middle ground context where no side possessed the power to dominate the other.

In Pennsylvania, the English colony famous for its fair treatment of Indians, it is not clear that a true middle ground emerged.[56] When William Penn's Quaker colonists arrived in 1690, the Delawares already had moved westward, leaving vacant land for Quakers and Anabaptists to occupy. Because of geographic separation and the pacifism of the colony's early settlers, violent conflict was delayed for a couple of generations in Pennsylvania. During this interlude, if a middle ground emerged, it was attenuated and abbreviated. The steep ridges and valleys of the Alleghenies proved a formidable obstacle for go-betweens. During the middle decades of the eighteenth century, trade was interrupted as Scotch-Irish Presbyterians and German Lutheran farmers poured into the backcountry. Uninterested in accommodating Indians and determined to take possession of the land, they obliterated through violence the tenuous forms of mutual exchange connecting Indians and Europeans. They massacred Conestoga Indians in Lancaster in 1763 and nineteen years later killed Indians who had been Christianized by Moravians.

Even as middle grounds were demolished in New England and Virginia and stillborn in Pennsylvania, they were being created elsewhere.[57] An early middle ground emerged between the Iroquois, the Dutch, and the French in the upstate New York region during the mid-seventeenth century. Another arose in the Great Lakes region during the same period. In a place beyond the effective control of empires and world systems, Algonquians and French Catholic people cocreated a multidimensional network of cross-cultural ties that enabled them to engage in reciprocal forms of exchange.[58] New economic and political arrangements facilitated trade and alliance. And new or significantly modified rituals and myths helped people handle contact with strangers. In the Great Lakes region and in Canada, generations of involvement in the fur trade brought together the French and Indians to create new peoples called the métis.[59] Meanwhile, in the Southeast, yet another middle ground was created after the founding of Carolina by Anglicans in 1670 and the founding of Mobile by French Catholics in 1699. This one lasted throughout the eighteenth century and involved a variety of Europeans, Africans, and dozens of Indian groups, including the Cherokees, Chickasaws, Choctaws, and Creeks. It led, too, to the creation of hybrid cultural forms as well as bicultural people. As I showed earlier, this middle ground was destroyed in Creek country in 1814 by U.S. military invasion. Other middle grounds existed in the central and western United States, but space does not permit discussion of those here.[60] My point is that a narrative focused on contact will find the concept of the middle ground useful.

As our narrative examines the impact of contact on religious life in different historical contexts, it also will consider the impact of uneven power relations. Our history will examine the religious history of slaves and slaveowners, of men and women, of the majority population and of minorities, of the politically dominant and those who were disenfranchised. But our history, because it focuses on colonialism, also will study and compare the religious histories of non-native colonizers and colonized native peoples. A productive way to do this is to study religious life in various regions where middle grounds had existed, but later were destroyed. As the Creek case study suggests, the concept of the "underground" may be useful to describe the religions of colonized or politically oppressed peoples. It certainly fits the experience of Pueblo,

Plains, and Northwestern peoples who hid their religious societies for generations from condemning non-native authorities and priests. Additionally, the history of missions will be important, for it was often only after an Indian people was subjugated militarily that missionaries settled in their territory.[61]

On the side of the colonizers, as power relations between natives and non-natives became more uneven through the nineteenth century, dominant non-natives tended to downplay the impact of contact on themselves and exaggerate it regarding Indians. The myth of the vanishing Indian, fading before "white civilization," took hold of the public imagination and was memorialized in art, popular culture, entertainment, and even on coins. Among other things, dominant non-Indians used images of Indian men and women to work out their own gender issues. The images of western Indians, particularly Plains Indians, transported men to a mythic realm, a violent land called the West, which was imagined largely without women. Here unfettered white men killed roaming red men. A full treatment of non-Indian religion in the Victorian period would need to examine the relation of this antidomestic myth to "domesticated" religious formations such as Methodism, with its focus on the family altar and its glorification of the piety of the good mother.[62]

By the end of the nineteenth century, the military conquest of the continent was completed, images of Indians had replaced real Indians in the public imagination, and a white, Protestant nationalism had become the dominant cultural orientation. As Albanese has shown, Public Protestantism blurred the boundary between the values of the state and those of Protestantism. This fusion posed challenges for Jews, Catholics, other non-Protestant groups, and for those Protestants like the Amish and Fundamentalists who did not want religion linked to the affairs and fate of the nation-state. But perhaps the harshest impact of the fusion was on Native Americans. Many of their religious practices were outlawed, including the Ghost Dance, the Sun Dance, potlatch ceremonies, and the sacramental use of peyote. Native Americans have yet to enjoy full and equal religious freedom.[63]

A good focus for this section of the narrative is to concentrate on a single year, 1890. This year marks a turning point, for it was the moment when "Anglo-Saxon" colonialism reached its apogee in North America. This was the year of the Wounded Knee Massacre, when U.S. troops slaughtered Lakota Ghost Dancers. It was the year when the Indian population of the United States reached its nadir. It was but a few years past the date (1887) when the federal government passed the Allotment Act, legislation designed to pulverize Indian land holdings and obliterate their cultural identity. (As Robert Clinton notes, "This policy alone reduced the remaining Indian land base from 138 million acres to 42 million acres in fifty years."[64]) It was but a few years shy of the year in which lynchings of African Americans reached their greatest frequency (several hundred a year). It was in the era in which Jim Crow was established, a half dozen years before *Plessy v. Ferguson*. It falls close to the World Parliament of Religions at the Columbian World's Fair (1893), an event richly revealing of how white American Protestants understood themselves and others during an age of empire. Finally, 1890, the year of Sitting Bull's murder, represents the year when the American continental empire was consolidated, the "frontier" closed. From this date onward, American expansionists would have to look elsewhere to satisfy land-grabbing impulses—to Hawaii, to the Philippines, to Panama.

By 1890, many white Americans had become imperialistic, race-obsessed, and perhaps xenophobic. This did not stop the country, however, from becoming more pluralistic. Subsequent decades brought the influx of millions of eastern and southern European immigrants, as well as an increase in Asian immigration and a more extensive encounter with Asian religions.[65] A history centered on contact would have much to say concerning these encounters, the compromises forged, the repulsions and seductions that took place. Among other things, it would probe how these newcomers challenged the cultural dominance of Anglo-Protestants, redefined who was accepted as an American, and expanded the range of religious practices tolerated, sometimes by translating their own traditions into forms acceptable to the dominant population. It also would consider how Protestants responded to these immigrants. Jews and Catholics had been in North America as long as other Europeans, but never accepted as full citizens. Anti-Catholic movements had surfaced before the Civil War, and anti-Semitism had been a constant aspect of Christianity. As new waves of immigrants arrived, a nativistic reaction took place among Protestants, and new, more restrictive, immigration laws were passed.

In the middle of the next century, World War II changed everything. Movements of decolonization around the globe led to the creation of dozens of indigenous nation-states, and inspired subaltern groups in America to seek full citizenship and acceptance. Different groups met with varying degrees of success. Postwar prosperity enlarged the American middle class in terms of sheer size but also in terms of the range of ethnicities represented. Economic inequality diminished. Judaism and Catholicism joined Protestantism as mainstream faiths. Afro-Christians, although Protestants, were not as welcomed, but some boundary testing did occur. The civil rights movement, beginning with efforts to desegregate Pullman porters and branches of the armed forces, and extending to other aspects of public life, challenged some forms of race-based political and social discrimination. These trends and others, including the massive expansion of higher education and the spread of rock-and-roll youth culture, blended to produce in the United States the political struggles, cultural wars, and religious crusades of the sixties.

Interpreting the impact of the sixties on American religious history will be a critical part of any history centered on contact and colonialism. If a single year were picked for concentrated attention, it might be 1965. During that year, the United States increased its involvement in the Vietnam War, sending the first combat troops, then later greatly bolstering their numbers. Once again the United States committed itself to the violent repression of an anticolonial movement organized by a non-European people in a region over which the United States had no legitimate sovereignty. Bellicose rhetoric, which had been developed in nineteenth-century military campaigns against Plains Indians, was applied against the Vietcong. In a move emblematic of this continuity, western film star John Wayne exchanged his cowboy boots for those of a Green Beret (1968). In 1965, however, the United States already was becoming divided over the Vietnam War and conflicted about the future of state-supported white supremacy in the South and elsewhere. Teach-ins began in 1965, and the Civil Rights Act had become law the previous year. Once again, immigration laws provided a telling index of the nation's openness to cultural contact and non-Protestant religions. In 1965, U.S. immigration laws changed, opening the doors to much greater numbers of Asian and Latino newcomers. Their influx increased religious diversity in the United States at a time when American religious communities were already bitterly divided over the Vietnam War and state-supported segregation. A lively decade animated by absorbing public contests, the sixties was also an era punctuated all too often by the brutal murders of non-WASP leaders who had challenged the boundaries by which ethnics, workers, and minorities had long been segregated—John Kennedy in 1963, Malcolm X in 1965, Robert Kennedy and Martin Luther King, Jr., in 1968.

During the sixties, American Indians gained new political and legal

tools and renewed their religious traditions. In 1966, Congress authorized recognized Indian polities "to file suit in federal district court, ir-
respective of the amount in controversy, for claims arising under the
Constitution, laws, or treaties of the United States."[66] In response, in
1967, Philip S. Deloria organized the Pre-Law Summer Institute at the
American Indian Law Center, Inc., to encourage Indian scholars to become attorneys. This effort contributed to a great increase in the number of Indian lawyers and the filing of many important claims. Inspired
by the civil rights movement's successes and empowered by their new
legal standing, Indians challenged colonialism in the United States, creating "the first sustained decrease and partial reversal in American
colonialist policies toward Indians." As Robert N. Clinton states, they
reasserted their own sovereignty and regained some "political control
over their economic and cultural destinies."[67]

At many moments in the past, religion had provided the form
through which Indians expressed their deepest desires and constructed
their collective identities—for instance, the anticolonial prophetic
movements, the Ghost Dance, the peyote religion, the restored Sun
Dance. This continued to be the case in the latter decades of the twentieth century, as Indians fought for the repatriation of sacred objects,
the bones of their ancestors, the inviolability of sacred sites. Yet just
as every minuscule advance of a nondominant group seems to produce
a massive backlash (such as intransigent white resistance to desegrega-
tion during the sixties and seventies, and more recently to affirmative
action), so the struggles of Indians have encountered opposition. Part of
that opposition is grounded in mythic beliefs held by non-natives about
Indians. Indeed, something like a religion—an endlessly repeated set of
mythic images and unquestioned values that orient behavior—informed
many of the responses of non-Indians to Indians and their struggles.
Shaped by this quasi religion, non-natives had been trained to think of
the United States as a legitimate nation with unproblematic sovereignty
over its entire territory and of Indians as mythic figures from America's
past whose images may be used in ways either demeaning (the Washington Redskins) or romantic (New Age white shamans). Trapped in these
patterns of thought and profiting economically from their continued
exploitation of the images, beliefs, and lands of Indians, non-natives
have a difficult time letting go of the benefits of colonialism. Belatedly,
archaeologists return the bones of Indian ancestors to their descendants.
Belligerently, white citizens challenge Indians' rights to fish or hunt
in the Great Lakes and the Northwest, although treaties protect these

rights. With astounding insensitivity, sports franchises continue to use Indian mascots. And with persistent intolerance, state and federal authorities undermine Indian religions by allowing sacred sites to be "developed." Not surprisingly, colonialist patterns remain alive in federal law as well and influence court decisions related to Indian land claims and religious freedom. Our narrative would chronicle these contests and divergences, which might be described as a clash between religions of postcolonial resistance and religions of neocolonial appropriation.

Finally, the last chapter of our survey would consist of a careful examination of the symbolism of the National Museum of the American Indian. (I have in mind here a close reading of the sort authored by Edward Linenthal on the National Museum of the Holocaust.[68]) The National Museum of the American Indian is being built on the last site remaining on the Mall in Washington, D.C., and scheduled to open as one millennium ends and another begins; a study of its design, rationale, and articulation with American civil religion would make a fitting way to cap a survey focused on contact and colonialism. Intended to change forever how Americans view Native Americans, the museum, like our survey, is committed to a postcolonial vision of America's past and its future.

The narrative I have sketched would be quite different from previous ones. It would cover a much greater time period, take contact and colonialism seriously, shed light on many neglected aspects of American religious history, and encourage new perspectives on topics already treated in standard histories. Yet in proposing this approach, I do not mean to say it represents the only way to narrate a postcolonial story. There are other ways to tell a story focused on contact and colonialism. For instance, we could narrate American religious history in reverse, beginning with the present and working our way back. Specifically, a survey could begin with current conflicts over religion. In a very real sense, these are the conflicts that our history of contact and colonialism has destined us to experience. They are the distillates of American history. They provide excellent starting points.

One could begin a course or textbook on American religious history with a discussion of the text of the Supreme Court's decision in *Oregon v. Smith,* a case involving the dismissal of a state worker because of his participation in worship services of the Native American Church.[69] Beginning in this way would convey several valuable lessons. It would signal to students and readers that Native Americans are contemporaries.

It would provide a focused way to examine American pluralism and some of the conflicts that result. It would convey to readers and students that the definition of religion is highly contested. It would remind us that these definitions matter in people's lives. It would underscore the importance of the Supreme Court and the separation clause of the Constitution in the history of religions in America. It would show that the study of religion is interdisciplinary, reliant on history, anthropology, literary studies, oral history, legal studies, and other approaches. It would show that the study of religion concerns issues of contemporary significance. Further, the case itself makes fascinating reading. There are many excellent essays on this decision, including some by Native Americans, which could be used to help students understand the broad issues and historical background.[70]

A narrative beginning with this case could then move backward and outward, asking questions such as the following: What is the peyote religion? Where did it come from? When did it spread? How can the consumption of peyote be considered a religious act? What makes anything religious? When did European-Americans arrive in Oregon? What was their religious background? How was U.S. sovereignty extended over Indian peoples? Why was the First Amendment written? Have there been other instances where contests over religious freedom occurred? Why are many religious Jews, Catholics, and Protestants alarmed by the Supreme Court's decision? Such questions could lead to a study of many of the themes and issues that always have been important in the historiography and theory of religion, yet they also could be used to accent the importance of the themes of contact and colonialism. All the while, because we began our story with a contemporary case, students and readers would have the sense that American religious history is not about studying the past alone, but also about understanding the present.

As we rethink the story of American religious history, we should keep in mind Sydney Ahlstrom's question, "How did America come to its present moral and spiritual condition?" One illuminating answer may come in the form of a story of religions in contact in the context of colonialism. Such an approach would encourage us to think of Native American religions as dynamic meaning systems that responded to historical changes, for example, life in the context of a middle ground or an underground. This view would protect us against the conventional trope of disappearing Indians, and prepare us for stories of political renewal and religious innovation among Native Americans. An ap-

proach centered on contact and colonialism also could illumine the religious life of Europeans, Africans, and Asians in America. It might help
us understand how and why they reinterpreted their Old World traditions. On the one hand, we would consider how Jews, Catholics, Muslims, and Hindus modify their own institutions and values in response
to those of the Protestant majority. On the other hand, we would examine how the Protestant majority responds to the rise of pluralism. An
emphasis on contact and colonialism might encourage us to examine
instances in which newcomers fused their ancestral traditions with
other religions (for example, Yoruba religion blended with Catholicism
to produce Santería) or created new traditions which gave Native
Americans great symbolic value (Mormons, Spiritualism, New Age). By
paying attention to contact and colonialism, we might understand more
fully how America has come to its present moral and spiritual condition. We might then grasp how Indians could be resurgent and reclaiming their rights, even as non-natives continue to act as if Indians have
vanished. Understanding contact and colonialism we could understand
how uneven power relations have affected diverse religions, and left Indians among the poorest, most disenfranchised people in the country.
This would help us understand better the cultural wars, political controversies, and moral struggles of the present—and perhaps enable us to
anticipate those to come as Americans continue to deal with colonialism
and its legacies. Lastly, this approach might help us identify those moments of convergence that did not end in conflict, those contacts not
ruined by colonialism. Is it too much to hope that our field will not
merely document the history of transitional middle grounds and subver-
sive undergrounds, but help to establish a firm and lasting common
ground where all Americans can meet to build a more just, postcolonial
future?

SEVEN

Voices from the Attic

The Canadian Border and the Writing of American Religious History

WILLIAM WESTFALL

The Canadian border, that seemingly endless and ethereal line that marks America's northern frontier, offers an intriguing perspective on the religious history of the United States.[1] The two countries this border divides—at once so very different and so hauntingly similar—have played an important part in each other's religious and cultural lives. Their intricate story of defiance and exchange presents several valuable insights not only into the histories of each country but also into the ways these histories have been interpreted. As we approach this border the religious histories of the two countries begin to move in parallax, setting long-standing assumptions about religion and nation in a new and critical light.

To appreciate the insights that a Canadian perspective can bring to this project, however, one must first reflect for a moment on the object of Canada's gaze. To resite the writing of American religious history— as Thomas A. Tweed has explained in his introductory essay—raises a number of fundamental questions about both America and the process of historical narration itself.[2] How are narratives constructed? What have been the dominant narratives of American religious history? And especially in this instance, what is American about the writing of American religious history? By returning briefly to these questions we can draw out some of the basic assumptions that have informed the writing of American religious history, and, more important, situate Canada in relation to these assumptions and the debates they have enkindled.

American religious history, Nathan O. Hatch has recently pointed out, emerged as a coherent field of study in the 1960s in large part because the historians who constructed the narratives that defined (and then dominated) the field approached their task from a common cultural position.[3] The great tradition in American religious history (turning slightly the title of Winthrop S. Hudson's famous study) drew heavily on the consensus paradigms of American culture. In Hatch's words, these historians were "consensualists, believing in a common American character, and most held a positive, affirmative reading of the overall achievement of American culture and its religion."[4] Indeed, these values became so deeply embedded in their work that the history of American religion not only marched to the rhythms of consensus, it graced and lined each chorus of the national hymn this cultural paradigm intoned.

The symmetry between the history of nation and the history of religion can be seen at many points. Both told the story of the evolution of a single body of coherent ideas over an extended period of time. More specifically, as consensus historians searched for a common American intellectual experience, historians of American religion set out to articulate a dominant American religious tradition. And, by rooting the religious history of the United States in a defining Puritan moment, historians of religion provided one of the intellectual and ideological foundations on which consensus historians could secure their stories. The bonds that linked identity, America, and religion provided at the same time an ideological mechanism for selecting and ordering these narratives, reinforcing the proscriptive tendencies of consensus culture. Those individuals, groups, or regions who were not at the centre of the American religious tradition—who for a variety of reasons did not participate fully in the national consensus—took on the trappings of heretics and outsiders, and for this reason could be ignored or placed on the margins of the dominant discourse. And finally the historians of American religion not only treated the triumph of consensus as a positive achievement but also helped to identify how this consensus had been achieved. Without state regulation or legal coercion a wide variety of religious groups had come to share a common body of social, political, and religious values. In religion, as in life itself, the beneficial air of freedom and competition was able to mute conflict over time and almost effortlessly nurture a distinctive American religious culture. Viewed in this way, the ties between religion and consensus achieved a positive synergy. Working together like the tracks of a railway, they set out to carry this anointed nation to its millennial destiny.[5]

Thirty years on, however, it is the "great tradition" itself that has become the centre of a sustained scholarly critique—although it is a measure of the strength of this long-standing representation of American religion and culture that it has taken at least a generation of American historians to deconstruct it. By now the criticisms that encircle the old narrative accounts are well known.[6] Critics have focused on the process of selection (identifying especially those groups who are excluded from the older discourse), the process of ordering (how individuals, groups, and regions are assigned positions of dominance and subordination within the narratives), and to a much lesser extent the structure of the story itself (the postmodern problematics of writing national history). This collection of essays is part of this larger cultural critique, for it takes the criticisms of the older interpretations of American religious history as points of departure to explore new ways of narrating the religious history of the United States.

It is at this point that Canada may begin to contribute to this important scholarly undertaking, for this country stands in a unique relation to both the history of American religion and the search to find new ways of narrating that history. In the first instance Canada's historical experience casts certain important themes in the standard accounts of American religion in a different (and much darker) light. Looking back in time from the Canadian border one is immediately impressed by the predatory possibilities of the equation of religion and nation. If the great tradition of American religious history affirmed the link between the Protestant religion and the American identity, Canadian history reveals just how often this association has served to sanction American expansion abroad. Standing above the United States, Canada hears the public voice of American religion, at least in the first instance, as a convenient benediction to the popular creed of American manifest destiny, continually raised aloft in the shrill jingoism of the politicians, promoters, and carpetbaggers who have cast their covetous eyes on Canada's fair domain. The consensus paradigm downplayed the significance of conflict within America, representing the history of the United States as a unified and harmonious experience. Through Canadian eyes, however, the aggressive posture of American history becomes clear, and if the values that are carried abroad also thrive at home, then this northern perspective strongly suggests that the dominance of certain groups and values within American culture may have been the result of conflict rather than its absence.

By the same token the ability of Canada to survive these excursions has marked one of the boundaries of American culture and set a limit on America's assumptions about its own righteousness. Canada's survival also introduces the second contribution that a Canadian perspective might offer to this enterprise.[7] From the far side of the Canadian border one looks at America from the outside. While many like to presume that the Canadian-American border is as obscure as it is long, a more careful reading of history reveals that this border has been (and continues to be) very real. Canada is a foreign country in which the materials of nation building have been put together in a way that is different from the United States.

For this reason crossing the Canadian border becomes an important historical act. The seemingly free interchange of American tourists and Canadian shoppers has perhaps obscured the fact that many individuals and groups have crossed this border for very tangible (and often very religious) reasons, and the journeys these people have taken (in both directions) offer valuable insights into the history of each country. The reality of the Canadian border imparts social and cultural significance to the act of crossing from one side of it to the other. However perfunctory the rituals of border crossings may be, certain things change as one moves across the line—as those tourists who rage against having to leave their firearms behind have discovered.

This essay focuses on the border and these border crossings not only because they are an important and largely unexplored part of the historical record, but also because they provide a new way of looking at the history of religion in North America. Like most novel perspectives, the view from this site reveals new things about history and suggests new ways of telling the story. Put another way, this essay focuses on the edge of two national histories rather than their centres; it examines the boundary between two different histories because this site offers new ways of seeing and explaining what has taken place on both sides of that line.

To appreciate the Canadian perspective, then, let us ascend to this rather unpilgrimmed religious site and survey the frontier that demarcates this analysis of religion and culture. What does the boundary between the two countries signify? What does it separate and how has it been crossed? What do the boundary and these border crossings have to declare about what has taken place on both sides of this line? What counsel may this perspective offer about renarrating the religious history of the United States?[8]

Mapping the Border

In 1827 John Strachan, archdeacon of York, launched an appeal to raise funds for the University of Upper Canada. This fledgling institution—which in time became the University of Toronto—had just received a royal charter, and Strachan was anxious to inform his audience of the important role this Anglican establishment was sure to play in the future development of British North America. To this end he began to frame a long and sustained critique of American religion and culture. In his eyes one of the primary reasons for creating such a university was the absolute necessity of protecting young men from the contagion of American values. Without their own institution of higher learning, he pointed out, the future leaders of the colony would be obliged to attend American institutions, where they would be taught little more than anarchy in politics and infidelity in religion. Instead of securing education upon a rational and enlightened morality—"the domestic, the social and religious virtues"—American institutions linked education to an assertive and injurious nationalism, seeing it as their primary duty to elevate all things American and "breathe hatred of everything English."[9]

Strachan's central theme—the moral and religious inferiority of American society—became a persistent motif in Canadian national thought.[10] At this point, however, we need not explore in any detail the accuracy of these remarks. More important to this analysis is the way Strachan was mapping a particular religious and cultural geography. Situated in the provincial capital of York, which was renamed Toronto a few years later, this Anglican cleric was determined to draw a hard and fast line between the British colonies in North America and the new country that was taking shape on the other side of the border. By shielding the future leaders of Canada from the baneful influences of American religion and politics, the colony would be able to pursue a course of history that was different from the one being followed by the United States. To make America a good neighbour, the archdeacon was determined to build a good fence.

The religious line that Strachan was trying to etch along the American frontier, with British establishmentarianism on one side and American anarchy on the other, should not be taken as the ruminations of some paranoid Scottish reactionary who had purposefully blinded him-

self to all the wonderful benefits that America could bestow. His determined effort to defend the border grew directly out of his own and his
new homeland's historical experience. Less than fifteen years before
Strachan penned these words, American armies were invading Canada
and pillaging the provincial capital (the British retaliated by burning
Washington and Buffalo). Strachan himself had helped to lead the
defence of the colony and used this occasion to articulate a nationalist
creed that would become one of the cornerstones of Canadian imperial
thought in the Victorian period.[11]

In the years following the war Britain spent millions of pounds for-
tifying with earth and stone the border that Strachan had been working
so assiduously to delimit along religious and cultural lines. These military preparations were, in turn, reinforced in the early Victorian period
by important demographic shifts in the Canadian population as wave
upon wave of British settlers overwhelmed the old American population
that had settled Upper Canada and the Maritime colonies in the period
immediately following the American Revolutionary War.[12] These changes
left Canada at the time of Confederation with two primary cultural
groups—British and French Canadians—who for all their differences
shared both a strong fear of the United States and a determination to
create in the area to the north of the St. Lawrence valley and the Great
Lakes a new country that rejected what they regarded as the anarchic
and irreligious assumptions of American culture.[13] The border marks
genuine difference: for Americans, Canada was meant to be foreign territory.

The strength and clarity of this border have important methodologi-
cal implications for this study. For one, they tend to set this essay apart
from the other contributions to the volume. If one of the major goals in
our project is to find ways of bringing into American history those individuals and groups who have been excluded or marginalized by the
older narratives, then Canada must stand apart from such a reconciliation. Canadians as a group should not be counted among those Nathan
Hatch describes as the "outsiders, subcultures, and the vast population
of women, native and African Americans that the consensus school
overlooked or subordinated to the main story of American religion."[14]
While Canada and the United States have shared many things, Canada
is a different country with its own history and its own patterns of historical narration. From this perspective it is appropriate that Canada
should remain outside the gates of American historiography.

At the same time, the clarity of this national boundary gives Canada a special role as we try to find new ways of narrating the history of religion in United States. Situated on the other side of an international boundary, Canada brings a comparative perspective to the issues at hand.[15] The question is not how American religious history would be reconfigured were Canada seen as a part of that experience, but rather what insights are provided by the Canadian historical experience, and especially the Canadian religious experience, for seeing the history of American religion in a different way. Similarly, what insights can be gained for historians of American religion from the ways Canadians have tried to interpret their own historical experiences? In this sense, Canada offers to this project a parallel historical discourse, one that is waiting no doubt to be deconstructed by another gathering of scholars—perhaps with an historian of American religion offering such a project a voice from below the stairs.

Boundaries between nations, however, are complex historical constructions. In this case the defiance with which so many Canadians have greeted the incursions of American religion and culture speaks to only one aspect of the relationship between these two nations. While it is essential to acknowledge the solidity of the international boundary—so well marked by the battles of armies and of ideologies—it is just as important to emphasize that this border has been crossed on countless occasions. Put simply, the fact that the border has marked such important differences has given people and ideas on both sides good reasons for moving across it. Borders not only keep nations apart, they also join them together.

Once again John Strachan can help us to see the border in this second way. While his pen was working so hard to sketch a permanent and effective barrier between two different societies, his day-to-day activities were redefining the boundary between British North America and the United States in different terms. History shows that he "crossed" this border on several occasions. American universities, for example, may well have poisoned the minds of the young, but when Strachan became the first bishop of Toronto in 1839 he found that some of his own clergy had graduated from these highly suspect institutions. Nor did his loathing of America stop him from trying to recruit missionaries for his new diocese from the ranks of the American Episcopal Church, and he lamented the fact that American ordination vows made it almost impossible for these clergy to serve God (and the Queen) within the British Empire. He also was quite prepared to send one of his own clergy, the Reverend William McMurray, on several highly successful forays into the United States to raise money for his new educational endeavour, that bastion of everything true blue and British, the University of Trinity College.[16] And when the bishop set out to reorganize the political and administrative structure of the United Church of England and Ireland in Canada, he drew heavily on the experience of the American Episcopal Church and especially the initiatives of Bishop Hobart of New York, whose life he celebrated in a famous letter he wrote (and then had published) to his old friend in Scotland, the Reverend Thomas Chalmers.[17] It also might be pointed out that when Strachan set out from Scotland for Upper Canada in 1799, he broke his journey for a few days in New York City where he tried to establish a network of contacts to which he might turn were his prospects disappointed in the British dominions to the north.[18]

Once again Strachan's initiatives introduce an important pattern within Canadian (and American) history. The way he reached across the line was by no means unique; while the border was being fortified against American religion and culture, Canada and Canadians were crossing that same border with seeming impunity. It is well known, for example, that thousands of European immigrants treated Canada as little more than a stopover on their way to the United States—and many English and French Canadians joined this exodus to the south, seeking prosperity among the factories and farms of New England and the mid-western states.[19] Even the "national policies" of immigration, railway construction, and tariff protection that Canada adopted in the decades after Confederation to realize its vision of becoming the second modern transcontinental nation-state in North America were largely modelled on the policies that the United States had adopted to develop its own vast territorial domains. Indeed, one important goal of this national policy—to fill the Canadian prairies with producing farmers—was achieved by importing agriculturalists not only from Britain, Poland, and the Ukraine but also from Kansas, Nebraska, and the Dakotas.[20]

These border crossings introduce a second major theme in a new narrative of religion constructed at this site. Here the focus shifts from how the border separates two countries to the way it draws them together—from the differences between nations to the relationships that have formed between what is on either side of the line. Once again there are patterns to the way the border has been crossed, and these patterns provide insights into the history, especially the religious history, of the two countries.

Although religion has often served to divide the two countries, it also has provided the reason for many individuals and groups to move from one country to the other. Throughout the history of English-speaking Canada, for example, several prominent Adventist, Pentecostal, and Fundamentalist figures have chosen to move from Canada to the United States. The list of those crossing the border is long and impressive. John Taylor, an active member of one of the first Methodist class meetings in Toronto, was converted by Mormon missionaries from upper New York state. He then joined the great trek west and in time succeeded Brigham Young to become the third president of the Mormon church;[21] the Reverend Richard Hutchinson, a British Wesleyan missionary, left Canada to become a prominent Millerite and Adventist writer;[22] Clem Davis moved down the coast from Victoria, British Columbia, to Hollywood, California, where he proclaimed himself "Canada's prophetic salesman"—a moniker he emblazoned on the side door of his motor. And Aimee Semple McPherson, born into the verdant Protestant culture of Oxford County, Ontario, began her career with the Salvation Army in Canada before becoming a Pentecostal, taking up a ministry of healing, and moving to the United States. Her Los Angeles revivals made her America's most famous woman revivalist, and the movement she founded, the International Church of the Foursquare Gospel, became one of the most prominent groups in the complex history of American Pentecostalism.[23]

One may even be so bold as to identify a similar movement within the French and Irish branches of the Roman Catholic Church in Canada. When the Reverend Charles Chiniquy, the apostle of temperance in French Canada, became too great a problem for the church in Quebec, he was exiled to the diocese of Chicago where he was sent to work among his compatriots in the French Canadian colony at Kankakee, Illinois. There, quarrels with the local Irish hierarchy forced him to leave the Catholic Church altogether and he subsequently returned to Canada as a Presbyterian minister, in which guise he turned his extraordinary evangelical gifts to denouncing the harlotry of the Church of Rome.[24]

Charles Edward Coughlin was born in Hamilton, Ontario, educated at St. Michael's College, University of Toronto, and became a member of the most prominent and respected Catholic religious order in the city, the Congregation of St. Basil. In 1926, after teaching a few years at Assumption College in Windsor, Ontario, Father Coughlin moved to Michigan, where he established the Radio League of the Little Flower. An extraordinarily successful religious broadcaster, he became a major figure on the American religious right, filling the airwaves with anti-Semitic pro-Nazi propaganda, leading a movement to defeat Franklin Delano Roosevelt, and campaigning to keep America out of World War II.[25]

The religious histories of the two countries also provide ample evidence of individuals and groups who have crossed the border in the other direction. At several points in American history, for example, Canada has provided a safe haven for those who have felt compelled to flee America. The loyalists (or American Tories) who found themselves on the wrong side of the Revolutionary War felt deeply betrayed by American promises of justice and reconciliation. Driven out of the revolting colonies, many chose to start life anew in what remained of British North America. Their journey into the wilderness of the old colony of Quebec took on the aura of a biblical exodus and provided the new English-speaking communities they helped to found with what became the myth of their own genesis.[26]

Blacks escaping slavery followed the underground railway to its terminus in southwestern Ontario. Here they established settlements that became an important part of the fabric of Canadian life. These journeys to freedom tell an important story, for they make it clear that the boundary between slavery and freedom was not drawn along the Mason-Dixon line. To cross from slave state to free was to cross from southern slavery to northern racism and offered no guarantee of asylum. The journey to safety did not end until these people had passed out of the United States altogether.[27]

Canadian history also has witnessed a long procession of pacifists and war resisters who have crossed the border into Canada from the United States. In 1800 Timothy Rogers led some forty Quaker families from Vermont to Upper Canada, settling on a land grant in the backwoods townships of King, Whitchurch, and East and West Gwillimbury. He initiated a pattern of religious migration that would in time bring large communities of religious pacifists to Canada, not only from the United States but also from Britain, Europe, and South America.[28] While the reasons behind these migrations are complex, the religious and political environment Canada offered to these groups clearly played a major role in their decision to come. The first lieutenant governor of Upper Canada, John Graves Simcoe, personally invited Mennonites, Tunkers, and Quakers to settle in the colony by promising them exemption from military duties, promises that were recognized officially by the first Parliament of Upper Canada in the Militia Bill of 1793. Even the practice of imposing a small fine in lieu of militia drill was removed

under the reform administration of 1849. These specific legal enact-
ments were clearly valued much more highly than were the more abstract guarantees of freedom of religion and freedom of speech which,
in theory, enjoyed full constitutional protection in the United States.[29]
A similar evaluation of the comparative safety of the two societies also
was made by the large number of war resisters whose opposition to
American imperialism led them to Canada—journeys that may have begun for other reasons but quickly took on strong religious overtones.

These border crossings, which could be developed into the episodes
of this new border narrative, tell an important story about the religious
histories of the two countries. Here, however, one must approach these
stories with care. I doubt seriously, for example, if one can explain these
journeys by simply attributing certain religious characteristics to one
country or the other. I would be hard pressed to identify substantial differences between the theological doctrines of Canadian and American
Pentecostals or to discern critical differences between the tenets of Canadian and American pacifists. Indeed, it is clear that North American
Fundamentalists are linked by a series of formal and informal networks
that carry ideas and information back and forth across the border. Nor
can one tie the larger movements that these ideas sustained to only
one of these countries. Religious pacifism is not a Canadian creation;
American history has been distinguished by the work of many individuals and groups who have opposed the violence of imperialism and racism. Similarly, supposedly American movements—such as Adventism,
Pentecostalism, and Fundamentalism—have enjoyed (as George Rawlyk
has recently demonstrated) a long and rich history in Canada.[30] The Canadian adherents of these religious groups were not some sort of religious aliens plunked down in the midst of the great hyperborean forest
who were searching desperately to find their way home.

At the same time, it is clear that religious movements have assumed
different positions within the religious landscape of each country.
While Fundamentalists have enjoyed a long and important history in
Canada, they have tended to be overshadowed by an informal Protestant
alliance of Anglicans, Presbyterians, and Methodists that came to dominate English Canadian religious life in the mid-Victorian period. (Some
would argue this Protestant influence lingers still.) The power of ultra-
montanism to control the centre of the Roman Catholic Church in Canada may well have served a similar function within Canadian Catholicism. The fractures within American religion, however, have provided
much more space for the sustained growth of movements that Canadian

history has pushed more towards the margin. This may explain why a whole host of Canadians who have inhabited these regions of the Canadian religious spectrum have chosen, often after working for many years in Canada, to take up their calling in the United States, where their preachings seem to be able to sustain a much stronger currency.

Movements across the border in the other direction may well offer similar insights into American culture. Once again the same characters and forces appear on either side of the line. While Canadians like to see themselves as a tolerant and peaceable people, one need not look deeply into Canadian history to find ample evidence of the nativism and racism that Canadians prefer to associate with their neighbours to the south. The abhorrent record of the Canadian government in keeping out Jewish refugees who were fleeing Nazi Germany was unrivalled in the Western world.[31] At the same time, racism and nativism in Canada have had much greater difficulty in linking their ideologies to a single notion of nationhood, although it has not been from a want of trying. Not knowing what "Canada" is makes the term *unCanadian* problematic.

American nationalism has tended to be more rigid. All seem to agree that there is a true American, although there is considerably less agreement about exactly who that person might be. Nationalism of this type has been highly proscriptive, and throughout American history it has made minorities—be they racial, religious, or political—extraordinarily wary, for as intolerance hones itself on the creed of nationalism it becomes a terribly swift sword. Americans have had to leave the United States because they have been labelled "unAmerican." Somewhat ironically they may have found themselves welcomed in Canada for the same reason.

These networks and patterns also amplify a theme that both Mark A. Noll and Robert T. Handy have identified in their studies of the history of religion in North America. In comparing Canada and the United States, these scholars have discerned both patterns of similarities and patterns of differences—patterns that seem to fold into each other as differences provide a way of seeing similarities, and similarities help to identify differences. The relationship between the two countries, which appears on the surface to be so straightforward, upon closer examination becomes extraordinarily complex.[32]

Crossing the border sets these larger patterns in motion. A long history of putting similar materials together in different ways has created two compatible yet different religious cultures. This has encouraged a certain type of religious movement across the border, as groups are drawn in both directions by another world that is different from their own but one in which they still can recognize many of the social markers. History tends to sort out individuals and groups according to the differences between these cultures. The migrations, then, not only mark important differences between the religious histories of the two countries, but they also tend to reinforce these differences over time. If the wall between the two countries seems to be very high, it also has many gates. At the border one passes through a fine filter—or perhaps through a well-polished mirror.

Standing at the border one also can witness another kind of religious pilgrimage. Northrop Frye has argued eloquently that every nation gives allegiance to a religious and cultural ideal. Buried at the deepest levels of the cultural imagination, these national visions often speak to the nation that should have been rather than the one that is, to the history that should have taken place rather than the one that did.[33] Both Canada and the United States have been enchanted by such visions, and along the border one can watch a curious metaphysical interplay as these ideals and visions cross from one country to the other.

At several points in time each country has projected an image of itself on the other. Imperialism, to cite an obvious and persistent example, can be seen as the most extreme form of this process in that it sets out to erase difference by imposing the vision of one nation on another. As we have seen, however, Canadian timber often has proved too hard a wood for Americans to fell, and it is perhaps the persistence of Canada that has forced this process of projection to assume a different (and much more fascinating) form. Perhaps the very proximity of these two countries has allowed the one to serve as a metaphysical counterpoint to the other.

It is something of a truism in Canadian culture that the definition of a Canadian begins with the words, "compared to Americans we are . . . ," but the dualisms implicit in this response run deeply into the cultures of both countries. In the same way that heroes dance most exquisitely with villains, so each country has projected its absences on the other, placing on the other side of the line the hopes (and horrors) that its own cultural development have in some way denied or repressed. From this perspective people have crossed the border, in both real and imaginary terms, not to escape from the cultural values of their former homeland but in the belief that they might be able to find (or suffer) in the new country the dreams and visions they could not realize at home.

Throughout Canadian history, for example, Canadians have constructed an imaginary America that has represented in their minds the paradise of freedom and prosperity that Canada had promised to provide but, at least in their eyes, has failed to achieve. To point out that freedom and prosperity are illusory for many Americans simply confirms the observation that such projections speak more to absences within Canada than to a "real" America. This kind of projection has occurred across the Canadian social and political spectrum—from radicals looking at America as the democratic New Jerusalem to right-wing groups who march under the banner of American free markets as they set out to dismantle the Canadian state.

At times Canada has played a similar role in America's image of itself, coming to embody for many people the real America that their own country had abandoned or could no longer find. Henry Alline, a New England preacher, left his native land to lead a great awakening in the colony of Nova Scotia. Deeply disillusioned by the events leading up to the American Revolution, he reshaped his messianic visions around his newfound home, telling the poor and outcast of Nova Scotia, as Gordon Stewart and George Rawlyk have so skillfully explained, that they were a people highly favoured of God who must now take up the religious destiny that God had once entrusted to New England. Rawlyk has also explained how Alline's new light revivals helped to give this region a distinct (and decidedly unAmerican) identity.[34]

Henry Alline's transposition—the way he articulated Canada's destiny in relation to someone else's failure—recurs with an eerie regularity in the fables of Canada's national identities. Figuring prominently in both the loyalist ideology of defeat and the French Canadian ideology of *la survivance* is the belief that each group has a God-given mission to preserve a religious ideal that has been violated in the revolutionary outrages of their former homelands. By escaping the American and French revolutions (and the enlightenments they embodied), they are able to continue a history begun but abandoned somewhere else; the real history of America and France takes place in Canada.

The romance of these conservative eschatologies—while the modern world is going one way, Canada is going another—has proved enormously attractive to outsiders. Near the start of the century Frederick Philip Grove, a German immigrant, left Europe for the New World in search of the real America. But in the United States he found the natural world of Rousseau hopelessly corrupted by the materialism of contemporary American life. His journey then led him to Canada, where he celebrated the social and spiritual values of the new communities on the prairies, and through his stories he helped to translate this agricultural ideal into a strong regional identity.[35] Louis Hémon made a similar spiritual journey. He came to Quebec from France hoping to find in the Lac St. Jean region the primitive spirituality that urbanization and industrialization had obliterated in his native country. Like Grove in Manitoba (or Gauguin in Pont Aven), Hémon created a mythical landscape—in this case one inhabited by a faithful and enduring Catholic peasantry—that reinforced the conservative ideology that had drawn him to Quebec.[36]

Many of the American projections of Canada, be they of a wasteland where socialists are allowed to run free or of a land of safe streets and pristine air where the Mounties always get their man, tell us more about America than they do about life on the other side of the line.[37] Although statistics may demonstrate that Canadians are a civil and law-abiding folk, I imagine it is the long history of the kinds of events that have most recently taken place in Waco, Oklahoma City, and Detroit that sustains our reputation as a peaceable kingdom.[38] Canada provides a reference point for evoking American dreams and nightmares (which are generally cut from the same cloth).

The self-reflexive quality of these images, however, do not make them any the less valuable, for the semiotics of these projections across the border offer further insights into the religious histories of the two countries. Here these images of the other return us to the construction of the cultural image of the national self—or perhaps to the disjunction between national religious ideals and historical practice. As we have come to expect when we look at the border, we find patterns of similarity and patterns of difference.

Each country has tried to align itself with what it understood to be God's plan for the world. The ideologies of nationhood that both countries have proclaimed are deeply religious—informed and structured by the sense of time and place that was so much a part of the Christian worldviews that shaped Western culture at the time of their birth.[39] But while both societies held out the vision of becoming a Christian nation, the paths they took to reach this goal led them in different directions.

If the Christian religion tries to reconcile freedom and order—to create and nurture at the same time—the Canadian vision of the Christian commonwealth has tended to privilege the latter over the former. Creating order out of a Gothic world is Canada's eternal quest. Perhaps this effort has reduced the power of this national vision to appeal to large masses of people at an intensely personal level and explains in part the attraction that the more experimental features of American religion have held out to so many Canadians. At the same time, the tendency of the American vision to privilege freedom over restraint[40] not only imparts to this vision a sense of drama and immediacy—ready to enter and change history like a thief in the night—but also may suggest why so many Americans project onto Canada the sense of peace and order that their own culture seems to devalue.

In American eschatology, as in the old consensus paradigm of American culture, there can be only one redeemer nation; but every individual and group in America has the freedom, indeed the obligation, to define this kingdom for themselves and reject all that has gone before. To say that America makes all things new also means that new things become old very quickly. Perhaps the immediacy and individualism of this cultural matrix make the vision it so boldly proclaims impossible to realize. Many eyes may have seen the glory of the coming of the Lord, but Americans seem destined to sing time and again only the first verse.

Canada projects a mirror image. Here the vision of nation appeals to history (albeit to the path that others did not take) rather than to abstract values, such as freedom. The postmillennialism of Canadian time declaims the gradual unfolding of Christ's kingdom on earth—perhaps so gradually that this kingdom merges almost imperceptively into the secular landscape around it.[41] Indeed, without the fanfare of trumpets and shouts of glory we might not know that the kingdom even exists. If Americans search for the kingdom that never comes, Canadians may have built the kingdom but are unaware of the redeemer who chats casually in their midst. Mark Noll perceptively places this theme in a comparative context when he points out, with an irony Canadians would certainly appreciate, that during the nineteenth century Canada may well have become the "Christian nation" that America always had wanted to be, the illusive grail that the writers of American religious history always sought but could never find. "The search for Christian America," he writes, "is over. It is Canada."[42]

Narrating National Histories

This essay has tried to look at the history of religion in North America from the Canadian border, from the edge of a national history rather the centre. In the process it has outlined some of the themes that might inform a new narrative written from this perspective. By examining the border between Canada and the United States and studying the process of moving across it, a new kind of story emerges, one that offers many insights into the history of the two countries the same border divides.

One important question, however, still remains to be considered. This collection explores the history of American religion by looking at that history from several sites. The Canadian border is one such site. At the same time the contributors have tried to explore new ways of narrating a national religious history. After rejecting the older narratives of American religious history, we have asked what new narratives might arise to take their place. What, then, do the border and these crossings offer as we consider this final question? If this essay has focused on the edge of two national histories, what then does the edge have to say about the centre?

In the first instance the view from the Canadian border reaffirms in a new setting a point that many other critics have made. Here again we find groups of Americans who must be brought into the history of religion in America. While American religious history has celebrated all those who have come to America seeking freedom, the religious journeys of Americans *leaving* the United States rarely appear (if at all) in the standard accounts of American religion. American religious history seems to presume that when Americans leave the United States they leave American history altogether, lost forever in the black hole that begins on the other side of the border. This essay has tried to suggest that their stories of exile offer an important commentary on the history of American religion as a whole.

How to bring these groups into a new national narrative, however, raises a more substantial issue. To call for the inclusion of characters who were not privileged by the older stories begs the question of the terms on which they can be welcomed into American history. While one can imagine that some groups and regions within America can be accommodated by adopting a more pluralistic notion of America and American culture, some might find it singularly difficult simply to pull up another chair at the rich banquet of American culture. Many of the Americans who left the United States—the loyalists, the slaves, and the pacifists—did so in large part because they faced inherent structural divisions within American society, divisions that a more pluralistic representation of American religion and culture may not be able to transcend. This conflict highlights a major problem that in my view has not been addressed adequately in the debates over the writing of the history of American religion. After acknowledging the reality of diversity and conflict, how does one then conceptualize difference within the writing of a national history? The same problem also is of pressing concern for historians of class, colour, and gender as categories of analysis that once seemed uniform become susceptible to a seemingly infinite process of division and subdivision.

Looking back it was relatively easy for those historians who wrote within the great tradition to define a national religious history, because the consensual assumptions within which they worked placed clear boundaries on what it meant to be American. If one was different or moved outside these boundaries then one stepped outside the story and, in effect, ceased to be American. Acknowledging difference as real and structural undercuts this symmetry and perforce raises the question that seems to haunt the depths of any attempt to redefine American history. If one reconstructs American religious history in relation to class, region, gender, and a host of other identifying factors, can one still talk meaningfully of an *American* religious history? Can one still talk meaningfully of a single national narrative?

Here one seems caught in the perfect double bind. To emphasize difference yields many new religious narratives, but the national component of these histories may be nothing more than the fact that they all describe something that took place at least to some degree in the United States. To search for common national themes, however, raises the opposite problem. While it draws one towards a new national narrative, it also downplays the differences and diversity one set out in the first place to acknowledge.

If the way in which the Canadian border has been crossed calls on scholars to consider very differently the issue of difference, then what has happened on the other side of the line may offer a few helpful suggestions about how the renarration of American history may proceed. In Canada the writing of national histories always has had to face basic structural differences. The type of society that grew up on the other side of the line that Strachan and others tried to draw so boldly had to confront right from the start several radical dualities—French and English, Protestant and Catholic, native and newcomer, centre and periphery, worker and owner. These profound differences have forced most historians who write national history to adopt metaphors and language that acknowledge the reality of basic and perhaps irreconcilable differences. The staples thesis, for example, that analyzed Canadian development in terms of the exploitation of a succession of natural products was constructed on the tensions between hinterlands and metropolitan centres; regionalism, in turn, acknowledged the inherently unequal

division of power within the Canadian nation-state; biculturalism rejected the idea of a single dominant social and cultural group; while
multiculturalism proclaims as a positive good a seemingly endless process of redefining the term *Canadian*. Canadian historians have had to
write their histories from the edge, because those edges are at the centre
of the Canadian nation-state. It is by focusing directly on difference that
they are able to identify how a nation of differences can in fact cohere.

These observations help to explain why in Canada words such as *nation* and *identity* are so often used in the plural,[43] for in the writing
of Canadian history the word *Canada* can be highly problematic. Historians in Canada have to write the history of Canada knowing that the
meaning of the word changes continually—that Canada cannot be understood apart from the constellation of differences and tensions that
form and re-form the meaning of nation at each moment in time. In
Canada historians have had to learn not to take a national framework
for granted.[44]

These tensions and differences can impart an ironic tone to Canadian
culture and may help to explain why Canada has been called a truly
postmodern country.[45] In Canada the only truth we hold to be self-evident is that no truth is self-evident. They also may explain why Canada
can offer such an interesting and valuable counterpoint to America.
Like things relegated to the attic—clothes that have gone out of fashion, novels with long-forgotten heroes, and even perhaps the odd relation whose sanity may be a few pennies short of a pound—Canada
recalls a different way of seeing the world and offers to the family
downstairs a way of reformulating views that for too long it has taken
for granted. If America is now seeking ways to encompass difference
within nationhood, it might well begin by lighting a candle and rum-
maging around upstairs on a cold winter's day.

Exchanging Selves, Exchanging Souls

Contact, Combination, and American Religious History

CATHERINE L. ALBANESE

In the mid-1840s, still in his twenties, Bohemian-born rabbi Isaac Mayer Wise—later to be acknowledged leader of the Jewish Reform movement in America—was riding the railroad in New York state. As he tried to read from a small copy of the Pentateuch with two Aramaic translations and a commentary, his Yankee seatmate grew more and more curious. He wanted to know about Wise's book and about its languages and translations, and Wise explained as best he could. The two got to talking, and the Yankee learned that Wise only recently had arrived in the United States. "Ah, now I know who you are; you are a Jewish bishop," the man declared. Wise recounted what happened next: "I explained to him that the Jews had no hierarchy, but he drew a New Haven newspaper out of his pocket and showed me black on white that a Jewish bishop, Wess or Wiss, who had lately arrived from Jerusalem, had dedicated the synagogue in New Haven." Wise, neither bishop nor Jerusalemite nor dedicator of the New Haven synagogue (he had only preached there), protested in vain. The foreign rabbi had acquired an American identity, and—when later he arrived in Syracuse—he found that the newspaper there already knew it: "N. traveled yesterday from Albany to this city in company with the Jewish Bishop Wess or Wiss (the pronunciation of the name is uncertain), who has lately arrived from Jerusalem."[1]

Another time a country missionary and his wife wanted to meet Wise because, as the man said, "he had never seen a Jew." That task accomplished, the missionary apparently could not contain himself; he let loose a barrage of religious witness in order "to speak in the name of the Lord." But, at least according to his own account, Wise turned out to be better at religious confutation than the missionary. Placing the Hebrew Bible and the Greek New Testament in front of his adversary, he announced, "Here is the Bible. Pray, show me what you may have to object to my Judaism." What followed was Wise's victory: "He confessed that he could read neither the one nor the other, and I attempted to show him how he had learned to know the Bible from the unreliable source of a translation, and that, therefore, he must not discuss Biblical questions with me."[2]

On still a third occasion, in 1850, while Wise was functioning as rabbi at the Bethel congregation in Albany, New York, he became involved in a bitter struggle for control with Louis Spanier, the synagogue's elected president, or parnass. As Wise upheld and Spanier fought violently against the cause of Reform Judaism, Wise found his official preaching garb missing from the synagogue one Sabbath and on another received a message from the parnass not to preach. Blow followed blow in a continuing dispute until it broke through the walls of the synagogue to involve the legal system of the state of New York and the attorney general's office. In the climactic episode of their battle, at one synagogue service that challenged Spanier's authority, the parnass physically obstructed Wise and then struck him with a fist so that Wise's cap fell from his head. Wise, who was arrested, remembered that people "acted like furies" and the synagogue became a "flaming conflagration." The sheriff and his posse who arrived to restore order were "forced out," and then everybody else "surged out of the house" into the street.[3]

Taken together, the three snapshots of Wise—Jewish bishop, missionary's foil, and leader of a faction in a New York synagogue's civil war—invite entry into a world of religious interchange that is often undernoticed and underexplored. Each of the incidents in which Wise functioned as principal actor cast him in a role that was inflected differently, with a distinguishable religious horizon framing the drama in separable ways. Hovering as backdrop for the first was the rumored world of Roman Catholicism, where bishops presided and hierarchies organized religious life. Coming closer in the second episode was the brash and confident world of nineteenth-century Protestant evangelicalism, with militant revival forces ready to do battle for the Lord. And in the third, another sort of battle erupted within the intimacy of a small

Jewish congregation. In the Germany and eastern Europe of the past, the rabbi would have reigned supreme, but now the strident echoes of a new land (democracy and religious freedom) and new religious ways (Protestant congregational polity) had brought the authority of the rabbi down.

Whatever else they are about, each of the three episodes from the life of Isaac Mayer Wise are about religious contacts and exchanges in which pluralism and its results must be understood as controlling principles. The exchanges are not exactly symmetrical, and each manifests in a way that seems slightly askew—but the untidiness of the three, their disorderliness, if you will, signals acts in an extended play that tells a new story of religion in America. This tale is one of meeting and change. It is one in which the encounter with the other becomes the invited or (mostly) uninvited gift that transforms the contacting parties—or the gift rebuffed, which still comes back to haunt. And it is one in which transformation comes, sometimes, even through the agencies of third and fourth parties who drift like ghosts on the edge of the cultural horizon.

We may perhaps take a cue from French anthropologist Marcel Mauss. In his provocative *Essai sur le don* (*The Gift*), first published in 1925, Mauss compared a series of cultures past and present to argue that the ritual exchange of gifts functioned as a way to define the social order. Societies avoided war by trading, and in many instances they refined their trading by supplanting written contracts with alliances and gifts. Here they felt the heavy pressure of what became cultures of obligation—pressure to give, to receive, and to repay. According to a Maori proverb, the rule was, Mauss said, "Give as much as you receive and all is for the best."[4]

So gifts, markets, alliances, and constraints were of a piece, part of a continuous social process that maintained the requirements for societal order. Gifts came with strings and prods attached. They extended velvet gloves but masked iron hands beneath. To give a gift meant to coerce with a moral agency that overlay the actual exchange. To receive a gift meant a transaction that might or might not have been equal, and it could also mean possession of what, in effect, had been stolen. Mauss himself was clear about the presence of nonmaterial factors within the created order, pointing to the "various determinants, aesthetic, moral, religious and economic, and the material and demographic factors, whose sum is the basis of society and constitutes the common life."[5]

In this context, it may be a parable in architectural brick that Boston's Faneuil Hall and America's "cradle of liberty"—site of patriot meetings in the Revolutionary War era and abolitionist meetings in the nineteenth century—began life in 1742 as a public market. Below its second-floor speaker's rostrum, where goods of the spirit were opened and passionately traded, was the large material emporium where society's most basic requirements were met in the thriving port of Boston. In Faneuil Hall, one could find fish and freedom for sale. There one could find, literally, tea and sympathy—and also inequality.

Keeping in mind the view from Boston's harbor and from Faneuil Hall, then, insights about gifts and their ambiguities lose their French glow and acquire a distinctly American aura. Mauss in his own work found striking congruities between the societies he studied and the French and other European societies of his time.[6] Following Mauss's insight into an American setting—in which actors were involved seemingly *de nouveau* in creating and patterning their acts—we can look to exchanges between strangers as so many gifts they gave one another. These gifts possessed material market meanings: they instructed representatives of other cultures according to the fund of signification provided by each. But they also contained moral and spiritual capital: over the gesture of a practice shared, they carried the ultimate and proximate habits of mind and life that composed a culture at the moment of being shared.

From a specifically religious perspective, religious exchanges between strangers become cases of what R. Laurence Moore might call "selling God." American religious leaders, he thought, had "learned to operate effectively in the marketplace of American culture"; they had "made that marketplace respond to their concerns," and this was "no mean feat."[7] As for leaders, so for followers and for loners. And when native and would-be Americans met and communicated about their religious ways, they discovered that, as Mauss observed of the Maori, "to give something is to give a part of oneself."[8] So the material gift was also a market exchange and sometime dominative tool in a vast bazaar of the spirit. What was being sold was self and soul. What was being bought was new and combinatory American religions and religion.

This is to argue that, whatever their ascribed religious identity, Americans were professing religions that bore the signs of contact with those who were other and different. American religions were *changed* religions, and they were *new* religions, even if they evoked the stuff of tradition and the trappings of former cultures and times. In this context, discourses about syncretism and "new"—meaning "alternative"—religions are suspect, and what they obscure most of all is the social and spiritual landscape of religious change. Historiographies of consensus begin to unravel, and contested sites for New World pot-latches take their place. Gifts are made and remade; they weigh heavily or lightly; they mask oppression and also subvert it. They signal new narratives of contact and combination.

Indian Episodes

A natural place to begin the story of how all of this worked is with American Indians, earliest residents and partners to processes of exchange. Along the North and Middle Atlantic Coast, Indian contact with Europeans came, initially, through traders and, by the dawn of serious English settlement, their microbes. In the 1610s the plague and in the 1630s the smallpox decimated Indian communities and nations, leaving small, isolated, and seriously demoralized populations. Shamanic powers failed, and the growing encroachment of foreigners outside Indian communities loomed over against the internal havoc wreaked by disease. Cultural collapse seemed imminent, and Indians, at the mercy of disease and foreigners, were strenuously seeking a cure.[9]

No surprise, therefore, that Indians proved vulnerable to Christian teaching and that in New England Puritan missionaries had their modicum of success.[10] But what needs to be added to the picture of "praying Indians" succumbing to the baptismal waters is that if Indians were constrained by circumstance to convert to Christianity, they also did so on their own terms and for their own needs.

Take, for example, the work of the much celebrated John Eliot who, aided by the Society for the Propagation of the Gospel in New England, established a total of fourteen towns of Indian converts, beginning with Natick, Massachusetts, in 1650. In "praying towns" like Natick, the gospel came blatantly with English civilization attached. This conversion scenario is easily read as surrender to a superior culture according to its stipulations, and on many levels that judgment seems correct. Ethnohistorian James Axtell has pointed out, however, that praying towns could function as Indian strategies for survival. Faced with cultural groupings and communities that had dwindled critically and stood in danger of extinction, Indians could band with other native groups in similar circumstance. But the price was higher than many wanted to pay—biological survival in exchange for the death of cultural praxis and ceremony, kinship relations and ways of life. Enter, then, the gatherings that became the praying towns, in which, saved both from their English enemies and from fusions with other tribes, Indian communities could maintain a semblance of their former lives. "By accepting the Christian minister or priest as the functional equivalent of a native shaman and by giving traditional meanings to Christian rites, dogmas, and deities," wrote Axtell, "the Indians ensured the survival of native culture by taking on the protective coloration of the invaders' religion." Indeed, the Indians became, in Axtell's market metaphor, satisfied "cultural customers."[11]

One can question the sanguine reading here and elsewhere—perhaps nowhere more than in eighteenth-century California with its San Diego Indian revolt of 1775 and the Franciscan Junipero Serra's string of missions reinforced by the presence of Spanish military nearby. There the friars got rich on vineyards tended by forced Indian labor, and, as Sherburne Cook writes, "all pretense of voluntary conversion was discarded."[12] Still, at Mission Santa Barbara and other places in the Serra missions, one could see Indian motifs and designs adorning native chapels, and the sacramental spirituality of the Roman church blended with the ceremonial richness of Indian cultural life.[13]

Moreover, contact worked both ways. Beneath the guise of the victorious European extinguishing native cultures and proceeding more or less intact, another tale asks to be told. It is a story about the permeability of any culture and about the conscious and unconscious ways that Indian cultures with their spiritual powers pried open spaces in the seemingly impermeable walls of European civilization. Here the Anglo-American case in point is especially instructive, for the English—considerably more than the Spanish or the French—practiced an ideal of cultural separation. Antimiscegenation held a strong place in English colonial conquest ideology, even if racial conceptions preoccupied the English in their relationship to Indians considerably less than in their relationship to blacks.[14]

Hence, for all the Anglo-American fear of combination, hints of it in specifically religious terms surfaced in seemingly improbable places, forming, sub rosa, part of the fundament in the architecture of an emerging American religious culture. Amanda Porterfield has raised questions about putative shamanic elements in Puritan religion in the context of Algonquian praxis, looking, for example, at the visionary experiences of Puritan saints and the ways that praying, preaching, reading, and writing could function as a shamanic language of power. Porterfield is careful not to argue cause and effect. But staring, even from the safe distance of literature, into the flames of an Algonquian shaman's fire can lead at least to queries about the Indian horizon of awakenings and revivals among the Puritans and other European colonists. Dissociated states, as Ann Taves has shown, are not the comfortable discourse of Western Christian theology.[15]

Meanwhile, there was English trader Thomas Morton of Ma-re Mount. In the 1620s, the existence of his settlement in what is now Quincy, Massachusetts, was a thorn in the side of the Separatist Puritan settlement at Plymouth colony. Morton violated Puritan order by his trading practices with Indians (it was said that he even sold them guns) and by the rumored sexual congress with Indian women practiced at his "plantation." As Ann Taves notes in Chapter 1, Morton and his men erected a maypole. It was not an unconnected symbol—a materialized memory, surely, of the English countryside but also an evocation of pagan rituals of fertility. Thomas Morton's story ended in arrest and deportation by Miles Standish and his men, and it was only from England's rainy shore that Morton could have another word. Significantly, in his *New England Canaan,* published in 1637 to defend the life ways of Ma-re Mount, he argued that union between Indians and the English would bring renewal through the fusion of the vital physical powers of Indians and the civilized intellectual ones of Christians.[16]

Apparently others—even among the Puritans—shared at least some of Morton's sentiment. The New England establishment was regularly embarrassed by whites who, captured in Indian raids or wars, refused to come home when a ransom had been negotiated for them. They chose to remain part of Indian societies, adopted by native peoples to take the place of their own kin lost to war or disease. Former Puritans and now-white Indians, they liked the freedoms they found among Indians; they flourished in their midst.[17]

Contact with Indians found overt representation again, though less straightforwardly, in the Revolutionary War era, when the Sons of Liberty and the Sons of Tammany exploited Indian society to take "Saint Tammany" as cultural icon of their cause. According to popular account, Tammany was Tamanend, a Delaware Indian chief thought to have bid welcome to the newly immigrated William Penn and to have exchanged the land that later came to be known as Pennsylvania for a series of practical gifts. The lore about Tammany grew as—like an early set of tall tales about a Davy Crockett or Daniel Boone—it recounted his amazing deeds and exploits on behalf of whites and all of humankind.[18]

The object of ceremonial attention by 1771 on Tammany Day (Mayday), when colonists dressed as Indians and danced their maypole dances to honor him, Tammany inspired an ample share of ritual songs and poems of celebration. He became the patron of Pennsylvania troops in the Revolutionary War, and by 1778 even George Washington and his army honored Tammany Day by dressing as Indians, singing and dancing around maypoles, and dramatizing his presence. When, after the war, Tammany societies flourished for a time, they copied what they knew of Indian cultures by dividing their membership into thirteen "tribes" with a "sachem" over each and a "grand sachem" over all. Meeting places were called wigwams, and a lunar calendar as a conscious adaptation of Indian time keeping was employed. Tammany societies appropriated the trappings of Indian religions and cultures, as they were understood, mimicking them to express cultural independence from Europe in political and economic contexts. Even when Tammany societies faded in the nineteenth century, one still continued in New York, headquartered in the 1850s at Tammany Hall as the well-remembered Democratic machine organization of the city and the time.

Something of the Tammany societies' impulse and inspiration continued, too, in men's societies that were Indian-identified, such as Lewis Henry Morgan's secret and brief Order of the Iroquois in 1845 and the more sustained Improved Order of Red Men from 1834. By 1850, according to Mark Carnes, the latter group's Grand Lodge went on record declaring that the construction of "effective rituals" constituted its principal business, but the order languished through a series of ritual revisions lasting to the Civil War period. Then, in 1868, it began to offer an Adoption degree that proved the remaking of its fortunes. In the middle of the 1870s, the order was welcoming 10,000 new members annually. "By 1900," Carnes wrote, "approximately 350,000 Red Men were finding their way into wigwams of the order each week. Its annual receipts exceeded a million dollars."[19]

The initiation ceremony that apparently turned so many toward the Red Men featured an extended contemplation of death with a "sachem" as officiant, invoking the Great Spirit on behalf of the new initiate. There were a kindling of actual fire, a donning of moccasins, and a dramatic enactment of an encounter with Indian "hunters" who prepared to burn the initiate at the stake, even as a still more elaborate scenario was enacted in a ritual of adoption.[20] Middle class, urban, and frequented by erstwhile business associates, the lodges of the Red Men were inhabited by mainstream white Protestant men.

If the Indian had become culture broker and, with innuendos of racism, principle of association for them, the figure of the red man functioned similarly for Anglo-Protestants who found their way, less conventionally, into nonmainstream religious groups. From the late 1830s, well before the Red Men had their heyday, members of Shaker communities, who were undergoing a time of revival, claimed to be regularly visited by Indian spirits. In his account of nineteenth-century religious communities, John Humphrey Noyes, himself founder of the Oneida Perfectionists, gave a rare, practical glimpse of a visitation, quoting at length from a source in the Shaker society at Watervliet, New York, during the winter of 1842–43. "Eight or nine sisters became possessed of the spirits of Indian squaws," the sojourner wrote, "and about six of the brethren became Indians." There were "whooping and yelling and strange antics," he told, and—visible only to spirit eyes—the eating of "succotash" with fingers, in wooden dishes on the floor.[21]

Later, American spiritualists joined the ranks of those who said they spent religious time with Indians. After the Civil War, especially, stylized rituals of spirit communication developed, and in the twentieth century Indians were reported to be functioning in key roles. "Indian chiefs" were expected presences at séance gatherings, serving as "gate keepers" to protect mediums by keeping out unwelcome spirits. Moreover, regulars at séances eventually received the names of their own specially designated Indian chiefs as guardians.[22] By century's end, it remained for the children of the New Age to burn sage and sweet grass and to make sweat lodge ceremonies virtually identifying ritual badges for their movement. Indian people could protest in vain about the cooptation of their religious practices by New Age Indian "wannabes," as white Americans signaled their search for closeness to the land and for spiritual transformation. There were ironies and conspiracies of innocence here, gifts that were commandeered and exchanges that were lopsided and unequal. Still, the legacies of contact were real, and they told a story different from those of monochromatic consensus or simple dominance and submission.

Catholic Encounters

Roman Catholics became involved in ambiguous gift exchanges with native peoples on American shores as early as 1492, when the Italian Christopher Columbus with three crews of Spaniards touched anchor in the Bahamas. What Jay P. Dolan calls the "marriage between conquest and conversion" became a standard arrangement in the fifteenth and sixteenth centuries as Spanish ritual crosses were planted in the Americas to signal the coming of gospel and gun.[23] Here the transition from warring to gift giving was fragilely wrought in a Catholic pale of trade and settlement that stretched through the territories of New France and New Spain, as Catholic missionaries and native peoples struggled through acts of contact.

As political power settled out and Anglo-Protestants ruled, Catholic encounters with strangers took new turns in the former Atlantic seaboard colonies and their western extensions. Earliest Catholic presence among Anglo-Protestants in America had come with Leonard Calvert of the Baltimore clan, who arrived as first governor of the Maryland colony in 1634. With him, the *Ark* and the *Dove* brought two Jesuit priests and a lay brother, and they were joined soon afterward by a third priest and second brother. At first the Jesuits evangelized among the Indians with familiar goals of converting them to "civility" as well as to Roman Catholic Christianity. By 1645, however, when Protestants from Virginia invaded Maryland and deposed the Calverts, Jesuit mission ventures among the Indians ended. The continuing religious contacts of Roman Catholics were to be with Anglo-Protestants.[24]

From the first, the Calvert plan had been to make that religious contact minimal, with written instructions that "all Acts of Romane Catholique Religion . . . be done as privately as may be" and that Roman Catholic settlers be told "to be silent upon all occasions of discourse concerning matters of Religion." The plan worked poorly though, and Protestant hostilities toward Calvert and Catholic presence did not fail to surface, as the later history of the colony showed.[25] With the exception of Pennsylvania, conditions were likewise unfavorable for Catholics in the other colonies. A brief era of toleration ended in Rhode Island in 1664, and the period of toleration in New York before the Revolution also was brief. Thus, it was the religious settlement forced by political circumstance in the new United States that initiated widespread legal toleration of Roman Catholicism—and this only gradually, as state governments fell into line behind the federal model. Moreover, Catholics had continuing reasons to be wary of Protestant power, whatever the formal declarations of the law.

To complicate matters for Roman Catholics further, the contact situations they met were internal as well as external. As Catholics from widely disparate ethnic groups found themselves members of the same American church, they were forced to recognize their kinship even as they often wanted to stress their difference. English, French Canadian, German, and Irish Catholics were hardly easy comrades, and by the end of the nineteenth century when they were joined by southern and eastern Europeans the stresses were even more noticeable. A small and continuing African American presence in the church and a rapidly growing Latino population added further to ethnic diversity and to strain.

Robert Orsi's account of the twentieth-century *festa* devoted to Our Lady of Mount Carmel by Italian Americans in Harlem, New York, is an instructive case.[26] As Italian Harlem gave way to the Spanish brand, the July *festa* with its flamboyant public procession transporting a statue of the Madonna through the streets meant, more and more, Orsi argued, an expedition into "foreign" territory controlled, especially, by Puerto Ricans. Dark-skinned and ambiguously understood as "black," the Puerto Ricans evoked Italian American memories and fears of their own ambiguity in Anglo-America, where initially their swarthy complexions had been cause for racial comment. In their turn, Puerto Ricans reciprocated by conspicuously ignoring the *festa*.

In contrast, when another dark-skinned people, the Haitians, began to enter Harlem in appreciable numbers, Italian Americans gave them a decidedly different reception. The Haitians found in the Madonna and the Carmel church ritual support for their own mixed practice of Catholicism and *vodou*. The Madonna granted miracles to the Haitians, it was said, and the appearance of the Haitians themselves was understood, as Orsi recounted, "as something of a mystery and miracle, an uncanny event."[27] That the Haitians spoke French and could command the Latin language of the liturgy on occasion were credits in their cause. And, finally, in an act of denial, Italian Americans did not consider the Haitians black. As if in a laboratory report on ethnic—and racial—contact and conflict, Italian Americans displayed the subtleties of the meeting of Catholic with Catholic across lines of language and culture. They deflected attention away from the Anglo-Protestant world that has occupied so much of American religious historiography to point to processes of exchange where gifting and its refusal went on behind and beyond a specifically Protestant gaze. Yet in their concern regarding ethnic and racial identity—their preoccupation with "blackness"—they hinted at memories of their contact with Protestant America and the exchanges that it brought.

Contact with Protestant America led not merely to inner conflict, though. There also could be exercises of active emulation: from a Catholic immigrant's stance, Protestants, who were people of power and definers of the socially real, could be good to imitate. For evidence, consider the lay-trustee conflicts of the late eighteenth and antebellum nineteenth century and the Americanist controversy after the Civil War. In the case of the former, congregational church governance—the kind of polity in which an individual congregation called its pastor and in effect hired and fired him—became the envy of the Catholic laity and the ambiguous gift of Anglo-Protestantism to them. Moreover, envy and gift mingled with ethnic tensions and antagonisms within the American church. In the case of the Americanist controversy, ethnic quarrels blended with ideologies of American freedom and activist democracy to yield a "phantom heresy."

As early as the 1780s, in the wake of the American Revolution and its republican ideology, New York and Philadelphia Catholics were moving toward a lay-trustee system of church governance. Here those members of a parish who rented pews elected trustees annually to represent them by presiding over practical affairs within a congregation. Along the frontier in the New West as well, Catholic laity banded together, elected representatives, and purchased land for church buildings. But control of practical affairs escalated into a desire for control of policy and personnel, and soon decision making regarding clergy was claimed by lay trustees. At St. Peter's Church in New York City, for example, the congregation divided over the pastoral virtues of two Irish-born Capuchin priests, Charles Whelan and Andrew Nugent.[28]

Even more seriously, in Philadelphia the German national parish at Holy Trinity Church, founded at the initiative of German lay immigrants and reluctantly approved by Archbishop John Carroll, elected the German Capuchin John Charles Helbron as their pastor over Carroll's objections. And when Irish lay trustees assumed control of church finances in Norfolk, Virginia, in 1808, they went on to challenge the authority of the archbishop of Baltimore over the appointment of French pastors. Not only did they appeal to the pope (Pius VII) and to the Roman Congregation for the Propagation of the Faith, but they turned as well to Virginia state officials, to the United States Congress, and to President Thomas Jefferson.[29]

American nationalism intermixed with ethnic loyalties in the Americanist controversy later in the century, too.[30] Read backward, from Pope Leo XIII's encyclical letter *Testem Benevolentiae* of 1899, the Americanist controversy was about a series of opinions favoring themes of activism, individualism, and freedom and condemned as "Americanism" by the pontiff. Read backward, thus, the Americanist controversy was about a phantom heresy disclaimed, about a group of church leaders who pronounced themselves free of taint when papal innuendos were in the air. But read forward from an American contact situation tangled and retangled by complex connections between Catholics from diverse national groups and between Catholics and non-Catholics, Americanism became a phantom of another sort. It became a case study in the contact politics of the 1880s and 1890s and a series of jostling matches between liberals and conservatives.

Significantly, liberals, who were expansionists, wanted to embrace the American way *and* wanted ethnic edges to smooth away within their own church. They wanted English (not German), the language of the land, *and* hailed the public schools. They upheld the normative social ideologies reflected in the rule of abstinence *and* sought the handshake of man with fellow man in Protestant-dominated fraternal societies *and* vied for the joined arms of man with fellow (Protestant and ethnic) man in the Knights of Labor. As significantly, conservatives, who were contractionists, fought for the preservation of immigrant selves consolidated in separate national groups, segregated by religion, and reserved in their contact with other (Catholic national and Anglo-Protestant) groups, who were kept as much as possible at arm's length.

What Catholic followers, as groups distinct from their leaders, thought in all of this is difficult to decipher. But we can look for hints and suggestions by checking into their reading habits. For Irish Catholics, the largest group, perhaps the popular nineteenth-century novels of Mary Sadlier can provide a clue. By late century, Catholic writing in general was moderately big business. Colleen McDannell tells that in the 1890s some 1,183 Roman Catholic books were produced by sixty-eight firms,[31] and fiction writing loomed large among these publications. Sadlier, who helped her husband run a New York publishing house, stood among a group of perhaps twenty-six postbellum women novelists who helped their fellow religionists maintain a sense of separate Catholic identity.

Among other themes, Sadlier's novels told what being the object of Protestant evangelical concern felt like from an Irish Catholic vantage. In her 1862 production, *Old and New; or, Taste Versus Fashion*, for example, Isaac Wise's real-life encounter with a Protestant missionary as played out fictively in other keys. Here mission representatives described how Irish and Italian children were "degraded" and "utterly abandoned." Their parents, beyond the mission's ability to aid, were "hopeless" and addicted to "idleness, drunkenness, blasphemy, and, in short, everything bad." But one Irishwoman they met countered their Protestant gifts with Catholic rebuff. "The devil was the first Protestant," she declared. She went on to denounce Protestant missionaries as "all a set of humbugs, going about preaching religion to them that had the true religion, if they only had the grace to practice it." The missionaries would be "fitter" if they stayed home darning stockings "than trying to inveigle poor children from their lawful parents, and get them in by hoo[k] or by crook" to their mission.[32]

Whether it was humbug or not, Catholic working- and middle-class immigrants were set to endure the officious attention of their Anglo-Protestant evangelical neighbors in a contest for what the contact between ethnic groups would mean. Would the gift be the bestowal of evangelical Protestantism in the Anglo mode? Would it be the habits of mind and life—what Pierre Bourdieu calls the *habitus*—that accompanied that particular gift?[33] Would the gift eventuate in different outcomes from those originally intended? Would Protestants become Catholics? Would both groups reevaluate the religious claims that bound them and drift away into indifference? Or would they join or invent other religions to accommodate their needs at new times and junctures, religions that were gifts of the contact and the spin-offs it initiated?

These are questions that will remain mostly unanswered here, but one hint that the contact was at least a two-way street for religious exchange is provided by Boston's earlier-century Unitarians. These scions of the American establishment sent their children, when they could, to Roman Catholic private schools. The Unitarians harbored fantasies of the Catholic Middle Ages, and in the 1830s the pages of their newspaper the *Christian Register* often carried admiring pieces on medieval themes. Indeed, the Boston paper was widely tolerant—admitting early Transcendentalist writers to its pages and noticing their doings, admiring Emanuel Swedenborg, and generally inquiring about religious difference. Its expansionism was a straw in the wind, a prognostication of a liberal Protestant future, when the borders of religious doctrine would no longer hold firm and the exchange of religious gifts would create new and different religious futures. In short, as Jenny Franchot has observed of antebellum Protestant American literature in general, it revealed "how an intricately metaphorized Catholicism operated in effect as a strategically confused language of spiritual desire and ethnic repudiation for middle-class Anglo-Americans."[34] Negative encounters, like the fictional one in the Sadlier novel, masked a deep ambivalence and a hidden positive charge.

Protestant Relations, African American Ports of Call, Jewish Alliances, and Asian Junctures

The story must contract from an impressionistic outline to only traces of a sketch here as we make our way through a spendthrift catalog of religious performances and peoples. Indian and Catholic choreographies of contact and equivocal gifting already hint at what to expect. Among Protestants, for a first example, it will not do to stop with exchanges with non-Protestant strangers of the native or the immigrant sort. For Protestant pluralism has itself been vastly overlooked, and Protestant pluralism was extensive. Even on Boston Commons in the seventeenth century, the Puritans could not be sure a Quaker would not intrude. And Quaker gifts were not welcome, as the hangings of four Quakers between 1659 and 1661 attested.[35]

In the colony of New York, in contrast, gifts were better appreciated and received. With its pluralism inherited from New Netherland times, New York was home to the Dutch Reformed and Dutch Lutherans as well as English Puritans and Quakers, New England Congregationalists and Presbyterians, some Anabaptists, French-speaking Walloons and French Huguenots, and other Protestants and non-Protestants as well. "By the time the English conquered the colony, in 1664," wrote Richard W. Pointer, "no greater mixture of religions, nationalities, races, and tongues could be found anywhere in colonial America. And in the years that followed, New York's religious diversity only broadened."[36]

Well over a century after New Amsterdam became New York, in the wake of the American Revolution cooperative religious projects among Protestants abounded, with missions, publications, and prayer activities as key examples. By 1794, the New York Society for Promoting Christian Knowledge and Piety, which counted members who belonged to seven different denominations, was offering assistance to missionaries, distributing Bibles and tracts among the poor, and helping to start up schools. Two years later the New York Missionary Society, the earliest nondenominational missionary agency in the United States, came into existence with ministerial and lay members working together. Baptists in the New York Baptist Association were not unusual in 1803 when they thought that "the dear people of God in different parts and among different denominations are pursuing the same precious cause with increasing zeal." They dismissed "prejudice and party spirit" as "on the margin of oblivion," with Christianity now "become a common cause." In short, as Pointer has told, the large majority of New York Protestants found their pluralism to be, in theological terms, "a biblically acceptable expression of the various parts of Christ's one body."[37]

Meanwhile, for the nation at large, the urge to missionize the West was especially good at evoking a cooperative spirit among Anglo-Protestants. By 1801 Presbyterians and Congregationalists were joining together in home mission efforts in their Plan of Union. On the frontier, especially, pulpits were exchanged, lay and clerical workers from the two denominations labored side by side, and believers even counted themselves members of both. In the camp meeting revivals that spread across the New West at the time, evangelists from four or five different denominations could be found preaching in separate enclaves on a common meadow. Baptists, Methodists, Presbyterians, "Christians" (Disciples of Christ), and even Shakers competed for converts and exchanged invective. They also cooperated in evolving a corporate evangelical style, and they shared a set of cosmological and epistemological assumptions for support.

We gain an inkling of how the process worked in the discourse dilemmas of early nineteenth-century Methodists. Russell E. Richey has persuasively argued the case for the plurality of languages with which Methodists struggled to name and organize religious experience and expression within the denomination. "The central problem," he writes, "was that of living with these languages, accommodating them to one another, translating among them. Language vexed Methodist loyalty to the past and adjustment to change."[38] What needs to be underscored here, though, is that the four languages Richey found in early Methodism were products of the contact—goods that they had received and integrated in and through an economy of religious exchange.

The first language that Richey identified was a shared evangelical argot with a vocabulary of experiential religious piety in which people had "melting" times, were knit by "love," and waited for the Holy Spirit to "fall" on a gathered group. The second language, from English Methodist founder John Wesley, was one of "methodical" organization, telling, Richey said, of "class, society, itinerancy, circuits, holiness, . . . love feast, quarterly meeting, conference"; in America, it also became a badge of Methodist difference and a gift that could be shared. The third language, however, was more consciously adaptive, as, after 1784, American Methodists used an episcopal language of deacons, elders, and bishops to give themselves a sense of church identity and organized denominational status. And the fourth language, which Richey identifies as the product of a later time in the mid-nineteenth century, employed a republican idiom taken from the nation's political ideology to yoke Methodist imperatives to themes of national destiny and desire.[39]

As Richey's second language of organization already tells, Methodist contact worked outward as powerfully as it worked inward. The language of class and circuit, of holiness and love feast, fed into a common religious fund that strongly shaped the future of the nation's evangelicalism. So, too, did the Arminian theology of American Methodism—with its positivism and optimism regarding human effort and its effects—as it eroded a Calvinist antimission heritage and gave its blessing to mission zeal. Beyond that, Wesley's perfectionist leanings were underlined on the American side of the Atlantic as they blended with other cultural currents to yield a general perfectionist cosmology. In America, John Humphrey Noyes's Oneida Perfectionists with their brave, new experiment of complex marriage would owe a large debt to the Methodists, as would denizens of Reformed Christianity who joined with Methodists in an independent Holiness-Pentecostal movement.[40]

If perfectionism among Methodists and others gave a go-ahead to mission zeal, that general missionary impulse helped to spur religious contact especially between evangelical Protestants and African Americans. The First Great Awakening already had counted black converts among those who embraced Christianity, and by 1760 the presence of African American Christians had surely become noticeable. But in the nineteenth century Methodists and Baptists succeeded among slaves and free blacks as earlier Anglicans never had. In considerable part, whites gave the Christian gift with conscious manipulation—as a way to control their slaves and ensure submissive slave societies. But African Americans were not blind to the elements of resistance and rebellion contained in the Christian message and especially in its apocalyptic strands, as the experiences of Denmark Vesey (1822) and Nat Turner (1831) attest. In a developed *habitus* that was far more prevalent, though, African Americans in the American South themselves created a combinatory Christian faith that is often hailed as an "invisible institution." Here the contact meant a mingling of what Charles H. Long has called West African structures of consciousness (the slaves generally came from West Africa) with the historical experience of involuntary

presence in America and the overt language of Christian belief and practice.[41]

In this process a common West African belief in a noninterfering
high God, who was not ritually involved, could support a theodicy in
which slavery could be accepted as a fact of life without imputing God.
And West African ritual habits involving active possession states, when
intermediary Gods mounted and "rode"—like horses—individual
devotees, could lend themselves to revival praxis in strongly toned conversion experiences. Baptist worship as embraced by African Americans
in the American Southwest could echo traditional African ritual frames
and rhythms that transported from melancholy to ecstasy. Spiritual
churches in New Orleans, with their female leadership, could welcome
the Holy Spirit and also the spirit guides of American spiritualism and
Haitian *vodou*.[42]

In this context to speak of an "African spiritual holocaust," as Jon
Butler has, may obscure as much as, or more than, it reveals.[43] Intact
religious systems may not have survived the contact, but their underlying structures surely did. These intellectual, emotional, and physical
ways of being in the world governed the way blacks faced their New
World encounters, what they took, what they gave, and how and what
they combined. Some joinings of distinctively African and Christian elements were obvious, as in *vodou*, in Cuban Santería, and in other Afro-
Caribbean religions that made their way, with twentieth-century Caribbean immigrants, into East Coast cities such as New York and Miami.[44]

Yet many of the combinations present earlier in the United States by-
passed Christian themes or radically transformed them in religious survivals that bore little, if any, relationship to organized religion. Traditions of root work and conjure, use of the Bible itself as a conjure book,
folk fables passed on as in the Brer Rabbit tales, old shamanic memories
of magical human flight revived to assuage the pain of slavery—much
of the time none (or, as with the Bible, only some) of this could be cast
within a Christian mold.[45] Still, all such practice and discourse involved
religious combination, as elements from the past were adapted and re-
invented under new circumstances.

That the contact between blacks and whites worked both ways is nowhere more evident than in the origins and transformations of the spiritual in what became a black master art and genuinely American musical
culture, a process that has been traced effectively by Lawrence W.
Levine.[46] However, if white Americans were principal partners for the
African contact, they were surely not the only ones. Cultural amalga-

mation between Africans and Indians, for example, could be found in Cape Cod and some New England towns, in New York City, Long Island, and the Hudson River Valley, in small tri-ethnic (black, Indian, white) enclaves in Delaware, Maryland, Virginia, and North Carolina, and, especially, in South Carolina and Georgia.

Although interaction between blacks and Indians was discouraged by whites in the South, for fear of combined insurrections, numbers of slaves found sanctuary in Indian communities as Joel Martin notes in chapter 6. Gary Nash has suggested that "so common was Afro-Indian contact in the Southern colonies that the term *mustee* was added to the Southern vocabulary in order to categorize the offspring of African and Indian parents."[47] And the tracks of the exchange were left, at least, in a discourse that the two peoples shared. Joel Chandler Harris's *Uncle Remus* stories with their Brer Rabbit exploits, for example, paralleled similar tales that were told in Cherokee and Creek societies. Trickster tales and animal stories from African-American and southeastern Indian cultures, generally, shared thematic content and a common fund of popular wisdom and spirituality.[48]

Trickster tales on an American landscape bespeak the role of culture heroes in creating the practical cosmos of a richly pluralist society, and in America, there were culture heroes too numerous to count. If the African diaspora with its culture heroes resulted in a multifaceted complex of New World religious exchanges, so, too, did the American diaspora of the Jews. We already have met Isaac Mayer Wise traveling the trains in upper New York state and fielding inquiries and blows from assorted strangers and former friends. Wise's exchanges took on the high drama of his public persona in his autobiographical reminiscences, but other Jewish gifts and exchanges were as important. Wise's contemporary, Isaac Leeser, for example, upheld traditional orthodoxy against Wise's Reform leadership. For Leeser and others, though, religious contraction and consolidation were relative commodities. At Philadelphia's Sephardic Mikveh Israel Congregation, well before Wise's arrival in America, the twenty-three-year-old Leeser—not officially a rabbi but reader for the congregation—began to preach regularly from 1829. "At that period, the duties of the minister were confined to the conducting of the public worship in the synagogue and elsewhere," he later recalled, "and it was not accepted that he should be at the same time a preacher and exhorter."[49] Preaching was not the only adaptation from the evangelical Protestant mode that could be attributed to Leeser; he also advocated use of the English language and supported Rebecca

Gratz in the initiation of a Sunday school in Philadelphia in 1838. A year later, he published a catechism to help replace texts like the scripture lessons from the Christian Sunday School Union, used in Gratz's school—as Rosa Mordecai remembered—by "pasting pieces of paper over answers unsuitable for Jewish children."[50]

Leeser went on to inaugurate a traditionalist journal, the *Occident and American Jewish Advocate* in 1843. But by 1844, he was editorializing in favor of the distinctly nontraditional idea of a *"federative* union." Later he adapted and elaborated an earlier plan for union formed with Louis Salomon, leader of Philadelphia's Ashkenazic Congregation Rodeph Shalom. Then, with the support of a third Philadelphia synagogue, Beth Israel, the plan, which called for a national Jewish congress, was published and endorsed in the pages of the *Occident*.[51] Jews at the time were not ready for "traditionalist" Leeser's unionist plans on an American federal model. Still, the long-term trajectory of American Judaism would be one of religious expansionism.

Joseph L. Blau has stressed the compatibilities between traditional Judaism and Anglo-Protestant America, pointing, for example, to the similarities between a Jewish biblical ethic that viewed scripture under the character of law and a Calvinist one with its own lawyerly grasp of the Old Testament.[52] Judaism, Blau argued, embodied a series of major characteristics of American religion: its protestantism, its pluralism, its moralism, and, especially, its voluntaryism. In Blau's terms, "protestantism" (lower case) meant the religious impulse toward creedal freedom, the allowance of multiple conclusions. A foundational characteristic of historic Protestantism (upper case), it was also, said Blau, a significant part of a Jewish tradition that did not put its premium on religious creed to begin with. In contrast, pluralism directed attention away from conclusions and toward beginnings, operating on the premise that all originating points in religion possessed equal validity. Even with their ideology of chosenness, Jews had historically known significant experience with cultural pluralism, and they had thrived in the pluralistic matrix of America.

Again, the moralism that Blau named was for him an expression of an American pragmatism that put its stock in "immediate practical consequences," a habitual stance that was reflected in a Jewish social concern for goodness. And voluntaryism—for Blau the right of people living in a free society to choose freedom *from* religion—became in his reading of immigrant Jewry an American Protestant gift that was received with enthusiasm. Evoking a model of Judaisms in America, he concluded that it was voluntaryism most of all that shaped Jews into "an American Jewry made in the reflection of American cultural and religious patterns."[53]

So there were Jewish atheists and socialists in America, and there were Jews who enthusiastically endorsed Freemasonry. There were Black Jews and Jewish Humanists and a Jewish founder and membership for the Ethical Culture Society. In the twentieth century, Jews marched beside blacks and liberal Protestants in the civil rights movement of the sixties and helped to found the National Association for the Advancement of Colored People. Meanwhile, beginning with the Puritan collective vision of their society as the New Israel, Jewish threads had been woven into the general fabric of American religion. It was true that on the cultural seesaw of the nation's history, Judaism was at times figured as the enemy—in clear patterns of anti-Semitism and refusal of the gift. At other times, though, Judaism to the contrary figured the warmth and security of family and home, as in advertising slogans such as the invitational, "You don't have to be Jewish to love Levy's Jewish Rye bread."[54]

Significant numbers of unhyphenated Americans, apparently, liked consuming Jewish gifts. They also were ardent consumers of Asian ones, and their consumption was hardly limited to Chinese and Japanese culinary productions. For what many Americans consumed from the Orient—before, for the most part, they encountered Asian peoples themselves—was Eastern culture and religion. In the years following the Revolution, American ships sailed for Asian ports, returning with Chinese and Indian goods to grace households and shops in New England and Middle Atlantic coastal cities. Along with the material culture of Asia came some of its sacred texts, and there was a smattering of interest among elites.[55] It remained for the nineteenth century, however, to see a more serious interest in Asian peoples and their religions develop on the part of non-Asian Americans. It may have been a straw in the wind that, in 1801, a handbook claiming to describe the religions that had arisen since the dawn of the Christian era included, in its third edition, a thirty-page section on the religions of Asia. Hannah Adams's *A View of Religions* reflected the sources and knowledge of its time as well as the shock, for her, of the Asian encounter. The "incredible tortures" of a Hindu yogi revolted the author. She confessed that "a minute description of the voluntary sufferings of the Indian devotee" brought "increasing horror" to the mind and froze "the astonished reader to a statue, almost as immoveable as the suffering penitent."[56]

Still, Adams had worked hard to present all that was known, spending time reading at booksellers' quarters because she could not afford the price of the books that she needed. She also had worked hard to be fair. Her interest presaged that of the New England Transcendentalists nearly four decades later and, after that, a steady procession of Anglo-American inquirers. Thus, when Edward Elbridge Salisbury lectured on the history of Buddhism at the American Oriental Society's first annual meeting in 1844, he stood at the launch of a Victorian American romance with things Buddhist. Here, as Thomas A. Tweed has shown, Buddhism was read by Anglo-American converts and sympathizers as supportive of the best in American individualism, optimism, and activism.[57] As in a Judaism that found the part of itself that fit the exchange rate in American society, the new Buddhism of these Americans was transmuted into the coin of the realm.

After these beginnings, the postbellum Gilded Age brought the presence of Asia and its religions still closer to Anglo-America. By 1878, Helena Blavatsky and Henry Steel Olcott, cofounders of a still-infant Theosophical Society, set sail for India and, especially for Olcott, began a serious commitment to Buddhism. What had started as a spiritualist reform society with a preoccupation with the occult now stretched to include the study of Asian religions, even if the study was premised on an underlying orientalism that read Buddhism in unconscious Western and Theosophical terms.[58] Then, by 1893, as numbers of Chicagoans perused the pages of the Chicago *Daily Inter Ocean* with its reports on the World's Parliament of Religions, a sizable population of non-Asian Americans was becoming superficially acquainted with Asian religions for the first time.

The parliament had been held in conjunction with the Columbian Exposition marking the four-hundred-year anniversary of European contact with the Americas and bringing twenty-seven million visitors from seventy-two nations.[59] Racism and colonialism pervaded the exposition, reflected in its hegemonic construction of the White City—a specially designed assemblage of buildings—and its relegation of non-American "others" to grounds outside it as so many exhibits at which fair-goers might ogle. The parliament itself, with 150,000 spectators over seventeen days, was held away from the White City in downtown Chicago.[60] But the parliament shared the condescension and colonialism of the fair toward the world's peoples.[61] So the translation of Asian—religions or peoples—read "exotic," and accounts of Swami Vivekananda's orange and crimson robes and accompanying turban made impressions as strong or stronger than the subtleties of what he taught. A contemporary poem by Minnie Andrews Snell, appearing in a Chicago journal, the *Open Court,* offered a useful summary of popular surmise. In "Aunt Hannah on the Parliament of Religions," Snell's Aunt Hannah confessed how she "listened to th' Buddhist, in his robes of shinin' white," then "heered th' han'some Hindu monk, drest up in orange dress, / Who sed that all humanity was part of God—no less."[62]

Still, despite the superficialities and cultural imperialism, important exchanges occurred, and Asian parliament representatives in their speeches often inverted the assumptions of conference organizers.[63] They also used the occasion as a springboard for later missionary work in America. In fact, the parliament was, as Kenten Druyvesteyn argued, a watershed for Eastern religions in the United States.[64] Meanwhile, on the West Coast, the ethnic presence of Asia was visible and, with it, traditional Asian religions. Chinese immigrants had come as early as the 1840s, bringing Buddhism, Taoism, and Confucianism intermingled as they were in their own culture. Japanese missionaries accommodated their own people in Hawaii from 1889 and in California a decade later, carrying Pure Land Buddhism with its devotion to Amida Buddha and hope of attainment, after death, of the Pure Land, or Western Kingdom. Here the contact was easy to trace institutionally in titles, designations, and the most visible signs of American accommodation. The Jodo Shinshu (Pure Land) movement in America became, from 1899 to 1944, the North American Buddhist Mission; after that, it was the Buddhist Churches of America. Regular services were inaugurated, unlike the pattern of devotion in the Buddhist temples of Japan, and Buddhist "bishops" came to oversee American worship, even as Sunday schools flourished along with the Sunday services.

Hence, as all of this already testifies, the American contact produced two characteristic forms of Asian religions overall. *Export* religions were embraced by non-Asian Americans; *ethnic* religions were observed by Asian immigrants and/or their children. Often the two forms were widely divergent, with export versions stressing philosophy, meditation traditions, and esoterica, and ethnic forms concerned with ritual and cultural praxis. Moreover, the gifts of the contact often spawned combinations that perhaps surprised even the participants. When, for example, the International Society for Krishna Consciousness (ISKCON) found itself dwindling after its American countercultural heyday in the late sixties and seventies, it was Asian Indian immigrants who rescued the Hare Krishna movement after most of the non-Asian converts had gone.[65]

Other South Asians, who built lavish temples to grace the American landscape, often found themselves more observant of their traditions in this nation than they had been in India. They used religion as a carrier of culture, and they worked to preserve language, tradition, art, music, and folkways over the sign of the Gods. Concerned for their children in huge and crime-ridden American cities and worried about an American moral culture they often found decadent, they turned to the new temples they erected as tools for cultural contraction, for the maintenance of islands of integrity in an America they found too culturally and religiously promiscuous. Yet, as Joanne Punzo Waghorne's study of the Sri Siva-Vishnu Temple in suburban Washington, D.C., has shown, South Asians could not go home again religiously. The suburban temple in Lanham, Maryland, was neither an intact replica of South Asia nor a totally American creation. Rather the temple's design—with its split-level construction that forced a non-Indian separation of sacred rituals from more ordinary cultural activities—openly articulated theological change.[66] Built into the material reality of the temple, the new distinctions were a product of the contact; they signaled a change in the habits of mind and life that constituted religious culture for these South Asian Indians.

Contacts and Combinations

As the Asian experience underscored, religious mixing was surely the name of the spiritual game in the United States. And as this account already has suggested, the creation of new religions proved a continual product of the contact. One can work through the data of early and antebellum America and on through the Gilded Age, the Progressive Era and World War I, through the Depression years and World War II, past the Eisenhower age of consensus, the hippie times of the sixties, and on into the New Age and the coming of age of Generation X, marking the new religious forms. Shakers and the "Publick Universal Friend" (Jemima Wilkinson),[67] Mormons and "Christians" in the new Disciples of Christ, Millerites and Adventists, Christian Scientists and New Thoughters, Spiritualists and Theosophists, adherents of UFO movements and shamanic visionaries of whatever sort: all have tales to tell about contact, encounter, exchange.

Outside the American context, writing about the religions of Japan, Allan G. Grapard has argued for the importance of association and what he has called "combinative" religion. For Grapard, treating Japanese "religions" as separate entities was artificial and thoroughly dubious. "Associations," he writes, "occurred at the institutional, ritual, doctrinal, and philosophical levels everywhere throughout Japanese history and formed the backbone not only of what has been called religion but also of Japanese culture in general." They were, in fact, "a fundamental element of the Japanese tradition." It was imperative "that artificial separations between supposedly independent systems of meaning not be applied to the past, and that ways and means of expressing the changing composition of combinative systems of belief be developed."[68]

Like the Japanese, religious Americans throughout the nation's history have been what Grapard would call "combinativists." But for Americans there was at least one obvious difference. What the Japanese casually acknowledged in the overt practice of a blended religious culture became, in America, a secret obscured. And religious exchange obscured and unrecognized as such became religious exchange denied, an ideology of purity and self-containment proclaimed in its stead. The text read church and sect and denomination, standing separate and intact; only the subtext read new and combinative religion. Still, the subtext has been, throughout American history, clear, consistent, and compelling. The social function of religion as exchange has not gone away but continued. Thus to speak of "new" religions in the United States as so many also-rans, as a coterie of curiosities to be pigeonholed under the banner of "syncretism," is to miss a very large point. The shape and operation of American religious life—all of it—is best described under the rubric of religious combination. To target some faiths for the designation while overlooking all the rest is like noticing the tip of the religious iceberg while ignoring what lies below.

To say this another way, as Tamar Frankiel did in the seventies regarding the California Indians, we need to think about religions in America not so much as syncretistic but more as "additive."[69] This is because to evoke the presence of syncretism is to suggest the non-normal and marginal, the unnatural and exotic. More, it is to imply a loss of self and soul, to call under judgment a decomposition of sorts. It is to say, in so many words, that elements of original and "pure" religions have surrendered their previous integrity in bowdlerized and inferior blends that represent a religious devolution. To talk about "combination" or "addition" (and a related shedding of the no-longer-relevant), in contrast, is to move the analysis toward a different set of assumptions and assessments. It is to talk about a natural cultural process that occurs whenever and wherever contact comes. It is to own that—unless religious systems are relics to be admired in a taxonomy of the sacred that comes with museum shelves—they let go and add on; they lose; they gain; they exchange. In the economy of the gift and the gifted, this is simply religion as usual. And when, as in the history of this nation, the chances for contact between religious cultures multiply immeasurably, so, too, do the gifts and gifted.

Moreover, as stories of gift givers and receivers in American society already hint, we need to be willing to expand our theoretical perspectives to include a view of combinatory religions as what Leonard Norman Primiano would call "vernacular" religions. Here vernacular religions are religions "as they are lived." The fine print of this statement is that such lived religions are always combinations and recombinations in which "official" traditions are sanded down and glued on, so to speak, to create a customized religious structure that fits the overall context of a life.[70] This view circumvents the distinction between elite and popular religion and focuses, instead, on a common that is shared. It catches in the act the processes of religious exchange that form the sacred economies of the culture. It collects snapshots, like those of Isaac Mayer Wise, that help us see how religions work and how they grow and change.

What the snapshots suggest, further, is that American religions and religious people—combinative and vernacular as they are—are also eminently practical. Religious praxis means *what is done,* and what is done often looks like a complex choreography of largely intuitive moves. The choreography yields a background cosmology and epistemology and a foreground series of balancing acts between social and cultural lines of force and the people who work them. Sometimes the choreography is danced out in a more or less lightly inflected theme: exchanges have been smooth and easy; gifts have been given and received with delight. At other times the dance has looked more like a martial arts "push hands" demonstration between opposing but intimately connected actors: the "harmony" has arisen out of a balance of tensions. And still other times one or another dancing partner has gone down. The gift has been smashed; "harmony" has become a pseudonym for hegemony; there are cuts and bruises, twisted knees, and more.

In all of this, the view is one that invites attention to choreographies of contact and combination. In them, the historical gaze must move continually from side to side and focus from place to place. Practitioners of the martial arts tell us that one way to be focused—different from attending to a single, relatively discrete object—is to move continuously and to follow the series of connected actions as one moves. Following the moves that American actors make in religious contact situations on such a model can yield considerably different plots and performances from those that are part of the standard historiographical repertoire. Accounts of gifts given and received can move the story forward, chart ambiguities and offenses, provide occasions for interpretive challenge, and offer opportunities for insight. Tracking the gifts can bring us back to Faneuil Hall, reminding us that—in America as elsewhere—even spirits go to market, and even spirits, whatever their constraints, purchase gifts.

Notes

1. This story, "Indian History," is included in a small assortment of tales collected by Hedvig Tetens Evans in the 1950s. They were narrated by four Seminole informants—Billy Bowlegs, the Reverend Daniel Beaver, the Reverend Billy Osceola, and Frank Tiger. Christian influences are evident in this and other narratives recorded in this brief collection. Hedvig Tetens Evans, ed., "Seminole Folktales," *Florida Historical Quarterly* 56 (April 1978): 473–94.

2. Several fine sociological studies have tried to map the contemporary religious landscape in the United States. Among the most useful studies for understanding the trends I mention here are Wade Clark Roof and William McKinney, *American Mainline Religion: Its Changing Shape and Future* (New Brunswick, N.J.: Rutgers University Press, 1987); Robert Wuthnow, *The Restructuring of American Religion: Society and Faith since World War II* (Princeton: Princeton University Press, 1988); and Phillip E. Hammond, *Religion and Personal Autonomy: The Third Disestablishment in America* (Columbia: University of South Carolina Press, 1992). On Hindus and Buddhists in America, before and after 1965, and a review of the literature on the topic, see Thomas A. Tweed, "Asian Religions in the United States: Reflections on an Emerging Sub-Field," in Walter Conser and Sumner Twiss, eds., *Religious Diversity and American Religious History: Studies in Traditions and Cultures* (Athens: University of Georgia Press, forthcoming). For a helpful overview of the post-1965 immigrants, see Peter Kivisto, "Religion and the New Immigrants," in William H. Swatos, Jr., ed., *A Future for Religion? New Paradigms for Social Analysis* (Newbury Park, Calif.: Sage Publications, 1993), 92–108. For some survey data on the contemporary period, see George Gallup, Jr., and Jim Castelli, *The People's Religion: American Faith in the 90s* (New York: Macmillan, 1989), and

Barry A. Kosmin and Seymour P. Lachman, *One Nation under God: Religion in Contemporary American Society* (New York: Harmony Books, 1993).

3. Lawrence W. Levine, "Clio, Canons, and Culture," *Journal of American History* 80 (December 1993): 867. Vincent G. Harding, who also quotes Levine, deals with similar issues in "Healing at the Razor's Edge: Reflections on a History of Multicultural America," *Journal of American History* 81 (September 1994): 571–84. Harding focuses his analysis on one recent attempt to offer a different narrative of American history, Ronald Takaki's *A Different Mirror: A History of Multicultural America* (Boston: Little, Brown, 1993). Peter Novick has offered an insightful account of the historical profession in the United States, which includes a discussion of the post-1960s period, in *That Noble Dream: The "Objectivity Question" and the American Historical Profession* (Cambridge: Cambridge University Press, 1988), 415–629. After I finished this introduction, I discovered a recent book on history writing that deals with many of the same issues in a lucid and suggestive way: Joyce Appleby, Lynn Hunt, and Margaret Jacob, *Telling the Truth about History* (New York: W. W. Norton, 1994).

4. On the history of the writing of American religious history see the helpful overview by Henry W. Bowden, "The Historiography of American Religion," in Charles H. Lippy and Peter W. Williams, eds., *Encyclopedia of the American Religious Experience* (New York: Charles Scribner's, 1988). For one account of religious history writing in the United States since the 1960s see Henry Warner Bowden, *Church History in an Age of Uncertainty: Historiographical Patterns in the United States, 1906–1990* (Carbondale: Southern Illinois University Press, 1991), 164–218. For helpful analyses of the textbook surveys of American religion see Leonard I. Sweet, " 'Ringmasters,' 'Blind Elephant Feelers,' and 'Mules': The Textbook Literature of American Religious History," *Critical Review of Books in Religion, 1988* (Atlanta: Journal of the American Academy of Religion and the Journal of Biblical Literature, 1988), 89–118, and Stephen J. Stein, " 'Something Old, Something New, Something Borrowed, Something *Left to Do*': Choosing a Textbook for Religion in America," *Religion and American Culture* 3 (summer 1993): 217–27. Following William R. Hutchison and many others, I define "mainline" Protestants as those belonging to seven influential denominations—Congregationalists, Episcopalians, Presbyterians, Disciples of Christ, United Lutherans, and the white divisions of Baptist and Methodist families. William R. Hutchison, ed., *Between the Times: The Travail of the Protestant Establishment in America, 1900–1960* (Cambridge: Cambridge University Press, 1989), 4. I have argued elsewhere that a Protestant establishment has had influence even in areas that have been celebrated and condemned for their diversity in the late twentieth century; see Thomas A. Tweed, "An Emerging Protestant Establishment: Religious Affiliation and Public Power on the Urban Frontier in Miami, 1896–1904," *Church History* 64 (September 1995): 412–37. The debate about narratives, on one level, is a professional one. It is about academic turf, graduate training, and professional bonds. But more is going on at the personal level: the debate is also about collective memory, social power, and personal identity. That facet helps

to explain the intense emotions that the issues generate for some participants in the public debates about who's in and who's out of anthologies and textbooks.

5. By the term *America* we refer to the political boundaries of the United States at the time we wrote this book. At the same time, some contributors consider developments outside those borders, in other parts of the hemisphere, for example; and many essays show how stories about religion cross political boundaries. Part of our goal, then, is to place developments in different geographical contexts. If other specialists in the United States share that view, and so want conversation with residents and scholars of other nations in the hemisphere, we will need to work together toward a new language. Many residents and scholars of Latin America are offended when the term *America* is used to refer only to the United States. They too, in their terms, are "Americans." In this introduction, I use the term *U.S.* most often. Occasionally, for stylistic purposes, I shift to *America* or *American,* but I remain conscious of the problem.

6. In this volume, we decided to let our competing narratives of U.S. religion stand—and not to try to compose a single grand narrative from these accounts. In a way, our strategy follows that used by William Faulkner in *The Sound and the Fury,* in which four narrators positioned variously tell the story of an old Southern family in Mississippi. William Faulkner, *The Sound and the Fury,* the corrected text (1929; New York: Modern Library, 1992). Some historians have advocated a similar narrative strategy. See Peter Burke, "The History of Events and the Revival of Narrative," in Peter Burke, ed., *New Perspectives on Historical Writing* (University Park: Pennsylvania State University Press, 1992), 239. See also Richard Price, *Alabi's World* (Baltimore: Johns Hopkins University Press, 1990). In that book, Price narrates events in eighteenth-century Surinam through four "voices": black slaves, Dutch administrators, Moravian missionaries, and the historian himself.

7. James D. Bratt has made a similar point about the need to attend to "elements of story"—character, plot, and setting. I highlight motif more than he does. See James D. Bratt, "A New Narrative for American Religious History?" *Fides et Historia* 23 (fall 1991): 19–30. Although narratives usually are linked with time, some literary theorists—for instance, M. Bakhtin, Julia Kristeva, and Susan Friedman—have talked about the "spatialization" of narratives. The purpose of much of this theoretical writing has been to find new ways of including the reader and the historical context in narrative interpretation. As it will become clear, that is not my primary purpose here. M. M. Bakhtin, *The Dialogic Imagination,* ed. Michael Holquist (Austin: University of Texas Press, 1981), 84–85; Julia Kristeva, *Desire in Language: A Semiotic Approach to Literature and Art,* ed. Leon S. Roudiez (New York: Columbia University Press, 1980), 36–37, 65–69; Susan Stanford Friedman, "Spatialization: A Strategy for Reading Narrative," *Narrative* (January 1993): 12–23.

8. W. H. Dray, "On the Nature and Role of Narrative in Historiography," *History and Theory* 10 (1971): 157. Despite continuing interest in the analysis of structures rather than stories about events, in the past few decades some observers have noticed a revival of narrative among historians. See Lawrence Stone, "The Revival of Narrative," *Past and Present* 85 (1979): 3–24. With the

authors of *Telling the Truth about History,* I suggest that in one sense narrative did not need reviving. It has been implicit, even explicit, in the structural analyses of social historians, and (I would add) it certainly has been present in what we tell students in the classroom. Teachers, and syllabi, tell stories. Appleby, Hunt, and Jacob, *Telling the Truth about History,* 231.

9. On this distinction, see W. H. Walsh, " 'Plain' and 'Significant' Narrative in History," *Journal of Philosophy* 55 (1958): 479–84; Louis Mink, "Narrative Form as a Cognitive Instrument," in Robert H. Canary and Henry Kozicki, eds., *The Writing of History* (Madison: University of Wisconsin Press, 1978), 144. Scholars in several fields have been debating the nature of narrative for the last several decades. Key disputants include social-scientifically oriented historians like Fernand Braudel, hermeneutically oriented philosophers like Paul Ricoeur, semiotically oriented literary theorists like Roland Barthes, linguistically oriented analytic philosophers like William Dray, and "postmodernist" theorists such as F. R. Ankersmit. One helpful overview of the debates is found in Hayden White, "The Question of Narrative in Contemporary Historical Theory," *History and Theory* 23 (1984): 1–33. See also the summaries in Wallace Martin, *Recent Theories of Narrative* (Ithaca: Cornell University Press, 1986), 71–75, 222–23; Paul Ricoeur, *Time and Narrative* (Chicago: University of Chicago Press, 1984), 1:91–174; and Appleby, Hunt, and Jacob, *Telling the Truth about History,* 231–37. The debate continues in the pages of many journals, for instance *History and Theory.*

10. The quotation is from Martin, *Recent Theories of Narrative,* 72. See also White, "The Question of Narrative," 24. White has argued that constructing historical narratives involves "projecting onto the facts of the plot-structure of one or another of the genres of literary figuration." While I disagree with White's claim that there are only four modes of emplotment—romance, tragedy, comedy, or satire—it certainly seems true that "emplotting" of some sort takes place in most historical work. On emplotment, see Hayden White, *Metahistory* (Baltimore: Johns Hopkins University Press, 1973), 7. For a sympathetic and judicious analysis of literary approaches to historical narratives, especially in the work of Hayden White and Dominick LaCapra, see Lloyd S. Kramer, "Literature, Criticism, and Historical Imagination: The Literary Challenge of Hayden White and Dominick LaCapra," in Lynn Hunt, ed., *The New Cultural History* (Berkeley: University of California Press, 1989), 97–128.

11. I realize that "evidence" can be understood in a variety of ways. On this point, see James Chandler, Arnold I. Davidson, and Harry D. Harootunian, eds., *Questions of Evidence* (Chicago: University of Chicago Press, 1994). In describing the strongest version of the "constructivist" view I have in mind theorists such as Hayden White and postmodernist interpreters like F. R. Ankersmit. Since most postmodernist theorists and historians are highly suspicious of narrative form, the stance I take in this introduction and the position of the contributors is not postmodernist, at least on that issue. To argue for the view of historical narrative that I advocate here is to place ourselves between two types of thinking about the writing of history. These two positions have been labeled in various ways—modernist and postmodernist, realist and idealist, criterial and linguistic, espistemological and narrativist. For one useful account

of the two ideal-typical positions by one who advocates the postmodernist, see F. R. Ankersmit, "The Dilemma of Contemporary Anglo-Saxon Philosophy of History," in F. R. Ankersmit, ed., *Knowing and Telling History: The Anglo-Saxon Debate* (Middletown, Conn.: Wesleyan University Press, 1986), 1–27. "For the modernist," Ankersmit claims, "evidence is in essence the evidence that something happened in the past. The modernist historian follows a line of reasoning from his sources and evidence to a historical reality hidden behind the sources." For postmodernists, he suggests, nothing rests "behind" the sources: it is constructions all the way down. Ankersmit, "Historiography and Postmodernism," *History and Theory* 28 (1989): 144–45. For criticisms of Ankersmit's article and the author's response see Perez Zagorin, "Historiography and Postmodernism: Reconsiderations," *History and Theory* 29 (1990): 263–74, and F. R. Ankersmit, "Reply to Professor Zagorin," *History and Theory* 29 (1990): 275–96. For another carefully argued "modernist" view see Raymond Martin, "Objectivity and Meaning in Historical Studies: Toward a Post-Analytic View," *History and Theory* 32 (1993): 25–50. See also W. J. Van Der Dussen and Lionel Rubinoff, eds., *Objectivity, Method, and Point of View: Essays in the Philosophy of History* (Leiden: E. J. Brill, 1991). On the history of the concern for "objectivity" in the historical profession in the United States see Novick, *That Noble Dream*. See also the interesting response by Thomas Haskell, "Objectivity Is Not Neutrality: Rhetoric Versus Practice in Peter Novick's *That Noble Dream*," *History and Theory* 29 (1990): 129–57.

12. One theological ethicist who read this in draft suggested that even my silly examples of false empirical assertions might appear meaningfully in stories that were narrated for particular purposes and a particular community. Personal correspondence, Stanley Hauerwas, 13 June 1994. Perhaps Hauerwas is right. Maybe someone for some reason might want to present Whitefield as a Jesuit missionary, for instance. Generally, however, I stand by my suggestion that empirical errors, unless they are intentional and strategic, diminish the persuasiveness of narratives.

13. Donna Haraway, *Simians, Cyborgs, and Women: The Reinvention of Nature* (New York: Routledge, 1991), 183–201; Yi-Fu Tuan, *Space and Place* (Minneapolis: University of Minnesota Press, 1977), 161; *The Oxford English Dictionary*, 2d ed., s.v. "narrate."

14. Robert Baird, *Religion in America*, a critical abridgement with introduction by Henry Warner Bowden (1844; New York: Harper and Row, 1970). It is important to note that our chosen focus is the "comprehensive" surveys, from Baird's account to the most recent textbooks. Our criticisms, then, are not directed at the authors of the many articles and books that have interpreted narrower ranges of American religious history, although some of the same patterns appear there too. Several fine studies, especially in the past twenty-five years, already have moved in the direction we suggest in this volume. In a sense, we are trying to synthesize and build on illuminating work already done in American religious history, and our efforts parallel those of scholars in other fields in the humanities and social sciences to reconsider the basic stories they tell. Of course, by highlighting a collection of texts here I am constructing a "canon" of sorts. For those familiar with the field, however, I hope that my choices do

not seem arbitrary. I acknowledge a canon that already shapes the field as much as I construct one.

15. Peter W. Williams, *America's Religions: Traditions and Cultures* (New York: Macmillan, 1990), 265–74; Edwin Scott Gaustad, *A Religious History of America*, rev. ed. (New York: Harper and Row, 1990); Catherine L. Albanese, *America: Religions and Religion*, 2d ed. (Belmont, Calif.: Wadsworth, 1992), 324–49; Winthrop Hudson and John Corrigan, *Religion in America*, 5th ed. (New York: Macmillan, 1992), 4–5.

16. Many fine local and regional studies have appeared, and a few scholars have called for interpreters to attend more carefully and fully to regional variation. See Samuel S. Hill, "Religion and Region in America," *Annals of the American Academy of Political and Social Science* 480 (July 1985): 132–41, and Jerald C. Brauer, "Regionalism and Religion in America," *Church History* 54 (September 1985): 366–78.

17. Mark A. Noll, *A History of Christianity in the United States and Canada* (Grand Rapids, Mich.: Eerdmans, 1992); Robert T. Handy, *A History of the Churches in the United States and Canada* (New York: Oxford University Press, 1976). Note also that in *America*, Albanese includes a world map entitled "The Religious Peopling of the United States" (ii–iii) that clearly establishes a wider geographical context for U.S. developments. Jon Butler, "The Future of American Religious History: Prospectus, Agenda, and Transatlantic Problematique," *William and Mary Quarterly* 42 (1985): 167–83; David W. Wills and Albert J. Raboteau, "Rethinking American Religious History: A Progress Report on 'Afro-American Religious History: A Documentary Project,'" *Council of Societies for the Study of Religion Bulletin* 20 (September 1991): 57–61; David Wills, "Forum: The Decade Ahead in Scholarship," *Religion and American Culture* 3 (1993): 15–22; Herbert E. Bolton, *Wider Horizons of American History* (Notre Dame, Ind.: University of Notre Dame Press, 1967), 1–54. Bolton's essay "The Epic of Greater America" was the presidential address of the American Historical Association in 1932, and it first appeared in print the following year.

18. My understanding of social space has been shaped by the writings of scholars in geography, sociology, history, literary theory, and philosophy. Michel Foucault talked about social spaces and sites, and used geographical metaphors; see especially Foucault's "Of Other Spaces," *Diacritics* 16 (spring 1986): 22–27, and his "Questions on Geography," in Colin Gordon, ed., *Power/Knowledge: Selected Interviews and Other Writings, 1972–1977* (New York: Pantheon, 1980), 63–77. Also useful were Edward Soja, *Postmodern Geographies* (London: Verso, 1989); Michel de Certeau, *The Practice of Everyday Life,* trans. Steven F. Rendall (Berkeley: University of California Press, 1984), 91–130; Rhys Isaac, *The Transformation of Virginia, 1740–1790* (1982; New York: Norton, 1988); Henri Lefebvre, *The Production of Space,* trans. Donald Nicholson-Smith (Oxford: Blackwell, 1991). Mary Louise Pratt's term *contact zones* also seems useful, although the social spaces I refer to are more than sites of "colonial encounters," which are her focus. See Mary Louise Pratt, *Imperial Eyes: Travel Writing and Transculturation* (London: Routledge, 1992), 6. Much of my thinking about both geographical and social space has been influenced by the writings of Yi-Fu Tuan, especially *Space and Place.* Unlike Tuan and de Certeau,

I do not make distinctions between "space" and "place." Here I use them synonymously. My understanding of religion is shaped not only by the work of the geographer Tuan, but also by scholars in the history of religions and anthropology. Jonathan Z. Smith, for instance, also emphasizes place in his theory of religion; see his *Map Is Not Territory* (1978; Chicago: University of Chicago Press, 1993), 290–91. By emphasizing the interpenetration of "public" and "private" spaces I am agreeing with Martin Marty's remarks in "Religion: A Private Affair, in Public Affairs," *Religion and American Culture* 3 (summer 1993): 115–27.

19. Sydney E. Ahlstrom, *A Religious History of the American People* (New Haven: Yale University Press, 1972); Sidney E. Mead, "By Puritans Possessed," *Worldview* 16 (April 1973): 49–52; Mary Farrell Bednarowski, *American Religion: A Cultural Perspective* (Englewood Cliffs, N.J.: Prentice-Hall, 1984). In Albanese's and Williams's books, "popular" or "cultural" religion also receive treatment (Albanese, *America*, 463–500; Williams, *America's Religions*). See also Peter Williams, *Popular Religion in America: Symbolic Change and the Modernization Process in Historical Perspective* (1980; Urbana: University of Illinois Press, 1989).

20. George M. Marsden, *Religion and American Culture* (New York: Harcourt Brace Jovanovich, 1990), 5.

21. The "germ" theory I mention here was very influential in the late nineteenth century among historians in general in the United States, not just those who wrote about religion. Leonard Woolsey Bacon, *A History of American Christianity*, American Church History Series (1897; New York: Scribner's, 1900), 399. Such narrative lines might emphasize, as Baird's did, the commercialization, urbanization, and civilization of the "vast wilderness" that the first immigrants encountered. Storytellers might define the American "environment" in various terms, not just geographical, and trace the efforts of religious men and women—mostly elite men—to "develop" their tradition in a cultural context that fostered religious liberty, democratic individualism, and the voluntary principle. As Henry Bowden has noted, not only Baird but also Philip Schaff (1855) and Daniel Dorchester (1888) wove such plots by drawing on organic motifs. Bowden, "Historiography"; Philip Schaff, *America: A Sketch of Its Political, Social, and Religious Character*, ed. Perry Miller (1855; Cambridge, Mass.: Harvard University Press, 1961); Daniel Dorchester, *Christianity in the United States from the First Settlement Down to the Present* (New York: Phillips and Hunt, 1888). The motif survives in contemporary narratives in an indirect and limited way as scholars aim to "portray the role of religion in all *stages* of this country's *development*" (emphasis added). Gaustad, *Religious History of America*, ix.

22. Frederick Jackson Turner, *The Frontier in American History* (1920; New York: Holt, Rinehart, and Winston, 1962). See also Wilbur R. Jacobs, *On Turner's Trail: 100 Years of Writing Western History* (Lawrence: University of Kansas Press, 1994); Peter G. Mode, *The Frontier Spirit in American Christianity* (New York: Macmillan, 1923); William Warren Sweet, *The Story of Religion in America* (1930; New York: Harper and Brothers, 1939). Narrators who appeal directly or indirectly to this motif sometimes have referred to the

expansion and constriction of space. Albanese mentions this image in passing in her *America*. It is a central organizing principle in Gaustad's narrative of American religious history, which combines that image with a political one about empire. The story moves through "exploration," "colonization," "expansion," and "empire," and concludes with "the age of limits." See Albanese, *America*, 517; Gaustad, *Religious History of America*, vii–viii. Although the image of the frontier is associated with a thesis that is now largely discredited, taken metaphorically, its influence persists in some recent surveys. The motif appears in the text by Hudson and Corrigan as they discuss urbanization, industrialization, and the "new frontiers" facing the churches. It figures even more prominently in Peter Williams's story as he describes adjustments connected with the "end of the frontier and the rise of the city" and "old and new frontiers" associated with American Indian, African American, and new religious movements. In his interpretation, "the city was the frontier of late nineteenth century and early twentieth centuries in America." As these and other recent survey writers have used it, the frontier has become an image for various sorts of challenges that religious groups have faced as they have adapted to and shaped the American cultural landscape. See Hudson and Corrigan, *Religion in America*, 282; Williams, *America's Religions*, 227–319, 228.

23. Henry K. Rowe, *The History of Religion in the United States* (New York: Macmillan, 1924). Characters and motifs are related. As Jon Butler has noted, many influential motifs have been drawn largely from Puritanism—Calvinism, evangelicalism, declension, secularism, laicization, democracy, and American exceptionalism. See Butler, "Historiographical Heresy: Catholicism as a Model for American Religious History," in Thomas Kselman, ed., *Belief in History: Innovative Approaches to European and American Religion* (Notre Dame, Ind.: University of Notre Dame Press, 1991), 286. Butler's suggestion that we consider using six "Catholic" themes to write U.S. religious history should be given careful consideration. In a suggestive article Nathan O. Hatch has exhorted scholars to consider Methodist motifs, and I have proposed a model that derives from the history of Asian religions in America. Nathan O. Hatch, "The Puzzle of American Methodism," *Church History* 63 (June 1994): 175–89; Tweed, "Asian Religions in the United States." One midwestern Lutheran, a prominent scholar in the field, confessed to me that he too wondered where his group was in the Puritan-based story. Motifs drawn from the history of Lutheranism might reveal patterns obscured in other stories. Similarly, David Wills has made the case that race—or relations between blacks and whites—could serve as an illuminating motif. See David Wills, "The Central Themes of American Religious History: Pluralism, Puritanism, and the Encounter of Black and White," *Religion and Intellectual Life* 5 (fall 1987): 30–41. The usual cautions about the use of ideal types apply here. The types I sketch are intended as interpretive tools. I do not claim that they exhaust all possible motifs. Nor does any single narrator fit a type perfectly. Further, most narrators draw on more than one motif. Narratives, in turn, might have characteristics of more than one type. For example, it is difficult to classify Clifton E. Olmstead's narratives in terms of these four motifs. At least three distinct interpretive threads run through his story directly or indirectly. He emphasized the "adaptation" of

American religions from the "Old World" in a "New World" environment. Also, appealing to an image associated with the stages of growth of butterflies, he suggested that the "saga of American religion is one of metamorphosis." Finally, like many narrators since the 1970s, Olmstead talked about "diversity" and "diversification." To undercut any overly rigid use of my typology even further, it is helpful to note that Olmstead even introduced other motifs, such as bringing order out of disorder. See Clifton E. Olmstead, *Religion in America: Past and Present* (Englewood Cliffs, N.J.: Prentice-Hall, 1961), 3, 160.

24. The connection here between the center/periphery image and political concerns is neither accidental nor insignificant. As Jonathan Z. Smith has argued in a different context: "The language of 'center' is preeminently *political*. . . . It is a vocabulary that stems, primarily, from archaic ideologies of kingship and the royal function." Jonathan Z. Smith, *To Take Place: Toward Theory in Ritual* (Chicago: University of Chicago Press, 1987), 17. R. Laurence Moore highlighted "insiders" and "outsiders" and drew on images of a center and a periphery, although he challenged prevailing commitments about the centrality of Protestantism, in *Religious Outsiders and the Making of Americans* (New York: Oxford University Press, 1986).

25. Julia Mitchell Corbett, *Religion in America,* 1st ed. (Englewood Cliffs, N.J.: Prentice-Hall, 1990), 14. Albanese, *America,* 16–17.

26. Corbett's second edition continues to organize religions into a center and a periphery and draws on an identity/difference motif, but she abandons "mainstream" language for talk about "consensus religion." She explicitly addresses the issue in chap. 1: "The mainstream-sectarian-marginal designation used in the First Edition of this book was not wholly satisfactory. Although it does show how these religious categories relate to the larger culture, the word 'mainstream' has a normative ring, and 'sectarian' and 'marginal' have correspondingly negative overtones." Corbett, *Religion in America,* 2d ed. (1994), 10.

27. Marsden, *Religion and American Culture,* 5.

28. Martin Marty, *Pilgrims in Their Own Land: Five Hundred Years of Religion in America* (Boston: Little, Brown, 1984). Sidney E. Mead noted the significance of space and place, in *The Lively Experiment: The Shaping of Christianity in America* (New York: Harper and Row, 1963), 7. A Catholic scholar called for more attention to migration: Jay P. Dolan, "The Immigrants and Their Gods: A New Perspective in American Religious History," *Church History* 57 (March 1988): 61–72. I argue for the usefulness of the motifs of place and migration in "Asian Religions in the United States" and in the postscript of *Our Lady of the Exile: Diasporic Religion at a Cuban Catholic Shrine in Miami* (New York: Oxford University Press, forthcoming).

29. Bronislaw Malinowski, *Argonauts of the Western Pacific* (London: Routledge and Kegan Paul, 1922); Marcel Mauss, *The Gift: Forms and Functions of Exchange in Archaic Societies,* trans. Ian Cunnison (1954; New York: W. W. Norton, 1967); James Axtell, *The Invasion Within: The Contest of Cultures in Colonial North America* (New York: Oxford University Press, 1985).

30. The social "location" of the narrator—her or his class, gender, ethnicity, region, religion, and personal history—also shapes the account, often in ways that neither reader nor writer notices. For instance, all of the contributors to

this book are highly educated, middle-class academics of European descent, and no doubt that has had some influence on the shape of our essays, as have our own distinct life experiences. In this section I do not focus on the social location or personal history of narrators. Rather, I emphasize the setting of story. In my view, however, more self-consciously autobiographical reflections also have a place in historical narration, even if we do not offer them here.

31. Extending Westfall's insights, then, we might narrate a tale that attended more closely to the movements of migrant workers, missionaries, soldiers, diplomats, and tourists who temporarily or permanently crossed the national borders.

CHAPTER 1: SEXUALITY IN AMERICAN RELIGIOUS HISTORY

1. Charles W. Hackett, "Inquisition Testimonies, 1629–1671" in David H. Snow, ed., *The Native American and Spanish Colonial Experience in the Greater Southwest* (New York: Garland, 1992), 1: 209; Thomas Morton, *New English Canaan,* ed. Charles Francis Adams, Jr. (Boston: The Prince Society, 1883; reprint 1967), 279.

2. Hackett, "Inquisition Testimonies," 207–8.

3. The different outcomes are due, at least in part, to the very different relations between church and state in New England and New Spain. In the former, the opinion of church and state—as manifest in the Puritan clergy and Governors Bradford and Winthrop—was largely united against Morton, such that Morton, whose renegade singularity makes even Roger Williams pale by comparison, was expelled from New England to stand trial in England on rather flimsy charges. In the latter, the conflict between Mendizábal and the Franciscans was simply one of the more vicious instances in decades of conflict between governors and friars in New Mexico. The rivalry effectively undercut Spanish authority, both civil and ecclesiastical, vis-à-vis the Pueblo and created an opening for successful, if limited, revolt against both Spanish religion and Spanish rule. See Richard Drinnon, *Facing West: The Metaphysics of Indian-Hating and Empire-Building* (1980; New York: Schocken, 1990), 9–20; France V. Scholes, "Civil Government and Society in New Mexico in the Seventeenth Century," *New Mexico Historical Review* 10, 2 (April 1935): 71–111; on Mendizábal in particular, see France V. Scholes, "Troublous Times in New Mexico, 1659–1670," *New Mexico Historical Review* 12, 2 (April 1937): 152–64.

4. Robert Handy, *A Christian America: Protestant Hopes and Historical Realities* (New York: Oxford University Press, 1971); Martin E. Marty, *The Righteous Empire: The Protestant Experience in America* (New York: Dial, 1970); Sydney E. Ahlstrom, *A Religious History of the American People* (New Haven: Yale University Press, 1972), 506, 560, 566; Mark A. Noll, *A History of Christianity in the United States and Canada* (Grand Rapids, Mich.: Eerdmans, 1992); Winthrop Hudson and John Corrigan, *Religion in America: An Historical Account of the Development of American Religious Life,* 5th ed. (New York: Macmillan, 1992); Catherine L. Albanese, *America: Religions and Religion,* 2d ed. (Belmont, Calif.: Wadsworth, 1992), 85, 96, 98, 102, 374–75.

5. The idea that sexuality is both produced through and constituted by discourse goes back to Michel Foucault's pioneering *History of Sexuality* (New York: Pantheon, 1978). For a concise overview of the relationships between sex, gender, and sexuality as well as recent efforts to historicize sexuality, see Eve Kosofsky Sedgwick, "Gender Criticism," in Stephen Greenblatt and Giles Gunn, eds., *Redrawing the Boundaries: The Transformation of English and American Literary Studies* (New York: Modern Language Association of America, 1992), 271–302.

6. David Biale, *Eros and the Jews: From Biblical Israel to Contemporary America* (New York: Basic Books, 1992), 37–40, 46–48, 54–55; the quotations are on 59.

7. John Boswell, *Same-Sex Unions in Pre-Modern Europe* (New York: Villard Press, 1994), 108.

8. James A. Brundage, *Law, Sex, and Christian Society in Medieval Europe* (Chicago: University of Chicago Press, 1987), 128, 131.

9. Boswell, *Same-Sex Unions,* 112.

10. Brundage, *Law, Sex, and Christian Society,* 430–33; Boswell, *Same-Sex Unions,* 169, 178.

11. James A. Brundage, "Adultery and Fornication: A Study in Legal Theology," in Vern L. Bullough and James A. Brundage, *Sexual Practices and the Medieval Church* (Buffalo: Prometheus Books, 1982), 134; John Boswell, *Christianity, Social Tolerance, and Homosexuality* (Chicago: University of Chicago Press, 1980), 321–23.

12. Brundage, Appendix 3: "Survivals of Medieval Sex Law in the United States and the Western World," in *Law, Sex, and Christian Society,* 608–17.

13. Steven Ozment, *When Fathers Ruled: Family Life in Reformation Europe* (Cambridge, Mass.: Harvard University Press, 1983), 100, 215–16 nn. 4 and 6.

14. Henry Abelove, *The Evangelist of Desire: John Wesley and the Methodists* (Stanford: Stanford University Press, 1990), 49–73.

15. Roger Williams, *A Key into the Language of America,* ed. John J. Teunissen and Evelyn J. Hinz (Detroit: Wayne State University Press, 1973), 142–45, 185. Of the Massachusetts, Morton notes that "they seeme to have as much modesty as civilized people, and deserve to be applauded for it" (*New English Canaan,* 145).

16. Williams, *A Key into the Language,* 86, 203, 205–6.

17. Bert Salwen, "Indians of Southern New England and Long Island: Early Period," in *Handbook of North American Indians* (Washington, D.C.: Smithsonian Institution Press, 1984), 15:164.

18. "Declaration of Joseph Brondate, 1601," in George P. Hammond and Agapito Rey, eds. and trans., *Don Juan de Oñate: Colonizer of New Mexico, 1595–1628,* 2 vols. (Albuquerque: University of New Mexico Press, 1953), vol. 2: 627, quoted in Ramón Gutiérrez, *When Jesus Came, the Corn Mothers Went Away: Marriage, Sexuality, and Power in New Mexico, 1500–1846* (Stanford: Stanford University Press, 1991), 11–12.

19. Recent attempts by anthropologists to clarify the use of the term *ber-*

dache emphasize the distinction between the berdache as a "third gender" and homosexuality. While many berdache did engage in homosexual relations, this behavior is not understood by anthropologists as a defining feature of the role. See Charles Callender and Lee M. Kochems, "The North American Berdache," *Current Anthropology* 24, 4 (1983): 443–70.

20. Gutiérrez, *When Jesus Came*, 35.

21. Thomas Shepard, *The Sincere Convert,* in *The Works of Thomas Shepard* (New York: AMS Press, 1967), 28–29; Thomas Shepard, *The Paradoxes of Puritan Piety: Being the Autobiography and Journal of Thomas Shepard,* ed. Michael McGiffert (Amherst: University of Massachusetts Press, 1972), 98.

22. On adultery as a theme in New England piety, see Amanda Porterfield, *Female Piety in Puritan New England* (New York: Oxford University Press, 1992), 28–29.

23. Shepard, *Paradoxes,* 41, 72.

24. Ibid., 45–46.

25. Stephanie Coontz, *The Social Origins of Private Life: A History of American Families, 1600–1900* (New York: Verso, 1988), 80.

26. Gutiérrez, *When Jesus Came,* 194, 190.

27. Williams, *A Key into the Language,* 84; Morton explicitly compares the Massachusetts Indians to the wild Irish at several points—see, for example, *New English Canaan,* 134; Audrey Smedley, *Race in North America: Origin and Evolution of a Worldview* (Boulder: Westview Press, 1993), 86.

28. While there was considerable interest in dissociating conversion and Frenchification among the Jesuits missionaries in New France, their approach was not supported by the theologians at home, and "the general conceptual framework in which colonial missions operated remained officially unchanged." Cornelius Jaenen, *Friend and Foe: Aspects of French-Amerindian Cultural Contact in the Sixteenth and Seventeenth Centuries* (New York: Columbia University Press, 1976), 157.

29. William R. Hutchison, *Errand to the World: American Protestant Thought and Foreign Missions* (Chicago: University of Chicago Press, 1987), 24.

30. Thomas Shepard, *Clear Sun-shine,* 62, quoted in James Axtell, *The Invasion Within: The Contest of Cultures in Colonial North America* (New York: Oxford University Press, 1985), 169, 170.

31. Quoted in Charles Wilson Hackett and Charmion Shelby, *Revolt of the Pueblo Indians,* 2 vols. (Albuquerque: University of New Mexico Press, 1942), 2:239–40; similar testimony is offered by others, see for example, 1:23–24, 2:235, 244, 247–48, 345–46, 360–61.

32. Kwame Anthony Appiah, *In My Father's House: Africa in the Philosophy of Culture* (New York: Oxford University Press, 1992), 10–13, 37–45.

33. Smedley, *Race in North America,* 106–7.

34. Jon Butler, "Enlarging the Bonds of Christ: Slavery, Evangelicalism, and the Christianization of the White South, 1690–1790," in Leonard I. Sweet, ed., *The Evangelical Tradition in America* (Macon, Ga.: Mercer University Press, 1984), 87–112.

35. Smedley, *Race in North America,* 211.

36. George M. Fredrickson, *White Supremacy: A Comparative Study in American and South African History* (New York: Oxford University Press, 1981), 101.

37. Contrast, for example, Gary B. Nash, *Red, White, and Black: The Peoples of Early America* (Englewood Cliffs, N.J.: Prentice-Hall, 1974), 276–97, who argues that New World circumstances were sufficient to account for differences, with Smedley, *Race in North America*, who does not.

38. Smedley, *Race in North America*, 139.

39. Harriet A. Jacobs, *Incidents in the Life of a Slave Girl* (Cambridge, Mass.: Harvard University Press, 1987).

40. Ann Taves, "Spiritual Purity and Sexual Shame: Religious Themes in the Writings of Harriet Jacobs," *Church History* 56, 1 (1987): 59–72.

41. Ralph Henry Gabriel, *Elias Boudinot: Cherokee and His America* (Norman: University of Oklahoma Press, 1941), 61.

42. From the special report of the agents of the Cornwall School, 17 June 1825, quoted in ibid., 76–77. Although initially opposed, Harriet's parents came to believe (as did Harriet herself) that their daughter's desire to marry Elias Boudinot and serve with him as a missionary to the Cherokees reflected the will of God and gave their blessing. Harriet's father, writing to one of his disgruntled sons-in-law, refused to comment on what he believed to be the many unjust accusations leveled at Harriet, his wife, and himself by his relatives, sufficing it to say that "it is through pride and prejudice — that all this clamour has been raised *against Indians* and the least that can be said and done against Christian connections of any colour I believe to be best." Benjamin Gold (father of Harriet) to Herman Vaill (son-in-law), September 1825, quoted in ibid., 87–88.

43. Theda Perdue, ed., *Cherokee Editor: The Writings of Elias Boudinot* (Knoxville: University of Tennessee Press, 1983), 10.

44. Hutchison, *Errand,* 67.

45. Karen Lystra, *Searching the Heart: Women, Men, and Romantic Love in Nineteenth-Century America* (New York: Oxford University Press, 1989), 119; see especially 275 n.5, for a discussion of the "repressive hypothesis" in the history of sexuality in the Victorian era.

46. Linda Gordon, *Woman's Body, Woman's Right: A Social History of Birth Control in America* (New York: Penguin, 1978), 95–115; Janet Brodie, *Contraception and Abortion in 19th-Century America* (Ithaca: Cornell University Press, 1994), last chap.

47. Brodie; *Contraception;* Gordon, *Woman's Body,* 47–71; Lystra, *Searching the Heart,* 78; John D'Emilio and Estelle B. Freedman, *Intimate Matters: A History of Sexuality in America* (New York: Harper and Row, 1988), 173–78.

48. Lystra, *Searching the Heart,* 92, 99–100.

49. Frances E. Willard, *Glimpses of Fifty Years* (Boston: G. M. Smith, 1889), 639–42; Carolyn DeSwarte Gifford, *Writing Out My Heart: Selections from the Journal of Frances Willard, 1855–1896* (Urbana: University of Illinois Press, 1995), 115–16.

50. Relationships between Unitarian women ministers are discussed in Cynthia Grant Tucker, *Prophetic Sisterhood* (Boston: Beacon Press, 1990), and between women missionaries in Jane Hunter, *Gospel of Gentility: American*

Women Missionaries in Turn-of-the-Century China (New Haven: Yale University Press, 1984).

51. William McLoughlin, *The Meaning of Henry Ward Beecher: An Essay on the Shifting Values of Mid-Victorian America* (New York: Knopf, 1970), 4, 56. On Beecher's theology more generally, see ibid., 55–97, and Marie Caskey, *Chariot of Fire: Religion and the Beecher Family* (New Haven: Yale University Press, 1978), 208–48.

52. McLoughlin, *Meaning of Beecher,* 90–91; Lystra, *Searching the Heart,* 249.

53. McLoughlin, *Meaning of Beecher,* 96 (emphasis added).

54. Ibid., 92–96.

55. On the sacralization of the home, see Colleen McDannell, *The Christian Home in Victorian America* (Bloomington: Indiana University Press, 1986), 45–49. On the feminization of images of Jesus, see Ann Douglas, *The Feminization of American Culture* (New York: Knopf, 1977).

56. Jenny Franchot has suggested that liberal Protestant efforts to "familiarize and feminize the Deity were prevented from becoming eroticized by the expulsion of bodily excesses onto Catholic spirituality," in *Roads to Rome* (Berkeley: University of California Press, 1994), 124. We might generalize this to suggest that it was the displacement of unchecked sexuality onto others that allowed Protestants to feminize their images of Jesus and God and sacralize their images of the home and romantic love without eroticizing them.

57. On Catholicism, see Ray Allen Billington, *The Protestant Crusade, 1800–1860* (New York: Rinehart and Co., 1938), 361–67; and Franchot, *Roads to Rome.* On nineteenth-century Indian captivity narratives, see June Namias, *White Captives* (Chapel Hill: University of North Carolina Press, 1993), 97–112. On Mormonism, see Charles A. Cannon, "The Awesome Power of Sex: The Polemical Campaign against Mormon Polygamy," *Pacific Historical Review* 43, 1 (1974): 61–82 and Leonard J. Arrington and Jon Haupt, "Intolerable Zion: The Image of Mormonism in Nineteenth Century American Literature," *Western Humanities Review* 22, 3 (1968): 243–60. On alcoholic husbands, see Ruth Bordin, *Women and Temperance: The Quest for Power and Liberty* (Philadelphia: Temple University Press, 1981), and Elizabeth Pleck, *Domestic Tyranny: The Making of Social Policy against Family Violence from Colonial Times to the Present* (New York: Oxford University Press, 1987).

58. Gustive O. Larson, *The "Americanization" of Utah for Statehood* (San Marino, Calif.: Huntington Library, 1971), 56. The Republican party platform of 1856 claimed that it was the "duty of Congress to prohibit in the territories those twin relics of barbarism—Polygamy and Slavery" (Cannon, "Awesome Power," 62).

59. Harriet Beecher Stowe's preface to T. E. H. Stenhouse, *Tell It All* (Hartford, Conn., 1874), quoted in Cannon, "Awesome Power," 62; Frances Willard, "Introduction," to Jenny Froiseth, *The Women of Mormonism; Or, The Story of Polygamy as Told by the Victims Themselves* (Detroit: G. G. Paine, 1882), v–xv; *Springfield Union* (Mass.), quoted in Larson, *"Americanization" of Utah,* 207.

60. *Deseret News,* 20 Nov. 1878, 8–9, quoted in ibid., 88; *New York Herald,* quoted in ibid., 68–69.

61. Jill Mulvay Derr, " 'Strength in Our Union': The Making of Mormon Sisterhood," in Maureen Ursenbach Beecher and Lavinia Fielding Anderson, eds., *Sisters in Spirit: Mormon Women in Historical and Cultural Perspective* (Urbana: University of Illinois Press, 1987), 179; Larson, *"Americanization" of Utah,* 88, 212; Joan Smyth Iversen, "A Debate on the American Home: The Antipolygamy Controversy, 1880–1890," in John C. Fout and Maura S. Tantillo, eds., *American Sexual Politics* (Chicago: University of Chicago Press, 1993), 123–40.

62. D'Emilio and Freedman, *Intimate Matters,* 85–108.

63. Rebecca Latimer Felton, Newspaper clipping, Felton Papers, Hargrett Rare Book and Manuscript Library, University of Georgia Libraries, Athens, Georgia.

64. Evelyn Higginbotham, *Righteous Discontent: The Women's Movement in the Black Baptist Church, 1880–1920* (Cambridge, Mass.: Harvard University Press, 1993), 202.

65. M. E. Billings, *Crimes of Preachers* (1881; New York: Truthseeker Pub., 1883), 75. On the Avery trial, see David R. Kasserman, *Fall River Outrage* (Philadelphia: University of Pennsylvania Press, 1986).

66. Altina L. Waller, *Reverend Beecher and Mrs. Tilton: Sex and Class in Victorian America* (Amherst: University of Massachusetts Press, 1982); Ann-Janine Morey builds on Waller's account of the incident in *Religion and Sexuality in American Literature* (New York: Cambridge University Press, 1992), 104–40; and Marie Fortune compares Beecher and contemporary clergymen based on Waller's account, in *Is Nothing Sacred?* (San Francisco: Harper and Row, 1989). Richard Wightman Fox, "Intimacy on Trial: Cultural Meanings of the Beecher-Tilton Affair," in Richard Wightman Fox and T. J. Jackson Lears, eds., *The Power of Culture: Critical Essays in American History* (Chicago: University of Chicago Press, 1993), 113, 130–31. There is also general agreement that this sort of passionate intimacy did not exist within either the Beecher or the Tilton marriage and did exist for some time between Henry and Theodore as well as between Henry and Elizabeth. Laughter apparently erupted in the courtroom when Beecher testified that at the end of one intense encounter with the Tiltons, "I kissed him and he kissed me, and I kissed his wife and she kissed me, and I believe they kissed each other" (Fox, "Intimacy," 116).

67. Higginbotham, *Righteous Discontent,* 185–228; David Wills, "Womanhood and Domesticity in the A.M.E. Tradition: The Influence of Daniel Alexander Payne," in David Wills and Richard Newman, eds., *Black Apostles at Home and Abroad* (Boston: G. K. Hall, 1982).

68. Higginbotham, *Righteous Discontent,* 192–97.

69. Alfreda M. Duster, ed., *Crusade for Justice: The Autobiography of Ida B. Wells* (Chicago: University of Chicago Press, 1970), 43–45.

70. Ida B. Wells, *A Red Record: Lynchings in the United States* (Chicago: Donohue and Henneberry, 1895), 10–11; Jacquelyn Dowd Hall, *Revolt against Chivalry: Jessie Daniel Ames and the Women's Campaign against Lynching*

(New York: Columbia University Press, 1979), 203–6; Martha Hodes, "The Sexualization of Reconstruction Politics: White Women and Black Men in the South after the Civil War," in *American Sexual Politics*, 59–74.

71. Peter Gardella, *Innocent Ecstasy: How Christianity Gave America an Ethic of Sexual Pleasure* (New York: Oxford University Press, 1985), 36.

72. Ibid., 9.

73. Ibid., 18–19.

74. Francis P. Kenrick, *Theologia Moralis*, 3 vols. (Philadelphia: Eugenium Cummiskey, 1841–43), 3:319, quoted in Gardella, *Innocent Ecstasy*, 36.

75. Gardella, *Innocent Ecstasy*, 37.

76. Lawrence Foster, *Religion and Sexuality: Three American Communal Experiments of the Nineteenth Century* (New York: Oxford University Press, 1981), 144–45, 198–99.

77. Ibid., 208–11.

78. Jan Shipps, *Mormonism: The Story of a New Religious Tradition* (Urbana: University of Illinois Press, 1985), 125.

79. Quoted in Biale, *Eros and the Jews*, 148.

80. Ibid., 141–42; the quotation is from 144.

81. Ann Braude, "The Jewish Woman's Encounter with American Culture," in Rosemary Ruether and Rosemary Keller, eds., *Women and Religion in America*, 3 vols. (San Francisco: Harper and Row, 1981–86), 1:150–59.

82. Biale, *Eros and the Jews*, 161.

83. Ellen Chesler, *Woman of Valor: Margaret Sanger and the Birth Control Movement in America* (New York: Simon and Schuster, 1992), 208, 211–13, 320–21; the quotation is from 208.

84. Ibid., 318–20.

85. William G. Cole, "Protestantism and Sex," in Albert Ellis and Albert Abarbanel, eds., *The Encyclopedia of Sexual Behavior*, 2 vols. (New York: Hawthorn Books, 1961), 2:887.

86. Robert Blair Kaiser, *The Politics of Sex and Religion: A Case History in the Development of Doctrine, 1962–1984* (Kansas City, Mo.: Leaven Press, 1985), 1–6.

87. David J. Garrow, *Liberty and Sexuality: The Right to Privacy and the Making of Roe v. Wade* (New York: Macmillan, 1994), 196–269.

88. As late as the mid-twentieth century, thirty-one states had laws forbidding interracial marriage. By the 1960s, seventeen states, all in the South, still prohibited interracial marriage. When a Virginia court found an interracial couple guilty of miscegenation in 1967, the judge stated in his opinion that "Almighty God created the races white, black, yellow, malay and red, and He placed them on separate continents. And but for the interference with His arrangement there would be no cause for such marriages. The fact that He separated the races shows that He did not intend for the races to mix." William B. Rubenstein, ed., *Lesbians, Gay Men, and the Law* (New York: New Press, 1993), 391–93. For a discussion of twentieth-century religious reactions to intermarriage, see Joseph R. Washington, Jr., *Marriage in Black and White* (Boston: Beacon Press, 1972).

89. Technically, Judge Levinson remanded the case back to a lower court where the state is (as of this writing) required to show a compelling interest in precluding same-sex marriage before the current law can be upheld. Ken Kobayashi [Courts Writer], "Analysis," *Honolulu Advertiser,* 7 May 1993.

90. There has been considerable change at the state level outside the South, much of it precipitated by the decriminalization of all sexual activity between consenting adults in the model penal code formulated in the fifties. Rubenstein, *Lesbians,* 136 n.1.

91. Ibid., 135, 143.

92. James Davidson Hunter, *Culture Wars: The Struggle to Define America* (New York: Basic Books, 1991), 95.

93. Ibid., 89–106.

CHAPTER 2: RITUAL SITES IN THE
NARRATIVE OF AMERICAN RELIGION

1. Robert Bellah's classic article, "Civil Religion in America," first appeared in *Daedalus* in 1967; for easy access to it see Russell E. Richey and Donald G. Jones, *American Civil Religion* (New York: Harper, 1974), 21–44. Bellah's work was foreshadowed by W. Lloyd Warner in *The Family of God: A Symbolic Study of Christian Life in America* (New Haven: Yale University Press, 1961). Such studies have been amplified by, among others, Conrad Cherry's documentary history *God's New Israel* (Englewood Cliffs, N.J.: Prentice-Hall, 1971), and Catherine L. Albanese's *Sons of the Fathers: The Civil Religion of the American Revolution* (Philadelphia: Temple University Press, 1976). See also the discussion of civil religion in John F. Wilson's *Public Religion in America* (Philadelphia: Temple University Press, 1979). In addition, Charles Reagan Wilson has identified the southern version of civil religion, the "Religion of the Lost Cause," in *Baptized in Blood: The Religion of the Lost Cause 1865–1920* (Athens: University of Georgia Press, 1980); Sean Wilentz has written about working-class versions of the civic rituals in *Chants Democratic: New York City and the Rise of the American Working Class 1788–1850* (New York: Oxford University Press, 1984); see also Roy Rosenzweig, *Eight Hours for What We Will: Workers and Leisure in an Industrial City* (New York: Cambridge University Press, 1983). Monographs on ritual in the American setting go back to Ronald L. Grimes, *Symbol and Conquest: Public Ritual and Drama in Santa Fe, New Mexico* (Ithaca: Cornell University Press, 1976). Studies that feature ritual prominently in historical contexts include Tamar [Sandra S. Sizer] Frankiel, *Gospel Hymns and Social Religion: The Rhetoric of Nineteenth Century Revivalism* (Philadelphia: Temple University Press, 1978); Robert Anthony Orsi, *The Madonna of 115th Street: Faith and Community in Italian Harlem, 1880–1950* (New Haven: Yale University Press, 1985); Susan Davis, *Parades and Power: Street Theater in Nineteenth Century Philadelphia* (Philadelphia: Temple University Press, 1986); Rhys Isaac, *Worlds of Experience: Communities in Colonial Virginia* (Williamsburg, Va.: Colonial Williamsburg Foundation, 1987); David Hall, *Worlds of Wonder, Days of Judgment: Popular Religious Belief in*

Early New England (New York: Knopf, 1989); Leigh Schmidt, *Holy Fairs: Scottish Communions and American Revivals in the Early Modern Period* (Princeton: Princeton University Press, 1989); David Glassberg, *American Historical Pageantry: The Uses of Tradition in the Early Twentieth Century* (Chapel Hill: University of North Carolina Press, 1990); and A. Gregory Schneider, *The Way of the Cross Leads Home: The Domestication of American Methodism* (Bloomington: Indiana University Press, 1993).

2. Among anthropologists, Clifford Geertz's "Religion as a Cultural System," in M. Banton, ed., *Anthropological Approaches to the Study of Religion* (London: Lavistock Publications, 1966), and his *Islam Observed: Religious Development in Morocco and Indonesia* (New Haven: Yale University Press, 1968) were highly influential among scholars of religion, as was Victor Turner's *The Ritual Process* (Chicago: Aldine, 1969). Recent theorists have gone considerably beyond these works, however; see, in particular, Jonathan Z. Smith, *To Take Place: Toward Theory in Ritual* (Chicago: University of Chicago Press, 1987); Catherine Bell, *Ritual Theory, Ritual Practice* (New York: Oxford University Press, 1992); and Thomas Csordas, *The Sacred Self: A Cultural Phenomenology of Charismatic Healing* (Berkeley: University of California Press, 1994).

3. Clifford Geertz has been a leading figure among anthropologists who use drama as a central metaphor for ritual. Since his 1966 article, "Religion as a Cultural System," ritual has been central to his analyses; his fieldwork in Indonesian culture has often used dramatic cultural performances as central foci for analysis. An example in an American setting is Grimes, *Symbol and Conquest*. Bell, however, has launched significant criticisms against using the metaphor of drama, and its extension in performance theory, to understand ritual. See Bell, *Ritual Theory*, 42–43. For our purposes here, the metaphor is meant to suggest the power of embodied action; certainly it should not be taken to mean that rituals require an explicit physical frame such as a stage, but neither does the focus on embodiment exclude verbalizations in ritual. Ritual use of language is distinctive, however. It is often repetitive or rhythmic (for example, repeated "Amens"), takes the form of performative utterances (such as the "I do" in marriage vows), or relies heavily on formulaic frameworks (like the Puritan "jeremiad" as a sermonic form).

4. See especially Bell, *Ritual Theory*, for the emphasis on embodiment and the term *practices* (from Pierre Bourdieu); and Csordas, *Sacred Self* (who also draws on Bourdieu as well as Merleau-Ponty), for the emphasis on orientation and open-ended processes.

5. For an excellent discussion of this point, see Bell, *Ritual Theory*, chap. 5: "The Ritual Body."

6. Liminality was most fully described, with its paradoxical structures of power/powerlessness, by Victor Turner in his important work *The Ritual Process*, adapted from the threefold pattern of initiation outlined by Arnold Van Gennep in his classic book, *The Rites of Passage* (1909; London: Routledge and Kegan Paul, 1960).

7. I use "imagine" here in line with Csordas's interpretation of imagery as

a self-process that orients the person in relation to different aspects, or "sub-selves," that exist in memory (Csordas, *Sacred Self*, chaps. 4–6). The imaginative process behind the African-American mandala may bear some resemblance to the charismatic ritual of "healing of memories," although the latter is more therapeutically inclined.

8. For an excellent discussion, see James Axtell, "The White Indians of Colonial America" and "The Scholastic Philosophy of the Wilderness," in *The European and the Indian: Essays in the Ethnohistory of Colonial North America* (New York: Oxford University Press, 1981). On the latter point Axtell notes, for example, that Cotton Mather complained people were learning three vices from the Indians: idleness, lying, and indulgence toward children, the latter of which he called "an epidemical miscarriage of the country" (ibid., 160, 281). Among scholars of early North American culture contact, Axtell treats religion quite fully; his results, however, have been questioned by some Native American scholars. Therefore, in addition to his work, one should look at Karen O. Kupperman, *Settling with the Indians: The Meeting of English and Indian Cultures in America, 1580–1640* (Totowa, N.J.: Rowman and Littlefield, 1980); Wilbur Jacobs, *Dispossessing the American Indian* (1972; Norman: University of Oklahoma Press, 1985); and Jack D. Forbes, *A World Ruled by Cannibals: The Wetiko Disease of Aggression, Violence, and Imperialism* (Pittsburgh: Duquesne University Press, 1979). Many other scholars have examined Native American and European assumptions; for sources that include vivid examples from primary texts, see Gordon Brotherston, *Image of the New World: The American Continent Portrayed in Native Texts* (London: Thames and Hudson, 1979), and Ronald Wright, *Stolen Continents: The Americas through Indian Eyes since 1492* (Boston: Houghton Mifflin, 1992).

9. Axtell, *European and Indian*, 119.

10. A particularly vivid portrait of the demands on Puritans for constant devotion, beyond the conversion experience, appears in Charles Hambrick-Stowe, *The Practice of Piety: Puritan Devotional Disciplines in Seventeenth Century New England* (Chapel Hill: University of North Carolina Press, 1982); and Hall, *Worlds of Wonder,* particularly chap. 1 on literacy and the Bible, and chap. 4 for a discussion of confession.

11. Axtell, *European and Indian*, 122. Hall, *Worlds of Wonder*, 70. As many commentators have observed in comparing Protestant to Catholic ritual attitudes, focus on the Word reduced the use of the several senses, requiring containment of the body rather than symbolizing or dramatizing emotion and sensation outwardly. "Rational" discourse was presumed to be the model. For an early discussion with reference to America see Warner, *The Family of God,* chap. 3: "The Protestant Revolt and Symbolism."

12. The Jesuits created a few separate communities, called "reserves," but they also worked by developing a Christian faction within the native village, with the intent of getting the Christians into positions of influence. There, baptism was often deferred longer than among the Franciscans, until the convert was believed to be strong in the faith so he or she would be able to resist the contempt of former fellows in the village (Axtell, *European and Indian*, 69–71).

13. Reports suggest that Jesuits used punishment only rarely, whereas Franciscans used it fairly regularly depending on the policy of the senior missionary. The Jesuit model was different, of course, in that the priests frequently lived within the community and sometimes accepted certain Native American customs in order to win converts.

14. On the notion of civility, see Richard P. Gildrie, *The Profane, the Civil, and the Godly: The Reformation of Manners in Orthodox New England, 1679–1749* (University Park: Pennsylvania State University Press, 1994). On these developments see also Hall, *Worlds of Wonder.* For a recent treatment of the eighteenth-century revolution in consumer demand and the public media in relation to revivalism, see Frank Lambert's *"Pedlar in Divinity": George Whitefield and the Transatlantic Revivals, 1737–1770* (Princeton: Princeton University Press, 1994).

15. Schmidt, *Holy Fairs,* 78, 91.

16. This line of thinking suggests several areas of investigation. For example, what were the patterns of ritual in local revivals, where people underwent radical experiences not while "on pilgrimage" but in the familiar space of their own home church? It may be significant that, as Edwards records in his "Narratives of Surprising Conversions," he sometimes has to *go out* to visit a person in his or her home who is fainting, catatonic, or talking wildly. Clearly, as revivals proceed, the Methodist class meeting and the Presbyterian conference meeting are means by which the laity promote the revival outside the realm of the public worship service, often unobserved by the eye of the minister. The nature of the preachers' role in the revival also deserves more investigation. Alan Heimert, in his seminal *Religion and the American Mind* (Cambridge, Mass.: Harvard University Press, 1966), chap. 4, held that changes in preaching to a more straightforward, forceful style full of dramatic images and impressive metaphors were the hinge of the Great Awakening. But more investigation is needed to relate this style to other specific changes in ritualization.

17. For comparison, see Marilyn J. Westerkamp, *Triumph of the Laity: Scots-Irish Piety and the Great Awakening, 1625–1760* (New York: Oxford University Press, 1988), 211. On the strength of localism of colonial society up to the American Revolution, see the classic studies of Michael Zuckerman, *Peaceable Kingdoms: New England Towns in the Eighteenth Century* (New York: Knopf, 1970), and Bernard Bailyn, *The Ideological Origins of the American Revolution* (Cambridge, Mass.: Harvard University Press, 1967). As Heimert pointed out, however, the revivalistic Calvinists were developing a concept of the harmony of different "modes" of religion which eventually allowed them to conceive of an idea of the "common good" or the "general will of the community" (Heimert, *Religion and the American Mind,* 17–18, 402–5). For the strengthening of local churches in the Second Great Awakening, see Terry D. Bilhartz, *Urban Religion and the Second Great Awakening: Church and Society in Early National Baltimore* (Rutherford, N.J.: Fairleigh Dickinson University Press, 1986), 140.

18. Bilhartz, *Urban Religion,* 75.

19. Scholars have long suggested that the First Great Awakening contributed to a heightened white Protestant awareness, tied to an inherited Puritan sense

of millennial mission; see especially Heimert, *Religion and the American Mind,* 403–5, and Westerkamp, *Triumph of the Laity,* 212–13. The John and Abigail Adams correspondence is quoted by Sacvan Bercovitch in "The Typology of America's Mission," *American Quarterly* 30, 2 (summer 1978): 150. For further development see Bercovitch's *The American Jeremiad* (Madison: University of Wisconsin Press, 1978). See also Bercovitch's *The Rites of Assent: Transformations in the Symbolic Construction of America* (New York: Routledge, 1993). For further discussion of the definition of new symbols in revolutionary times, see Albanese, *Sons of the Fathers.*

20. Bilhartz, *Urban Religion,* 140.

21. For a sense of the range of experiences of bodily action in the frontier revivals (many familiar from the First Great Awakening), see Paul K. Conkin, *Cane Ridge: America's Pentecost* (Madison: University of Wisconsin Press, 1990), 109–31. Voluntary practices included loud singing, exhorting, hand shaking, engaging in prayer matches and mass confessions, shouting, dancing; involuntary ones included falling, rolling, jerking, barking, "holy laughter," and having visions.

22. Not all ecstasy is revolutionary. If it becomes a criterion for group membership or status, it can be conservative, like the Puritan conversion experience or later Pentecostal "gifts of the Spirit." Emotional experiences in general need a different approach from their usual treatment as catharses. In my view, emotions are aspects of the ritualized body just as much as standing or kneeling, or chanting or singing in prayer. Examples include such varied expressions as family mourning rites, the agony of the mystic, the weeping crowds at the elevation of the host in the Roman Catholic Eucharist, or hymns that bring tears to the eyes. Emotions in such contexts are usually not under voluntary control and may represent some slight degree of dissociation. However, they can become patterned responses through the establishment and repetition of ritual acts that evoke them.

23. See for example Nathan O. Hatch, *The Democratization of American Christianity* (New Haven: Yale University Press, 1989). Meanwhile, as democratic ideology grew in popularity and the idea of church-state separation took hold, most states disestablished their churches. As Roger Finke argues elsewhere in this volume, such "deregulation" is a powerful catalyst in opening up new religious possibilities.

24. Walter F. Pitts, *Old Ship of Zion: The Afro-Baptist Ritual in the African Diaspora* (New York: Oxford University Press, 1993), especially chaps. 3 and 4; Donald G. Mathews, *Religion in the Old South* (Chicago: University of Chicago Press, 1977), 215.

25. John F. Watson, quoted in Hatch, *Democratization,* 155.

26. For treatment of hymns and testimonials as ritualized expressions, see Frankiel, *Gospel Hymns.* The power of testimony is still not well understood, but accounts of revivals often witness to the domino effect, so to speak, of testimonials. For example, as Paul Conkin relates, Barton Stone's telling a story of revivals, "as so often before . . . led to an almost immediate eruption of physical exercises roughly similar to those he described" (*Cane Ridge,* 70).

27. An older but still helpful treatment of the "prophet" is Kenelm Bur-

ridge's *New Heaven, New Earth* (New York: Schocken, 1969), which discusses millennial movements; his *Mambu: A Study of Melanesian Cargo Movements* (1960; New York: Harper, 1970) is a monograph that describes such a prophet.

28. See, for example, Louis J. Kern, *An Ordered Love* (Chapel Hill: University of North Carolina Press, 1981), and Lawrence Foster, *Religion and Sexuality: Three American Communal Experiments of the Nineteenth Century* (New York: Oxford University Press, 1981). On the Seventh-day Adventists, see in particular Ronald L. Numbers, *Prophetess of Health: A Study of Ellen G. White* (New York: Harper, 1976), and Malcolm Bull and Keith Lockhart, *Seeking a Sanctuary: Seventh-Day Adventism and the American Dream* (San Francisco: Harper and Row, 1989), especially chap. 10. On Mormons, see Klaus J. Hansen, *Mormonism and the American Experience* (Chicago: University of Chicago Press, 1981), especially 104, where he compares Mormons with Shakers and Oneida Perfectionists. On medicine and health, see Robert Fuller, *Alternative Medicine and American Religious Life* (New York: Oxford University Press, 1989).

29. Michael Barkun notes that this same period generated attempts to isolate and rehabilitate social deviants through institutions: the asylum, the penitentiary, the almshouse, the orphanage. Michael Barkun, *Crucible of the Millennium: The Burned-Over District of Western New York in the 1840s* (Syracuse: Syracuse University Press, 1986).

30. A significant study that relates the development of American Methodism to this ideology is Schneider, *The Way of the Cross Leads Home*. An earlier work that connects domesticity to hymnody is Frankiel, *Gospel Hymns* (1978). Among others, see Mary P. Ryan, *Empire of the Mother: American Writing about Domesticity, 1830 to 1860* (New York: Haworth Press, 1982); Colleen McDannell, *The Christian Home in Victorian America, 1840–1900* (Bloomington: Indiana University Press, 1986); Barbara Leslie Epstein, *The Politics of Domesticity: Women, Evangelism, and Temperance in Nineteenth Century America* (Middletown, Conn.: Wesleyan University Press, 1981). For a Roman Catholic comparison, see Ann Taves, *The Household of Faith: Roman Catholic Devotions in Mid-Nineteenth Century America* (Notre Dame, Ind.: Notre Dame University Press, 1986). Studies of Jewish domestic practice and ideology would probably reveal a great deal about assimilation, or resistance to it, among various groups of American Jews. A seminal treatment of "domesticity" as a category for understanding American religion, and particularly the evangelical tradition, is Ann Douglas, *The Feminization of American Culture* (New York: Alfred A. Knopf, 1977), although Douglas has been criticized for seeing "feminization" as a negative development; see the essay on gender by Ann Braude in this volume. Mark Carnes has suggested that many upwardly mobile middle-class men reacted against the domestication of American religion by creating their own strictly male rituals and even a perception of deity that was more powerful and less intimate. See Mark Carnes, *Secret Ritual and Manhood in Victorian America* (New Haven: Yale University Press, 1989).

31. Among recent treatments, see John A. Andrew III, *From Revivals to Removal: Jeremiah Evarts, the Cherokee Nation, and the Search for the Soul of America* (Athens: University of Georgia Press, 1992). Andrew examines the dy-

namics of revivals and change in sensibility, followed by the move toward reform societies and missionary work as a way of generating proper feeling and behavior.

32. Mathews, *Religion in the Old South*, 26. As Mathews has noted, southern Methodists were somewhat different and perhaps more "northern," with little of the Baptist interest in theological disputations and forming tight, closed communities. More open to communion with other Christians, they focused on intrachurch structure and morality.

33. For an examination of similar rituals in the former Confederate regions, see Wilson, *Baptized in Blood*.

34. Similar movements, particularly in the arts and literature, have been identified as "anti-modernist" by T. J. Jackson Lears in *No Place of Grace: Antimodernism and the Transformation of American Culture, 1880–1920* (New York: Pantheon, 1981). Americans' ambivalent relationship to nature has been discussed in depth by Catherine L. Albanese in *Nature Religion in America: From the Algonkian Indians to the New Age* (Chicago: University of Chicago Press, 1990). The attempt to put a new face on American history is suggested by Rodman Wanamaker's proposal to put an American Indian statue in New York harbor next to the Statue of Liberty. Since the "vanishing race" was no longer a threat to civilization, they could now be honored. The Educational Bureau of Wanamaker's Clothing Store (Philadelphia) also sponsored filming expeditions among Native Americans. See Manfred E. Keune, "An Immodest Proposal: A Memorial to the American Indian," *Journal of American Culture* 1 (1978): 788–86.

35. See Neal Gabler, *An Empire of Their Own: How the Jews Invented Hollywood* (New York: Crown, 1988).

36. As Robert Orsi has shown, Italian ritual dramas eventually became involved even in papal politics and opposing "Americanism" within the church. See Orsi, *Madonna of 115th Street*. On related issues, see also R. Laurence Moore, "Managing Catholic Success in a Protestant Empire," in *Religious Outsiders and the Making of Americans* (New York: Oxford University Press, 1986).

37. For example, Isaac Wise's early reforms, which became models for others, included eliminating from the liturgy some medieval poems and using German and English hymns, abolishing the sale of synagogue honors, sitting during the Torah reading, introducing a (mixed) choir and, a little later, the family pew. Wise at first adopted the latter for pragmatic reasons, so that his new congregation would not have to spend money on remodeling the church building they bought in 1851 (and similarly with the first synagogue in New York to have mixed seating in 1854). However, this aspect soon became a mark of "modernity" and equality with Christianity in Judaism's presumed attitudes toward women. For discussion, see Jonathan D. Sarna, "Mixed Seating in the American Synagogue," in Jack Wertheimer, ed., *The American Synagogue: A Sanctuary Transformed* (New York: Cambridge University Press, 1987), 23.

38. Russia's "modernization" program in the mid-nineteenth century had attempted to lure Jews into Jewish, government-supported schools which allowed Jewish education but also taught secular subjects. The bitter struggles

between traditional and "enlightened" Jews over this subject, together with the clear trend toward assimilation among students who went to these schools, had established firm attitudes among eastern Europeans about mixing their culture with that of non-Jews.

39. Despite the emphasis on mind, however, it was still necessary to discipline the body to its nonexistence, and certain of the positive thinkers developed exercises for the ear and eye, senses of taste, touch, and smell, as well as for nerves and paying attention.

40. Donald Meyer, in *The Positive Thinkers: Religion as Popular Psychology from Mary Baker Eddy to Oral Roberts* (New York: Pantheon, 1980), 165, cites Frank Haddock's *Power of Will* (1907) as an example. For general treatments of the metaphysical movements, see Stephen Gottschalk, *The Emergence of Christian Science in American Religious Life* (Berkeley: University of California Press, 1973); Robert Peel, *Christian Science: Its Encounter with American Culture* (New York: Holt, 1958); J. Stillson Judah, *History and Philosophy of the Metaphysical Movements in America* (Philadelphia: Westminster, 1967); and Charles Braden, *Spirits in Rebellion* (Dallas: Southern Methodist University Press, 1963). On Buddhism in America, see Thomas A. Tweed, *The American Encounter with Buddhism, 1844–1912: Victorian Culture and the Limits of Dissent* (Bloomington: Indiana University Press, 1992). Another important related movement was Theosophy, which had a few communities in America. See Judah's *History and Philosophy;* Bruce F. Campbell, *Ancient Wisdom Revived: A History of the Theosophical Movement* (Berkeley: University of California Press, 1980); Emmett A. Greenwalt, "The Point Loma Community in California 1897–1942," Ph.D. dissertation, University of California, Los Angeles, 1949; and Robert V. Hine, *California's Utopian Colonies* (San Marino, Calif.: Huntington Library, 1953).

41. For a treatment of this dimension, see the chapter on Nazarene founder Phineas Bresee in Tamar [Sandra S.] Frankiel, *California's Spiritual Frontiers: Religious Alternatives in Anglo-Protestantism 1850–1915* (Berkeley: University of California Press, 1988).

42. A recent work suggests the connection of certain key figures in Pentecostalism to the mesmeric tradition; see McDannell, *Christian Home.*

43. As T. J. Jackson Lears has pointed out in *No Place of Grace,* gender relations had already been changing since the turn of the century. Women were advocating new feminine models from the suffragette to the outdoors type; the diaphragm was invented, which aided birth control. For a summary of the Jazz Age influences, see Itabari Njeri, "Trickle-Down Culture," *Los Angeles Times Magazine,* 28 August 1994, 53–54, citing jazz critic Stanley Crouch. Jill Watts has commented on similar themes in her article on the popular 1936 film *Klondike Annie:* "Constructions of Western Religion on the Screen: Mae West as Sister Annie," presented at the Seminar on American Dreams, Western Images, William Andrews Clark Memorial Library, University of California, Los Angeles, May 1994.

44. Hasidism, a movement within traditional Orthodoxy, had emerged in eastern Europe in the middle and late eighteenth century, and by the nineteenth

was a major force in many European towns. Thus it was contemporary with Methodism, and its emphasis on intimate groupings of followers, self-examination, the importance of song and prayer, and joy in worshiping and serving God indeed bears many similarities to Methodism and other Protestant forms of pietism.

CHAPTER 3: WOMEN'S HISTORY *IS* AMERICAN RELIGIOUS HISTORY

1. I would like to thank members of the Comparative Women's History Seminar at the University of Minnesota, especially Riv-Ellen Prell and M. J. Maynes, and members of the American Religion and Culture Workshop at Princeton University, especially Marie Griffith, as well as Colleen McDannell for helpful comments on drafts of this essay and Michael McNally for research assistance. Tom Tweed provided inspiration, insight, persistence, and expert editing through many drafts.

2. Robert G. Pope, *The Half-Way Covenant: Church Membership in Puritan New England* (Princeton: Princeton University Press, 1969), chap. 8; Mary Maples Dunn, "Saints and Sisters: Congregational and Quaker Women in the Early Colonial Period," and Gerald Moran, " 'Sisters' in Christ: Women and the Church in Seventeenth-Century New England," both in Janet Wilson James, ed., *Women in American Religion* (Philadelphia: University of Pennsylvania Press, 1980); Richard D. Shiels, "The Feminization of American Congregationalism, 1730–1835," *American Quarterly* 39 (1981): 45–62; Donald Mathews, *Religion in the Old South* (Chicago: University of Chicago Press, 1977), 47; Mary Ryan, *The Cradle of the Middle Class: The Family in Oneida County, New York, 1790–1865* (New York: Cambridge University Press, 1983), 75–83; C. Eric Lincoln and Lawrence H. Mamiya, *The Black Church in the African-American Experience* (Durham, N. C.: Duke University Press, 1990).

3. Because the Catholic Church counts as members all who receive baptism, its membership in the United States has the same proportion of females as the general population, 51 percent. This figure tells little about involvement with or sustenance of the church, so categories such as vocations and participation in religious practice are more useful. Larger female majorities in these categories are documented in Mary J. Oates, "Organized Voluntarism: The Catholic Sisters in Massachusetts, 1870–1940," in *Women in American Religion,* and idem, "Organizing for Service: Challenges to Community Life and Work Decisions in Catholic Sisterhoods, 1850–1940," in Wendy E. Chmielewski, Louis J. Kern, and Marlyn Klee-Hartzell, eds., *Women in Spiritual and Communitarian Societies in the United States* (Syracuse: Syracuse University Press, 1993); Robert Anthony Orsi, " 'He Keeps Me Going': Women's Devotion to Saint Jude and the Dialectics of Gender in American Catholicism, 1929–1965," in Thomas Kselman, ed., *Belief in History* (Notre Dame, Ind.: University of Notre Dame Press, 1991).

4. Robert Wuthnow and William Lehrman, "Religion: Inhibitor or Facilitator of Political Involvement among Women?" in Louise A. Tilly and Patricia Gurin, eds. *Women, Politics, and Change* (New York: Russell Sage Foundation,

1990), 300–322; Rodney Stark and William Sims Bainbridge, *The Future of Religion: Secularization, Revival, and Cult Formation* (Berkeley: University of California Press, 1985); Roger Finke and Rodney Stark, *The Churching of America, 1776–1990* (New Brunswick, N.J.: Rutgers University Press, 1992), 33–35, 66–71; Cedric Cowing, "Sex and Preaching in the Great Awakening," *American Quarterly,* 30 (fall 1968): 624–44; Barbara E. Lacey, "Gender, Piety, and Secularization in Connecticut Religion, 1720–1775," *Journal of Social History* 24 (summer 1991): 799–821.

5. Beverly Thomas McCloud, "African-American Muslim Women," in Yvonne Haddad, ed., *The Muslims of America* (New York: Oxford University Press, 1991), 177–87; Marshall Sklare, *Conservative Judaism: An American Religious Movement* (Glencoe, Ill.: Free Press, 1955), 86–88; Leon A. Jicks, *The Americanization of the Synagogue, 1820–1870* (Hanover, N. H.: Brandeis University Press, 1976).

6. Marcia K. Hermansen, "Two-Way Acculturation: Muslim Women in America between Individual Choice (Liminality) and Community Affiliation (Communitas)," in *Muslims of America,* 199; Rita Gross, *Buddhism after Patriarchy: A Feminist History, Analysis and Reconstruction of Buddhism* (Albany: SUNY Press, 1993); Anne Carolyn Klein, *Meeting the Great Bliss Queen: Buddhists, Feminists, and the Art of the Self* (Boston: Beacon Press, 1995). See also Thomas A. Tweed, *The American Encounter with Buddhism, 1844–1912* (Bloomington: Indiana University Press, 1992), 85–87.

7. Many studies support similar findings for Europe. See, for example, Suzanne Desan, *Reclaiming the Sacred: Lay Religion and Popular Politics in Revolutionary France* (Ithaca: Cornell University Press), 210–15; William A. Christian, Jr., *Person and God in a Spanish Valley* (New York: Seminar Press, 1972); Olwen Hufton, "The Reconstruction of a Church 1796–1801," in Gwynne Lewis and Colin Lucas, eds., *Beyond the Terror: Essays in French Regional Social History, 1794–1815* (Cambridge: Cambridge University Press, 1983), 21–52; Hugh McLeod, *Religion and the People of Western Europe, 1789–1970* (Oxford: Oxford University Press, 1981), 28–35, found that female majorities characterize both Catholic and Protestant countries. Michel Vovelle locates the rise of a female majority to the eighteenth century, but he documents gender parity in enthusiasm for the mass only for a brief moment in 1710, with female majorities in evidence both before and after. Michel Vovelle, *Piété baroque et déchristianisation en province au XVIII siècle* (Paris: Editions du Seuil, 1978), 134. Beyond Europe comparative data are currently difficult to obtain.

8. Mary Farrell Bednarowski, "Outside the Mainstream: Women's Religion and Women Religious Leaders in Nineteenth-Century America," *Journal of the American Academy of Religion* 48 (June 1980): 207–31; Catherine Wessinger, ed., *Women's Leadership in Marginal Religions: Explorations Outside the Mainstream* (Urbana: University of Illinois Press, 1993).

9. Ann Braude, *Radical Spirits: Spiritualism and Women's Rights in Nineteenth-Century America* (Boston: Beacon Press, 1989); idem, "The Perils of Passivity: Women's Leadership in Spiritualism and Christian Science," in *Women's Leadership in Marginal Religions.*

10. Dunn, "Saints and Sisters," 37; Orsi, " 'He Keeps Me Going.' "

11. Nathan O. Hatch, *The Democratization of American Christianity* (New Haven: Yale University Press, 1989), 10.

12. References to women and gender that affect the narrative are so infrequent in surveys on American religion that there is no need to list particular texts. A survey text that mentions women more frequently than most is Peter W. Williams, *America's Religions: Traditions and Cultures* (New York: Macmillan, 1990). A thematic (rather than narrative) text that includes women is Mary Farrell Bednarowski, *American Religion: A Cultural Perspective* (Englewood Cliffs, N. J.: Prentice Hall, 1984).

13. Dunn, "Saints and Sisters," 37.

14. Shiels, "Feminization of American Congregationalism."

15. Harry S. Stout and Catherine A. Brekus, "Declension, Gender, and the 'New Religious History,' " and Gerald Moran, " 'Sinners Are Turned into Saints in Numbers': Puritanism and Revivalism in Colonial Connecticut," both in Philip R. Vandermeer and Robert P. Swierenga, eds., *Belief and Behavior: Essays in the New Religious History* (New Brunswick, N.J.: Rutgers University Press, 1991). Stout and Brekus conclude that feminization *did* occur following the Revolutionary War. However, the membership statistics they present for the First Church of New Haven reveal a relatively constant sex ratio in which women outnumber men by more than two to one from 1680 to 1980. The only years in which they found male majorities were 1639 to 1659.

16. Perry Miller, *The New England Mind: From Colony to Province* (1953; Boston: Beacon Press, 1961), 34.

17. Ibid., chap. 2.

18. Barbara Welter, "The Feminization of American Religion: 1800–1860," in Mary Hartman and Lois Banner, eds., *Clio's Consciousness Raised* (New York: Harper Torchbooks, 1973), 138; Ann Douglas, *The Feminization of American Culture* (New York: Knopf, 1977); Cotton Mather, *Ornaments of the Daughters of Zion* (Boston: Samuel Phillips, 1691), 56; Shiels, "Feminization of American Congregationalism."

19. Betty A. De Berg, *Ungodly Women: Gender and the First Wave of American Fundamentalism* (Minneapolis: Fortress Press, 1990).

20. See, for example, Jeffrey K. Hadden and Anson Shupe, eds., *Secularization and Fundamentalism Reconsidered* (New York: Paragon House Books, 1989), and Stark and Bainbridge, *Future of Religion*.

21. Paul E. Johnson, *A Shopkeeper's Millennium* (New York: Hill and Wang, 1978), 4–6; George Gallup, Jr., "Fifty Years of Gallup Surveys on Religion," *Gallup Report* 236 (May): 4–14.

22. John Murray Cuddihy, *The Ordeal of Civility: Freud, Marx, Lévi-Strauss and the Jewish Struggle with Modernity* (1974; New York: Delta, 1976), 34 and passim; see also idem, *No Offense: Civil Religion and Protestant Taste* (New York: Seabury Press, 1978).

23. Edmund S. Morgan, *The Puritan Family: Religion and Domestic Relations in Seventeenth-Century New England* (New York: Harper and Row, 1966); Laurel Thatcher Ulrich, "Virtuous Women Found: New England Minis-

terial Literature, 1668–1735," in *Women in American Religion;* Lona Malm-sheimer, "Daughters of Zion: New England Roots of American Feminism," *New England Quarterly* 50 (September 1977): 484–504; Carol F. Karlsen, *The Devil in the Shape of a Woman: Witchcraft in Colonial New England* (New York: Vintage Books, 1989); David Hall, *Worlds of Wonder, Days of Judgment* (New York: Knopf, 1989), 32–34, 128–30.

24. Susan Juster, *Disorderly Women: Sexual Politics and Evangelicalism in Revolutionary New England* (Ithaca: Cornell University Press, 1994); Margaret Mason, "The Typology of the Female as a Model for the Regenerate in Puritan Preaching, 1690–1730," *Signs* 2 (1976): 304–15; Barbara Leslie Epstein, *The Politics of Domesticity: Women, Evangelism and Temperance in Nineteenth-Century America* (Middletown, Conn.: Wesleyan University Press, 1981).

25. Barbara Welter, "The Cult of True Womanhood: 1829–1860," *American Quarterly* 18 (1966): 151–74.

26. Colleen McDannell, "Catholic Domesticity, 1860–1960," in Karen Kennelly, C.S.J., ed., *American Catholic Women: A Historical Exploration* (New York: Macmillan, 1989), 48–80; Ann Braude, "The Jewish Woman's En-counter with American Culture," in Rosemary Ruether and Rosemary Keller, eds., *Women and Religion in America* (San Francisco: Harper and Row, 1981), 1:156; Evelyn Brooks Higgenbotham, *Righteous Discontent: The Women's Movement in the Black Baptist Church, 1880–1920* (Cambridge, Mass.: Har-vard University Press, 1993); Peggy Pascoe, *Relations of Rescue: The Search for Female Moral Authority in the American West, 1874–1939* (New York: Oxford University Press, 1990); Margaret Lamberts Bendroth, *Fundamentalism and Gender: 1875 to the Present* (New Haven: Yale University Press, 1993); Cott, "Passionlessness," 163.

27. Christine L. Krueger, *The Reader's Repentance: Woman Preachers, Woman Writers, and Nineteenth-Century Social Discourse* (Chicago: University of Chicago Press, 1992).

28. The literature documenting this tendency is legion. See, for example, Carroll Smith-Rosenberg, "Beauty, the Beast, and the Militant Woman: A Case Study in Sex Roles and Social Stress in Jacksonian America," in *Disorderly Con-duct* (New York: Oxford University Press, 1985), 109–28; Epstein, *Politics of Domesticity;* Mary Ryan, "A Woman's Awakening: Evangelical Religion and the Families of Utica, New York, 1800–1840," in *Women and Religion in America,* and idem, "The Power of Women's Networks: A Case Study of Female Moral Reform in Antebellum America," *Feminist Studies* 5 (spring 1979): 66–88; Nancy F. Cott, *The Bonds of Womanhood: "Woman's Sphere" in New England, 1780–1835* (New Haven: Yale University Press, 1977); Patricia R. Hill, *The World Their Household: The American Women's Foreign Mission Movement and Cul-tural Transformation, 1870–1920* (Ann Arbor: University of Michigan Press, 1985); Elaine J. Lawless, *Handmaidens of the Lord: Pentecostal Women Preach-ers and Traditional Religion* (Philadelphia: University of Pennsylvania Press, 1988).

29. Nancy F. Cott, "Passionlessness: An Interpretation of Victorian Sexual Ideology, 1790–1850," *Signs: Journal of Women in Culture and Society* 4 (1978): 219–36.

30. Ulrich, "Virtuous Women Found"; Bendroth, *Fundamentalism and*

Gender, 110; Karlsen, *The Devil in the Shape of a Woman;* De Berg, *Ungodly Women.*

31. Ryan, "Power of Women's Networks"; Smith-Rosenberg, "Beauty, the Beast, and the Militant Woman," 109–28.

32. Jean Fagin Yellin, *Women and Sisters: The Anti-Slavery Feminists in American Culture* (New Haven: Yale University Press, 1989); Jean Fagin Yellin and John C. Van Horne, eds., *The Abolitionist Sisterhood: Women's Political Culture in Antebellum America* (Ithaca: Cornell University Press, 1994); Epstein, *Politics of Domesticity.*

33. R. Pierce Beaver, *American Protestant Women in World Mission: A History of the First Feminist Movement in North America* (Grand Rapids, Mich.: Eerdmans, 1980); Barbara Welter, "She Hath Done What She Could: Protestant Women's Missionary Careers in the Nineteenth-Century," in *Women in American Religion;* Elizabeth Howell Verdesi, *In but Still Out: Women in the Church* (Philadelphia: Westminster Press, 1976), chap. 3; Hill, *The World Their Household.*

34. Sonya Michel and Seth Koven, eds., *Mothers of a New World: Maternalist Politics and the Origins of the Welfare State* (New York: Routledge, 1993).

35. Barbara Brown Zikmund, "Women and Ordination," in Rosemary Skinner Keller and Rosemary Radford Ruether, eds., *In Our Own Voices* (San Francisco: Harper San Francisco, 1995), 292–340.

36. Wuthnow and Lehrman, "Religion: Inhibitor or Facilitator?"

37. Lynn Davidman, *Tradition in a Rootless World: Women Turn to Orthodox Judaism* (Berkeley: University of California Press, 1991).

38. See, for example, Marie Caskey, *Chariot of Fire: Religion and the Beecher Family* (New Haven: Yale University Press, 1977).

39. Ryan, "A Woman's Awakening," 91; Stout and Brekus, "Declension, Gender, and the 'New Religious History,'" in *Belief and Behavior,* 29.

40. Lincoln and Mamiya, *The Black Church,* 304–6.

41. Gail Bederman, "'The Women Have Had Charge of the Church Work Long Enough': The Men and Religion Forward Movement of 1911–1912 and the Masculinization of Middle-Class Protestantism," *American Quarterly* 41 (September 1989): 432–65.

42. Mark C. Carnes, *Secret Ritual and Manhood in Victorian America* (New Haven: Yale University Press, 1989); Douglas, *Feminization of American Culture;* E. Anthony Rotundo, *American Manhood* (New York: Basic Books, 1993), 172.

43. Lincoln and Mamiya, *The Black Church,* 304–6.

44. Colleen McDannell, "Going to the Ladies' Fair: Irish Catholics in New York City, 1870–1900," in Timothy Meagher and Ronald Baylor, eds., *The New York Irish* (Baltimore: Johns Hopkins University Press, forthcoming).

45. James J. Kenneally, *The History of American Catholic Women* (New York: Crossroads, 1990), 66.

46. Oates, "Organized Voluntarism," and idem, "Organizing for Service"; Mary Ewens, O.P., *The Role of the Nun in Nineteenth-Century America* (1971; Salem, N.H.: Ayer, 1984), 35–64.

47. Oates, "Organized Voluntarism," 150.

CHAPTER 4: THE ILLUSION OF SHIFTING DEMAND

1. Andrew Reed and James Matheson, *A Narrative of the Visit to the American Churches* (London: Jackson and Walford, 1835), 2:137, 141; for the reaction of other European visitors to the new religious economy, see Milton Powell, ed., *The Voluntary Church: American Religious Life (1740–1865) Seen through the Eyes of European Visitors* (New York: Macmillan, 1967).

2. Philip Schaff, *America: A Sketch of Its Political, Social, and Religious Character*, ed. Perry Miller (1855; Cambridge, Mass.: Harvard University Press), 11, 96, 99; Robert Baird, *Religion in America; or, An Account of the Origin, Progress, Relation to the State, and Present Condition of the Evangelical Churches in the United States. With Notices of the Unevangelical Denominations* (1844; New York: Arno Press, 1969), 409.

3. Baird, *Religion in America*, 607, 610; Schaff, *America*, 99, 102.

4. Sidney E. Mead, *The Lively Experiment: The Shaping of Christianity in America* (1963; New York: Harper and Row, 1976); Franklin Littell, *From State Church to Pluralism* (Chicago: Aldine, 1962). Although Robert T. Handy does not treat the voluntary principle as the central motif in his survey *A History of Churches in the United States and Canada* (New York: Oxford University Press, 1976), he does explain how religious liberties helped to "remould the churches" during the Revolutionary era and stresses the importance of voluntarism during the early nineteenth century.

5. Sidney E. Mead, "By Puritans Possessed," *Worldview* 16 (April 1973): 49–52.

6. Mead writes: "The Constitution is the rule-book of the game we are playing. . . . {and the] provisions in the Bill of Rights have the form of abstract general principles." Sidney E. Mead, *The Nation with the Soul of a Church* (1975; Macon, Ga.: Mercer University Press, 1985), 107.

7. Jay P. Dolan explains how parish missions were used to recruit new members and activate the inactive in *Catholic Revivalism: The American Experience, 1830–1900* (Notre Dame, Ind.: University of Notre Dame Press, 1978).

8. Immediately prior to this statement, Mead described the reader as an "absent hearer"; see *The Nation with the Soul of a Church*, vi.

9. See Roger Finke, "Religious Deregulation: Origins and Consequences," *Journal of Church and State* 32 (1990): 609–26.

10. Mead, *Lively Experiment;* William G. McLoughlin, *New England Dissent, 1630–1833*, 2 vols. (Cambridge, Mass.: Harvard University Press, 1971); James A. Beckford, *Cult Controversies: The Societal Response to New Religious Movements* (London: Tavistock Publications, 1985); Thomas Robbins and James A. Beckford, "Religious Movements and Church-State Issues," in D. Bromley and J. Hadden, eds., *Handbook of Cults and Sects* (Greenwich, Conn.: JAI Press, 1993), 199–218.

11. See Rodney Stark and William Sims Bainbridge, *The Future of Religion: Secularization, Revival, and Cult Formation* (Berkeley: University of California Press, 1985); Finke, "Religious Deregulation"; Roger Finke and Rodney Stark, *The Churching of America 1776–1990* (New Brunswick, N.J.: Rutgers University Press, 1992).

12. A religious dissenter from Connecticut offered this biting assessment in 1791: "Preachers that will not preach without a salary found for them by law are hirelings who seek the fleece and not the flock"; as quoted in McLoughlin, *New England Dissent*, 2:927.

13. Francis Grund, *The Americans in Their Moral, Social, and Political Relations* (1837), as excerpted in Powell, *The Voluntary Church*, 74–83.

14. The estimates are taken from Roger Finke and Rodney Stark, "Turning Pews into People: Estimating Nineteenth-Century Church Membership," *Journal for the Scientific Study of Religion* 25 (1986): 180–92; and Rodney Stark and Roger Finke, "American Religion in 1776: A Statistical Portrait," *Sociological Analysis* 49 (1988): 39–51.

15. See Finke, "Religious Deregulation."

16. John Leland spoke for many dissenters when he wrote, "The very idea of toleration is despicable; it supposes that some have a pre-eminence above the rest to grant indulgence"; as quoted in Anson Phelps Stokes, *Church and State in the United States* (New York: Harper and Brothers, 1950), 3:355.

17. McLoughlin, *New England Dissent*, 1:363; Madison quoted in Leo Pfeffer, *Church, State, and Freedom* (Boston: Beacon Press, 1953), 81.

18. See Nathan O. Hatch, *The Democratization of American Christianity* (New Haven: Yale University Press, 1989).

19. Peter Cartwright, *Peter Cartwright: The Backwoods Preacher* (Cincinnati: Cranston and Curts, 1856), 123.

20. Frank Lambert, " 'Pedlar in Divinity': George Whitefield and the Great Awakening, 1737–1745," *Journal of American History* 77 (1990): 812–37, and idem, *Pedlar in Divinity: George Whitefield and the Transatlantic Revivals, 1737–1770* (Princeton: Princeton University Press, 1994); Harry S. Stout, *The Divine Dramatist: George Whitefield and the Rise of Modern Evangelism* (Grand Rapids, Mich.: Eerdmans, 1991).

21. Hatch, *Democratization*, 9. Hatch writes that between 1775 and 1845 the "number of preachers per capita more than tripled" and "twice the number of denominations competed for adherents." This growth in preachers was due to the surging supply of sectarian ministers. "Congregationalists, which had twice the clergy of any other American church in 1775, could not muster one-tenth the preaching force of the Methodists in 1845" (ibid., 4). When studying the Second Great Awakening in Baltimore, Terry D. Bilhartz concluded that instead of searching for "clues from the demand side of the equation, perhaps Baltimore's awakening more simply can be understood as 'supply-side religion'"; Bilhartz, *Urban Religion and the Second Great Awakening* (London: Associated University Press, 1986), 99.

22. David Hempton, *Methodism and Politics in British Society, 1750–1850* (Stanford: Stanford University Press, 1984), 104; idem, "Methodism and the Law, 1740–1820," in A. Dyson and E. Barker, eds., *Sects and New Religious Movements*, in *Bulletin of the John Rylands Library* 70 (1988): 93–107, where Hempton notes that "how far Methodism should be allowed to shelter under the umbrella of the Church of England . . . became one of the most controversial legal problems of the period between 1740 and 1820" (94).

23. Hatch, *Democratization*, 50. When American itinerant Lorenzo Dow

attempted to introduce the camp meetings to Great Britain, he found strong support from the people and sharp opposition from the hierarchy: "they warned the Methodists against me, to starve me out . . . [and] they offered to pay my passage home, if I would quit the country, and promise never to return, which in conscience I could not do"; see Lorenzo Dow, *History of Cosmopolite or The Four Volumes of Lorenzo Dow's Journal, Sixth Edition* (Wheeling, Va: Joshua Martin, 1849), 256.

24. W. R. Ward, *Religion and Society in England, 1790–1850* (New York: Schocken Books, 1972), 5.

25. In Halifax, for example, the Church of England offered a higher percentage of its seats free (29 percent) than did the New Connexion General Baptists (14 percent), the Wesleyan Methodists (19 percent), the New Connexion Methodists (7 percent), or the Primitive Methodists (12 percent). Only the Wesleyan Reformers offered all of their four hundred seats free. See Horace Mann, *Religious Worship: England and Wales* (London: Her Majesty's Stationery Office, 1853).

26. Finke and Stark, *The Churching of America*. For data on Methodist membership in Great Britain see Robert Currie, Alan Gilbert, and Lee Horsley, *Churches and Churchgoers: Patterns of Church Growth in the British Isles since 1700,* (Oxford: Clarendon Press, 1977), 161–65.

27. See Lawrence A. Young, ed. *Assessing Rational Choice Theories of Religion,* (New York: Routledge Press, 1996).

28. Sydney E. Ahlstrom, *A Religious History of the American People* (Garden City, N.Y.: Image Books, 1975), 612; Martin E. Marty, *A Nation of Behavers* (Chicago: University of Chicago Press, 1976), 71. Marty used the words *seismic shift* when he described to sociologists the recent decline of the mainline churches. See his forward to Dean R. Hoge and David A. Roozen, eds., *Understanding Church Growth and Decline: 1950–1978* (New York: Pilgrim Press, 1979), 10. Winthrop S. Hudson, *Religion in America,* 3d ed. (New York: Charles Scribner's Sons, 1981), 439. Hudson did note a few continuities between the new evangelicals and those of the past, but he was quick to point out the many differences.

29. Mark A. Noll, *A History of Christianity in the United States and Canada* (Grand Rapids, Mich.: Eerdmans, 1992), 469; George M. Marsden, *Religion and American Culture* (New York: Harcourt Brace Jovanovich, 1990), 261. Marsden listed three additional "reasons for growth": first, "traditional religion provided . . . a simple critique of the perceived failures of liberal American culture"; second, "the small-group strategies of the charismatics and others"; and, third, "the reemergence of the South as a full participant in national life" (261–62).

30. The alternative is when the culture conforms to the standards of the religious movement and the tension is reduced. For example, the Mormons' prohibitions against members smoking or consuming caffeine are in less tension with the culture today than two decades ago.

31. H. Richard Niebuhr recognized that this process was inherent to the life of sects, though he had little to say about how it affected church growth: "Rarely does a second generation hold the convictions it has inherited with a

fervor equal to that of its fathers. . . . Compromise begins and the ethics of the sect approach the churchly type of morals." See Niebuhr, *The Social Sources of Denominationalism* (1929; Hamden, Conn.: Shoe String Press, 1954), 20.

32. Stark and Bainbridge, *Future of Religion;* Finke and Stark, *The Churching of America.*

33. Scholars studying individual denominations often treat this process as a general cultural trend, rather than a trend within a single organization. This has led many to interpret organizational secularization as support for a general historical trend of secularization.

34. William Warren Sweet, *The Story of Religion in America* (1930; New York: Harper and Row, 1950), 424; Martin E. Marty, *Righteous Empire: The Protestant Experience in America* (New York: Dial, 1970), 244.

35. Warren H. Wilson, "The Church and the Rural Community," *American Journal of Sociology* 16 (1911): 668–93. For an excellent review of the reformers' activities, see James H. Madison, "Reformers and the Rural Church, 1900–1950," *Journal of American History,* 73 (1986): 645–68.

36. John Hargreaves, "The Rural Community and Church Federation," *American Journal of Sociology* 20 (1914): 249–60; Bureau of the Census, *Religious Bodies: 1926,* 2 vols. (Washington, D.C.: Government Printing Office, 1930).

37. Edmund deS. Brunner, *Village Communities* (New York: George H. Doran, 1927), 73, 76. See also Finke and Stark, *The Churching of America,* chap. 6.

38. See Winthrop Hudson and John Corrigan, *Religion in America,* 5th ed. (New York: Macmillan, 1992). Though many would not consider them "surveys" of American religious history, several recent books on American religion provide rich illustrations of this pluralism. Catherine L. Albanese, *America: Religions and Religion,* 2d ed. (Belmont, Calif.: Wadsworth, 1992); Julia Mitchell Corbett, *Religion in America* 2d ed. (Englewood Cliffs, N.J.: Prentice-Hall, 1994); Peter W. Williams, *Popular Religion in America* (1980; Urbana: University of Illinois Press, 1989).

39. See Finke and Stark, *The Churching of America,* chap. 6; H. Paul Douglass, *Church Unity Movements in the United States* (New York: Institute of Social and Religious Research, 1934); H. Paul Douglass and Edmund deS. Brunner, *The Protestant Church as a Social Institution* (New York: Russell and Russell, 1935).

40. J. Gordon Melton, "How New Is New? The Flowering of the 'New' Religious Consciousness since 1965," in David G. Bromley and Phillip E. Hammond, eds., *The Future of New Religious Movements* (Macon, Ga.: Mercer University Press, 1987); Finke and Stark, *The Churching of America,* chap. 7; Roger Finke and Laurence R. Iannaccone, "Supply-Side Explanations for Religious Change," *Annals, AAPSS* 527 (1993): 27–39.

41. For further discussion on how the narrative might be shifted away from the traditional mainline, see R. Laurence Moore, *Religious Outsiders and the Making of Americans* (New York: Oxford University Press, 1986), and Nathan O. Hatch, "The Puzzle of American Methodism," *Church History* 63 (June 1994): 175–89.

42. For a more complete discussion of this approach, see Finke and Stark, *The Churching of America*, and R. Stephen Warner, "Work in Progress toward a New Paradigm for the Sociological Study of Religion in the United States," *American Journal of Sociology* 98 (1993): 1044–93.

43. For a more complete discussion, see Warner, "Work in Progress toward a New Paradigm."

44. For a more complete discussion, see Finke, "Religious Deregulation."

45. Stephen L. Carter, *The Culture of Disbelief* (New York: Basic Books, 1993).

46. See, for example, Finke and Iannaccone, "Supply-Side Explanations for Religious Change"; Laurence R. Iannaccone, Roger Finke, and Rodney Stark, "Deregulating Religion: Supply-Side Stories of Trends and Change in the Religious Marketplace," *Economic Inquiry,* forthcoming.

CHAPTER 5: EASTWARD HO!

1. Samuel Mills to Gordon Hall, 20 December 1809, in Gardiner Spring, *Memoirs of the Rev. Samuel J. Mills,* 50, cited in Clifton Jackson Phillips, *Protestant America and the Pagan World: The First Half Century of the American Board of Commissioners for Foreign Missions, 1810–1860* (Cambridge, Mass.: Harvard University Press, 1969), 89.

2. Phillips, *Protestant America,* 89–92. On missionary success in Hawaii, see William Hutchison, *Errand to the World* (Chicago: University of Chicago Press, 1987). Obookiah's life was memorialized by Lyman Beecher on *A Sermon Delivered at the Funeral of Henry Obookiah* (1818), and by Edwin W. Dwight, in *Memoirs of Henry Obookiah, a Native of Owyhee, and a Member of the Foreign Mission School* (1818).

3. Phillips, *Protestant America,* 90–91. See also the American Board of Commissioners for Foreign Missions (ABCFM) tract *A Narrative of Five Youths from the Sandwich Islands Now Receiving an Education in this Country* (1816); and John Whitehead, "Hawai'i: The First and Last Far West?" *Western Historical Quarterly* 23, 2 (May 1992): 153–77. Whitehead relates that Hawaiians formed part of the labor force that constructed the ABCFM mission in Oregon Territory for the Whitman party in the 1840s (163).

4. The term *Pacific Rim* itself has an important history, and its contemporary use often connotes specific political, racial, or economic groupings. My use here is geographic and political, referring to the present-day regions of the United States that border the Pacific Ocean. My larger interest in this essay, however, includes not only the terrain now encompassed by the national borders, but also the histories of those peoples who have migrated to the region from other places, including other areas of the Pacific, as well as the conceptual role that the region has played in the religious worldviews of those who became citizens of the United States. While these are, in theory, separable concerns, a survey that takes seriously the significance of the Pacific Rim must grapple with all of them.

5. Herbert Eugene Bolton was the often unheralded scholar who, in the

1930s, emphasized the importance of viewing American history in a hemi-spheric perspective. He emphasized that doing so would necessarily illuminate the various movements, from the south, north, east, and west, that had created the societies of North America. See Bolton, "The Epic of Greater America," in his *Wider Horizons of American History* (1939; reprint, Notre Dame, Ind.: University of Notre Dame Press, 1967). See also Patricia Nelson Limerick, "Dis-orientation and Reorientation: The American Landscape Discovered from the West," *Journal of American History* 79, 3 (December 1992): 1021–49. Vincent G. Harding has recently suggested that American historians need to reconsider the variety of vantage points for narrating the history of the nation, in "Healing at the Razor's Edge: Reflections on a History of Multicultural America," *Journal of American History* 81, 2 (September 1994): 571–84.

6. Winthrop S. Hudson and John Corrigan, *Religion in America*, 5th ed. (New York: Macmillan, 1992), 252–53, 277, 408; Martin E. Marty, *Pilgrims in Their Own Land: Five Hundred Years of Religion in America* (1984; New York: Penguin Books, 1985), 430, 452.

7. See Thomas A. Tweed's *The American Encounter with Buddhism, 1844–1912: Victorian Culture and the Limits of Dissent* (Bloomington: Indiana University Press, 1992). Tweed very helpfully distinguishes Euro-American appropriations of Buddhism from its Asian-American manifestations, without passing judgment on the cultural "authenticity" of either one. My point is not to call for study of a "pure" religious tradition, since Chinese and many other Asians were hardly "pure" in their adherence to Buddhist principles, but to sug-gest that by focusing almost exclusively on Euro-American appropriations of these traditions, we are ignoring the vast majority of actors in the story.

8. Edwin Gaustad, *A Religious History of America*, new rev. ed. (1966; San Francisco: Harper and Row, 1990), 162, 221.

9. Patricia Nelson Limerick, "The Multicultural Islands," *American His-torical Review* 97, 1 (February 1992): 121–35; and idem, "Disorientation and Reorientation," 1022.

10. Yi-Fu Tuan, "Humanistic Geography," *Annals of the Association of American Geographers* 66, 2 (June 1976): 269. See also Gregory J. Levine, "On the Geography of Religion," *Transactions of the Institute of British Geogra-phers* 11 (1986): 428–40; David E. Sopher, "Geography and Religions," *Pro-gress in Human Geography* 5 (1981): 510–24; and Roger Stump, "The Geog-raphy of Religion: Introduction," *Journal of Cultural Geography* 7 (1986): 1–3.

11. The use of sacralization as a theoretical construct is obviously not the only significant aspect of religion on the Pacific Rim, nor is its usefulness limited to this particular region. Indeed, I would hope that scholars of other regions might take it up as a means of highlighting certain themes in religious history (how often, for instance, do we speak of New England Puritanism as a regional religion?). I find it especially useful as a way of emphasizing the religious dimen-sions of intercultural movements, contacts, and conflicts, as well as a means of stressing the importance of the Pacific region to a narration of American reli-gious history. In recent years there has been increased interest among students of migration and diaspora in these sorts of questions. However, sacralization

has only begun to be analyzed systematically by scholars of religious history, and has yet to be used as a conceptual framework in survey histories of American religion.

12. Walter A. McDougall, *Let the Sea Make a Noise: A History of the North Pacific from Magellan to MacArthur* (New York: Basic Books, 1993), 73.

13. William L. Thomas, Jr., "The Pacific Basin: An Introduction," in Herman R. Friis, ed., *The Pacific Basin: A History of Its Geographical Exploration* (New York: American Geographical Society, 1967), 2–3. It should be noted, however, that the Pacific Ocean, with over twenty-five thousand islands, is considerably more populated than the Atlantic. See also Arrell Morgan Gibson, completed with assistance by John S. Whitehead, *Yankees in Paradise: The Pacific Basin Frontier* (Albuquerque: University of New Mexico Press, 1993), 13–17.

14. Barry M. Gough, *Distant Dominion: Britain and the Northwest Coast of North America, 1579–1809* (Vancouver: University of British Columbia Press, 1980), 2–3.

15. Ralph S. Kuykendall, *The Hawaiian Kingdom, 1778–1854: Foundation and Transformation* (Honolulu: University of Hawaii Press, 1947), 3; Gordon R. Lewthwaite, "Geographical Knowledge of the Pacific Peoples," in *Pacific Basin,* 85–86.

16. David J. Weber, *The Spanish Frontier in North America* (New Haven: Yale University Press, 1992), 263; for figures on Hawaii, see David Stannard, *Before the Horror: The Population of Hawai'i on the Eve of Western Contact* (Honolulu: Social Science Research Institute, University of Hawaii, 1989). Then, as now, California not only had the highest population density of any area of North America, with approximately three hundred thousand people, but also was the most culturally and linguistically diverse area of the continent (Weber, *Spanish Frontier,* 247; see also Albert Hurtado, *Indian Survival on the California Frontier* [New Haven: Yale University Press, 1988]). Stannard's recent and controversial study of Hawaiian population figures has revised earlier estimates of the population (two to three hundred thousand) significantly: he estimates that there were perhaps eight hundred thousand natives in the islands (vii–xiv).

17. Scholars speculate that Hsu Fu may have journeyed as far as Japan. See Chiao-Min Hsieh, "Geographical Exploration by the Chinese," in *Pacific Basin,* 88.

18. Gibson, *Yankees in Paradise,* 42; Weber, *Spanish Frontier,* 19–24. David D. Hall alerts us to a Puritan world that may be fruitfully compared with the Spanish one in *Worlds of Wonder, Days of Judgment: Popular Religious Belief in Early New England* (Cambridge, Mass.: Harvard University Press, 1990).

19. Herbert E. Bolton, "Defensive Spanish Expansion and the Significance of the Borderlands," in *Wider Horizons,* 65.

20. James R. Gibson, *Imperial Russia in Frontier America: The Changing Geography of Supply of Russian America, 1784–1867* (New York: Oxford University Press, 1976), viii.

21. To avoid the pitfall of privileging the movers (as opposed to the indigenous peoples), the motif of migration must be balanced by that of the cultural contact fostered by movement. Once movement has occurred, it is important that we assess the perspectives of all participants in that encounter, and not

assume that the migration itself furnishes a singular viewpoint. For examples of studies that attempt a multiperspectival account, see William Cronon, *Changes in the Land: Indians, Colonists, and the Ecology of New England* (New York: Hill and Wang, 1983); Ramón Gutiérrez, *When Jesus Came, the Corn Mothers Went Away: Marriage, Sexuality, and Power in New Mexico, 1500–1846* (Stanford: Stanford University Press, 1991); Richard Price, *Alabi's World* (Baltimore: Johns Hopkins University Press, 1990); and Weber, *Spanish Frontier.*

22. The term *colonization* is intended to offset the more benign and even celebratory connotations of the term *cultural contact* by suggesting the elements of coercion that invariably accompany situations of contact. An expanding literature on transnational colonialism reveals the extent to which meetings among cultures have rarely involved simple exchanges on a level political playing field. See, for example, Nicholas B. Dirks, ed., *Colonialism and Culture* (Ann Arbor: University of Michigan Press, 1992). For an example that reiterates the concept of American colonialism, see Helen Matthews Lewis, Linda Johnson, and Don Askins, eds., *Colonialism in Modern America: The Appalachian Case* (Boone, N. C.: Appalachian Consortium Press, 1978).

23. I refer here to the ways in which the desire to condemn historical abuses of power, usually on the part of Europeans or Americans, often ironically leads scholars to focus exclusively on politics and nation building as the negative force against which local peoples must invariably react. I argue for striking a balance by acknowledging the realities of political domination, while also exploring the aspects of people's lives—sacralization often being among them—that are not exclusively determined by the politics of nation-states. See Margaret J. Wiener, *Visible and Invisible Realms: Power, Magic, and Colonial Conquest in Bali* (Chicago: University of Chicago Press, 1995) for an illuminating example of this approach.

24. American motivations, to be sure, can be held up to ethical scrutiny at many points. And numerous studies, by focusing exclusively on the notion of "manifest destiny" or the drive for internal self-improvement reflected in the evangelical revivals of the antebellum era, ignore the plain fact of American aggression toward other peoples that characterized this period, long after what we ordinarily call the "colonial era" had ended. It had not ended for many people. As D. W. Meinig notes, American expansion was not only a westward movement but also an outward drive, although Americans themselves (and their scholarly descendants) tend to avoid most evidence of the vast empire controlled from the Atlantic Coast. It was an empire that coerced and subjugated peoples, often through religious means, from North Carolina to Hawaii. Yet put simply, that is not the whole story. See Meinig, *Continental America, 1800–1867,* vol. 2 of *The Shaping of America* (New Haven: Yale University Press, 1993), 169, 185, 192.

25. Despite the greater numbers of indigenous peoples in the Americas during this period, they were not homogeneous in any meaningful sense. The contours of cultural relations between Spaniards and Indians varied widely from place to place, and the dynamics of these encounters were dependent in large measure on the will and resources of the native populations. Our understanding

of the religious dimensions of these encounters, particularly those on the Pacific, is scanty. The *encomienda* system was the first labor system (aside from slavery) imposed by the Spanish on native populations.

26. Bolton, "Defensive Spanish Expansion," 56; and idem, "The Epic of Greater America," in *Wider Horizons,* 9. The universities of Mexico and Lima were both founded in 1551.

27. Weber, *Spanish Frontier,* 8. The Puritans did not count the native inhabitants or their slaves as citizens, and thus our story of Puritanism often excludes what was, at least initially, the majority population of the region.

28. Ibid., 94, 111–12.

29. Ibid., 113–14; Gutiérrez, *When Jesus Came,* chap. 2.

30. Weber, *Spanish Frontier,* 116–17.

31. It is revealing to note the similarities to the apocryphal tale of the Nez Perce Indians, who were said to have traveled from the Northwest to St. Louis in order to request Christian instruction.

32. Bishop Gregory Afonsky, *A History of the Orthodox Church in Alaska (1794–1917)* (Kodiak: St. Herman's Theological Seminary, 1977), 12–30. See also Susan Wiley Hardwick, *Russian Refuge: Religion, Migration, and Settlement on the North American Pacific Rim* (Chicago: University of Chicago Press, 1993); Sergei Kan, "Russian Orthodox Brotherhoods among the Tlingit: Missionary Goals and Native Response," *Ethnohistory* 32, 3 (1985): 196–223; E. M. B. Mattson, "Orthodoxy and the Aleuts: The Historical Significance of the Russian Orthodox Mission in Alaska," M.A. thesis, University of Idaho, 1985; S. A. Mousalimas, *The Transition from Shamanism to Russian Orthodoxy in Alaska* (Providence, R.I.: Berghahn Books, 1995); and M. Oleska, ed., *Alaskan Missionary Spirituality* (New York: Paulist Press, 1987).

33. Oleska, *Alaskan Missionary Spirituality,* 35–38. On the Russian attempt to colonize Hawaii, see R. A. Pierce, *Russia's Hawaiian Adventure, 1815–1817* (Kingston, Ont.: Limestone Press, 1965).

34. This may have been true of both Protestant Americans during the California gold rush and Japanese Buddhists in the early years of migration to Hawaii. See Laurie F. Maffly-Kipp, *Religion and Society in Frontier California* (New Haven: Yale University Press, 1994), chap. 5, and Louise H. Hunter, *Buddhism in Hawaii: Its Impact on a Yankee Community* (Honolulu: University of Hawaii Press, 1971), 80–81.

35. For Russian, Spanish, British, and American migrants (and for Asians, as we shall see later), these overwhelmingly male migrations also led to the weakening of institutional religions in newly colonized areas, not because women are naturally more religious than men, but because in many of these cultures women have sustained the ritual activities most closely associated with the endurance of community life.

36. Although space does not permit full treatment of Protestant missions in Oregon and Washington, those religious encounters represent an important aspect of the larger story that would require discussion in a narrative. Classic accounts of early missionaries in the Northwest include Clifford M. Drury, *Marcus and Narcissa Whitman, and the Opening of Old Oregon,* 2 vols. (Glendale, Calif.: A. H. Clark, 1973), and Robert J. Loewenberg, *Equality on the Oregon*

Frontier: Jason Lee and the Methodist Mission, 1834–1843 (Seattle: University of Washington Press, 1976).

37. Whitehead, "Hawai'i," 162.

38. Phillips, *Protestant America*, 96.

39. Ibid., 102 (cited in Jones to Marshall, Oahu, 5 May 1826, Josiah Marshall Papers, Harvard University).

40. Gibson, *Yankees in Paradise*, 281–82.

41. Whitehead, "Hawai'i," 164, 167; Phillips, *Protestant America*, 102–3.

42. Patricia Limerick has predicted that Hawaii's cultural diversity may provide a model for the future of the nation as a whole: "The Hawaiianization of the nation is, in this sense, the wave of the future" ("Multicultural Islands," 135).

43. Laurie F. Maffly-Kipp, "At Home on the Theological Equator: Protestant Reform and Religious Pluralism in California, 1848–1882," unpublished manuscript.

44. Ibid.; see also Michael Engh, *Frontier Faiths: Church, Temple and Synagogue in Los Angeles, 1846–1888* (Albuquerque: University of New Mexico Press, 1992).

45. The emergence of the Young Men's Buddhist Association was just one indicator of the ways an Asian religious tradition conformed to Euro-American patterns. Influence also ran the other direction, and at times, Protestant religious institutions were reshaped by Asian immigrants to fill their own needs. Much more work needs to be done to understand the complex interactions between Asian and Euro-American religions on the Pacific Rim. See Wesley Woo, "Chinese Protestants in the San Francisco Bay Area," in Sucheng Chan, ed., *Entry Denied: Exclusion and the Chinese Community in America, 1882–1943* (Philadelphia: Temple University Press, 1991).

46. On Indian survival and adaptation, see Hurtado, *Indian Survival,* and Maffly-Kipp, *Religion and Society,* chap. 5.

47. Rick Fields, *How the Swans Came to the Lake: A Narrative History of Buddhism in America* (Boulder: Shambhala Publications, 1981), 74–75; Ronald Takaki, *Strangers from a Different Shore: A History of Asian Americans* (Boston: Little, Brown, 1989), 121. Of the 63,199 Chinese in the United States in 1870, only 4,566 were women (Takaki, *Strangers*, 121).

48. Hunter, *Buddhism in Hawaii*, 69–71; Tetsuden Kashima, *Buddhism in America: The Social Organization of an Ethnic Religious Institution* (Westport, Conn.: Greenwood Press, 1977).

49. Any comparison such as this requires some caution: The historical circumstances encountered by Africans and Asians were, needless to say, vastly different. But I believe it can serve a useful purpose to examine them comparatively; we may begin to see aspects of each that have previously escaped notice.

50. Hunter, *Buddhism in Hawaii*, 35.

51. Ibid., 33, 42–47, 80–85. Planters in early twentieth-century Hawaii, fearful that higher wages on the mainland would entice workers, actively encouraged the work of Buddhist priests and even donated land for the construction of temples. In 1907, after an immigration bill was passed to restrict Japanese out-migration and protect the planters, the flurry of temple construction

slowed considerably (ibid., 69–71). There are intriguing parallels to be drawn between the Anglican phase of African American missions in the early eighteenth-century South and the story of Japanese Buddhists.

52. Ibid., 64.

53. Ibid., 190; see also Limerick, "Disorientation and Reorientation," 1038–41. On the sacralization and colonization of Japanese communities in California, see Brian M. Hayashi, *"For the Sake of Our Japanese Brethren": Assimilation, Nationalism, and Protestantism among the Japanese of Los Angeles, 1895–1942* (Stanford: Stanford University Press, 1995), and Valerie J. Matsumoto, *Farming the Home Place: A Japanese American Community in California, 1919–1982* (Ithaca: Cornell University Press, 1993).

54. For a helpful overview of religious traditions throughout the entire western region of the United States, see D. Michael Quinn, "Religion in the American West," in William Cronon, George Miles, and Jay Gitlin, eds., *Under an Open Sky: Rethinking America's Western Past* (New York: W. W. Norton, 1992).

55. Newell S. Booth, Jr., "Islam in North America"; John Y. Fenton, "Hinduism"; C. Carlyle Haaland, "Shinto and Indigenous Chinese Religion"; and Charles S. Prebish, "Buddhism"; all in Charles H. Lippy and Peter W. Williams, eds., *Encyclopedia of the American Religious Experience* (New York: Scribner's, 1988); Gregory Johnson, "The Hare Krishna in San Francisco," in Charles Y. Glock and Robert N. Bellah, eds., *The New Religious Consciousness* (Berkeley: University of California Press, 1976); E. Allen Richardson, *East Comes West: Asian Religions and Cultures in North America* (New York: Pilgrim Press, 1985).

56. George J. Sanchez, *Becoming Mexican American: Ethnicity, Culture, and Identity in Chicano Los Angeles, 1900–1945* (New York: Oxford University Press, 1993), 9. See also Juan Flores and George Yudice, "Living Borders/Buscando America: Languages of Latino Self-Formation," *Social Text* 8, 3 (1990, no. 24): 57–84.

57. Sanchez, *Becoming Mexican American*, especially chap. 7. There is much more to be said about religion and the Latino presence on the Pacific; because of space restrictions this account has focused more extensively on Asian migrations.

58. Richard W. Etulain, "Regionalizing Religion: Evangelicals in the American West, 1940–1990," in Raymond M. Cooke and Richard W. Etulain, eds., *Religion and Culture: Historical Essays in Honor of Robert C. Woodward* (Albuquerque, N.M.: Far West Books, 1991), 87–95.

59. On the reinterpretation of scripture, see Armand L. Mauss, *The Angel and the Beehive: The Mormon Struggle with Assimilation* (Urbana: University of Illinois Press, 1994); on Mormon outreach to the Pacific, see Gibson, *Yankees in Paradise*, 287–88, and R. Lanier Britsch, *Unto the Islands of the Sea: A History of the Latter-Day Saints in the Pacific* (Salt Lake City: Deseret Books, 1986). Gibson reveals that in 1843, Joseph Smith sent a scouting party from Nauvoo, Illinois, to survey the Pacific Basin; by 1846, the church claimed membership in ten settlements on Pacific islands.

60. On Islam, see Yvonne Yazbeck Haddad and Jane Idleman Smith, *Muslim Communities in North America* (Albany: SUNY Press, 1994); Prebish, "Buddhism," 676, 679. This current interest can be fruitfully compared to a history of contact and interest between Americans and adherents of Eastern religious traditions; see Tweed, *American Encounter with Buddhism.*

CHAPTER 6: INDIANS, CONTACT, AND COLONIALISM IN THE DEEP SOUTH

1. Catherine L. Albanese, *America: Religions and Religion,* 2d ed. (1981; Belmont, Calif.: Wadsworth, 1992); Denise Lardner Carmody and John Tully Carmody, *Exploring American Religion* (Mountain View, Calif.: Mayfield 1990); Rosemary Ruether and Rosemary Skinner Keller, eds., *Women and Religion in America,* vol. 2: *The Colonial and Revolutionary Periods: A Documentary History* (San Francisco: Harper and Row, 1983); Peter Williams, *Popular Religion in America* (Carbondale: University of Illinois Press, 1989); Sam Gill, "Native American Religions," in Charles H. Lippy and Peter W. Williams, eds., *Encyclopedia of American Religious Experience: Studies of Traditions and Movements* (New York: Scribner's, 1988), 137-56.

2. See M. Annette Jaimes, ed., *The State of Native America: Genocide, Colonization, and Resistance* (Boston: South End Press, 1992); Ward Churchill, *Struggle for the Land: Indigenous Resistance to Genocide, Ecocide and Expropriation in Contemporary North America* (Monroe, Me.: Common Courage Press, 1993).

3. Other important Native American writers include Marilu Amiakta, Jeannette Armstrong, Rebecca Belmore, Gloria Bird, Kimberly Blaeser, Beth Brant, Michael Dorris, Louise Erdrich, Diane Gloney, Joy Harjo, Tomson Highway, Linda Hogan, Maurice Kenny, Daniel David Moses, Simon J. Ortiz, Wendy Rose, Greg Sarris, Vicki Sears, Ruby Slipperjack, Glenn J. Twist, Gerald Vizenor, and James Welch. See Louis Owens, *Other Destinies: Understanding the American Indian Novel* (Norman: University of Oklahoma Press, 1992); Arnold Krupat, ed., *New Voices in Native American Literary Criticism* (Washington, D.C.: Smithsonian Institution Press, 1993). The Indian literary renaissance is not confined within the borders of the United States, but includes Canadian Native artists as well. See Noel Elizabeth Currie, "Jeannette Armstrong and the Colonial Legacy," and Barbara Godard, "The Politics of Representation: Some Native Canadian Women Writers," *Canadian Literature* 124/125 (spring/summer 1990): 138-52, 183-225. Michael McNally suggested to me the important point regarding the artistic scene at the regional level.

4. Quoted in Richard Marius, "Liberty: Various Views," *Harvard Magazine* (January-February 1995): 118.

5. Other important Native American academics include Paula Gunn Allen, Betty Bell, Mary Churchill, Philip J. Deloria, Walter Echo-Hawk, Donald Grinde, Jr., Richard Grounds, Chris Jacks, M. Annette Jaimes, Oren Lyons, John Mohawk, Alfonso Ortiz, Louis Owens, Sara Parker, Michelene E. Pesan-

tubbee, Ines Talamantez, George Tinker, Robert Allen Warrior, and Richard West. See Ward Churchill, *Fantasies of the Master Race: Literature, Cinema and the Colonization of American Indians,* ed. M. Annette Jaimes (Monroe, Me.: Common Courage Press, 1992); Jaimes, *State of Native America;* Laura Coltelli, *Winged Words: American Indian Writers Speak* (Lincoln: University of Nebraska Press, 1990); Vine Deloria, *God Is Red* (New York: Grosset and Dunlap, 1973); Vine Deloria, Jr., and Clifford M. Lytle, *American Indians, American Justice* (Austin: University of Texas Press, 1983); Robert Allen Warrior, *Recovering American Indian Intellectual Traditions* (Minneapolis: University of Minnesota Press, 1994); Janet Silman, *Enough Is Enough: Aboriginal Women Speak Out* (Toronto: Women's Press, 1987).

6. Ward Churchill, "Perversions of Justice: Examining the Doctrine of U.S. Rights to Occupancy in North America," in *Struggle for the Land,* 33–83. Churchill's argument focuses on the "philosophical validity of U.S. legal claims." He begins by explicating the principles of the Discovery Doctrine established during the age of exploration. These principles, while often ignored by colonial powers, acknowledged the rights of indigenous peoples over their land. As they settled in North America, European colonists, including the English, felt compelled to enter into formal treaties with American Indians. Likewise, the new nation of the United States sought to enter into formal treaties with Indians, in part to establish itself as a legitimate country. This changed, however, as the United States sought to expand westward and encountered Native American sovereignty as "the preeminent barrier." What followed, according to Churchill, is a sorry history of legal subterfuge and obfuscation, stretching from John Marshall to Daniel Inouye, and all designed to justify the theft of Native American lands and resources. Using the model of "the classic relationship between colonizer and colonized," Churchill interprets and critiques major U.S. initiatives, including the "policy of extermination" (late nineteenth century), Major Crimes Act (1885), Dawes Allotment Act (1887), Indian Citizenship Act (1924), Indian Reorganization Act (1934), and Termination Act (1953).

7. Karl Kroeber, "American Indian Persistence and Resurgence," *Boundary 2* 19, 3 (1992): 1–25.

8. Stuart Klawans, "The Greatest Story Ever Told, Or, When Worlds Collide," *Village Voice* (November 1991): 10. For excellent recent works in ethnohistory, see Jacqueline Louise Peterson and Jennifer S. H. Brown, *The New Peoples: Being and Becoming Métis in North America* (Lincoln: University of Nebraska Press, 1985); James Merrell, *The Indians' New World: Catawbas and Their Neighbors from European Contact through the Era of Removal* (Chapel Hill: University of North Carolina Press, 1989); Richard White, *The Middle Ground: Indians, Empires, and Republics in the Great Lakes Region, 1650–1815* (New York: Cambridge University Press, 1991); Daniel Usner, Jr., *Indians, Settlers and Slaves in a Frontier Exchange Economy* (Chapel Hill: University of North Carolina, 1992); Ramón Gutiérrez, *When Jesus Came, the Corn Mothers Went Away: Marriage, Sexuality, and Power in New Mexico, 1500–1846* (Stanford: Stanford University Press, 1991); Daniel K. Richter, *The Ordeal of the*

Longhouse: The Peoples of the Iroquois League in the Era of European Coloniration (Chapel Hill: University of North Carolina Press, 1992); Matthew Dennis, *Cultivating a Landscape of Peace: Iroquois-European Encounters in Seventeenth-Century America* (Ithaca: Cornell University Press, 1993); John Demos, *The Unredeemed Captive: A Family Story from Early America* (New York: Alfred A. Knopf, 1994).

9. Other scholars who have contributed to the study of cultural contact include Jennifer S. H. Brown, James Merrell, Daniel Usner, Jr., Gregory Dowd, Theda Perdue, Mike Green, Ramón Gutiérrez, Daniel K. Richter, Matthew Dennis, and John Demos. Gary B. Nash, *Red, White, and Black: The Peoples of Early America* (Englewood Cliffs, N.J.: Prentice-Hall, 1974); D. W. [Donald William] Meinig, *The Shaping of America: A Geographical Perspective on 500 Years Of History* (New Haven: Yale University Press, 1986); Ronald T. Takaki, *A Different Mirror : A History of Multicultural America* (Boston: Little, Brown, 1993).

10. There are significant tensions between ethnohistorians and Native American intellectuals. These tensions may be resolved as more Indians become ethnohistorians and "take over the writing of their own history," but this has not yet happened. Marius, "Liberty: Various Views," 118. For an attempt to represent the differences between the two approaches as well as an initial attempt to reconcile them, see the special issue of *Historical Reflections* that I edited with M. Annette Jaimes: "The Scholarship of Cultural Contact: Decolonizing Native American History," *Historical Reflections/Réflexions Historiques* 21 (winter 1995).

11. James Axtell, *After Columbus: Essays in the Ethnohistory of Colonial North America* (New York: Oxford, 1988), 223.

12. I have argued this in "Before and beyond the Sioux Ghost Dance: Native American Prophetic Movements and the Discourse of the Study of Religion," *Journal of the American Academy of Religion* (winter 1991): 677–701.

13. Alabama alone recognizes four Creek tribes, with the largest being the Poarch Band of Creek Indians, located in Atmore, Alabama. This last group numbers 2,127. It also received federal recognition in the 1980s.

14. Jefferson Chapman, *Tellico Archaeology: 12,000 Years of Native American History* (Knoxville: Tennessee Valley Authority, distributed by University of Tennessee Press, 1985); Vernon J. Knight, *Mississippian Ritual,* (Ph.D. dissertation, University of Florida, 1981).

15. For instance, to the Caddo, according to George Sabo, "trade with Europeans does not appear to have differed substantially from Caddo trade relations with other Indians." In both types of contact, Caddos relied on the calumet ceremony and conferred on these interactions an essentially religious character. George Sabo III, "Encounters and Images: European Contact and the Caddo Indians," *Historical Reflections/Réflexions Historiques* 21 (spring 1995): 1–26.

16. Jerald T. Milanich, *Hernando de Soto and the Indians of Florida* (Gainesville: University Press of Florida and Florida Museum of Natural History, 1993); Charles Hudson, *The Forgotten Centuries: Indians and Europeans in the American South, 1521–1704* (Athens: University of Georgia Press, 1994).

17. John W. Verano and Douglas H. Ubelaker, eds., *Disease and Demography in the Americas* (Washington, D.C.: Smithsonian Institution Press, 1992); Vernon James Knight, Jr., "The Institutional Organization of Mississippian Religion," *American Antiquity* 51, 4 (1986): 675–87.

18. This religious system is described in Joel W. Martin, *Sacred Revolt: The Muskogees' Struggle for a New World* (Boston: Beacon Press, 1991), 17–45; William Bartram, *Travels through North and South Carolina, Georgia, East and West Florida, the Cherokee Country, the Extensive Territories of the Muscogulges, or Creek Confederacy, and the Country of the Choctaws* (1791; New York: Penguin, 1988), 393–95.

19. Bartram, *Travels,* 360; Caleb Swan, "Position and State of Manners and Arts in the Creek Nation, in 1791," in *Information Respecting the History Condition and Prospects of the Indian Tribes of the United States,* comp. Henry Rowe Schoolcraft (Philadelphia, 1855), 5:266–67.

20. For the metaphor of middle ground, see White, *Middle Ground,* 33. White applied the concept to one specific region; however, because he defines the concept broadly, it can be used to describe different contact situations.

21. Most Creek Indians thought monogamy could be monotonous, sanctioned divorce, and organized village life around matrilineal, matrilocal compounds where women controlled property and raised children with the help of male members of their clan and the children's fathers. See Swan, "Position and State of Manners," 5:273. In contrast, most Anglo-American Protestants celebrated the patrilineal, patriarchal nuclear family focused on a monogamous, heterosexual couple where fathers exercised authority over wives and children. This is not to say that the Protestant conception of the family was static or that only one type of family existed among Anglo-Americans. Within evangelical culture, for instance, women were gaining a new kind of authority as spiritual mentors to their husbands. See A. Gregory Schneider, *The Way of the Cross Leads Home: The Domestication of American Methodism* (Bloomington: Indiana University Press, 1993), 74–77, 174–78.

22. For an instance of cross-cultural conflict, see Benjamin Hawkins, *Letters, Journals and Writings* (Savannah, Ga.: Beehive Press, 1980), 1:47–48.

23. Carl Mauelshagen and Gerald H. Davis, trans., *Partners in the Lord's Work: The Diary of Two Moravian Missionaries in the Creek Indian Country,* Research Paper Number 21 (Atlanta: Georgia State College, 1969), 53.

24. Kenelm Burridge, *New Heaven, New Earth: A Study of Millenarian Activities* (New York: Schocken, 1969), 106, 107; Shahid Amin, "Gandhi as Mahatma: Gorakhpur District, Eastern UP, 1921–22," in Ranajit Guha and Gayatri Chakravorty Spivak, eds., *Subaltern Studies: Writings on South Asian History and Society, III* (Oxford: Oxford University Press, 1984), 1–61.

25. Samuel Coles Williams, ed., *Adair's History of the American Indians* (Johnson City, Tenn.: Watauga Press, 1930), 394.

26. Hawkins, *Letters,* 1:305.

27. Williams, *Adair's History,* 121; John Howard Payne, "The Green-Corn Dance," *Continental Monthly* (1862); Daniel F. Littlefield, Jr., *Africans and Creeks: From the Colonial Period to the Civil War* (Westport, Conn.: Greenwood Press, 1979), 9, 14, 15, 28; William S. Willis, "Divide and Rule: Red,

White, and Black in the Southeast," in Charles M. Hudson, ed., *Red, White, and Black: Symposium on Indians in the Old South* (Athens, Ga.: Southern Anthropological Society Proceedings, No. 5, 1970), 99–115; J. H. Johnston, "Documentary Evidence of the Relations of Negroes and Indian," *Journal of Negro History* 14 (1929): 21–43.

28. J. Leitch Wright, Jr., "Br'er Rabbit at the Square Ground," in *The Only Land They Knew: The Tragic Story of the American Indians in the Old South* (New York: Free Press, 1981), 248–78.

29. Journal of Lee Compere, 25 April 1828, American Indian Correspondence, Reel 98, American Baptist Historical Society, Rochester, N.Y.; Notes Furnished A. J. Pickett by the Rev. Lee Compere of Mississippi relating to the Creek Indians among whom he lived as a Missionary, Albert J. Pickett Papers, Notes upon the History of Alabama, section 24, Alabama Department of Archives and History, Montgomery, Ala.; Peter A. Brannon, "The Baptist Mission and Mr. Compere's Connection With It," *Arrow Points* 14, 3 (1929): 41–42; Daniel Sabin Butrick, "Jews and Indians" (circa 1840), Cherokee Missions, Miscellaneous, American Board of Commissioners for Foreign Missions, 18.3.3, vol. 3, pts. 1–3, Houghton Library, Harvard University, Cambridge, Mass.

30. "When my angel goes before you, and brings you in to the Amorites, and the Hittites, and the Perizzites, and the Canaanites, the Hivites, and the Jebusites, and I blot them out" (RSV, Exodus 23:23).

31. Rev. T. A. Morris, a Methodist bishop, summarized this widely shared conviction in his introduction to Henry C. Benson, *Life Among the Choctaw Indians and Sketches of the South-West* (Cincinnati: L. Swormstedt and A. Poe, 1860), 8. Morris wrote: "Now, it may be that this rapid disappearance [of Indians] before a superior race is in the order of an overruling Providence. It is declared in the book from which there is no appeal, 'For the nation and kingdom that will not serve thee shall perish; yea, those nations shall be utterly wasted.' Isaiah lx, 12. Heathenism and Christian civilization can never flourish as cotemporaries [sic] on the same soil. The life of one is the death of the other."

32. Many Protestants linked biblical tales of lost tribes with New World populations. Nineteenth-century Anglo-Americans who believed this included the followers of Joseph Smith and many non-Mormons as well. Daniel Butrick, a well-educated Presbyterian missionary among southeastern Indians, wrote several hundred pages comparing the religious systems of Jews and Indians, and concluded the religions and the peoples were related (Butrick, "Jews and Indians").

33. George E. Lankford, *Native American Legends: Southeastern Legends—Tales from the Natchez, Caddo, Biloxi, Chickasaw, and Other Nations* (Little Rock, Ark.: August House, 1987), 140–41.

34. James Wright to the Earl of Hillsborough, 4 July 1768, in Allen D. Candler and Lucien Lamar Knight, eds., *Colonial Records of the State of Georgia* (Atlanta: [state printers], 1904–16), 27:330. Of course, not all runaways found refuge in Muskogee. Some were ransomed by Muskogees for the reward offered by colonial officials. See John Donald Duncan, "Servitude and Slavery in Colonial South Carolina, 1670–1776," Ph.D. dissertation, Emory University, 1972,

630–32. As Peter H. Wood notes, running away was "a more frequent, more complicated and more politically significant act than was once imagined [by scholars]." Peter H. Wood, " 'I Did the Best I Could for My Day': The Study of Early Black History during the Second Reconstruction, 1960 to 1976," *William and Mary Quarterly,* 3d ser. 35, 2 (April 1978): 217. Pertinent studies of runaways include John J. TePaske, "The Fugitive Slave: Intercolonial Rivalry and Spanish Slave Policy, 1686–1764," in Samuel Proctor, ed., *Eighteenth-Century Florida and Its Borderlands,* (Gainesville: University Presses of Florida, 1975), 1–12; Daniel E. Meaders, "South Carolina Fugitives as Viewed through Local Colonial Newspapers with Emphasis on Runaway Notices, 1732–1801," *Journal of Negro History* 60 (1975): 288–319; Lathan A. Windley, "A Profile of Runaway Slaves in Virginia and South Carolina from 1730 through 1787," Ph.D. dissertation, University of Iowa, 1974.

35. Toni Morrison, *Beloved* (New York: Knopf, 1987).

36. Leslie Silko, *Ceremony* (New York: Viking, 1977).

37. Frederick E. Hoxie, ed., *Indians in American History : An Introduction* (Arlington Heights, Ill.: Harlan Davidson, 1988), 179.

38. See Martin, *Sacred Revolt,* 114–49.

39. Notes Furnished A. J. Pickett by the Rev. Lee Compere.

40. Joel W. Martin, "From 'Middle Ground' to 'Underground': Southeastern Indians and the Early Republic," in David G. Hackett, ed., *Religion and American Culture* (New York: Routledge, 1995), 127–45.

41. Like some white slaveholders, Creek chiefs feared that if African Americans had their own churches and preachers, they would be more difficult to control as slaves. Additionally, chiefs felt that if blacks became Christians, "the Indian would go and hear preaching and then the Kings of the towns would lose their authority" among their own people. Lee Compere to Rev. Dr. Bolles, 19 December 1828, American Indian Correspondence, Reel 98, American Baptist Historical Society Archives, Rochester, N.Y.

42. Ibid., 19 May 1828.

43. Peter A. Brannon, "Baptist Mission," 41. The Comperes' tenure at the church was short-lived as their support of the rights of the Creeks brought them into opposition with the Anglo-American settlers of Montgomery.

44. In 1839, a hapless couple traveled for several months and faced many dangers to reach the Creeks. Barely arrived in Little Rock, the American Baptist missionaries "were informed that no preaching was allowed in the Nation." Once among the Creeks, they were summoned to a council of the Nation and "ordered . . . to leave the country immediately." Diary of Releaf Mariah Smith Mason, 30 January 1839, American Baptist Historical Society Archives, Rochester, N.Y.

45. Richard Slotkin, *Regeneration through Violence: The Mythology of the American Frontier, 1600–1860* (Middletown, Conn.: Wesleyan University Press, 1973), 100, 179.

46. Quoted in Michael Paul Rogin, *Fathers and Children: Andrew Jackson and the Subjugation of the American Indian* (New York: Alfred A. Knopf, 1975), 147.

47. Catherine L. Albanese, "King Crockett: Nature and Civility on the American Frontier," *Proceedings of the American Antiquarian Society* 88 (1979): 225–50.

48. Alexander Beaufort Meek, *The Red Eagle: A Poem of the South* (Montgomery, Ala.: Paragon Press, 1914); Albert James Pickett, *History of Alabama, and Incidentally of Georgia and Mississippi, from the Earliest Period* (Birmingham, Ala.: Birmingham Book and Magazine Company, 1962), 611.

49. For a preliminary report on my findings, see Joel W. Martin, "Indian Sightings in Lancaster County: The Mythic, Religious Significance of 'Indians' for Non-Indians," *American Indian Religions: An Interdisciplinary Journal* 2 (spring 1994): 151–72.

50. Lakota Times (Rapid City, S. Dak.), 30 October 1991.

51. Churchill, *Fantasies of the Master Race.*

52. The following discussion of contemporary Creeks is based on J. Anthony Paredes, "Tribal Recognition and the Poarch Creek Indians," in J. Anthony Paredes, ed., *Indians of the Southeastern United States in the Late 20th Century* (Tuscaloosa: University of Alabama Press, 1992), 120–39.

53. Ibid., 137–38.

54. For New England, see Neal Salisbury, *Manitou and Providence: Indians, Europeans, and the Making of New England, 1500–1643* (New York: Oxford University Press, 1982); Francis Jennings, *The Invasion of America: Indians, Colonialism, and the Cant of Conquest* (Chapel Hill: University of North Carolina Press, 1975). For Virginia, see J. Frederick Fausz, "Patterns of Anglo-Indian Aggression and Accommodation along the Mid-Atlantic Coast, 1584–1634," in William Fitzhugh, ed., *Cultures in Contact,* (Washington, D.C.: Smithsonian Institution Press, 1985), 225–70; idem, "Fighting 'Fire' with Firearms: The Anglo-Powhatan Arms Race in Early Virginia," *American Indian Culture and Research Journal* 3 (1979): 33–50; idem, "The Powhatan Uprising of 1622: A Historical Study of Ethnocentrism and Cultural Conflict," Ph.D. dissertation, College of William and Mary, 1977; Helen C. Rountree, *Pocahontas's People: The Powhatan Indians of Virginia through Four Centuries* (Norman: University of Oklahoma Press, 1990), 1–103.

55. Jill Lepore, "Dead Men Tell No Tales: John Sassamon and the Fatal Consequences of Literacy," *American Quarterly* 46 (December 1994): 479–512.

56. For Pennsylvania, see Ives Goddard, "Delaware," in Bruce G. Trigger, ed., *Handbook of North American Indians, Northeast* (Washington, D.C.: Smithsonian Institution, 1978), 15:213–39; Clinton Alfred Weslager, *The Delaware Indians: A History* (New Brunswick, N.J.: Rutgers University Press, 1972).

57. For an examination of the short-lived Dutch-Indian middle ground (1624–64), see Lynn Ceci, "The Effect of European Contact and Trade on the Settlement Pattern of Indians in Coastal New York, 1524–1665: The Archaeological and Documentary Evidence," Ph.D. dissertation, City University of New York, 1977. For the Iroquois story, see Dennis, *Cultivating A Landscape of Peace;* Richter, *The Ordeal of the Longhouse;* Richard Aquila, *The Iroquois Restoration: Iroquois Diplomacy on the Colonial Frontier, 1701–1754* (Detroit:

Wayne State University Press, 1983); Francis Jennings, *The Ambiguous Iroquois Empire: The Covenant Chain Confederation of Indian Tribes with English Colonies from its Beginnings to the Lancaster Treaty of 1744* (New York: Norton, 1984).

58. White, *Middle Ground.*

59. For the métis, see Peterson and Brown, *The New Peoples,* and Jennifer S. H. Brown, *Strangers in Blood: Fur Trade Company Families in Indian Country* (Vancouver: University of British Columbia Press, 1980).

60. See, for instance, Willard H. Rollings, *The Osage: An Ethnohistorical Study of Hegemony on the Prairie-Plains* (Columbia: University of Missouri Press, 1992).

61. George E. Tinker, *Missionary Conquest: The Gospel and Native American Cultural Genocide* (Minneapolis: Fortress Press, 1993).

62. See Brian W. Dippie, *The Vanishing American: White Attitudes and U.S. Indian Policy* (1982; Lawrence: University Press of Kansas, 1991); Roy Pearce, *Savagism and Civilization* (Baltimore: Johns Hopkins University Press, 1965); Annette Kolodny, *The Lay of the Land: Metaphor as Experience and History in American Life and Letters* (Chapel Hill: University of North Carolina Press, 1975); Philip J. Deloria, "Playing Indian: Otherness and Authenticity in the Assumption of American Indian Identity," Ph.D. dissertation, Yale University, 1994; Schneider, *The Way of the Cross;* Lora Romera, "Vanishing Americans: Gender, Empire, and New Historicism," *American Literature* 63 (September 1991): 385–404.

63. For analyses of public Protestantism and civil religion, see Albanese, *America,* 396–462. For instances of efforts to outlaw Native American religion, see Omer Call Stewart, *Peyote Religion: A History* (Norman: University of Oklahoma Press, 1987); Douglas Cole and Ira Chaikan, *An Iron Hand upon the People: The Law against the Potlatch on the Northwest Coast* (Seattle: University of Washington Press, 1990); Curtis E. Jackson and Marcia J. Galli, *A History of the Bureau of Indian Affairs and Its Activities among Indians* (San Francisco: Rand E. Research Associates, 1977); Robert Michaelson, "The Significance of the American Indian Religious Freedom Act," *Journal of the American Academy of Religion* 52 (1984): 93–115.

64. Robert N. Clinton, "Redressing the Legacy of Conquest: A Vision Quest for a Decolonized Federal Indian Law," *Arkansas Law Review* 46; 77 (1993): 98.

65. See Thomas A. Tweed, *The American Encounter with Buddhism, 1844–1912 : Victorian Culture and the Limits of Dissent* (Bloomington: Indiana University Press, 1992).

66. Clinton, "Redressing the Legacy of Conquest," 90.

67. Ibid., 107.

68. Edward Linenthal, *Preserving Memory: The Struggle to Create America's Holocaust Museum* (New York: Viking Press, 1995).

69. Employment Div., Dept. of Human Resources of Oregon v. Smith, 494 U.S. 872, 110 S.Ct. 1595, 108 L.Ed. 2d 876 (1990), rehearing denied, U.S.110 S. Ct. 2605, 110 L.Ed. 2d 285 (1990).

70. See Christopher Vecsey, ed., *Handbook of American Indian Religious*

Freedom (New York: Crossroad Publishing, 1991). See also, essays on the theme of American Indian religious freedom in *American Indian Religions* 1: 1 (winter 1994).

CHAPTER 7: VOICES FROM THE ATTIC

1. Robertson Davies, *A Voice from the Attic* (Toronto: McClelland and Stewart, 1960), 3. I would like to thank all the contributors to this project—both authors and commentators—and especially Thomas Tweed, for their many helpful comments on earlier versions of this chapter. I also offer a special acknowledgement to my good friend, Professor Phyllis Airhart, who has always tried to keep me going in the right direction.

The religious history of Canada and the United States has been examined from somewhat different perspectives by two leading scholars of American religion, Robert T. Handy and Mark A. Noll. Both these men have not only written incisively on this subject, but also, through their personal generosity and strong support of scholars working in Canada (including this author), helped to nurture a subject too long ignored by the mainstream of Canadian historiography. In effect, not only have they written about religion in Canada and the United States, they have helped to make comparative religious studies possible. See Robert T. Handy, *A History of the Churches in the United States and Canada* (New York: Oxford University Press, 1976), and Mark A. Noll, *A History of Christianity in the United States and Canada* (Grand Rapids, Mich.: Eerdmans, 1992). See also Mark Noll, "Christianity in Canada: Good Books at Last," *Fides et Historia* 23 (summer 1991): 103; Robert T. Handy, "Dominant Patterns of Christian Life in Canada and the United States: Similarities and Differences," in William Westfall, Louis Rousseau, Fernand Harvey, and John Simpson, eds., *Religion/Culture: Comparative Canadian Studies, Études canadiennes comparées* (Ottawa: Association for Canadian Studies, 1985), 344–55; and Robert T. Handy, "Protestant Patterns in Canada and the United States: Similarities and Differences," in Joseph D. Ban and Paul R. Dekar, eds., *In the Great Tradition: Essays on Pluralism, Voluntarism, and Revivalism* (Valley Forge, Pa.: Judson Press, 1982), 33–51.

2. See also Hayden White, "The Question of Narrative in Contemporary Historical Theory, " *History and Theory* 23 (1984): 1–33; and idem, *The Content of the Form: Narrative Discourse and Historical Representation* (Baltimore: Johns Hopkins University Press, 1987).

3. Nathan O. Hatch, "The Puzzle of American Methodism," *Church History* 63 (June 1994): 175–89. His list of the historians who defined and shaped the great tradition includes Perry Miller, Samuel Eliot Morison, Ralph Barton Perry, Alan Heimert, Edmund Morgan, William McLoughlin, Sydney Ahlstrom, Timothy Smith, Henry May, H. Richard Niebuhr, John Smith, William Warren Sweet, Sidney Mead, Robert Handy, Winthrop Hudson, Jerald Brauer, and Martin E. Marty. Hatch gives special mention to three works: Ahlstrom's *A Religious History of the American People*, Mead's *The Lively Experiment*, and Marty's *Righteous Empire: The Protestant Experience in America*.

4. Hatch, "The Puzzle of American Methodism," 175–76. James D. Bratt reconstructs the great tradition in much the same way; see James D. Bratt, "A New Narrative for American Religious History?" *Fides et Historia* 23 (fall 1991): 19–30.

5. For other accounts of the development of this national Protestant historiography (as well as its shortcomings) see Bratt, "A New Narrative?" and Eldon G. Ernst, "Beyond the Protestant Era in American Religious Historiography," in *In the Great Tradition,* 123–45.

6. The shift from inside to outside is most brilliantly set out in R. Laurence Moore, *Religious Outsiders and the Making of Americans* (New York: Oxford University Press, 1986). For the general challenge to consensus history see Gene Wise, *American Historical Explanations: A Strategy for Grounded Inquiry* (Homewood, Ill.: Dorsey Press, 1973), and John Higham, "Changing Paradigms: The Collapse of Consensus History," *Journal of American History* (September 1989), 460–66.

7. Richard Van Alstyne is one of the few American historians to treat the border in this way; see Richard Van Alstyne, *The Rising American Empire* (Oxford: Basil Blackwood, 1960).

8. For a discussion of boundaries and cultural history see William Westfall, "On the Concept of Region in Canadian History and Literature," *Journal of Canadian Studies* 15 (summer 1980): 3–15, and Robert Lecker, ed., *Borderlands: Essays in Canadian-American Relations* (Toronto: ECW Press, 1991).

9. John Strachan, *An Appeal to the Friends of Religion and Literature in Behalf of the University of Upper Canada* (London: R. Gilbert, 1827), 5.

10. S. F. Wise and R. C. Brown, *Canada Views the United States: Nineteenth-Century Political Attitudes* (Toronto: Macmillan, 1967).

11. Carl Berger, *The Sense of Power: Studies in the Ideas of Canadian Imperialism, 1867–1914* (Toronto: University of Toronto Press, 1970).

12. G. M. Craig, *Upper Canada: The Formative Years, 1784–1841* (Toronto: McClelland and Stewart, 1963).

13. D. G. Creighton, *The Road to Confederation* (Toronto: Macmillan, 1964), and W. L. Morton, *The Critical Years: The Union of British North America, 1857–1873* (Toronto: McClelland and Stewart, 1964).

14. Hatch, "The Puzzle of American Methodism," 176, and Bratt, "A New Narrative," 23.

15. It is precisely this recognition that makes the two major scholarly works that have examined the religious histories of the two countries so insightful. Both Robert T. Handy and Mark A. Noll examine important themes in the history of religion in North America. In doing so they not only acknowledge the border but also see in it the opportunity to compare religious developments within two similar yet distinct societies, leading in each case to studies that can cast an informative light on the religious histories of both countries; see Noll, *A History of Christianity,* and Handy, *A History of the Churches.* See also Handy, "Dominant Patterns of Christian Life," 344–55; and idem, "Protestant Patterns," 33–51.

16. In appreciation of his work with the American church, Columbia College in New York City awarded McMurray an honourary degree. *Dictionary of*

Canadian Biography, s.v. "William McMurray," XII, 680–82. See also T. A. Reed, *A History of Trinity College, 1852–1952* (Toronto: University of Toronto Press, 1952).

17. William Westfall, *Two Worlds: The Protestant Culture of Nineteenth Century Ontario* (Montreal: McGill-Queen's University Press, 1989), especially chap. 4; John Strachan, *A Letter to the Rev. Thomas Chalmers, D.D., Professor of Divinity in the University of Edinburgh, on the Life and Character of the Right Reverend Dr. Hobart, Bishop of New York, North America* (New York: Swords and Stanford, 1832).

18. For an excellent overview of Strachan's career see: *Dictionary of Canadian Biography,* s.v. "John Strachan," X, 751–66. For an excellent study of cultural interchange along the border in the early nineteenth century see Jane Errington, *The Lion, the Eagle, and Upper Canada: A Developing Colonial Ideology* (Montreal: McGill-Queen's University Press, 1987).

19. Freda Hawkins, *Canada and Immigration* (Montreal: McGill-Queen's University Press, 1972).

20. Robert Craig Brown and Ramsay Cook, *Canada, 1896–1921: A Nation Transformed* (Toronto: McClelland and Stewart, 1974); Gerald Friesen, *The Canadian Prairies: A History* (Toronto: University of Toronto Press, 1984).

21. Thomas F. O'Dea. *The Mormons* (Chicago: University of Chicago Press, 1957). Taylor was with Joseph Smith when Smith was murdered, and Taylor was wounded as he leapt from the window of the lockup. O'Dea also points out that Brigham Young's brother Joseph was a lay preacher in Canada. Brigham, in fact, came to Canada to ask his brother's advice before he converted to Mormonism. See also Church of Jesus Christ of Latter Day Saints, Lethbridge Stake Historical Committee, *A History of the Mormon Church in Canada* (Lethbridge, Alb.: Lethbridge Herald, 1968).

22. The story of Hutchinson's conversion to the doctrines of William Miller can be found in the Canadian materials of the Wesleyan Methodist Church, Great Britain, Foreign Missions: British North America. Many of his pamphlets are preserved in the Jenks Memorial Collection of Adventist Materials in the Charles B. Phillips Library, Aurora College, Aurora, Ill.

23. For material on Canadian Fundamentalism and especially the careers of Davis and McPherson, see David Raymond Elliott, "The Intellectual World of Canadian Fundamentalism: 1870–1970," Ph.D. thesis, University of British Columbia, 1989. The cross-border theme is developed more fully in David R. Elliott, "Knowing No Borders: Canadian Contributions to American Fundamentalism," and Robert K. Burkinshaw, "Conservative Evangelicalism in the Twentieth-Century 'West': British Columbia and the United States," both in George A. Rawlyk and Mark A. Noll, eds., *Amazing Grace: Evangelicalism in Australia, Britain, Canada, and the United States* (Montreal: McGill-Queen's University Press, 1994), 349–74, 317–48. McPherson's life is also the subject of an excellent new biography; see Edith W. Blumhofer, *Aimee Semple McPherson: Everybody's Sister* (Grand Rapids, Mich.: Eerdmans, 1993).

24. For material on Chiniquy see Jan Noel, "Dry Patriotism: The Chiniquy Crusade," *Canadian Historical Review* 71 (June 1990): 189–207, and *Dictio-*

nary of Canadian Biography, s.v. "Charles Chiniquy," XII, 192–93. The titles of most Chiniquy's later tracts clearly reveal their content, for example: *The Church of Rome Is the Enemy of the Holy Virgin and Jesus Christ* and *President Lincoln's Assassination Traced Directly to the Doors of Rome.* On the tensions within North American Catholicism see: Roberto Perin, *Rome in Canada: The Vatican and Canadian Affairs in the Late Victorian Age* (Toronto: University of Toronto Press, 1990).

25. Alan Brinkley, *Voices of Protest* (New York: Vintage Books, 1983); J. Harold Ellens, *Models of Religious Broadcasting* (Grand Rapids, Mich.: Eerdmans, 1974).

26. Dennis Duffy, *Gardens, Covenants, and Exiles: Loyalism in the Literature of Upper Canada/Ontario* (Toronto: University of Toronto Press, 1982); Berger, *Sense of Power,* especially chap. 3.

27. Howard Law, " 'Self-Reliance Is the True Road to Independence': Ideology and the Ex-Slaves in Buxton and Chatham," *Ontario History* 77 (June 1985), 107–21; Robin Winks, *The Blacks in Canada* (New Haven: Yale University Press, 1971). Harriet Beecher Stowe uses biblical language to describe Canada as a land of refuge—"like the eternal shore." To say, however, that slaves found freedom in Canada is at best a relative statement and should not be taken to imply that racism did not (and does not) exist in Canada. At the end of the war many slaves returned to the United States, and those who stayed faced various forms of discrimination in Canada. It is also important to remember that at the end of the nineteenth century, when Canada was desperate for agricultural immigrants, African American farmers wanting to settle in the Canadian West were excluded, largely through administrative means. See Harold Troper, *Only Farmers Need Apply: Official Canadian Government Encouragement of Immigration from the United States* (Toronto: Griffin, 1972).

28. For an excellent discussion of early Quaker migrations to Canada see Albert Schrauwers, *Awaiting the Millennium: The Children of Peace and the Village of Hope* (Toronto: University of Toronto Press, 1993).

29. Thomas P. Socknat, *Witness against War: Pacifism in Canada, 1900–1945* (Toronto: University of Toronto Press, 1987).

30. G. A. Rawlyk, *The Canada Fire: Radical Evangelicalism in British North America, 1775–1812* (Montreal: McGill-Queen's University Press, 1994).

31. Irving Abella and Harold Troper, *None Is Too Many: Canada and the Jews of Europe* (Toronto: Lester and Orphen Dennys, 1982).

32. Noll, *A History of Christianity,* and Handy, *A History of the Churches.*

33. Northrop Frye, *The Modern Century* (1967; Toronto: Oxford University Press, 1991).

34. Gordon Stewart and George Rawlyk, *A People Highly Favoured of God: The Nova Scotia Yankees and the American Revolution* (Toronto: Macmillan, 1972); George Rawlyk, *Ravished by the Spirit: Religious Revivals, Baptists, and Henry Alline* (Montreal: McGill-Queen's University Press, 1984).

35. Frederick Philip Grove's novels include *A Search for America: The Odyssey of an Immigrant* (Toronto: McClelland and Stewart, 1971), *In Search of Myself* (Toronto: Macmillan, 1946), and especially *Over Prairie Trails* (Toronto: McClelland and Stewart, 1970). See also Russell Brown, "The Written Line,"

in *Borderlands,* 1–27; Dick Harrison, *Unnamed Country: The Struggle for a Canadian Prairie Fiction* (Edmonton: University of Alberta Press, 1977).

36. Louis Hémon, *Maria Chapdelaine* (New York: Macmillan, 1921).

37. See Pierre Berton, *Hollywood's Canada: The Americanization of Our National Image* (Toronto: McClelland and Stewart, 1975).

38. Fred Matthews, review of Seymour Martin Lipset's *Continental Divide: The Values and Institutions of the United States and Canada,* in *Journal of Interdisciplinary History* 21 (spring 1991): 719–21. See also William Kilbourn, ed., *Canada: A Guide to the Peaceable Kingdom* (Toronto: Macmillan, 1970), and James Doyle, ed., *Yankees in Canada: A Collection of Nineteenth-Century Travel Narratives* (Toronto: ECW Press, 1980).

39. While this discussion compares these visions within the Protestant cultures of the two countries, it is clear that Canadian Catholics, especially in Francophone Canada, were caught up in a similar vision. It is one of the deeper ironies of Canadian culture that these two religious groups, English Canadian Protestants and French Canadian Roman Catholics, who often represented each other as the devil incarnate, should articulate national religious ideologies that were so strikingly similar. Professor Roberto Perin and I are currently working on a study of this theme; William Westfall and Roberto Perin, "Protestant and Catholic: Religion, Culture, and the Creation of National Identities," paper presented at the biennial meeting of the Association of Canadian Studies in the United States, New Orleans, La., November 1993.

40. For a discussion of the relationship between freedom and coercion in American religion see Edwin S. Gaustad, "The Great Tradition and 'The Coercion of Voluntarism,' " in *In the Great Tradition,* 161–72.

41. It has always struck me that there is enormous significance in the fact that it was a Canadian, Sandford (later Sir Sandford) Fleming, who devised the international system of standard time.

42. Noll, "Christianity in Canada," 103.

43. Carl Berger, *The Writing of Canadian History: Aspects of English-Canadian Historical Writing, 1900 to 1970* (Toronto: Oxford University Press, 1976).

44. In Canada there is a strong tradition of antinational history that asserts, in effect, that the creation of Canada was a mistake. In English-speaking Canada this position was set out most fully by Goldwin Smith, *Canada and the Canadian Question* (Toronto: Hunter Rose, 1891); in French Canada the theme of *histoire noire* runs through the writing of many nationalist historians, and especially the work of Michel Brunet.

45. Linda Hutcheon, *The Canadian Postmodern: A Study of Contemporary English-Canadian Fiction* (Toronto: Oxford University Press, 1988).

CHAPTER 8: EXCHANGING SELVES, EXCHANGING SOULS

1. Isaac M. Wise, *Reminiscences,* trans. David Philipson, 2d ed. (New York: Central Synagogue of New York, 1945), in Jacob Rader Marcus, ed., *Memoirs of American Jews, 1775–1865* (Philadelphia: Jewish Publication Society of America, 1955), 2:104–5.

2. Ibid., 108.

3. Ibid., 120–25, 125–26.

4. Marcel Mauss, *The Gift: Forms and Functions of Exchange in Archaic Societies,* trans. Ian Cunnison (New York: W. W. Norton, 1967), 69. The recent thinking of my colleague Charles H. Long has sparked my own interest in the work of Mauss and its applicability to scenarios of religious contact.

5. Ibid., 81.

6. Ibid., 63–81.

7. R. Laurence Moore, *Selling God: American Religion in the Marketplace of Culture* (New York: Oxford University Press, 1994), 275. Moore's book, though, is written in a decidedly different key from this essay, since his concern is the commercialization and commodification of organized religion, while I focus here on the issue of the processes of contact and exchange in a pluralist society.

8. Mauss, *The Gift,* 10.

9. The classic exposition of the size of Native American populations before and after the European conquest is Henry F. Dobyns, "Estimating Aboriginal American Population: An Appraisal of Techniques with a New Hemispheric Estimate," *Current Anthropology* 7 (1966): 395–416. Useful accounts of the cultural meetings that ensued may be found in James Axtell, *The European and the Indian* (New York: Oxford University Press, 1981); idem, *The Invasion Within: The Contest of Cultures in Colonial North America* (New York: Oxford University Press, 1985); idem, *After Columbus: Essays in the Ethnohistory of Colonial North America* (New York: Oxford University Press, 1988); idem, *Beyond 1492: Encounters in Colonial North America* (New York: Oxford University Press, 1992); Francis Jennings, *The Invasion of America: Indians, Colonialism, and the Cant of Conquest* (Chapel Hill: University of North Carolina Press, 1975); Gary B. Nash, *Red, White, and Black: The Peoples of Early America* (Englewood Cliffs, N.J.: Prentice-Hall, 1974); and Neal Salisbury, *Manitou and Providence: Indians, Europeans, and the Making of New England, 1500–1643* (New York: Oxford University Press, 1982).

10. For a review of recent thinking on the success or failure of seventeenth-century Indian missions and an independent assessment, see James Axtell, "Were Indian Conversions *Bona Fide?,*" in *After Columbus,* 100–121.

11. James Axtell, "Some Thoughts on the Ethnohistory of Missions," in ibid., 54–55. See also idem, "Native Reactions to Invasion," in *Before 1492,* especially 116–18.

12. Sherburne F. Cook, *The Conflict between the California Indian and White Civilization* (Berkeley: University of California Press, 1976), 76. For a useful discussion of Roman Catholic–Indian mission contact, see Jay P. Dolan, *The American Catholic Experience: A History from Colonial Times to the Present* (Garden City, N.Y.: Doubleday, 1985), 15–68.

13. Sandra S. Sizer (Tamar Frankiel) explores some of the ways that the California Indians related to Franciscan Catholic religious practices in terms of their own ceremonial life in "Native Americans, Franciscans, and Puritans: Problems of Translation," an unpublished paper to which I am indebted.

14. For an argument that racial preoccupations were not important in early English colonial views of American Indians, see Karen Ordahl Kupperman, *Settling with the Indians: The Meeting of English and Indian Cultures in America, 1580–1640* (Totowa, N.J.: Rowman and Littlefield, 1980).

15. Amanda Porterfield, "Algonquian Shamans and Puritan Saints," *Horizons* 12, 2 (1985): 303–10; Ann Taves, "Knowing through the Body: Dissociative Religious Experience in the African- and British-American Methodist Traditions," *Journal of Religion* 73, 2 (April 1993): 220–22.

16. For a short and useful account of Ma-re Mount, see Salisbury, *Manitou and Providence,* 152–65.

17. See James Axtell, "The White Indians of Colonial America," in *European and Indian,* 168–206.

18. My treatment of Tammany and Tammany lore here and in what follows is indebted to Sarah McFarland Taylor of the University of California, Santa Barbara, whose unpublished paper "Customs, Costumes, and Ritual: Constructions of White 'Native' Identity and Origin in American History" explores the Tammany literature in greater depth than I can offer here. For more on Tammany, see Oliver E. Allen, *The Tiger: The Rise and Fall of Tammany Hall* (New York: Addison-Wesley, 1993); Edwin Kilroe, *Saint Tammany and the Origin of the Society of Tammany or Columbian Order in the City of New York* (New York: Columbia University Press, 1913); Carl Lemke, ed., *Official History of the Improved Order of Red Men: Compiled under the Authority from the Great Council of the United States by Past Great Incohonees, George Linsay of Maryland, Charles Conley of Pennsylvania, and Charles Litchman of Massachusetts* (Waco, Tex.: Davis, 1965); Gustavus Myers, *The History of Tammany Hall* (New York: Burt Franklin, 1917); and M. R. Werner, *Tammany Hall* (Garden City, N.Y.: Doubleday, Doran, 1928).

19. Mark C. Carnes, *Secret Ritual and Manhood in Victorian America* (New Haven: Yale University Press, 1989), 99, 97–99.

20. Ibid., 99–101.

21. John Humphrey Noyes, *Strange Cults and Utopias of Nineteenth-Century America* [*History of American Socialisms*] (1870; reprint, New York: Dover, 1966), 605.

22. See the discussion in J. Stillson Judah, *The History and Philosophy of the Metaphysical Movements in America* (Philadelphia: Westminster Press, 1967), 70.

23. Dolan, *American Catholic Experience,* 16.

24. For an account of the Jesuit contact with Indians in the Maryland colony, see James Axtell, "White Legend: The Jesuit Missions in Maryland," in *After Columbus,* 73–85.

25. Instructions of Cecil Calvert to his brother Leonard, as quoted in Dolan, *American Catholic Experience,* 74; see also 69–85.

26. Robert Orsi, "The Religious Boundaries of an Inbetween People: Street *Feste* and the Problem of the Dark-Skinned Other in Italian Harlem, 1920–1990," *American Quarterly* 44, 3 (September 1992): 313–47.

27. Ibid., 333.

28. For an estimate of the Protestantizing nature of what was happening, see the letter of John Carroll to the Trustees of St. Peter's Church, New York City, 25 January 1786, in John Tracy Ellis, ed., *Documents of American Catholic History, vol. 1, 1493–1865* (Wilmington, Del.: Michael Glazier, 1987), 152.

29. See Trustees of the Roman Catholic Congregation of Norfolk and Portsmouth, 14 January 1819, in ibid., 221–23, and the introduction by Ellis on 220.

30. My rereading of the Americanist controversy has been prompted in part by an unpublished paper by Monica Siems of the University of California, Santa Barbara: "Challenging the Consensus: Historiographical Reflections on the Americanist Controversy in the Catholic Church." See also R. Laurence Moore, "Managing Catholic Success in a Protestant Empire," in *Religious Outsiders and the Making of Americans* (New York: Oxford University Press, 1986), 48–71.

31. Colleen McDannell, "Catholic Women Fiction Writers, 1840–1920," *Women's Studies* 19 (1991): 386.

32. Colleen McDannell, " 'The Devil Was the First Protestant': Gender and Intolerance in Irish Catholic Fiction," *U.S. Catholic Historian* 8, 1 and 2 (winter/spring 1989): 51.

33. For the *habitus,* see Pierre Bourdieu, *Outline of a Theory of Practice,* trans. Richard Nice (Cambridge: Cambridge University Press, 1977).

34. Jenny Franchot, *Roads to Rome: The Antebellum Protestant Encounter with Catholicism* (Berkeley: University of California Press, 1994), xxii.

35. For a brief but useful account of Quaker fortunes in America and especially in New England, see Sydney E. Ahlstrom, *A Religious History of the American People* (New Haven: Yale University Press, 1972), 176–81.

36. Richard W. Pointer, *Protestant Pluralism and the New York Experience: A Study of Eighteenth-Century Religious Diversity* (Bloomington: Indiana University Press, 1988), 2.

37. Ibid., 134, 132, 121, 133.

38. Russell E. Richey, *Early American Methodism* (Bloomington: Indiana University Press, 1991), xi.

39. Ibid., xvi-xvii. The contact-and-exchange reading is my own interpretive gloss on Richey's material, but it is surely implicit in his carefully honed argument.

40. For the complex strands in the Holiness-Pentecostal movement, see Grant Wacker, "Pentecostalism," in Charles H. Lippy and Peter W. Williams, eds., *Encyclopedia of the American Religious Experience: Studies of Traditions and Movements* (New York: Scribner's, 1988) 2:934–36.

41. For a short and helpful introduction to themes of religion and rebellion in African American religious history, see Gayraud S. Wilmore, *Black Religion and Black Radicalism: An Interpretation of the Religious History of Afro-American People,* 2d ed. (Maryknoll, N.Y.: Orbis Books, 1983), especially 53–73. For the best study of the "invisible institution" among the slaves, see Albert J. Raboteau, *Slave Religion: The 'Invisible Institution' in the Antebellum South* (New York: Oxford University Press, 1978). Charles H. Long has argued the

case for West African structures of consciousness in numerous teaching situations throughout his career. For a related written discussion of some of his ideas that I cite here, see Charles H. Long, "Perspectives for a Study of Afro-American Religion in the United States," in *Significations: Signs, Symbols, and Images in the Interpretation of Religion* (Philadelphia: Fortress Press, 1986), 173–84.

42. See, for example, Walter F. Pitts, Jr., *Old Ship of Zion: The Afro-Baptist Ritual in the African Diaspora* (New York: Oxford University Press, 1993), and Claude F. Jacobs and Andrew J. Kaslow, *The Spiritual Churches of New Orleans: Origins, Beliefs, and Rituals of an African-American Religion* (Knoxville: University of Tennessee Press, 1991).

43. Jon Butler, *Awash in a Sea of Faith: Christianizing the American People* (Cambridge, Mass.: Harvard University Press, 1990), 129–63. In a work that predated Butler's by some six years, Gary B. Nash observed that "Africans in the English plantations [in America] adapted elements of African culture to the demands of a new life and a new environment. . . . This continuous infusion of African culture kept alive many of the elements that would later be transmuted almost beyond recognition. Through fashioning their own distinct culture, within the limits established by the rigors of the slave system, blacks were able to retain semiseparate religious forms, their own music and dance, their own family life, and their own beliefs and values" (Nash, *Red, White, and Black,* 211–12).

44. For elaboration, see Joseph M. Murphy, *Working the Spirit: Ceremonies of the African Diaspora* (Boston: Beacon Press, 1994), and idem, *Santería: An African Religion in America* (Boston: Beacon Press, 1988).

45. See, for example, Theophus H. Smith, *Conjuring Culture: Biblical Formations of Black America* (New York: Oxford University Press, 1994); Alan Dundes, ed., *Mother Wit from the Laughing Barrel: Readings in the Interpretation of Afro-American Folklore* (1973; reprint, Jackson: University Press of Mississippi, 1990), especially 357–427, 523–48; Langston Hughes and Arna Bontemps, eds., *Book of Negro Folklore* (New York: Dodd, Mead, 1958), especially 1–329; and Zora Neale Hurston, *Mules and Men* (1935; reprint, Bloomington: Indiana University Press, 1978).

46. See Lawrence W. Levine, *Black Culture and Black Consciousness: Afro-American Folk Thought from Slavery to Freedom* (New York: Oxford University Press, 1977), especially 19–30, 136–297. See also Don Yoder, *Pennsylvania Spirituals* (Lancaster, Pa.: Pennsylvania Folklife Society, 1961), 20–32. I am indebted to Leonard Norman Primiano for bringing the Yoder source to my attention.

47. Nash, *Red, White, and Black,* 296.

48. For a useful discussion that argues for a black provenance for these tales, see Alan Dundes, "African Tales among the North American Indians," in *Mother Wit,* 114–25. And for Cherokee examples of the phenomenon, see James Mooney, *Myths of the Cherokee,* Smithsonian Institution, Bureau of American Ethnology Nineteenth Annual Report, 1897–98, pt. 1 (Washington, D.C.: Government Printing Office, 1900); this work has been reprinted in James

Mooney, *Myths of the Cherokee and Sacred Formulas of the Cherokees* (Nashville, Tenn.: Charles and Randy Elder, Booksellers, in collaboration with Cherokee Heritage Books, 1982).

49. Quoted in Winthrop S. Hudson and John Corrigan, *Religion in America,* 5th ed. (New York: Macmillan, 1992), 176.

50. Rosa Mordecai, "Recollections of the First Hebrew Sunday School," *Hebrew Watchword and Instructor* 6 (1897), in Marcus, *Memoirs of American Jews,* 1:283.

51. See the account in Joseph L. Blau, *Judaism in America: From Curiosity to Third Faith* (Chicago: University of Chicago Press, 1976), 31–32.

52. Ibid., 112–13.

53. Ibid., 1–20, 20.

54. Quoted in ibid., 135. For a brief but germane discussion of anti-Semitism, see Catherine L. Albanese, *America: Religions and Religion,* 2d ed. (Belmont, Calif.: Wadsworth, 1992), 509–12.

55. For a useful discussion of eighteenth-century American contacts with Asia, see Carl T. Jackson, *The Oriental Religions and American Thought: Nineteenth-Century Explorations* (Westport, Conn.: Greenwood Press, 1981).

56. Hannah Adams, *A View of Religions in Two Parts . . . The Whole Collected from the Best Authors, Ancient and Modern,* 3d ed. (Boston: Manning and Loring, 1801), 409 n., quoted in Jackson, *Oriental Religions and American Thought,* 17.

57. For an elaboration of these themes, see Thomas A. Tweed, *The American Encounter with Buddhism, 1844–1912: Victorian Culture and the Limits of Dissent* (Bloomington: Indiana University Press, 1992).

58. For the early Theosophical Society as a Spiritualist reform movement, see Stephen Prothero, "From Spiritualism to Theosophy: 'Uplifting' a Democratic Tradition," *Religion and American Culture: A Journal of Interpretation* 3, 2 (summer 1993): 197–216; see also Bruce F. Campbell, *Ancient Wisdom Revived: A History of the Theosophical Movement* (Berkeley: University of California Press, 1980). For orientalism, cast in linguistic terms as creolization, see Stephen Prothero, *The White Buddhist: Henry Steel Olcott and the Nineteenth-Century American Encounter with Asian Religions* (Bloomington: Indiana University Press, 1996), especially 7–9, 176–82.

59. The best one-volume introduction to the World's Parliament of Religions is Eric J. Ziolkowski, ed., *A Museum of Faiths: Histories and Legacies of the 1893 World's Parliament of Religions* (Atlanta: Scholars Press, 1993).

60. John Henry Barrows, ed., *The World's Parliament of Religions: An Illustrated and Popular Story of the World's First Parliament of Religions, Held in Chicago in Connection with the Columbian Exposition of 1893* (Chicago: Parliament Publishing, 1893), 2:1558, quoted in Ziolkowski, *Museum of Faiths,* 8.

61. See the account of the parliament and its foundation in the "Columbian myth," in Richard Hughes Seager, *The World's Parliament of Religions: The East/West Encounter, Chicago, 1893* (Bloomington: Indiana University Press, 1995).

62. Minnie Andrews Snell, "Aunt Hannah on the Parliament of Religions,"

Open Court (12 October 1893), stanzas 4–5, quoted in Ziolkowski, *Museum of Faiths,* 17.

63. For an instructive account of this process, see Seager, *World's Parliament of Religions,* 94–120.

64. Kenten Druyvesteyn, "The World's Parliament of Religions," Ph.D. dissertation, University of Chicago, 1976.

65. On ISKCON, see Raymond Brady Williams, *Religions of Immigrants from India and Pakistan: New Threads in the American Tapestry* (Cambridge: Cambridge University Press, 1988), 130–37.

66. Joanne Punzo Waghorne, "The Hindu Gods in a Split-Level World: The Sri Siva-Vishnu Temple in Suburban Washington, D.C.," in Robert Orsi, ed., *Gods of the City* (Bloomington: Indiana University Press, forthcoming).

67. For the Universal Friend and her movement, see Herbert A. Wisbey, Jr., *Pioneer Prophetess: Jemima Wilkinson, the Publick Universal Friend* (Ithaca: Cornell University Press, 1964).

68. Allan G. Grapard, *The Protocol of the Gods: A Study of the Kasuga Cult in Japanese History* (Berkeley: University of California Press, 1992), 8.

69. Sizer [Frankiel], "Native Americans, Franciscans, and Puritans," 15. Frankiel cites Raymond White on Luiseno religious theory, which he described as tending to be "additive but not syncretistic" (Raymond White, "Religion and Its Role among the Luiseno," in Lowell Bean and Thomas Blackburn, eds., *Native Californians: A Theoretical Retrospective* [Ramona, Calif.: Ballena Press, 1976], 363).

70. Leonard Norman Primiano names and explores the meaning of vernacular religion in the first half of his "Intrinsically Catholic: Vernacular Religion and Philadelphia's 'Dignity,' " Ph.D. dissertation, University of Pennsylvania, 1993. See also idem, " 'I Would Rather Be Fixated on the Lord': Women's Religion, Men's Power, and the 'Dignity' Problem," *New York Folklore* 19, 1–2 (1993): especially 89; and idem "Vernacular Religion and the Search for Method in Religious Folklife," *Western Folklore* 54, 1 (January 1995): 37–56.

Selected Bibliography

NARRATIVE SURVEYS OF U.S. RELIGION

Ahlstrom, Sydney E. *A Religious History of the American People*. New Haven: Yale University Press, 1972.

Albanese, Catherine L.. *America: Religions and Religion*. 1981. 2d ed. Belmont, Calif.: Wadsworth, 1992.

Bacon, Leonard Woolsey. *A History of American Christianity*. American Church History Series. 1897. New York: Scribner's, 1900.

Baird, Robert. *Religion in America*. 1844. Critical abridgement by Henry Warner Bowden. New York: Harper and Row, 1970.

Bednarowski, Mary Farrell. *American Religion: A Cultural Perspective*. Englewood Cliffs, N.J.: Prentice-Hall, 1984.

Branagan, Thomas. *A Concise View of the Principal Denominations in the United States of America*. Philadelphia: J. Cline, 1811.

Carmody, Denise Lardner, and John Tully Carmody. *Exploring American Religion*. Mountain View, Calif.: Mayfield, 1990.

Carroll, H. K. *The Religious Forces of the United States Enumerated, Classified, and Described on the Basis of the Government Census of 1890*. New York: Christian Literature Co., 1893.

Clebsch, William A. *From Sacred to Profane America: The Role of Religion in American History*. New York: Harper and Row, 1968.

Corbett, Julia Mitchell. *Religion in America*. 1990. 2d ed. Englewood Cliffs, N.J.: Prentice-Hall, 1994.

Dorchester, Daniel. *Christianity in the United States from the First Settlement Down to the Present Time*. New York: Phillips and Hunt, 1888.

Gaustad, Edwin Scott. *A Religious History of America*. 1966. New rev. ed. San Francisco: Harper and Row, 1990.

Handy, Robert T. *A History of the Churches in the United States and Canada*. New York: Oxford University Press, 1976.

Hudson, Winthrop, and John Corrigan. *Religion in America: An Historical Account of the Development of American Religious Life*. 1965. 5th ed. New York: Macmillan, 1992.

Marsden, George M. *Religion and American Culture*. New York: Harcourt Brace Jovanovich, 1990.

Marty, Martin E. *Pilgrims in Their Own Land: Five Hundred Years of Religion in America*. Boston: Little, Brown, 1984.

Mode, Peter G. *The Frontier Spirit in American Christianity*. New York: Macmillan, 1923.

Moseley, James G. *A Cultural History of Religion in America*. Contributions to the Study of Religion, Number 2. Westport, Conn.: Greenwood Press, 1981.

Noll, Mark A. *A History of Christianity in the United States and Canada*. Grand Rapids, Mich.: Eerdmans, 1992.

Olmstead, Clifton E. *Religion in America: Past and Present*. Englewood Cliffs, N.J.: Prentice-Hall, 1961.

Rowe, Henry K. *The History of Religion in the United States*. New York: Macmillan, 1924.

Schaff, Philip. *America: A Sketch of Its Political, Social, and Religious Character*. 1855. Edited by Perry Miller. Cambridge, Mass.: Harvard University Press, 1961.

Sweet, William Warren. *The Story of Religion in America*. 1930. New York: Harper and Brothers, 1939.

Wentz, Richard E. *Religion in the New World: The Shaping of Religious Traditions in the United States*. Minneapolis: Fortress Press, 1990.

Williams, Peter W. *America's Religions: Traditions and Cultures*. New York: Macmillan, 1990.

ON NARRATIVE AND HISTORY

Ankersmit, F. R. "The Dilemma of Contemporary Anglo-Saxon Philosophy of History." In *Knowing and Telling History: The Anglo-Saxon Debate*, edited by F. R. Ankersmit. Middletown, Conn.: Wesleyan University Press, 1986.

———. "Historiography and Postmodernism." *History and Theory* 28 (1989): 137–53.

Appleby, Joyce, Lynn Hunt, and Margaret Jacob. *Telling the Truth about History*. New York: W. W. Norton, 1994.

Armstrong, Nancy, and Leonard Tennenhouse. "History, Poststructuralism, and the Question of Narrative." *Narrative* 1 (January 1993): 45–58.

Attridge, Derek, Geoff Benington, and Robert Young, eds. *Post-Structuralism and the Question of History*. Cambridge: Cambridge University Press, 1987.

Bakhtin, M. M. *The Dialogic Imagination*. Edited by Michael Holquist. Austin: University of Texas Press, 1981.

Burke, Peter. "The History of Events and the Revival of Narrative." In *New Perspectives on Historical Writing*, edited by Peter Burke. University Park: Pennsylvania State University Press, 1992.

Carr, David. *Time, Narrative, and History*. Bloomington: Indiana University Press, 1986.

Cronon, William. "A Place for Stories: Nature, History, and Narrative." *Journal of American History* 78 (March 1992): 1347–76.

Dray, W. H. "On the Nature and Role of Narrative in Historiography." *History and Theory* 10 (1971): 153–71.

Fell, A. P. " 'Epistemological' and 'Narrativist' Philosophies of History." In *Objectivity, Method, and Point of View: Essays in the Philosophy of History*, edited by W. J. van der Dussen and Lionel Rubinoff. Leiden: E. J. Brill, 1991.

Harding, Vincent G. "Healing at the Razor's Edge: Reflections on a History of Multicultural America." *Journal of American History* 81 (September 1994): 571–84.

Hunt, Lynn, ed. *The New Cultural History*. Berkeley: University of California Press, 1989.

Levine, Lawrence W. "Clio, Canons, and Culture." *Journal of American History* 80 (December 1993): 849–67.

Martin, Raymond. "Objectivity and Meaning in Historical Studies: Toward a Post-Analytic View." *History and Theory* 32 (1993): 25–50.

Martin, Wallace. *Recent Theories of Narrative*. Ithaca: Cornell University Press, 1986.

Mink, Louis. "Narrative Form as a Cognitive Instrument." In *The Writing of History*, edited by Robert H. Canary and Henry Kozicki. Madison: University of Wisconsin Press, 1978.

Moore, R. Laurence. "Insiders and Outsiders in American Historical Narrative and American History." *American Historical Review* 87 (April 1982): 390–412.

Novick, Peter. *That Noble Dream: The "Objectivity Question" and the American Historical Profession*. Cambridge: Cambridge University Press, 1988.

Ricoeur, Paul. *Time and Narrative*. Volume 1. Chicago: University of Chicago Press, 1984.

Rosaldo, Renato. *Culture and Truth: The Remaking of Social Analysis*. Boston: Beacon Press, 1989.

Stone, Lawrence. "The Revival of Narrative." *Past and Present* 85 (1979): 3–24.

Thelen, David, ed. "The Practice of American History: A Special Issue." *Journal of American History* 81 (December 1994).

Walsh, W. H. " 'Plain' and 'Significant' Narrative in History." *Journal of Philosophy* 55 (1958): 479–84.

White, Hayden. *Metahistory*. Baltimore: Johns Hopkins University Press, 1973.

———. *Tropics of Discourse: Essays in Cultural Criticism*. Baltimore: Johns Hopkins University Press, 1978.

———. "The Question of Narrative in Contemporary Historical Theory." *History and Theory* 23 (1984): 1–33.

Zagorin, Perez. "Historiography and Postmodernism: Reconsiderations." *History and Theory* 29 (1990): 263–96.

ON HISTORICAL NARRATIVES OF U.S. RELIGION

Ahlstrom, Sydney E. "The Problem of the History of Religion in America."
   Church History 39 (June 1970): 224–35.
Albanese, Catherine L. "Refusing the Wild Pomegranate Seed: America, Reli-
   gious History, and the Life of the Academy." *Journal of the American Acad-
   emy of Religion* 63 (summer 1995): 205–29.
Ash, James L. *Protestantism and the American University: An Intellectual Biog-
   raphy of William Warren Sweet.* Dallas: Southern Methodist University
   Press, 1982.
Bowden, Henry Warner. *Church History in the Age of Science: Historiographi-
   cal Patterns in the United States, 1876–1918.* Chapel Hill: University of
   North Carolina Press, 1971.
———. *Church History in an Age of Uncertainty: Historiographical Patterns
   in the United States, 1906–1990.* Carbondale: Southern Illinois University
   Press, 1991.
———. "The Historiography of American Religion." In *Encyclopedia of the
   American Religious Experience: Studies of Traditions and Movements,* ed-
   ited by Charles H. Lippy and Peter W. Williams. New York: Scribner's, 1988.
Bratt, James D. "A New Narrative for American Religious History?" *Fides et
   Historia* 23 (fall 1991): 19–30.
Brauer, Jerald C. "Regionalism and Religion in America." *Church History* 54
   (September 1985): 366–78.
———, ed. *Reinterpretation in American Church History.* Chicago: University
   of Chicago Press, 1968.
Butler, Jon. "The Future of American Religious History: Prospectus, Agenda,
   and Transatlantic *Problématique.*" *William and Mary Quarterly* 42 (April
   1985): 167–83.
———. "Historiographical Heresy: Catholicism as a Model for American Re-
   ligious History." In *Belief in History: Innovative Approaches to European
   and American Religion,* edited by Thomas Kselman. Notre Dame, Ind.: Uni-
   versity of Notre Dame Press, 1991.
Clebsch, William A. "A New Historiography of American Religion." *Historical
   Magazine of the Protestant Episcopal Church* 32 (1963): 225–57.
Dolan, Jay P. "The Immigrants and Their Gods: A New Perspective in American
   Religious History." *Church History* 57 (March 1988): 61–72.
Ernst, Eldon G. "Beyond the Protestant Era in American Religious Historiog-
   raphy." In *In the Great Tradition: Essays on Pluralism, Voluntarism, and
   Revivalism,* edited by Joseph D. Ban and Paul R. Dekar. Valley Forge, Pa.:
   Judson Press, 1982.
Gaustad, Edwin S. *Religion in America: History and Historiography.* AHA
   Pamphlets, volume 260. Washington, D.C.: American Historical Associa-
   tion, 1973.
Hatch, Nathan. "The Puzzle of American Methodism." *Church History,* 63
   (June 1994): 175–89.

Long, Charles H. "A New Look at American Religion." *Anglican Theological Review* 55 (7/1973): 117–25.

Lotz, David W. "A Changing Historiography: From Church History to Religious History." In *Altered Landscapes: Christianity in America, 1935–1985,* edited by David W. Lotz, Donald W. Shriver, Jr., and John F. Wilson. Grand Rapids, Mich.: Eerdmans, 1989.

Marty, Martin E., ed. *The Writing of American Religious History.* Munich: Saur, 1992.

May, Henry F. "The Recovery of American Religious History." *American Historical Review* 70 (October 1964): 79–92.

Mead, Sidney E. "The American People: Their Space, Time, and Religion." In *The Lively Experiment: The Shaping of Christianity in America.* New York: Harper and Row, 1963.

———. "By Puritans Possessed." *Worldview* 16 (April 1973): 49–52.

Moore, R. Laurence. "Protestant Unity and the American Mission—The Historiography of a Desire." In *Religious Outsiders and the Making of Americans.* New York: Oxford University Press, 1986.

Orsi, Robert A., George Marsden, David W. Wills, and Colleen McDannell. "Forum: The Decade Ahead in Scholarship." *Religion and American Culture* 3 (winter 1993): 1–28.

Stein, Stephen J. " 'Something Old, Something New, Something *Left to Do':* Choosing a Textbook for Religion in America." *Religion and American Culture* 3 (summer 1993): 217–27.

Sweet, Leonard I. " 'Ringmasters,' 'Blind Elephant Feelers,' and 'Mules': The Textbook Literature of American Religious History." *Critical Review of Books in Religion, 1988* (Atlanta: Journal of the American Academy of Religion and the Journal of Biblical Literature, 1988), 89–118.

Tweed, Thomas A. "Asian Religions in the United States: Reflections on an Emerging Sub-Field." In *Religious Diversity and American Religious History: Studies in Traditions and Cultures,* edited by Walter Conser and Sumner Twiss. Athens: University of Georgia Press, forthcoming.

Wills, David W. "The Central Themes of American Religious History: Pluralism, Puritanism, and the Encounter of Black and White." *Religion and Intellectual Life* 5 (fall 1987): 30–41.

———, and Albert J. Raboteau. "Rethinking American Religious History: A Progress Report on 'Afro-American Religious History: A Documentary Project.' " *Council of Societies for the Study of Religion Bulletin* 20 (September 1991): 57–61.

Wilson, John F. "A Review of Some Reviews of *A Religious History of the American People,* by Sydney E. Ahlstrom." *Religious Studies Review* (September 1975): 1–8.

Index

Compositor:	J. Jarrett Engineering, Inc.
Text:	10/13 Sabon
Display:	Sabon
Printer:	Haddon Craftsmen, Inc.
Binder:	Haddon Craftsmen, Inc.